OUR LAST HOPE

OUR LAST HOPE

Black Male-Female Relationships in Change

DELORES P. ALDRIDGE, PH.D

Ordering Information:

For orders and inquiries, please contact:
1-888-404-1388
www.goldtouchpress.com
book.orders@goldtouchpress.com

Printed in the United States of America

CONTENTS

PREFACE

An earlier version of this book, black Male-Female Relationships: A Resource book of Selected Materials was first published in 1989 by Kendall-Hunt Publishing Company. There was a perceived need for a book of readings about black males and females for the serious student, the scholar and the general reader. Today, the need continues to be there. While there has been much sound and fury concerning, first the black male, next, the black female, and finally, Black male-female relationships, the search for serious literature that pulls together a variety of scholarly-generated readings upon the latter subject continues to be difficult to locate. In fact, such volumes for explaining the nature of black male-female relationships many well be the last hope for understanding the development of these relationships with movement toward their survival.

The Earlier text grew out of the editor's research needs in pulling together materials for a companion text Focusing: Institutional and Interpersonal Perspectives on Black Male-Female Relationships which was published by Third World Press. Nowhere was there to be found a single source that covered the areas necessary to generate a macro systemic theory by which one could analyze black male-female relationships. While it cannot be claimed that the previous volume, not this present work, is exhaustive in its coverage of pertinent topics, it does attempt to expand upon the earlier volume including additions to old chapters as well as a new chapter on Afrocentric cultural issues with some focus on the hip hop. Finally, it provides a conclusion chapter which points to strategies which accompany understanding so that full advantage can be taken of our last hope for healthy black male-female relationships.

In selecting the eight topic areas for this work, a deliberate choice was made to include those areas which seemed to most accurately reflect the results of the situational inequities and sustained oppression that have continued to define the lives of black people in the USA.

Importantly, it must be emphasized, however, that so much has changed over the past decade since this book was first published. The public space and political climate have shaped many facets of American life. Accordingly, this book should be read in the context of the time of its original writing. Thus, while the descriptions and analyses provided were on point then black male-female relationships are fast becoming indistinguishable from other types of relationships in American society. Our Last hope for healthy relations with black partners of the opposite sex is vanishing.

INTRODUCTION

There continues to grow, though slowly, recognition of the need for quality research to be performed by scholars on black male-female relationships. While it is true that much research has been reported on black males or black females, there has been a curious omission of incisive work focusing upon the dyad. Many explanations could be advanced for this lacunae in the literature.

One of the problems is that much of the research has focused solely upon black males and, in addition, much of this research has been performed by white males. There appears to be a curious mental and perceptual flaw in many white scholars that enables them to research black males without adequate considerations of what has elsewhere been termed the institutionalized oppressive of what has elsewhere been termed the institutionalized oppressive ideology that fills every minute of a black male's life in America. The nature of blackness is, one might suggest, quite different from the nature of blackness as it structures the existence of American males.

Another problem lies in the sexiest nature of American society. White males tend to focus their research on black males, one suspect, in terms of a subconscious kind of male bonding which only interprets male activities as being meaningful material for research. Then, again, there is always the latent threat presented by the black male to the white male; research can be a way of binding this dangerous creature through conceptual bonds.

The rise of interest in the research oriented minds of scholars toward the black female follows the national tendency to grant women a grudging sense of importance in the American scene. But even here there has been a series of distortions through which one must work before anything meaningful can be accomplished through research. If one keeps in mind that the black male and the black female must continually live out their lives within social and psychological environment structured by an institutionalized oppressive ideology, it will be seen that the failure to include this overriding variable in the basic structuring of one's research simply results in further destructive myths, no matter what the degree of sophistication of one's statistical analyses.

This text represents an attempt to present a selection of the more meaningful work done by a majority of black scholars in the field of black males and black females. By no means can it be said that the contents represent the whole of the best works written in the field. And, while some of the works may contradict each other, they are valuable for such a volume which brings together various perspectives. What has been attempted is a selection of representative works that indicate approaches to important issues. As for the divisions presented, the choices have been defined by the critical nature of the issues chosen for inclusion.

We need, for example, to understand demographic aspects of black existence before choosing to follow a particular line of research on black males and females. We need to understand the powerful influence of primary groups upon and continuing socialization of black people. Given these insights, we have a basic preparation for asking meaningful questions concerning black race and gender. An exploration of psycho-social issue's needs, in turn, to be informed by the other sectional issues presented herein. Economic subordination is more sharply defined when one has a literacy based upon a critical reading of the total complex of meaningful issues. And of course. Religion needs to be sensitively understood and investigated as one of the basic socialization experiences in the lives of black people.

Yet, in spite of all that has been said above, there remains an incompleteness to the present volume. For the dyad of black male and black female presents a different unit of investigation from investigations of black males or black females. One suspects that black scholars will begin to give an increasing amount of attention to this vital dyad and move toward the creation of new and more meaningful definitions of black people in America. The value of the present volume rests in the attempt to make a statement about where we are. The total contents make a strong implication concerning there we need to arrive.

CHAPTER ONE
Toward An Understanding of Black Male-Female Relationships

In her seminal work, Delores P. Aldridge presents an intellectual Gestalt of the issues required to paint the overall canvas of the experiences and the meaning of the experiences of black males and black females. Beginning with a structural framework for examining male-female and demonstrate how these experiences are shaped in this model, named the lens Model in subsequent works. Black male scarcity, differential socialization of males and females sexism and its relationships to black women's liberation are some of the issues presented in the article. Modes of connecting, black women's liberation are some of the issues presented in the article. Modes of connecting, black women's perceptions and the critical need for quality research to be done with black people by black behavioral scientists complete the exposition of Aldridge's presentation.

A second work by Delores P. Aldridge and Willa M. Hemmons provides an Afrocentric perspective as a point of departure for the understanding of male-female violence. American society is defined by and derived from core or dominant values, which have differentially impacted its diverse populations. The Lens Model presented in this discourse focuses on these values as being counterproductive for black male-female relationships. Capitalism, racism, sexism and the Judeo Christian ethic comprise the four-prong institutional or structural value components of the Lens Model. This dynamic framework is instructive as it helps to understand domestic violence in black adult relationships so important in contemporary American society.

APPROACHING THE STUDY OF BLACK MALE-FEMALE RELATIONSHIPS

DELORES P. ALDRIDGE

There has been growth, albeit recent, in the literature of psychology and sociology concerning the black male and black female. The discretion of the literature has been such that there are two streams of writing, one devoted to the black female and another devoted to the black male. Representative of the first are such writers as Ladner (1972), Staples (1973), Lerner (1973, and Rodgers-Rose (1980). Wilkinson and Taylor (1977), Liebow (1967), and Gary (1981), among others have written concerning the black male.

What is curious, however, is a relative lack of social psychological works dealing with black males and females within the same endeavor. A case can be made, of course, for monadic rather than dyadic focus. The individual organism, stripped from its social ecosystem, is presented for critical analysis. One's vision is not beclouded by the intervening variable of the opposite gender. There remains, of course, the question of the ways in which the opposite gender has affected the overall characteristics of the monad under study. Man is born f woman and so is woman born of woman. Thus, it would seem that viewing black males and female within a social context or, bet yet, asocial psychological frame of reference enables one to generate a set of questions and insights differing from those drawn from black monadic studies.

When one begins to draw a border around the global concept of black males and females, it would appear important to concentrate upon communications that go toward defining black male/female relationship suggests a series of questions that form topics for the subject:

> *Why are male/female relationships important?*

> *Why is it significant to isolate as well as focus upon black male/female relations?*

What is a useful schematic and structural framework for examining male/female relationships?

What are the manifestations of the schematic and structural framework?

What are the implications of and recommendations for maintaining sound relationships and improving non-existent or weal relationships?

THE IMPORTANCE OF MALE/FEMALE RELATIONSHIPS

Karenga (1981) notes that male/female relationships are of fundamental and enduring concern and importance for several reasons: First, because of their indispensability to the maintenance and development of the species. Second, they are a barometer, i.e., measurement of our distance from the animal world in other words, our humanity. Third, they are an indicator of the quality of social life; the treatment of women in relationships and, by extension, in society becomes as Toure (1959:72) notes "…a mirror that reflects the economic and social conditions, the levels of political, cultural and moral development of a given country." Fourth, they are a measurement and mirror or personal development and identify a revelation of who persons really are. Fifth, they are a measurement of a people's capacity for struggle and social construction… as a fundamental unit of the nation, their strengths and weaknesses determine the nation's capacity to define, defend and develop its interest.

IMPORTANCE OF BLACK MALE/FEMALE RELATIONSHIPS

The issue of indispensability to the maintenance and development of the species within the context of black male and female relationships may be viewed both in terms of the nuclear family as well as the single parent family. There is a need for an increased amount of sensitive research focused upon the maintenance and development characteristics and outcomes of black female-headed families.

Within a social system frame of reference, one might ask whether the maintenance and development characteristics of black female headed families might not represent a type of response by black people to the overall messages they receive from white America." What is being suggested here is the black males, as a "subspecies," may need to be socialized by mothers rather than fathers insofar as their role behavior for future functioning in American society is concerned. Note, this is not an issue posed by the differential demography of black males compared to black females. Instead, it is a question that arises from demographic givens and becomes proper within the context of a social psychological frame of reference.

The black female-headed family, differing as it does from the mass media vidon of the nuclear family, operates in the eyes of many critics as a deficit model, one whose deviation from the official norm dooms it to internal dysfunctions and external maladaptation to the environment. Such a view is, of course, limited by the analytical focus of those who denigrate the black female-headed family. From a general system point of view (Berrien, 1968), it can be seen that the black female-headed family is, once again, an innovative black adaption to the social-economic and cultural pressures of the dominant society, an adaptation based in and growing from the scarcity of black males.

It is important to note that the maintenance and development of the species is carried on within the black female-headed family. But it is also important to not the need for, as noted above, sensible and sensitive research into the structure, dynamics and outcomes of role socialization in the black female-headed family. One suspects that there are strengths that have not yet entered the official vocabulary of the research literature.

Given the pressures upon black people in America, the continued maintenance and development of black children brought about through the love of black men and women for each other is, indeed, a critical measurement of the strength of black people. Yet, when one reviews the statement of Toure, cited above those male/female relationships are important and especially the treatment of women in relationships one needs to ask what the treatment of black women reflects in the national political, cultural and moral mirror of American society. One is forced to return, once again, to the image of the black woman as reflected in the ass media and even in that latest telecommunications format, musical video.

The standard of beauty that is communicated by television and only partly contradicted by such publications as Essence has, one suspects, much to do with setting the criteria of beauty for many black woman and black men. When it is considered that there are strict limitations on what is acceptable in black politics, culture and morality on the part of the dominant society, one might be moved to wonderment as to the survival of any black male/female relationship.

SIGNIFICANCE OF BLACK MALE/FEMALE RELATIONSHIPS

Social scientists, psychologists, novelists, political scientists, and psychiatrists have all discussed and examined the significance of black male/female relationships. The reader may want to examine the sociological writing (Staples, 1978; Jackson, 1978; Karenga, 1982; Scot, 1976; Hare, 1979), the psychological literature (Akbar, 1976; Tucker, 1979; Nobles, 1978); the writing of political scientists (Wilcox, 1979; Gary, 1981), the psychiatric literature (Welsing, 1974; Poussaint, 1979; Grier and Cobbs, 1968), and works of fiction (Wallace, 1979; Jordan, 1977). The gamut of perspectives has ranged from an Afrocentric mode (Asante, 1980; Akbar, 1976; Karenga, 1982) to a popularist model (Wallace, 1979).

What united all the writings cited above is the theme of black male/female relationships developing and surviving in the face of tremendous odds. At the same time, the presence of quite substantive historical problems whose characteristics have become more acute in the last several decades is also acknowledged. The lack of relationships due to the scarcity of black male (Jackson, 1971) and the mutually degrading games one plays in order to begin and sustain relationships (Staples, 1978) are but two of the present problems that threaten black male/female relationships. Even the quality and future of existing black male/female relationships remain open to continuing questions and challenges, given the social stress and strain of living in American society.

Despite what has been said about the problems of black male/female concerns, the writer is in agreement with Karenga (1982) that the following relevant facts need to form a background for future studies and research:

1. Black male/female relationships are probably no more problem ridden than other male/female relationships.
2. Life, itself, requires problems and the effort to solve those problems.
3. Many black male/female relationships are healthy; however, enough are in trouble to require a sustained critical view.
4. There are enough black males and black females without relationships so that discussion focused upon this fact needs furthering.
5. Any criticism of black male/female relationships is, at the same time and in equal measure, a criticism of American society the society that has shaped them to fit and "properly" function in it.

These five facts serve as a point of departure for any serious analysis of black men, black women and their relationships. To further underscore the point of view that argues that black people are products of their social conditions is to use the same argument for the connection between black relationships and social conditions. In order to properly understand black men and black women within the context of their relationships, one must understand the historical characteristics that have shaped them. Superimposed upon these variables is the complexity of mental, emotional and physical factors which have also shaped the behavior of black men and women.

A STRUCTURAL FRAMEWORK FOR EXAMINING BLACK MALE/FEMALE RELATIONSHIPS

American society is defined by and derived from four major structural and value systems; capitalism, racism, sexism, Judeo Christianity. Capitalism may be defined as a socio-economic system in which private ownership is the primary means for satisfying human needs. Another characteristic of capitalism is a strong and continuous pursuit of profit. The emphasis upon private ownership of things tends to often shape the view of human relationships, i.e., the conceptual conversion of human beings into things to be owned or similarly the profit motive in which people may subconsciously be viewed as objects for purchase and resale.

Racism may be defined as a system of denial and deformation of a people's history ad humanity based primarily on the specious concept of race and hierarchies of races. Racism in America was born form European feelings of racial superiority and bred within the moral contradiction between Christian concepts and economic beliefs. Slavery represented and attempt at dehumiliation of both the proponents as well as those who were enslaved, given the idea of Christianity. On their hand, slavery represented the extension of private ownership and profit theories into the realm of human relationships. In the contemporary world, neo-colonialism links capitalism and racism, resulting in nations that dominate and nations that are owned by the dominators. In this context, it is important to understand that capitalism and racism extend their influence from the intrapersonal system to the world system of human organization.

Sexism is the social system and resultant practice of using gender or sex as an ascriptive and primary determinant in the establishment, maintenance and explanation, i.e., justification, of relationships and exchanges. As a system, sexism is composed of assumptions and acts theories and practices which imply and impose unequal, oppressive and exploitive relationships based upon gender. When capitalism and racism are reviewed for their effects upon human relationships, it may be seen that sexism converts the dominated to a subordinate feminine stereotype, open and waiting to be used.

The Judeo-Christian tradition is a religious system which has its roots in Judaism and Christianity which draw heavily upon the cultural and social experiences of Jews, whites and males. The tradition encourages identification with males as leaders and heroes but more importantly it emphasizes the leader-hero tradition as being one with white males and their socio-economic experiences. A racist, sexist and Judeo-Christian macrosystem forms the basic framework from understanding black male/female relationships. From this understanding can be generated a set of questions germane to the topic of this paper:

What are the manifestations of the conceptual framework?

What are the values implied by the conceptual framework?

What are the concrete factors influencing male/female relations emerging out of a racist, sexist, capitalist, and Judeo-Christian society?

In the following discussions, the writer will attempt to respond to these questions.

FACTORS INFLUENCING THE QUALITY OF INTERACTION BETWEEN BLACK MALES AND BLACK FEMALES

Four factors shape the interactive nature of communication between black males and black females; the scarcity of black men, differential socialization of males and females, sexism and women's liberation, and the modes of connecting. Jackson (1971) focuses attention on the shortage of black males through a novel paradigm that black males have a higher rate of infant mortality, a shorter life expectancy, a high rate of accidents and homicide, a form a disproportionate segment of the prison population, and are a significant segment of the drug addict population. Staple (1978) reports that there is only one acceptable black male for every five black males. Data from the 1977 census indicates that there were 732,000 more black females than black males in the

22–24-year-old range during 1977. More recent census data show no close of the gap has occurred.

These statistics serve to underline certain grave consequences for black male/female relationships. The insufficient supply of eligible black males pits black women against each other in competition for the attention of this scarce resource. Secondly, many black men are aware of the imbalance and play a power game with black women, requiring them to accept the black male upon his terms. If black women fail to buy into the power game, interracial courtship is an option increasingly available to those who are so inclined. It comes as no surprise, of course, that the black woman sees interracial heterosexual relations as a personal rejection of her own desirability.

DIFFERENTIAL SOCIALIZATION OF MALES AND FEMALES

Jourard (1971) explored the deadening aspects of the male role, advancing the notion that the socially-defined male role requires men to appear tough, objective, striving, achieving, unsentimental, and emotionally unexpressive. If behind this social persona a man feels tender, if he cries, he will be viewed as unmanly by others the contradiction between the ways in which black men are expected to present themselves in small and large group situations and their real emotional feelings is a key to understanding the nature of being a black male in America. The learned residency of males to mask their true feelings makes it difficult for black men to achieve insight into and empathy with black women.

To the extent that women require expressions of intimate and personal emotions in exchange for their availability as social or sexual partners, the non-expressive or limited in expressiveness male may find himself in a difficult situation, observed Brathewaite. If he is to execute properly his role as a black man by associating with women who demonstrate their attraction to him, he must be fairly successful at something for which he has received contradictory signals that is to express emotions of gentleness, tenderness and verbal affection toward women while at the same time being strong, unexpressive and cool.

According to Braithewaite (1981), the high degree of verbal facility among black males makes it easier for them to create an initial impression of genuine feelings and, thus, they readily enter into relationships with women, as the relationship continues and the woman becomes familiar with the male's ways, it becomes increasingly difficult for the black male to camouflage his absence of genuine feelings for his partner. The male must constantly "fake it" and express sentiments he really does not feel. Perhaps this is part of the reason for seemingly unexpected physical attacks upon one's partner followed by loving apologies. Given that the male continuously runs the risk of "blowing his cover" with the outcome of a terminated relationship, the cardinal issue becomes plain. The issue is not one of entering relationships with women. The issue is one of sustaining relationships with women.

Tucker (1978) indicates that success with women is important to many men because they are engaged in covert competition with other men. The belief is that success will enable them to avoid ridicule and to be perceived as "hip." Given this process, women become targets and the communication structure by which they become targets assumes the status of an end in itself rather that a means to an end. The process is in many ways dysfunctional to black men. There is feeling that expression of emotions must not leave the man vulnerable. This rapidly passes over into the self-rejection of those emotions whose display might leave one vulnerable.

The pattern of initial contact and verbal gaming that is summarized above represents a well-patterned response to the teachings of capitalism and sexism. The woman becomes an object; one gains in profit as one "scores" on an increasing number of women. And, of course, the expression of a well as the possession of emotions that might reveal oneself as well as the women as feeling individual beings is contra productive to the capitalist mentality. At this point, one is tempted to wonder whether the "new morality" is not, in itself, a logical outgrowth of capitalism and sexism, e.g., the body becomes the object of buying and selling the inner person is reduced to a dancing (either in public or in the bedroom) object available for the man's pleasure.

Tucker suggest that women can help men by letting the latter know that they measure manhood not in terms of "cool" but in terms of responsiveness, support, care, and honesty. Black women can further help by encouraging black men to struggle and deal with their emotions rather than to conceal them. Black women need to share with black men an assurance that a man is found to be more attractive when he shares his feeling with them. And while it is true that black men may complain about women who force them to deal with issues, but ultimately, they respect such women far more than they do meek, complaint women who make no demands (Tucker, 1979). Given what has been said, one may conclude that self-disclosure is a major force influencing the quality of interaction between black men black women.

SEXISM AND WOMEN'S LIBERATION

Many scholars admit that sexism is present among black male and has the effect of inhibiting and corrupting meaningful relationship. In recent years, the criticism of sexism among black people has become an issue. It is an issue; however, that threatens the black community through assault upon the black male. Staples (1979) argue that female equality involves not only personal relationships, but also political and economic relationships. A substantial number of the inequalities perceived in male and female relationships need to be remedied through re-education of men and women toward changes in their sex-role socialization.

For black women, involvement in a feminist movement entails a tripartite battle against sexism, racism and capitalism. Racism and capitalism are forces that have subjected black women to political and economic subordination. Staples (1979) is among those who see feminism as a divisive force in an oppressed community such as black America. There are other points of view. Lorde (1979) supports feminism, arguing that since black women bear the brunt of sexism, it is in their interest to abolish it. She continues by suggesting that it is the responsibility of black women to decide whether or not sexism in the black community is pathological. According to Lorde, "Creative relationships of which Stales speaks are to the benefit of black males, considering the sex ration of males and females. Salaam (1979) contends that the struggle against sexism is not a threat to black masculinity. The forces that attack black women individually, institutionally and ideologically also assault black men.

On the other side of the question, many black men and women have spoken out against feminism (Larue; 1970; Duberman, 1975). The arguments they advance are:

Black people as a race need to be liberated from racism.

Feminism creates negative competition between the black male and the black female for economic security.

Feminism facilitates increased tension in the already strained interpersonal atmosphere in which black men and black women interact.

White women board the benefits of the struggle from black women.

One might argue, in the light of the many views presented above, that women's liberation as it is presently defined and implemented impacts negatively on the black liberation movement and on black male and female relationships. The essence of the writer's disagreement with women's liberation is the basically conservative mode of its beliefs and functions. Women's liberation operates within the capitalist tradition and accepts the end goals of sexiest white males; simply stated, women's liberation strives to place women on an equal par with men without considering whether the male position the white male position is basically a humanizing position.

Black women are victims of capitalism and sexism. How, then will the relations between black males and females be bettered through feminine adherence to a male-defined path? Black liberation involves male and female openly and courageously seeking mutual liberation; black liberation cannot have a luxury of a liberation movement operating inside the capitalist tradition and seeking goals defined by perpetuators of the sexist tradition. It will be seen, then, that black liberation, especially within black male and black female relations, has a far more complex task than women's liberation, black liberation seeks the establishment of a loving free movement within and between black males and black females that re-creates both parties and establishes a tradition that is non-capitalist, non-sexist and draws from the cultural experiences of the black people.

MODES OF CONNECTING

Black men and women often engage in relationships that are not in their mutual best interest. Karenga (1982) describes four modes through which black males and black females come together: 1) The Cash Connection, 2) The Flesh Connection, 3) The Force Connection, and 4) The Dependency Connection. Karenga (1982) defines a connection as "a short-term or tentative association which is utilitarian and alienated and designed primarily for the mutual misuses of each other's body. On the other hand, a quality relationship is a stable association defined by its positive sharing, it's mutual investment in each other's psychological well-being and development."

The "Cash Connection" is based upon a point of view epitomized by such statements as "everything and everybody has a price," "anything you can't buy ain't work having," what you invest assets into is yours," and "money is the measure of solutions to everything." The primary motivation in the dyadic relation controlled by the cash connection the presence of financial resources by at least one of the dyad's members. Women spar with other women over available men with money. In essence, men and women are looking at each other as potential "marks" in a petty confidence game.

The "Flesh Connection" is rooted in the new morality which characterizes much of contemporary society and is based predominantly on the pursuit of sex. This particular linkage focuses on the body and all the things one can do with all selected parts of it. It is not at all extreme to suggest that the flesh connection is basically a perverse connection, a corruptive reduction of the members of the dyad to definitions of self and other, primarily, in terms of the physical. A rejection of the boy is not at all intended here: instead, what is being said is that black males and females cannot afford to reduce themselves to an intrapersonal and interpersonal image that define them as slaves. For the slave is seen as a body capable of work, impregnation and reproduction. What is one must remember is that the final stage of colonization is the colonial taking over the attitudes of the colonizers and proceeding to maintain a colonial society based upon the colonizer's mentality? The flesh connection is, perhaps, the most damaging of connections for black males and black females since it is entirely contradictory to the basic canons of a healthy black liberation.

The "force connection" is predicated on the violent nature of society, part of the species' inheritance from its earliest ancestors. The force connection is fueled by the "macho' mentality of men who take what they are compelled to take as a result of their illusions of ownership. Lurking behind the macho mentality is particular self-view that is, once again, delimiting and, ultimately, insecure. It is delimiting in that viewing women as objects to be owned calls for the diminution of any self-view that suggest feeling and thoughts beyond those which enable one to own others. It is insecure since the very idea of a balanced self cannot abide within a self that is limited in its own definition as well as those whom it seeks to own.

The "dependency connection" results from entering into a relationship based upon any of the three preceding connections. The dependency connection is a different level, psychologically and sociologically speaking since it flows from negative connections rather than summarizes an initiating correction. It would be a mistake to call all dependency a negative form of interaction. Positive dependency can be the hallmark of what Karenga (1982) terms a stable association. Positive dependency flows form the growing strength of each member of the black dyad as they grow within themselves. If love is a process, rather than a "falling in," then it requires the presence of the other within each other as a rewarding stimulus for the individual "I" and the collective "we."

IMPLICATIONS

From the above discussion, one can proceed to recommendations for improving weak relationships, growing out of non-relationship states of being and maintaining sound relationships. Most of the social scientists referenced in this work have advanced theories for improving and maintaining relationships. The consensus being it is important that:

Social scientists develop and explore researchable questions examining the nature of the context in which black male/ female relationships are embedded:

Demographers focus attention on the scarcity of black males as a national phenomenon having potentially grave consequences for the race and having deleterious effects on black women;

Black men and women address unsatisfactory interpersonal relationships by participating in personal growth and human relations group sessions:

Universities develop and include a curse on male and female relationships as a part of their general education curriculum; and

Black national organizations place on their program agenda the issue of strategies for strengthening relationships between black men and black women.

If these theoretical constructs are pursued, one suspects that the socially-generated illnesses that define too many black male and black female relationships may begin, finally, to diminish and disappear.

The issue explored here should direct one's attention not only to black male and black female relationships, but to the foundation of American society. Although this chapter deals with the interpersonal and the intrapersonal, the implications are rooted within the two easily accepted and not too often examined Euro-American roots of this nation. As a nation, America practices upon weaker Third World countries precisely what men and women practice upon each other. Thus, although this paper is intended as a thesis in social psychology, the directional flow of its development is toward philosophy and, in particular, axiology- the study and criticism of values. Values are what shape one's perception of self and other as well as one's internal and external communication, not to mention the definition of social goals.

REFERENCES

Akbar, N. "Rhytmic patterns in African Personality." In L. King etc, al ((ed.) African Philosophy and Paradigms for research on Black Persons. Los Angeles: Fanon Center, 1976

Asante, M. AfroCentricity: The Theory of Social Change. Buffalo, N.Y.:Amulefi, 1980.

Berrien, F.K. General and Social Systems. New Brunswick, N.J.: Rutgers University Press, 1968

Braithwaite, R.L "Interpersonal Relations Between Black Males and Black Females." In L.E. Gary (ED.) Black Men. Beverly Hills, California: Sage Publications, 1981.

Duberman, L. Gender and Sex in Society, New York: Praeger, 1975.

Gary, L.E.(Ed.) Black Men, Beverly Hills, Calif.: Sage Publications, 1981.

Grier, W., and Cobbs, P. Black Rage. New York: Basic Books, 1968.

Hare, J. "Black Male-Female Relationships." Sepia (Noember 1979).

Jackson, J. "But Where Are the Black Men?" Black Scholar (1971) 4;34-41.

Jordan, J. Things That I Do in the Dark, New York: Random House.

Jourard, S. The Transparent Self. New York: Jan Nostrand, 1971.

Karenga, M. Introduction to Black Studies. Inglewood, California: Kawaida Publications, 1982.

Ladner, J. Tomorrow's Tomorrow: The Black Woman, New York: Doubleday, 1972.

LaRue, L.Black Liberation and women's Lib. Transaction, 19709, 8(1), 59-63.

Lerner, G. Black Women in White America. New York: Vintage Books, 1973.

Liebow, E. Talley's Corner. Bostone: Little, Brown and Co.,1967.

Lorde, A. "Feminism and Black Liberation." The Black Scholar (1979) 10 (8.9); 17-20.

Noble, J. Beautiful, also, Are the Souls of my Black Sisters: A History of Black Women in America.

Englewood Cliffs, N.J.: Prentice-Hall, 1978.

Poussant, A. "Whihte Manipulation and Black." The Black Scholar (1979) 10 (8.9); 52-55.

Rodgers-Rose, L. the Black Woman. Beverly Hills, Calif. 1980.

Salaam, J. "Revolutionary Struggle/Revolutionary Love." The Black Scholar (1979) 10(8.9); 20-24.

Scott, J. "Polygamy: A Futuristic Family Arrangements for African-Americans," Black Books Bulletin (1976); 13-19.

Staples, R. The Black Woman in America, Chicago: Nelson-Hall, 1973.

_____."Masculinity and Race: The Dual Dilemma of Black Men."Journal of Social Issues (1978) 34(1); 1969-183.

_____."A Rejoiner: Black Feminism and the Cult of Masculinity: The Danger Within." The Black Scholar (1979) 10(8.9).

Toure, S. Toward Full Feafricanizaton.Paris: Presence Africane, 1959.

Tucker, R, Why Do Black Men Hide Their Feelings? New Yourk: Dial Press, 1979.

Wallace, M. Black Macho and the Myth of the Superwoman. New York: Dial Press, 1979.

Welsing, F. "The Cress Theory of Color Confrontation and Racism." The Black Scholar (1974) 5; 32-40.

Wilcox, P. Is There Life for Black Leaders after ERA? Black Male/Female Relationshipss (1979) 2 (1); 53-55.

Wilkinson, D. and Taylor R.L. (Eds.) The Black male in America. Chicago: Nelson-Hall.

THE STRUCTURAL COMPONENTS OF VIOLENCE IN BLACK MALE-FEMALE RELATIONSHIPS

DELORES P. ALDRIDGE * WILLA HEMMONS

An Afrocentric perspective provides a point of departure for the understanding of black male-female violence. American society is defined by and derived from core or dominant values, which have differentially impacted its diverse populations. The Lens Model presented in this discourse focuses on these values as being counterproductive for black male-female relationships. Capitalism, racism, sexism, and the Judeo-Christian ethic comprise the four-prong institutional or structural value components of the Lens Model. This dynamic framework is instructive as it helps social scientists view domestic violence in black adult relationships from a different perspective. The Lens Model has a connection to the "scientific method" which purports detachment, objectivity, and impartiality.

While the literature coupling African Americans to a discussion of violence is prolific, the scholarship analyzing the dynamics of this relationship is scant (Aldridge, 1984, 1989, 1991; Rodgers-Rose, 1985). Even more tenuous is a ubiquitous reluctance on the part of social scientists to affect a discourse on both topics' violence and black male-female relationships in the context of their societal background (Aldridge, 1991). An analysis of this crucial relationship is essential to forming an accurate and comprehensive understanding of how, why and when, the purported interpersonal relationships between blacks of opposite gender explode or erode into violence. More tenuous still, is for the analysis of the relationship between black men and women to take place within a well formulated schema.

"The Structural Components of Violence in Black Male-Female Relationships." Aldridge, Delores P., and Willa Hemmons. Co-published simultaneously in Journal of Human Behavior in the Social Environment (The Haworth Social Work Practice Press, an imprint of the Haworth Press, Inc.) Vol. 4, No.4, 2001, pp. 209-226; and: Violence as Seen Through a Prism of Col red: Letha A. (Lee) See)

The Haworth Social Work Practice Press, an imprint of The Haworth Press, Inc., 2001. Reprinted with permission conceptual or theoretical framework. Indeed, it has been convenient for conventional European-centered wisdom to have discussions surrounding violence between black men and women devoid of a framework that includes institutional or structural factors. Such a non-contextual discourse lends itself to a "blaming the victim" (Ryan, 1965). In this perspective the female who is often the "victim" bears the burden of being at fault for here vulnerable situation. The fact that her circumstances, far from being situational are more the result of structural factors in the society are camouflaged by focusing primarily on Eurocentric, interpersonal "Who shot Jane?" or "dumping ground" approaches.

Karenga's (1982) observations of black male-female relationships are most instructive. He points out that these interactions are no more problem ridden than those of other groups, and that life itself, is characterized by conflicts and problem-solving. Further, he asserts that, while many black male-female relationships are sufficiently healthy, enough are in trouble or non-existent to require that they undergo a sustained critical examination. Karenga cautions however, that criticism of black male-female relationships must always be accompanied by an in-depth review of the structure of our social system, complete with all of the variables that shape and mold individuals and ultimately their relationships.

The purpose of this paper is to focus primarily on structural factors that influence violence in black male-female relations. In this writing the Lens Model as a conceptual framework for analyzing these relations will presented. Specifically, the paper will (1) look at the structural components that impinge upon black male-female relationships (2) present the Lens Model and discuss its usefulness as a theoretical construct (3) against the backdrop of the Lens model suggestions are made on ways of improving the relations between black males and females who must occupy the same space and live-in harmony in our society.

DEFINITION OF TERMS

Any discourse on black male-female relationships must ultimately begin with a definition of terms. For some, conjuring up memories of past atrocities involved in these relationships is not a useful undertaking-mainly because this is a calamitous, or at worse, hurtful process. However, an examination of past behavior can be cleansing and assist one to move one's life.

Obviously, the definition of black males and females require no explanation however "relationships" and violence" are more troublesome concepts and require specific, definitive, and candid appraisal. In this writing "relationships" transcends beyond courtship, dating, and even marriage, and moves into a threshold of connectedness, where there is no subordination but unity of purpose affected between two individuals.

Violence is defined in many ways. However, in the criminological literature it is more often defined in terms of physical force or as a threat or use of physical force-all or which may stem from antecedent acts and consequences to attain a given end (Steinmetz & Straus, 1974). In this paper however, the force of strained relationships, aggression, cruelty, and destructive acts may be directly traceable to the structure of the American society, which has severely oppressed each partner in black relationships. Although there are still ambiguities in the literature, the true definitions of "relationships" and "violence" seem to lie just below the surface of a paradigm, which will later be described as the "Lens Model."

In examining the societal structure that often impinge on black male and female relationships it can be seen that American society is defined by and derived from core or dominant values which have differentially impacted diverse sub cultural groups. The Lens perspective presented in this discourse focuses on these values as being counter-productive for an understanding of black male-female relationships. In the structure of this society, capitalism, racism, sexism, and the Judeo-Christian ethic comprise the four-pronged institutional or structural value components that focus on an understanding of these relationships (see Figure 1). The numbers in Figure 1 represent blurred vision of focusing on relationships. Twenty-twenty (20/20) vision moves away from 20/20, the focusing loses varying degree of sharpness. By focusing on capitalism racism, sexism and Judeo-Christianism, analysis can sharpen or assess differing degrees of impact on male-female relationships among African Americans and for that matter on any group in the American society.

Figure 1. The Lens Model for Focusing on Black Male-Female Relationships.

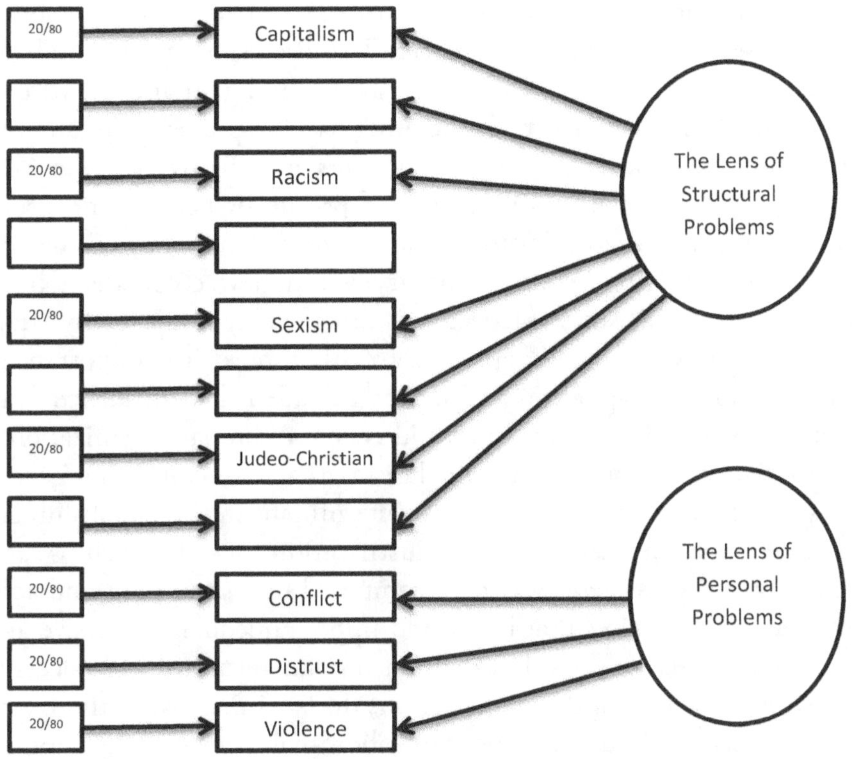

Note This Figure was designed by Dr. Delores P. Aldridge for the book, Violence as Seen through a Prism of Color. The Haworth Press, Inc., New York, NY.

Capitalism, which drives our economic system, may be defined as a socio-economic system in which private ownership is the primary means of satisfying human needs. One salient characteristics of capitalism is a strong and continuous pursuit of profit (Weber, 1950; Tawney, 1952; Marable, 1980). In capitalism the private ownership of goods and services lend to shape the view of human relationships. For example, the conceptual conversion of human beings into organisms to be owned, or an attitude in which people may subconsciously be viewed as objects for purchase and resale.

Concomitantly, racism may be defined as a system of denial and deformation of a people's history and humanity based primarily on the specious concept of race and hierarchies of races. Racism in America was born out of European feelings of racial superiority and is bred within the moral contradiction between Christian concepts and economic beliefs (see for example Max Weber, The Protestant Ethnic and the Spirit of Capitalism, 1950; Richard Tawney, Religion and the Rise of Capitalism, (1952). Slavery, on the other hand, represented an attempt at dehumanization of both the proponents as well as those who were enslaved. Slavery with its extension of private ownership and profit fragmented and almost destroyed the realm of all human relationships I this country. In the contemporary world new colonialism links capitalism and racism. Moreover, this linkage may result in any effort to affect an even-handed approach. In this context it is important to understand that capitalism and racism extended their influence from the interpersonal system to the world system of human organization.

Sexism is the political oriented "ism" that results in using gender or sex as an ascriptive and primary determinant in the establishment, maintenance, explanation, and justification of relationships and exchanges. As a system, sexism is composed of assumptions and acts, theories and practices that imply and impose unequal, oppressive and exploitative relationships based upon human relationships especially between black men and women it seems that sexism converts those who are dominate into an assortment of subordinate feminine stereotypes. Thus, they sitting targets to be "used."

The Judeo-Christian tradition is a religiously weighted system, which has its roots in Judaism and Christianity and draws heavily upon the cultural and social experiences of Jews, whites, and males. This tradition encourages identification with males as leaders and heroes. But more importantly, it emphasizes the leader-hero tradition as being one with elite males and their socio-economic experiences. Thus, any man who does not comply with such an ideal fall short within the value construct of American society. It is clear therefore, that a racist, sexist, capitalist, and Judeo-Christian macro systems form the basic structural value framework for analyzing black male-female relationships from an African centered or Afrocentric perspective (Aldridge, 1989).

AN AFRICAN CENTERED OR AFROCENTRIC PERSPECTIVE

In the journey toward the development of the "Lens Model" one needs to define all theoretical tenets that led to the development of this new framework. Thus, at this juncture the specific characteristics of the Afrocentric paradigm must be delineated. Nobles (1972, 1980), Akbar (1984), Baldwin (1985) and Asante (1988) are among contemporary scholars who have identified an Afrocentric approach to philosophy and human behavior and contributed to the development of what has come to be known as the Afrocentric paradigm. Dally, Jennings, Beckett and Leashore (1995), describe the Afrocentric approach as proposing that in Africa "cultural humanity is viewed as a collective rather than as individuals and that this collective view is expressed as shared concern and responsibility for the well-being of others (Akbar, 1984; Houston, 1990; Schiele, 1990).

The Afrocentric paradigm acknowledged feeling and emotions as well as rational and logical ways of thinking equally. Friendship, compassion, sharing, honesty, courage and self-control are among the other virtues of this perspective. It follows therefore, that the need for an African centered perspective in studying issues involving an African people is particularly salient when the dynamics of black male-female violence is so deeply mired in the function of the U.S. criminal justice system that is specifically designed to separate these two groups.

Ostensively, since blacks in the United States are in identified "out group," the function of the criminal justice system for black people whether alleged perpetrator or victim, has essentially been oppressive. Hence, it is postulated that the structural components of U.S. social institutions, including the criminal justice system prohibits the improvement of black male-female relationships. The resulting effects are expressed as violence, misuse, mistrust, and exploitation.

Furthermore, given the fact that both black men and women are an oppressed people, the harsh ramifications of societal policies and practices work a severe hardship upon the black community in general, and negate the notion of communism or "I am, because we are."

We turn now to a discussion of the "Lens Model" – which is the centerpiece of this chapter.

THE LENS MODEL: A CONCEPTUAL FRAME FOR ANALYZING BLACK MALE-FEMALE RELATIONSHIPS

A considerable number of writings have been published by African American and other scholar sin which they painstakingly addressed the breakdown in black male-female relationships from an Afrocentric perspective. These writing have been thought provoking, intellectually challenging, and polemics have emerged over whether the relationships have been unequal, exploitative, oppressive, and irresponsible. The writings although brilliant have produced no specific conceptual framework to help explain various aspects of the relationship phenomenon. The "Lens Model," an unadorned framework seeks to close that gap in the literature. It has multifaceted or eclectic attributes, which makes it a paradigm with considerable usefulness. Theis model was developed by first asking this question, what is a model? The literature is consistent neither in nominal definitions of what a model "is," nor in usage of the term. For example, Rubenstein and Haberstroh's (1960) discussing of organizational theory argue that a model gives "intuitive understanding" of the thing modeled: a model comes first, and contributes to theory-building. Miller (1956) reserves the term model for a formal identity between a conceptual system and an empirical one. According to Levi-Strauss (1953), social structure is to be regarded as a model. The Lens Model then, is a biological perspective that is crafted or "taylor-made" for usage in the social sciences. It selects the eyes as organs that can be employed to show that black males and females must see the same objects through the same pair of lenses.

According to the Webster Dictionary, a lens is a piece of glass, or other transparent object with two curved surfaces, or one plane and one curved surface. When brought together, the lens spread rays of light which is remarkably intensified. Using this definition, we see that historically, black men and women have experienced considerable difficulty attempting to come together or spread rays of light that will not "frost over," become cloudy, murky, or "out of focus." However, the societal structure has prevented them from shining bright as a couple by using every device at its disposal to keep the two groups divided to include amicable relations that would normally be exchanged with each other. The Lens Model addresses that deficiency.

OPERATIONALIZING THE LENS MODEL

A description of the Lens paradigm sets the stage for operationalizing this framework against a backdrop of black male-female relationships. Accordingly, the following postulates are set forth for this framework: (1) Black males and females have different experiences in a racist society and these are grossly different than those of white Americans. Accordingly, their relations must be viewed through the lens of a societal structure, which has denied and deformed black history and humanity based on the specious concept of race and hierarchies of race. (2) Sexual and gender oppression is a much an issue for African American males as it is for females. Thus, racism and sexism are interactive and inseparable as both are oppressed in similar yet different ways. Indeed, an analysis of sexism and the experiences of black men is needed which is different form the requirements of white men. The solving of this problem will cause the societal Lens to retract and for vision to become clear. (3) Demographics is a primary determinant of developing relationships between African American males and females. There is a significant shortage of available desirable, educated black men for black women to choose as mates. This shortage poses significant problems and prohibits the converging of the lens. (4) Capitalism and racism have generated situational inequities and sustained oppression which define the lives of people of African descent. These twin banes prohibit the Lens of society from becoming equal. (5) God-Christianism rooted in the social and cultural experiences of Jews, and white men provide images and models that encourage identification with white men as leaders, heroes. Thus, acting superior to black men and women causes the lens of the latter groups to misfocus, as they mistake the superficial for "the real thing." As can be seen therefore, the Lens Model analysis is a simple and comprehensive construct that enables practitioners to organize information in terms of relevance for change. It highlights areas of uncertainty, determines the feasibility of change and evaluates alternate interventions. At the heart of this paradigm is the conception that one's view of a situation is a dynamic force, and it is more powerful if black men and women will join efforts and work as a team rather than as separate entities, the case study of Mr. X will exemplify the point made so far in this writing.

THE CASE OF MR. X

Mr. X is a 26-year-old African American male and father of Doris X, age 6. He was accused of threatening his former wife, age 26 and her boyfriend when he came to pick up Doris for her regular weekly visit with him. As a dialysis patient Mr. X had never entered the home of this former wife and generally parked in the driveway and signaled by honking his car horn that he was waiting for Doris. The child's mother had always been ambivalent about the court ordered visitation rights, so on this day she had to prepared Doris for the visit with her father. After waiting in the car for an hour, Mr. X blew his horn continuously. Mrs. X' boyfriend came to the door and ordered him to cease the intimidation. Mr. X cursed at his former wife's boyfriend. At that point Mrs. X came to the door and he cursed at her also. Mrs. X called the police who arrested Mr. S for disturbing the peace. His bond was set at $30,000. Upon being contacted and apprised of the case a private attorney interviewed the arresting officers, the investigating detectives, bondspersons, judges, bailiffs and court clerks. Her objective was to obtain a release order for Mr. X to receive his dialysis treatment in order to prevent his lapsing into a coma. He was temporarily released with the understanding that he could not leave the city. This restriction made it impossible for Mr. X to travel to the college campus located 6 miles outside the city limit, where he had been awarded a scholarship to pursue a baccalaureate degree. The judge hearing the case had established a reputation as one who was "death on domestic violence." In fact, witness-victim advocated and court watchers who frequented his courtroom, as well as other judges in the municipality, remarked that he would not retract one inch from the "letter of the law." Mr. X's court appearance was not uneventful. During one session Mrs. X's boyfriend became unruly, had to be restrained, and was escorted from the court hearing. On another occasion the boyfriend attempted to physically assail Mr. X, the dialysis defendant. Finally, the case was dismissed. So, a case, which had begun in April 1999, had dragged on until mid-September. By then it was too late for Mr. X to properly enroll in college, so he lost his scholarship. He had not been able to comply with the conditions of his scholarship, which included making a campus visit, meeting with his advisor, and completing the final documents for enrollment. Additionally, with his arrest and court trial Mr. X could no longer write on this financial packet that he had no arrest record. Thus, with this case a young African man's potential for improving his life was sabotaged by a black female that was caught in a crossfire-between a former husband, and a current lover.

If the Lens Model were applied to this case from a purely Eurocentric view to black male-female violence one would most likely overlook the nuances of how the law was applied in this case. Such an approach would perhaps ignore how to economic, health and educational forces affected, in this instance the legal stages of the purported violence in black male-female relationships. Moreover, it is clear that there is need to consider the dynamics of black male-female violence form a Lens perspective-which means this case would be "viewed" through. Afrocentric lens which takes into consideration all the variables associated with this family conflict.

Many authors have written eloquently on the importance of black male-female relationships (Aldridge, 1989; Gordon, 1987; Hare & Hare, 1989; hooks, 1990, 1992; Karanga, 1982; Rodgers Rose and Rodgers, 1985). In sum, the perspective of these scholars is that if people have been oppressed, fragmented, dehumanized and demeaned by external forces, ultimately, they will begin to oppress, fragment dehumanize each other (Fanon, 1967; Aldridge, 1991; Rodgers-Rose and Rodgers,

1985) point out that black male-female relationships from the inception of their formation have been influenced by their societal environment Karenga (1982) posits:

Any criticism of black male-female relationships is at the same time and in equal measure a criticism of U.S. society which has shaped them to fit and function "properly" in it. Social conditions create both social consciousness and social conduct and failure to recognize this can lead one to see racial defects where social ones are more real and relevant. (1982, p. 291)

Results such as the case described above have led to the conclusion that, alternatives other than incrimination in situations involving domestic disputes should be pursued (Davis, 1998). This might be particularly true where the evidence is equivocal in as much as there is no apparent physical or mental injury and the situation has not been continuous. As Aldridge (1989 p.291) further indicates in her discourse:

Analyzes of the major defects in black male female relationships clearly reveal their social rather than genetic or purely personal basis. Thus, to understand the negatives of the relationship we must understand the negative characteristics of society which have shaped them.

ECONOMIC DISPARITY EXPERIENCED BY AFRICAN AMERICANS

In the case narrated above, the violence steaming from faulty black male-female relationships can be viewed from the Lens Model. This means that Mr. X's case could be viewed through lens that take into consideration the structural value systems of capitalism and racism which often operate synchronistically with each other (Glasglow, 1981; Mills, 1959; Marable, 1980). For example, the economic disadvantages faced by black men and women were exacerbated during the last half of the twentieth century. According to the U.S. Bureau of Census, the median family income of a family with a white male head of household was approximately $39,000 while a black female headed household results in a loss of almost $7,000 a year in annual income or $32,000. In general, families headed by blacks have incomes, which are sixty percent of those of whites (see Table 1). Thus, if the income disadvantages suffered by black family members is not frustrating, the prospects for economic improvements are serious. Despite, relatively low unemployment rates in the 1990s black people still were twice as likely to be unemployed than whites. Further, their poverty rates around the country averaged three times that of their white counterparts. Continuing this economic backdrop of black interpersonal dynamics, African Americans are still very conclusively shut out of the higher managerial level of corporate operations not to speak of ownership (Blackwell, 1991, p.303). Even if they mind their "P's" and "Q's" they still will be unable to move beyond token levels of middle management responsibility.

The economic situation is exacerbated likewise by two major political trends in the U.S. that plagued the post Reagan-Bush era (Blackwell, 1991, p. 483); One was the rampant explosion of million people, over half of whom are non-white origin, and the creation of essentially, a police state with a policy of zero tolerance for any black "deviance." The second was the passage of federal and state "Personal Responsibility" laws obliterating 'welfare' (as we know it). (42 U.S.C Sec. 601-678). However, no matter how inadequately implemented, eradicating any "safety-net" for millions of children-many of whom are non-white is brutal.

Hence, capitalism is the Lens through which any meaningful discussion of black-female violence must take into consideration. Black male-female relations do not take place in isolation. They are formed maintained and/or destroyed in a structural societal setting which is not geared toward the well-being of black men, black women, and their children.

Oliver (1994) suggests that the incidence of domestic violence is probably higher among blacks than among whites. Theoretically, he agrees with other African American scholars who contend that the

TABLE 1. Comparison of Summary Measures of Income by Selected Characteristics: 1989, 1997, and 1998.

| Characteristics | 1998 | | | Median Income in 1986 (in 1998 dollars) | | Median Income in 1989 (in 1996 dollars | | Percent Change in Real Income 1997 to 1998 | | Percent Change in Real Income 1989 to 1996 | |
| | Number (1,000) | Median Income | | Value (dollars) | 90 percent confidence interval (+/-) (dollars) | Value (dollars) | 90 percent confidence interval (+/-) (dollars) | Percent Change | 90 percent confidence interval (+/-) | Percent Change | 90 percent confidence interval (+/-) |
		Value (dollars)	90 percent confidence interval (+/-) (dollars)								
HOUSEHOLDS											
All households	103.874	38.885	378	37.581	286	37.884	344	*3.5	0.6	*2.6	0.8
Type of Household											
Family Household	71.535	47.469	410	46.053	394	45.343	413	*3.1	0.6	*4.7	0.8
Married Couple Families	54.770	54.276	530	52.486	388	50.702	458	*3.4	0.6	*7.0	0.9
Female Householder no husband present	12.789	24.393	655	23.399	657	22.662	60.	*4.2	2.0	*7.6	2.5
Male householder no wife present	3.976	39.414	1.633	37.205	1.201	39.717	1.607	*5.9	2.8	-0.8	3.5
Non-family households	32.339	23.441	467	22.043	347	22.568	22.568	363	*6.3	1.3	1.6
Female households	17.971	18.615	465	17.887	428	18.143	474	*4.1	1.8	2.6	2.2
Male householder	14.368	30.414	559	28.022	770	29.489	660	*8.5	1.8	*3.1	1.8

Race and Hispanic Origin of Householder											
All races	10.874	38.885	378	37.581	256	37.884	344	*3.5	0.6	*2.6	0.8
White	87.212	40.912	336	39.579	413	39.852	320	*3.4	0.7	*2.7	0.7
Non-Hispanic White	78.577	42.439	401	41.209	354	40.792	331	*3.0	0.6	*4.0	0.8
Black	12.579	25.351	653	25.440	720	23.950	789	-0.3	1.9	*5.8	2.7
Asian Pacific and Islander	3.306	46.637	2.135	45.954	2.102	47.337	2.007	1.5	3.2	-1.5	3.7
Hispanic Origin	9.060	28.330	896	792	28.631	28.631	882	*4.8	1.8	-1.1	2.7
Age of Householder											
15-24 years	5.770	23.564	730	22.935	822	24.401	755	2.7	2.4	-3.4	2.6
25-34 years	18.819	40.069	696	38.769	755	39.041	603	*3.4	1.3	*2.6	1.5
35-44 years	23.968	48.451	730	47.081	637	49.310	675	*2.9	1.0	-1.7	1.2
45-54 years	20.158	54.148	877	52.682	727	54.575	893	*2.8	1.1	-0.8	1.4
55-64 years	13.571	43.167	989	42.000	783	40.569	878	*2.8	1.5	*6.4	2.0
65 years and over	21.589	21.729	395	21.064	406	20.719	381	*3.1	1.3	*4.9	1.0
Nativity of the Householder											
Native born	92.853	39.677	390	38.229	381	(NA)	(NA)	*3.8	0.7	(X)	(X)
Foreign born	11.021	32.963	1.230	31.806	802	(NA)	(NA)	3.6	2.3	(X)	(X)
Naturalized Citizen	4.877	41.028	1.808	(NA)	(NA)	(NA)	(NA)	(X)	(X)	(X)	(X)
Not a citizen	6.143	28.278	1.199	27.379	971	(NA)	(NA)	3.3	2.8	(X)	(X)

Region											
Northeast	19.877	40.634	772	39.535	877	42.780	709	*2.8	1.5	-5.0	1.5
Midwest	24.489	40.609	600	38.913	747	37.685	642	*4.4	1.3	*7.8	1.5
South	36.959	35.797	500	34.880	580	33.933	471	*2.6	1.1	*5.5	1.0
West	22.549	40.983	681	39.772	910	40.705	696	*3.0	1.4	0.7	1.4
Residence											
Inside metropolitan areas	83.441	40.983	352	39.994	448	40.776	346	*2.5	0.7	0.5	0.7
Inside central cities	32.144	33.151	638	32.039	456	(NA)	(NA)	*3.5	1.5	(X)	(X)
Outside central cities	51.297	46.402	512	45.364	568	(NA)	(NA)	*2.3	0.8	(X)	(X)
Outside metropolitan areas	20.433	32.022	630	30.525	690	29.393	636	*4.9	1.5	*8.9	1.9
EARNINGS OF FULL-TIME YEAR-ROUND WORKERS											
Male	56.951	35.345	219	34.199	535	35.727	242	*3.4	0.9	*-1.1	0.6
Female	38.785	25.562	194	25.362	259	24.614	270	*2.0	0.7	*5.1	0.9
PER CAPITA INCOME											
All races	271.743	20.120	199	19.541	202	18.280	132	*3.0	0.7	*10.1	0.8

White	223.294	21.394	237	20.743	239	19.385	147	*3.1	0.8	*10.4	0.8
Non-Hispanic	193.074	22.952	268	22.246	271	(NA)	(NA)	*3.2	0.9	(X)	(X)
Black	35.070	12.957	322	12.543	346	11.406	253	*3.3	1.9	*13.6	2.1
Asian and Pacific Islander	10.867	18.709	1.094	1.126	1.128	(NA)	(NA)	1.1	4.4	(X)	(X)
Hispanic origin	31.689	11.434	410	10.941	393	10.770	294	*4.5	2.3	*6.2	2.7

* Statically significant change at the 90 percent confidence level.

* Revised to reflect the population distribution reported in the 1900 census.

[1] Data for American Indians. Eskimos, and Aleuts are not shown separately. Data for this population group are not tabulated from the CPS because of its small size.

[2] Hispanics may be of any race.

Source: U.S. Census Bureau. Current Population Survey, March 1990, 1998, and 1999.

Major reason for difference is due to racism. The internal devaluation of their self-worth as individuals precipitates much black violence, against other blacks, and toward whites. Since many blacks have little power to effect change, overwhelming obstacles and hopelessness produce high levels of frustration. Poussaint, (1972), p. 72) states that … "frustrated men may beat their wives in order to feel manly and thee violent acts are an outlet for a desperate struggle against feelings of inferiority." Oliver (1994), observes that beatings and arguments precipitated by a husband seem to occur particularly when there is a discrepancy between the demands on him as a provider and his ability to meet those demands. Consequently, his response is an attempt to regain status and respect for his role as head of the family.

Aldridge (1991) has employed her Lens Model to underscore how the structural value systems of capitalism, racism, sexism and Judoe-Christianism impose strains upon black male-female relationships. However, additional insights may be revealing. Karenga (1982, p. 292) contends that with blacks' strains can be expressed "as a transformation of the relationship into what can be described as 'connections.'" He posits that the four basic relationships in the U.S., and by extension between black males and females are: (1) the cash connection (2) the flesh connection (3) the force connection and (4) the dependency connection. But the economic motif in the U.S. transforms everyone into a commodity including the black female who according to this perspective can be bought and paid for because everyone has a price. In short, the "cash" connection causes black men and women to lose sight of each other as human beings and treat each other as market items. What Karenga (1982), is suggesting is that the connection allows both parties to exploit each other without remorse and teat each other in a heartless manner thus contributing to their mutual dehumanization without assessing their predicament through 20/20 vision.

TOWARD NEW MODALITIE IN BLACK MALE-FEMALE RELATIONSHIPS

New modalities in black male-female relationships demands that the quality relations between the two groups must grow out of a conscious struggle for change. A quality relationship is a stable association defined by its positive sharing and mutual investment in the emotional and psychological well-being of each other. African American women have the responsibility to select mates/partners who affirm their strengths, capabilities, and potentials. The complementary nature of the support provided by each member of the relationship sustains a resilience and a positive assertion of love, respect, and trust. It is thus incumbent upon the black male and female to find solutions to shield their relationship from violence. This means developing means to offset the interpersonal and institutional components imposed by the structure of the society, Hill-Collins (1991, p. 188) is among those who subscribe to the Lens Model by concluding that:

> … we need a holistic analysis of how race, gender and class oppression frame the gender ideology internalized by both African women and men. By deconstructing violence as a seemingly inevitable outcome of racism and sexism, other alternatives become possible, (p. 188)

In the Psychology of blacks: An Afro-American Perspective, White (1984, p. 73) captures the essence of the matter in the following description:

> The ideal male-female relationship within extended family networks and in the black community at large would be characterized by the Afro-American values of interdependence, cooperation, and mutual respect, without a fixed classification of household, economic and social responsibilities based on sex. Male-female relationships that are built on a bond of sharing, nurturance, tenderness and appreciation have the strong psychological foundation necessary to cope with the social and economic stresses that usually confront black couples living in a country dominated by Euro-Americans impact on male-female relationships.

In the future more research is needed to examine status devaluation as a racial group and how such status is expressed in violent behavior and what mediating factors control violence in some relationships while fostering it in others. Further, a crucial area of needed research is an analysis of employment trends and male-female violence. Does this violence increase as the rate of unemployment increases? What relationship exists, if any, between the type of status of occupations and the incidence of male-female violence? Finally, exploration of the relationship of strong religious orientation to violence would be a useful lens through which to examine the structural value system in the African American community.

CONCLUSION

The dynamic Lens Model allows social scientists to focus upon and approach an understanding of the complexity of the relations between black males and females. In the U.S. society, the integrity of being both black men and black women is constantly under assault. They both have sought refuge in the sanctity of their relationship with each other not recognizing that the long arm of the "master" has found its way into their bedroom. It will only take an intensive program of self-awareness and working together to gain some control of the political, economic, educational, health and communication institutions that help structure and determine the nature and quality of their relationship and to improve it. If the violence against the integrity of their personhood is taken away or diminished, likewise so will the violence which permeates their most intimate relationship be eliminated.

REFERENCES

Akbar, Naim. (1984). Afrocentric social services of human liberation. Journal of Black Studies, 14, 395-413.

Alsridge, Delores P. (1989). Black male-female relationships: A resource book of selected materials 9Ed.). Dubuque, Iowa: Kendall/Hunt Publishing Company.

______.(1991). Focusing: Black male-female relationships. Chicago: Third World Press.

______.(1984). Toward a theoretical perspective for understanding black male-feale realtionships. The Western Journal of Black Studies, 8, 184-191.

Allen, Walter R. (1981). "Moms, dads and boys: Race and sex differences in the socialization of male children. In Lawrence E. Gary (Ed.) Black Men. Beverly Hills, Calif.: Stat Publications, pp. 99-114.

Asante, Moleti. (1987). The afrocentric idea. Philadelphia: Temple Uniersity Press.

______.Afrocentricity. Trento, NJ: Africa World.

Blackwell, James E. (1991). The black community: Diversity and unity. Third Edition. New York: Harper Collins Publishers.

Daly, Alfrieda, Jeannette Jennings, Joyce O. Beckett, and Bogart R. Leashore (1995). Effective coping strategies of African Americans. Social Work, 40, 240-248.

Davis, Richard I. (1998). Domestic violence. Westport, CT: Praeger Publishers.

Fanon, Franz (1967). The wretched of the earth. New York: Grove.

Gelles, Richard J. (1993). Family violence. In introduction to Social Problems, C. Calhoun and G. Ritzer (Eds.) pp. 553-571.

Glasglow, Douglas (1981). The black underclass: Poverty, unemployment, and entrapment of ghetto youth. San Francisco, CA: Jossey-Bass Publishers.

Gordon, Vivian V. (1987). Black women, feminism, and black liberation: Which way? Chicago: Third World Press.

Hemmons, Willa. (1996). Black women in the new world order: Social justice and the African American female. Westport, CT.: Praeger Publishers.

Hill-Collins, Patricia. (1991). Black feminist thought: Knowledge, consciousness, and the politics of empowerment. New York: Routledge.

Hooks, bell. (1990). Ain't a Woman: black women and feminism. Boston: South End Press.

Houston, L.N. (1990). Psychological principles and the black experience. New York: University Press of America.

Karenga, Maulana. (1982). Introduction to black studies. Los Angeles: The University of Sankore Press.

Lev-Strauss, Claude. (1953). Social structure. In A.L. Kroeber (Ed.) Anthropology Today.
Chicago: The University of Chicago Press, pp. 524-553.

Marable, Manning (1980). How capitalism underdeveloped black America: Problems in race political economy and society. Boston. South End Press.

Miller, James G. toward a general theory for the behavioral sciences, in the state of the social sciences. Leonard D. White (ed), Chicago: The University of Chicago Press, pp. 29-65.

Mills, C. Wright (1959). The power elite. New York: Oxford.

Nobles, Wade W. (1980). African American family life: An instrument of culture. In H.P.

McAdoo (ed.), Black families (pp.77-86). Beverly Hills, CA: Sage Publications.

Oliver, William (1994). The violent social world of African American men. New York: Lexington.

Poussaint, Alvin (1972). Why Blacks Kill Blacks. New York: Emerson Hall.

Rodgers-Rose, LaFrancis and James T. Rodgers (1985). Strategies for resolving conflict in black male and female relationships. Plainfield, NJ: Traces Institute Publications.

Rubenstein, Albert H. and Chadwick J. Haberstroh (eds.) Some theories of organization. Homewood, IL: The Dorsey Press and Richard D. Irwin, Inc. Also see, Morgan, G. (Ed.).

Ryan, William. (1965). Savage Discovery: The Moynihan Report. Nation, November 22.

Schiele, Jerome H. (1990). Organizational theory from an Afrocentric perspective. Journal of Black Studies, 21, 145-161.

Social Security Act, 42 U.S.C. Secs. 401 et al. (As Amended 1996).

Steinmetz, Suzanne K. & Straus, Murray A. (1974). Violence in the family, New York: Dodd, Mead.

Tawney, Richard. (1952). Religion and the rise of capitalism. New York: Harcourt, Brace and Co., Inc.

U.S. Bureau of the Census. Current population survey, March 1990, 1998, and 1999.

Weber, Max. (1950). The protestant ethic and the spirit of capitalism, translated by Talcott Parsons. New York: Charles Scribner's Sons.

White, Josph L. The psychology of black: an Afro-American perspective. Englewood Cliffs, NJ: Prentice-Hall, 19884.

Young, Carlene. (1989). Psychodynamics of coping and surviving of the African American female in a changing world. Journal of Black Studies.

_____. (1986). Afro-Americans family: Contemporary Issues and implications for social policy. On Being black: An in-group analysis (ed.) David Pilgrim, Wyndham Hall Press.

CHAPTER TWO
Demographic Issues

Jacquelyn J. Jackson gives insight into contemporary demographic and sociological influences upon black males and black females. Her oft-quoted paper concerning the scarcity of black males explores social implications for black male and black female relationships, especially for the black family. It also provides a guide to regions where black males outnumber black females. And, while the male shortage is increasing there are ways to counteract the shortage. Lawrence Gary is more inclusive in his demographic treatise, choosing to focus upon the black male from a social and demographic profile of his existence in America. The social profile presented is envisioned as providing a framework for facilitating an understanding of the high psychosocial and economic risk status of black men that often leads to unhealthy adaptations. LaFrancis Rodgers-Rose completes the dyad through her focus upon demographic statistics of black females. While the data of the works mentioned above may appear to contradict each other at points, they included because of the extent to which they have been referenced in other sources.

The Aba D. Essuon work rounds out the chapter on demographics. It provides an update of the demographics from 1975 to 2000. This update allows for reflections on how ratios have changed or remained the same over time. In providing this analysis, variable have been added which include health issues due to HIV Aids and increased incarcerations as factors impacting male-female ratios.

BUT WHERE ARE THE BLACK MEN?

JACQUELYN JACKSON

The question, "But where are the males?" refers inevitably to that of the sex ratio (i.e., the number of males per every one hundred females). One highly significant gap in almost all contemporary scientific, pseudo-scientific, and ideological concerns about black women and especially about black female household heads – is that of the failure to consider the implications of the sex ratio itself. This gap can be attributed directly to the general tendency of social scientists and social policymakers to ignore the realities of the prevailing black sex ratios and concomitant factors, such as the aforenoted tendency of white females to seek black mates.

Such a gap is particularly deplorable in the social sciences, inasmuch as Oliver C. Cox focused specific in 1940. For present purposes, it is imperative to note that Cox indicated quite clearly the following:

1. Differences in the marital status of persons in different areas and communities may be due of differences in the ration of marriageable men to women; [2]
2. The racial sex ratio varies considerably in the different regional divisions of the United States;[3]
3. The percentage of Negro families married in cities is particularly sensitive to changes in the sex ratio, while the percentage of males married seems to respond almost not at all. [4]

Thus, as the black sex ratio rose, the percentage of black females who were married rose. As that sex ration declined, so did the percentage of married black females.

Table 1. Black Sex Ratios by Age and Geographical Location, 1970

		Geographical Location			
Age (years)	U.S.	Northeast [1]	North Central [2]	South [2]	West [2]
Total, all ages	90.8	87.5	91.3	98.8	97.6
Under 5	99.3	100.7	100.0	90.8	97.6
5-14	100.4	100.7	99.8	100.5	100.3
25-34	93.0	87.1	90.1	94.5	105.6
35-44	84.3	78.6	83.4	85.4	95.7
45-54	86.4	78.6	83.4	85.4	94.0
55-64	85.3	78.3	89.7	85.6	90.3
65+	76.4	71.7	81.4	76.2	76.3

1. Source of raw data: U.S. Department of Commerce/Bureau of the Census, 1970 Census of Population, Advance Report, "General Population Characteristics, United States," PC (V2)-1, U.S. Department of Commerce.
2. Northwestern states include Maine, New Hampshire, Vermont, Massachusetts, Rhode Island, Connecticut, New York, New Jersey, and Pennsylvania; North Central includes Ohio, Indiana, Illinois, Michigan, Wisconsin, Minnesota, Iowa, Missouri, North Dakota, South Dakota, Nebraska, and Kansa; the South includes Delaware, Maryland, District of Columbia, Virginia, West Virginia, North Carolina, South Carolina, Georgia, Florida, Kentucky, Tennessee, Alabama, Mississippi, Arkansas, Louisiana, Oklahoma, and Texas; and the West encompasses Montana, Idaho, Wyoming, Colorado, New Mexico, Arizona, Utah, Nevada, Washington, California, Alaska, and Hawaii.

Since 1940, the black sex ratio has actually worsened, if judged at least from the perspective of black females. Yet most contemporary literature is written as if there were one black male for each black female. That literature almost always fails to inquire about ale availability levels fo black females. Probably the most glaring example is The Moynihan Report. [5] Moynihan tended to assume that male unemployment was the critical factor affecting the proportion of female-headed households among blacks, but he failed miserably in dealing with the actual supply of black males for black females.

Census data clearly reveal that females have been excessive in the black population of the United States since at least 1850, or a period of more than 120 years. In 1850, the black sex ration was 99.1, rising slightly to 99.6 in 1860, but declining to 96.2 in 1870. In 1880, it was

97.8; and in 1920, 99.2. In 1900, 9836; in 1910, 98.9; and in 1920, 99.2. since 1920, the black sex ratio has decreased consistently, from 97.0 in 1930, to 95.0 in 1940, to 94.3 in 1950, to 93.3 in 1960, and, in 1970, to 90.8, or approximately 91 black males for every 100 black females. Thus for the past 50 years, black men have becoming scarcer and scarcer. It is not just the case that they are more likely to be missed in the Census counts, but that they are just not there.[6]

If no adjustment is made for age, at least 1, 069, 694 of the 11, 885, 595 black females in the population of the United States in 1970 would have been without available, monogamous mates. When age-adjusted and regional-adjusted data are presented, as shown in Table 1, the unadjusted pattern does not undergo any significant change. As can be seen in Table1, in the United States as a whole, black females are not more numerous than black males only within one age group, that of 5 to 14 years. They are more numerous in all of the remaining age groupings, and especially so during female childbearing ages. The same is true of the geographical divisions, with one exception occurring in the West among the 15- to 24-year-old grouping.

It is relevant now to inquire about alternative familial forms developed in the absence of a sufficient supply of males. Two of those forms, unnecessarily and irrationally viewed as "deviant" by the American white subculture, are those of female-headed households and illegitimacy. The nomenclature of "illegitimacy" is inappropriately applied to blacks, for any number of reasons, but the common usage of such a concept does not reflect a tendency of many whites to attempt to "desexify" blacks. It is quite important to add that the development of that term occurred at a time when white males exceeded white females in the United States as well. The application of the term was also grossly unfair to blacks who were already in the process of developing alternative familial forms in the absence of a sufficient supply of males, a condition not confronting whites until 1950.

The "problem" of female-headed households can only be perceived as a "problem" by those who act, again, as if there were identical supplies of males and females. When such is not the case, as it is clearly not in the case of blacks, then the phenomenon should be perceived as a rational alternative to an ineffective traditional system. It should be quite obvious that slavery is an insufficient factor to be used in explicating both illegitimacy and female-headed households, for, by the usual measures of family stability, as Frazier, has noted, black family stability continued progressively throughout the latter half of the nineteenth century and up until 1910. [7]

In fact, Census data show that in 1900, for persons 15+ years of age, there were no significant differences in marital statuses by race or by sex between black and white females and males. But since then, as the black sex ratio has decreases, the marital statuses of black females, in particular, have also been affected, as Cox demonstrated. [8] The marital statuses of black females have been far more sensitive that reducing sex ration that have those of black males, which leads us into an exploration of one of the relationships which may exist between black sex ratios and familial patterns, specifically that of female-headed households.

As that sex ratio has decreased, has proportion of female-headed households among blacks has increases, suggesting thereby that a possible causative factor for the latter may be the former. If we examine available 1970 data on the black sex ratio and the proportion of female-headed households among blacks in each state and the District of Columbia, what will emerge will be a significant inverse relationship between those two variables ($r = -.68$, $df = 49$, and $p > .001$) . In other words, as shown in Table 2, there is a tendency for the proportion of female-handed households to increase as the supply of males decreases. Conversely, when the supply of males increases, the proportion of female-headed households decreases. For example, the excess of black males over black females is greatest in Hawaii, where the proportion of black female-headed households ranks quite low. In fact, only two states (North Dakota and South Dakota) rank lower than Hawaii in the proportion of female-headed households among blacks. On the other hand, the sex ratio is lowest in New York (85.9, or approximately 86 males per every 100 females), and 32.1 percent of black families within the state were headed by females in 1970, exceeded only by Massachusetts, where 34.3 percent of black families were female-headed.

Despite the fact that black females are excessive in the black population, that excessive phenomenon is not equitably distrusted throughout the United States. In 19 states, black males outnumber females. Those states are Hawaii, Montana, North Dakota, Idaho, south Dakota, Utah, Alaska, Vermont, Maine, New Hampshire,

Wyoming, Washington, Colorado, Rhode Island, Minnesota, Arizona, New Mexico, Nevada and Oregon – none are southern states. They are also states containing extremely minute proportions of age (i.e., 65+ years) blacks, which suggests that they are probably less affected by the considerably shortened life expectancy rates of black males than is true of the remaining states. Thus, the proportion of widowed black females who may find it necessary to assume a status a household head is reduced.

This geographical disproportion in the distribution of black females and males also has consequences for familial patterns in that, as indicted above and as evident in Table 2, black females are generally least likely to be heads on households where the sex ratio is the highest. Thus, it may be that black male geographical mobility has been significantly different from that of black females, suggesting thereby two different types of policy alternatives for those concerned about the proportion of black female-headed households. One implication may well be that greater geographical mobility could be encouraged among black females, especially those in such states as New York, Massachusetts, Pennsylvania, Oklahoma, New Jersey, and Connecticut, where such encouragement would include the lure of significant opportunities for receipt of higher education, professional occupation, and incomes approximating at least the median income of all individuals in the United States. That might help move the "girls" to "where the boys are."

A second, but different type of implication, might well be the continuing development of alternative familiar forms, including that of polygyny, a system appropriate in the absence of a sufficient supply of males. Polygyny, of course, requires male participants with sufficient resources to maintain adequately several or more families. At the present time, almost no black males are economically equipped within the United States to participate in such a system, which forestalls any present concerns about the acceptability of such a system to black females. Nevertheless, as some keen observers have indicated in various private conversations with at least the writer, the legitimacy of polygyny could well benefit some females who are involved in "playing the polygyny," but who are denied legally any of the benefits to which they may otherwise be entitled.

For example, on a recent visit to Kampala, Uganda, the Vice Chancellor of Makerere University noted that in defense of polygyny, the women participating as spouses had a legal status of wife, not that of whore, slut, mistress, et cetera. Thus, not only did such wives not have illegitimate children, but both they and their children had legal protection under the law, which he regarded as a more "civilized" system than that existing in the "civilized" United States. He may have a point worth further investigation. In any case, it is quite clear that there is not one absolute system of marriage and family which must be adhered to at any cost and under any circumstance. Such is even the case among white Americans.

Table 2. Black Sex Ratios and the Percentage of Female-Headed Families and Their Rank Orders in the United States. 1970 [1]

State	Sex Ratio	% Female-Headed Families	Sex Ratio Rank[2]	% Female-Headed Families Rank[2]
Hawaii	192.5	7.1	1.0	3.0
Montana	169.2	24.2	2.0	16.0
North Dakota	160.3	2.9	3.0	1.0
Idaho	158.5	9.0	4.0	5.5
South Dakota	157.0	6.2	5.0	2.0
Utah	151.6	21.6	6.0	10.0
Alaska	147.3	7.8	7.0	4.0
Vermont	139.3	13.0	8.0	8.0
Maine	136.9	9.0	9.0	5.5
New Hampshire	130.4	9.9	10.0	7.0
Wyoming	114.2	13.2	11.0	9.0
Washington	113.0	23.1	12.0	12.0
Colorado	105.2	22.1	13.0	11.0
Rhode Island	102.5	31.7	14.0	49.0
Minnesota	102.4	28.5	15.0	36.5
Arizona	102.2	25.5	16.0	21.0
New Mexico	101.1	24.3	17.0	17.5
Nevada	100.8	23.6	18.0	13.0
Oregon	100.5	26.1	19.0	26.0
Kansas	97.9	27.2	20.0	29.0
Lowa	95.9	28.9	21.0	42.0

California	95.2	28.1	22.0	34.5
Virginia	94.7	23.7	23.0	14.0
Wisconsin	94.0	30.8	24.0	46.0
Michigan	93.6	25.7	25.5	22.5
Nebraska	93.6	30.5	25.5	45.0
Kentucky	93.0	27.9	27.0	33.0
Maryland	92.8	27.0	28.0	27.0
Indiana	92.7	24.7	29.5	19.0
Delaware	92.7	28.1	29.5	34.5
Texas	92.4	24.0	31.0	15.0
North Carolina	92.1	25.8	32.0	24.0
Florida	91.7	28.5	33.0	36.5
South Carolina	91.4	26.0	34.0	25.0
Ohio	90.6	27.1	35.0	28.0
Mississippi	90.1	25.7	36.0	22.5
Louisiana	90.0	27.6	37.0	32.0
Arkansas	89.8	24.3	38.0	17.5
Connecticut	89.7	30.4	39.0	43.5
New Jersey	89.5	30.4	40.0	43.5
Illinois	89.4	28.8	41.0	40.5
Oklahoma	89.3	31.1	42.0	47.0
Missouri	89.1	28.8	43.0	40.5
Massachusetts	88.6	34.3	45.0	51.0
Georgia	88.6	28.6	45.0	38.0
District of Columbia	88.6	28.7	45.0	39.0
Tennessee	88.3	27.9	47.5	30.0
Pennsylvania	88.3	31.3	47.0	48.0
Alabama	88.0	27.4	49.0	31.0
West Virginia	87.6	24.8	50.0	20.0
New York	85.9	32.1	51.0	50.0

1. Source of raw data: U.S. Department of Commerce/Bureau of the Census, 1970 Census of Population, Advance Report. "General Population Characteristics, United States," PC (V2) 1. U.S. Department of Commerce Washington, D.C. February, 1971.

2. Rank ordering for the sex ratio is from high to low. That is, the state with the highest sex ration (Hawaii) is ranked 1.0, while that with lowest (New York) is ranked 51.0. Ranked ordering for the percentage of female-headed households is from low to high. That is, the state with the lowest preparation (North Dakota) is ranked 1.0, while Massachusetts, with the highest, is ranked 51.0

WHITE SEX RATIOS

It has already been established that females have been excessive in the black population since 1850. Table 3, which provides a comparison of the black and white sex ratios, 1850-1970, shows clearly evidence permitting the statement already made those blacks have had a "headstart" on whites in developing alternative familial patterns in the absence of a sufficient number of males. Black are at least 100 years ahead of whites in this respect. A cursory examination of such variables as those of marital statuses, illegitimacy rates, and intermarriage rates is invaluable in noting certain trends depicting whites as becoming more like blacks.

Table 3. Black and White Sex Ratios, 1850-1970 [1]

| Year | Sex Ratios | |
	Black	White
1850	99.1	105.2
1860	99.6	105.3
1870	96.2	102.8
1880	97.8	104.0
1890	99.5	105.4
1900	98.6	104.9
1910	98.9	106.6
1920	99.2	104.4
1930	97.0	102.9
1940	95.0	101.2
1950	94.3	99.1
1960	93.3	97.3
1970	90.8	95.3

1. For whites in 1970, the data include non-blacks. Sex ratios were obtain from Census reports for the specified years.

Table 4 provides some limited information on two of the three variables referred to above, namely marital statuses and illegitimacy. If we examine female marital statuses, by race, from 1900 through 1970, we see that in 1900, when the black sex ratio was 98.6 an the white 104.9, there were no significant differences by race in marital statuses. In fact, a slightly higher proportion of the black females were returned as married, while a slightly larger proportion of the whites were returned as divorced, but slightly fewer as widowed. By 1940, when the black sex ratio had declined to 95.0 while that of the whites remained above 100, it is evident that the divorce rates by race were identical, while the widowhood rate was higher among blacks than whites. In addition, data available for person married with spouses present (not available in the 1900 Census) showed that the decreasing sex ratio had affected the proportion of black females likely to fall within that category, while the whites remained relatively unaffected.

In 1960, when the sex ratios among both blacks and whites had declined to 93.3 and 97.3 respectively, we actually find that a larger proportion of females in both racial groups were returned as married, with spouse present. By that year, their divorce rates were no longer identical, but both were rising, 3.6 among the blacks, and 2.7 among the whites, as compared with the 1940 rate of 1.7.

By 1970, with the sex ratios continuing to decline (90.8 among blacks, 95.3 among whites), it is clear that the proportion of females married; with spouse present had declined both among black and white females from the percentage given in 1960. In 1970, 9.8 percent fewer black females and 4.9 percent fewer white females were so classified. The major factor contributing to that change may, perhaps, be found in the increased proportion of those single, which is over twice as high among the black females, 1960-1970, than among the white females. In 1970, as it may be recalled, over nine black females out of every 100 would have been theoretically classified as being without monogamous males, true of only about five out of every 100 white females.

Thus, a partial explication of the differences in the marital statuses by race should not be sought, as is quite commonly done, within black family disorganization, but within the effects of sex ratios upon marital statuses. While the divorce rate in 1970 continued to be higher among black than among white females, the rate among the latter also continued to increase from 1960 to 1970.

Data in Table 4 depicting the percent of female-headed families do reveal, as expected, that the proportion of such families is considerably higher among blacks than among whites. However, the proportionate increase among blacks was less from 1960 to 1970 (119.6%) than it was from 1950 to 1960 (127.3%), whereas the proportionate increase among whites was greater in 1960-1970 (104.6%) than between 1950-1960, when it was 102.4 percent. Consequently, although the sex ratios were continuing to decline among both groups, the rate of increase in female-headed families among whites continued to rise between 1950-1970, while it had begun to decrease somewhat among blacks over the same time period.

A similar pattern emerges upon examination of the percentage changes occurring over time in two other variables the percent of own children living with both parents as the percent of all own children, and the percent change in estimated illegitimacy rates. In the case of the former variable, from 1960-1970, the percent of such children among both races declined, from 75 to 67 percent among blacks, and from 92 to 91 percent among whites, a decrease which may also be related to their decreasing sex ratios and increasing proportions of female-headed families.

Table 4, Selected Statistical Comparisons between Blacks and Whites

Characteristic	Black	White
Female Marital status		
1900, 15+ years of age		
% single	39.8	40.1
% married	55.5	55.4
% divorced	0.2	0.3
% widowed	4.3	4.0
1940, 15+ years of age		
% single	23.9	26.0
% married, spouse present	44.2	56.9
% divorced	1.7	1.7
% widowed	15.8	11.1
1960, 14+ years of age		
% single	22.3	18.7
% married, spouse present	51.8	65.2
% divorced	3.6	2.7
% widowed	14.0	12.0

1970, 14+ years of age		
% single	28.0	21.3
% married, spouse present	42.0	60.3
% divorced	4.3	3.4
% widowed	13.5	12.4
Percent of female-headed families		
1950	17.6	8.5
1955	20.7	9.0
1960	22.4	8.7
1966	23.7	8.9
1970	26.4	9.1
1971	28.9	9.4
Percent of own children living with both parents, as percent of all own children		
1960	75	92
1970	67	91
Percent change in estimated illegitimacy rates		
1940- 1944 to 1955- 1959	+166	+139
1955- 1959 to 1968	-8	+53

Sources of data U.S. Census Office, Census Reports, Vol. 2 Part 2, "Population," U.S. Govt. Printing Office Washington, D.C. 1902: U.S Bureau of the Census, Sixteenth Census of the United Stated: 1940, Vol. 1, "Population, Characteristics of the Population," U.S Govt. Printing Office, Washington, D.C 1943: U.S Bureau of the Census, U.S Gov. Printing Office, Washington D.C 1964. The Social and Economic Status of Negroes in the Commerce/Bureau of the Census, Washington, D.C July 1971: and Social and Economic Characteristics of the Population in Metropolitan and Nonmetropolitan Areas; 1970 and 1960. Current Population Reports, Series P 23 No, 37 U.S Govt. Printing Office, Washington, D.C. 1971.

While illegitimacy as usually defined remains higher among blacks than among whites, it is very interesting to note that illegitimacy rates have been declining among blacks, while increasing among whites, as also shown in Table 4. In other words, the rate of illegitimate births is rising among whites while their sex ratio is declining, which is a pattern not at all unlike that which transpired much earlier among blacks. Thus, it appears that as females become more excessive in the white population, the proportion seeking family forms deviating from the traditional is on the increase. In this sense and a very important sense, to be sure white are following trends mapped out earlier by blacks.

Whites, of course, have not yet "caught up" with blacks in developing various alternative patterns for several different reasons, with the most important one probably being that black females are yet more excessive in the black population than are those in the white population, and particularly so during the childbearing years of 15-44, as can be seen by inspecting the data provided in Table 5. For the years 15-44 inclusive, the sex ratios are much lower than among blacks than whites, and especially so for the years 25-44, as of 1970. Interestingly, however, for those 65+ years of age, the black sex ratio is actually higher than that of the whites, a finding readily explicable by the greater longevity of white females as compared with blacks and with white males. In passing, what may also be quite impressive about Table 5 is an inference that the significant differences in the sex ratios between blacks and whites are not reflected to the same extent in the differences in their illegitimacy rates. That is, given the fact again that white females are not as excessive in the white population as are black females within the black population, and considering also that white females have far greater access to black males as marital partners than do black females to white males, one must wonder why the white illegitimacy rate as high as it is among whites and as low as it is among blacks!

Table 5. Differences in the Black and White Sex Ratios, 15+ Years of Age, 1970 [1]

Age Group	Black	White	Difference
15-24 years	93.0	98.8	5.8
25-34 years	84.2	97.8	13.6
35-44 years	82.8	96.2	13.4
45-54 years	86.3	93.8	7.5
55-64 years	85.1	90.2	5.1
65+	76.4	71.9	-4.5

1. Source of raw data: U.S. Department of Commerce/Bureau of the Census, 1970 Census of Population, Advance Report, "General Population Characteristics, United States," PC (V2)-1. U.S. Department of Commerce, Washington, D.C., February, 1971.

SUMMARY AND CONCLUSIONS

By now it may be quite evident that there are at least three major and interrelated concerns running through this discourse about. "But where are the men?" with the most important one being that there simply are not enough men available for black women to assure their conformity to traditional pattern of sex, marriage, and family living, as defined for them by the white American subculture. More important, as the white sex ratio becomes more like that of blacks (as measured the age ranges of 15-44 years), it is quite clear that whites are increasingly utilizing patterns or models already developed by blacks, who have had a "headstart" of at least 100 years.

Ultimately, black women must be concerned with resolution of the issue of an insufficient supply of males, and aid in developing means of increasing that supply (which can take a variety of tactics, not the least of which is improving the life expectancies of black men) or, should that fail, providing viable alternatives to this "supply-and-demand" problem, one of which may be aiding in reducing the supply of black males available to white females, a practice, incidentally, which seems to affect an unduly high number of black coeds on major campuses throughout at least most of the northern and western parts of the United States.

In closing, then, the critical issues confronting many black women are not black matriarchy or black female emasculation of the male, but merely that of, "But where are the men?"

END NOTES

[1] Oliver C. Cox, "Sex Ratio and Marital Status Among Negroes," American Sociological Review, 5:937-947. Incidentally, no opportunity should be lost in pointing out a new that the significant contributions of Dr. Cox to American sociology, and particularly those valuable in knowing and understanding blacks, have been largely ignored by the white, male-dominated American sociological establishment. At the 1971 annual meeting of the Caucus of Black Sociologists, and Dr. James E. Conyers especially, the first

DuBois-Johnson-Frazier annual DuBois Award was conferred upon Dr. Cox in recognition of such contributions. Earlier, the first annual DuBois Award established by the Association of Social and Behavioral Scientist (founded 1935) was given to Dr. Cox in recognition of his distinguished achievements.

2. Ibid, p. 937
3. Ibid.
4. Ibid, p 938.
5. Daniel P. Moynihan, The Negro Family: A case for National Action, U.S. Government Printing Office, and Washington D.C.: 1965
6. It may be interesting to note that some discussions of this point have brought retorts that the males are there, but simply avoid being counted. The chief argument here is that even if all the black males throughout the United States were counted, the females would still remain excessive, due to a variety of reasons certainly warranting systematic investigations. Some, of course, are not there due to the unnecessarily high infant and childhood mortality rates especially affecting black males, while some others are dead, victimized by war and wanton killings.
7. E. Franklin Frazier, The Negro Family in the United States, University of Chicago Press: 1939. Here, perhaps, it should be noted that, contrary to a number of interpretations of Frazier, Frazier did not characterize matriarchy as the dominant family type among blacks.
8. Cox, op.cit.

A SOCIAL PROFILE

LAWRENCE E. GARY

In this chapter, consideration will be given to the social and demographic characteristics of black men in the United States. As mentioned earlier, there seems to be an impression in the minds of many people that the black community is composed primarily of black women and their children. In a provocative essay Jackson (1971) asked, "Where are the black men?" Although the ratio of black males to black females has been declining for many years, there were 12,108,000 black males in the United States in 1978. This figure represented 47.5 percent of the total black population (U.S. Bureau of the Census, 1979a).

There is no doubt that black men are an integral part of black communities. It is important for us to describe the current social conditions under which these men function in our society. More specifically, in this chapter, we plan to develop a profile on black men in terms of population growth and distribution, marital and family status, educational attainment, employment and income, and social participation. Health status is discussed in Chapter 2. Moreover, an in-depth analysis of education and training and economics id contained in Chapters 12, 13, and 14.

In developing this profile, it was necessary to exercise considerable judgment in selecting form the enormous body of available data. The primary data sources for this study include the U.S. Bureau of the Census, the U.S. Bureau of Labor Statistics, the U.S. Department of Justice (Federal Bureau of Investigation), and the National Center for Education Statistics. In addition, two government publications, the social and Economic Status of the Black Population in the United States 1790-1978 (U.S. Bureau of the Census, 1979b) and Social Indicator 1976 (U.S. Department of Commerce, 1977), have been most useful in developing this chapter. Since the data is this chapter were obtained from a variety of sources, one has to be aware of sampling errors (values from samples compared to those from complete

Enumeration f particular population groups) and nonsampling errors (refusals of respondents, undercounts of certain groups, poorly designed instruments, falsification of records, incorrect recording of information, and so forth). While appropriate, we shall mention data limitations as different information is presented.

In keeping with the basic theme of this volume, major comparisons will be made between black and white men, rather than between black men and women. In some cases, comparisons can be made only between blacks and whites. Moreover, much of the social data collected by various departments of the federal government have been categorized in terms of white nonwhite. When this the case, appropriate acknowledgement of this fact will be made, this social profile will provide a framework for helping us to understand the high psychosocial and economic risk status of black men in our society. Further, it will document the social frustration of black men that often leads to unhealthy adaptations. Finally, these social indicators will help us to see the interlocking relationship between black families and social institutions such as the economy, social services, education, the military, and the penal system.

POPULATION GROWTH AND DISTRIBUTION

As indicated earlier, in 1978, there were over 12 million black men, compared to 92 million white men. In other words, black males accounted for about 11.3 percent of the male population in the United States (U.S. Bureau of the Census, 1979a). In 1960, the black male populations were 9 million, compared to 78 million for white men. These data suggest that since 1960, the black male population has increased by 33.3 percent, whereas the white male population has increased by only 18 percent.

As indicated in Table 1, the age distribution of the black male population has shown some changes since 1960, in comparison to little change for the white male population. In 1978, the median age for black males was 23.2 years, but it was 29.4 years for white males. In other words, the black male population is younger than is the white male population. The proportion of the black male population below the age of 21 years was 48 percent, compared to 37 percent for the white male population in 1978. On the other hand, 10 percent of the white male population was 65 years and older, but the corresponding percentage for the black male population was only 7 percent in 1978. These data suggest that the age dependency ratio (the ratio of persons under 14 years of age and those persons 65 years of age and older defined as dependents to those persons between 14- and 65-years age defined as economically productive) is much higher for black males than it is for white males. In 1978, 36 percent of black males can be defined as being dependent, compared to 31 percent of white males.

Over the past hundred years, the U.S. Bureau of the Census has enumerated more black females than it has black males. The sex ratio (the number of males per 100 females) was 96.2 for the black community in 1870 and 90.6 in 1978 (E.S. Bureau of the Census, 1979a, 1979b). In comparison, the sec ratio was 95.3 for the white community in 1978. As implied in Table 1, the sex ratio is particularly problematic for the black community during the marriage and childbearing ages. However, this is not the case for the white community. Jackson (1971) has further analyzed sex ratio for the black community in terms of regions and states. She has shown that the sex ratio varies according to city, stage, and region, and that it has an impact on family

Table 1: Selected Population Characteristics of the U.S. Male Population by Race

	Black Male	White Male
1. Total Population in millions, 1978	12.0	92.0
2. Total Population in millions, 1970	10.0	87.0
3. Total Population in millions, 1960	9.0	78.0
4. Median age in years, 1978	23.2	29.4
5. Median age in years, 1970	21.0	27.6
6. Median age in years, 1960	22.4	29.4
7. Percentage of population under 22 years of age, 1978	48.0	37.0
8. Percentage of population 65 years of age 1978 and older,	7.0	10.0
9. Percentage of population considered dependents, 1978	36.0	31.0

10. Males per 100 females, 1978	90.6	95.3
11. Males under 14 years of age per 100 Females, 1978	101.6	104.8
12. Males 14-24 years of age per 100 Females, 1978	96.1	102.4
13. Males 25-44 years of age per 100 Females, 1978	84.0	98.8
14. Males 45-64 years of age per 100 Females, 1978	86.1	92.8
15. Males 65 years of age and older per 100 Females, 1978	71.2	67.9

SOURCE: U.S. Bureau of the Census. Statistical Abstract of the United States; 1979 (100th ed). Washington, DC Government Printing Office, 1979, pp. 28-29

stability and behavior. In Chapter 4, Braithwaite discusses the impact of the imbalance in the sex ratio on female and male relationships in black communities. Some caution must be exercised in accepting the census data with respect to the sex ratio. It has been shown that the U.S. Bureau of the Census undercounted the number of black people, especially black males, in the 1970 decennial census (Rodgers-Rose, 1980; Siegal, 1973; U.S. Department of Commerce, 1977). It has been suggested that the corrected sex ratio should be 95, instead of 91 (U.S. Bureau of the Census, 1979b).

MARITAL AND FAMILY STATUS

In 1975, 38 percent of the black male population 14 years of age and older was single, but only 28 percent of the white male population in this same age group was classified as single. What is interesting to note, as shown in Table 2, is that, in1940, black and white men had similar marital statuses. For white men 14 years of age and older, the percentage married.

Table 2: Marital Status of U.S. Males by Race

	Black Male	White Male
1. Percentage of male population 14 years Old and older single, 1975	38.0	28.0
2. Percentage of male population 14 years Old and older married, 1975	53.0	66.0
3. Percentage of male population 14 years Old and older divorced, 1975	4.0	3.0
4. Percentage of male population 14 years And older unattached (single, divorce, Widowed, etc.), 1975	46.0	33.0
5. Percentage of male population 14 years Old and older single, 1940	33.0	33.0
6. Percentage of male population 14 years Old and older married, 1940	61.0	61.0
7. Percentage of male population 14 years Old and older divorced, 1940	1.0	1.0
8. Percentage of male population 14 years Old and older widowed, 1940	6.0	4.0
9. Divorced males: all ages per 1000 married Persons with spouse present, 1975	83.0*	51.0
10. Divorced males 45-64 years of age per 1000 married persons with spouse present, 1975	116.0*	55.0
11. Percentage of male population 14 years Old and older widowed, 1975	4.0	2.0

SOURCE: U.S. Bureau of the Census. The Social and Economic Status of the Black Population in the United States 1790-1978. Washington, DC: Government Printing Office, 1979, 99. 109-111; and U.S. Department of Commerce. Social Indicators 1976. Washington, DC: Government Printing Office, 1977, p.68.

*Data refer to Black and other racial minorities.

Increased from 61 in 1940 to 66 in 1975. However, for black men the trend was the reverse; that is, there was a decrease in the percentage of married black men, black men are more likely to be divorced than are white men. In 1978, 6.9 percent of black males 18 years of age and over were divorced, compared to 2.4 percent in 1960 and 3.6 percent in 1970 (U.S. Bureau of the Census, 1979a). As shown in Table 2, divorce has become more common and widowhood less common for both groups between 1940 and 1975. It should be noted that income, education, region and age will have an impact on the divorce rate for a given population group, but a discussion of these issues is beyond the scope of this chapter (Glick, 1970; Glick and Norton, 1979).

The Data tend to suggest that there has been a significant increase in the number and percentage of black men who are single. When one combines single, divorced, or widowed into a category of unattached or not married, the data in Table 2 show that, in 1975, 46 percent of black males over 14 years of age are so classified, compared to 33 percent for white males. This larger percentage of unmarried black males will have an impact on male and female relationships and on the need for social and mental health services for this high-risk group. Further, as is pointed out in Chapters 2 and 8, marital status is correlated with health behavior and other adaptation strategies. Studies (Carter & Glick, 1976; Glick & Norton, 1979; Rosen et al., 1979; Gove, 1972) have consistently shown that unmarried (single, divorced, or widowed) persons are at a greater risk than married

Table 3: Marital Status of U.S. Males by Race

	Black Male	White Male
1. Percentage of own children living with both parents, 1960	75.0	93.0
2. Percent of own children living with both parents, 1970	65.0	91.0
3. Percentage of own children living with both parents, 1978	49.4	85.7
4. Percentage of all families, husband-wife type, 1960	74.1	98.2
5. Percentage of all families, husband-wife type, 1970	68.1	88.7
6. Percentage of all families, husband-wife type, 1978	56.1	85.9
7. Percentage of all families, male-headed, no wife present, 1960	4.1	2.7
8. Percentage of all families, male-headed, no wife present, 1978	3.7	2.3

9. Percentage of all families, male-headed, no wife present, 1978	4.6	2.5
10. Percentage of husband-wife families where husband is 14-34 years old, 1960	28.0	27.0
11. Percentage of husband-wife families where husband is 65 years Old and older, 1960	11.0	12.0
12. Percentage of husband-wife families where husband is 14-34 years old, 1975	32.0	30.0
13. Percentage of husband-wife families where husband is 65 years Old and older, 1975	13.0	14.0

SOURCE: U.S. Bureau of the Census. The Social and Economic Status of the Black Population in the United States 1790-1978. Washington, DC: Government Printing Office, 1979, p.103, 105, 107, 175, and 178.

Persons for all types of social and health and health disabilities (mental illness, drug and alcohol abuse, arrest, imprisonment, unemployment, homicide, and so forth).

Although the social science literature has tended to focus on the black male's absence from his family, it should be noted that in 1978 there were 5.8 million black families in the United States, of which the majority (56.1 percent) were two-parent families; that is, both husband and wife are present (U.S. Bureau of the census, 1979b). Moreover, in the same year, approximately 4.6 percent of all families were headed by men, with no wife present. As indicated in Table 3, black families are more likely to have no husband present than are white families, between 1960 and 1978, black husband-wife families declined from 74.1 percent to 56.1 percent of all black families. By contrast, for whites the decline in husband-wife families has not been as significant. For example, in 1960, 89.2 percent of all white families were of the husband-wife type; in 978 this family type had declined to 85.9 percent. In 1978, 85.7 percent of white children lived with both parents, compared to 49.4 percent for black children. In both white and black communities, there has been a decline in the percentage of children who live with both parents. However, the decline is much more significant for black families. The data suggest that for both blacks and whites the proportion of children living with both parents seems to be related to income (U.S. Bureau of the Census, 1979b). For example, in 1975, for black families with incomes under $4,000, only 17 percent of the children lived with both parents, but for those families with incomes of $15,000 and more, 86 percent lived with their parents. A similar income effect is noted for white families, although at all income levels white children are more likely to live with both of their parents than are black children.

In general, these data suggest that there has been a significant change in the structure of the traditional family unit in the black community. First, a large number of black men are not getting married, in addition, there is an increase in the divorce rate among black men. While income, age, and regional factors influence marital and family status, it is becoming increasingly clear that family fragmentation is more pronounced in black communities than it is white communities. Part II of this volume discusses in some detail the consequences of these changes on family relationships.

EDUCATION AND TRAINING

Education is considered to be a very important value in black communities (Doddy, 1963; Gary & Favors, 1975; Staples, 1976). To a large extent, many black see education as fundamental to their gaining the necessary economic resources for maintaining a reasonable quality of life. School enrollment rates for black males are about the same as these for whites, especially since 1960 (See Table 4). Commenting on the school attendance behavior of black people; the U.S. Bureau of the Census (1979b: 86) concludes:

> *In the past 25 years (1950-1975), substantial increases have been noted in the proportion of black youth enrolled in school above the compulsory attendance age... The growth in enrollment experienced by the age group 5 to 13 years old is due both to the increased availability of kindergarten classes to blacks... and to increase participation rates at the compulsory school ages 7 to 13.*

The extension of formal schooling to black men has resulted in a decline in the illiteracy rate from 10 percent in 1959 to 4 percent in 1969, as indicated in Table 4. In 1978, the median years of school completed was 11.6 for black males, compared to 12.6 for white males. Although black male' school enrollment rates are very similar to those for white males, black males continue to lag behind their white counterparts on a variety of educational attainment measures including median years of school completed, percentage of high school graduates, percentage of college graduates, and literacy rates. In an article, "Boys: Endangered Species," Raspberry (1979) reviews some of the behavioral and institutional problems that boys must face as they advance through the public school system.

Table 3: Educational Profile of Males by Race in the United States

	Black Male	White Male
1. Median years of school completed, 1960	7.7	10.7
2. Median years of school completed, 1970	9.6	12.0
3. Median years of school completed, 1978	11.6	12.6
4. Percentage of illiterate in population 14 years old older, 1959	10.0*	2.0
5. Percentage of illiterate in population 14 years old and older, 1969	4.0	1.0
6. Percentage of persons 5 to 29 years old enrolled in school, 1960	66.0	69.0
7. Percentage of persons 5 to 29 years old enrolled in school, 1970	69.0*	70.0
8. Percentage of persons 5 to 29 years old enrolled in school, 1975	69.0*	64.0
9. Percentage of high school dropouts among persons 14 to 24 years old, 1970	30.4	14.4
10. Percentage of high school dropouts among persons 14 to 34 years old, 1977	20.0	12.4
11. Percentage of persons 25 years old and older, less than 4 years of high school, 1970	67.5	42.8
12. Percentage of persons 25 years old and older, less than 4 years of high school, 1979	50.8	29.7
13. Percentage of persons 25 years old and older with 4 years of high school, 1970	22.2	30.9

14. Percentage of persons 25 years old and older with 4 years of high school, 1979	29.5	33.1
15. Percentage of persons 25 years old and older with 4 years of college or more, 1979	8.3	21.4
16. Percentage of persons 25 years old and older with 4 years of college or more, 1970	4.6	15.0
17. Percentage of total persons 14-34 years of age enrolled in college by race, 1978	44.3	52.9
18. Percentage of total persons 14-34 years of age enrolled in college by race, 1970	48.5	60.2

SOURCE: U.S. Bureau of the Census. Statistical Abstract of the United States 1979 (100th ed.). Washington, DC: Government Printing Office, 1979, pp. 145, 159; U.S. Bureau of the Census. The Social and Economic Status of the Black Population in the United States 1790-1978. Washington, DC: Government Printing Office, 1979, p.89, 92-93; National Center for Education Statistics. Digest of Education Statistics 1979. Washington, DC: Government Printing Office, 1979, p.66; and U.S. Department of Commerce. Population Profile of the United States: 1979. Current Population Reports, 1980, Series P-20, No. 350, p.17.

*Data refer to Black and other racial minorities.

In Chapter 13, Patton provides additional insight into this problem. Given the negative attitude of the public school system toward black males, as indicated in Table 4, it should be no surprise that their dropout rate was 20.0 percent, compared to 12.4 for white males in 1977.

As shown in Table 4, the data indicate that black men have been making gains in higher education, but they still lag behind their white counterparts. For example, in 1979, 8.3 percent of black men 25 years of age and older had four years or more of college, compared to 21.4 percent for white men in that age group. Although there has been an increase in the number of black men enrolled in college, they are quite a distance from reaching parity with white men. In 1978, 1.0 million black adults were enrolled in college; of this number, 452,000 were black men (U.S. Bureau of the Census, 1979a). In other words, black males represented 44.3 percent of the black adults enrolled in college. For the white community males accounted for 52.9 percent of the adult college enrollment. While black men and women are near parity in regard to college enrollment, black men still lag behind white men. Once enrolled in college, black men experience a variety of problems. In Chapter 14, Fleming examines the impact of higher education on black males.

EMPLOYMENT AND INCOME

How educational attainment benefits black men is a continuing question that is asked by many in the black community. Yankelovich (1979:31) in an easy entitled "Who Gets Ahead in America," answered the question in the following manner:

> *If you are "finishing" and have been persuaded to stay in school because "finishing high school will help you find a better job later on, "forget what you have been told. Even for whites the economic advantages of finishing high school without going on to college are marginal at best; for blacks, they count for almost nothing.*

These conclusions are based on findings from a study conducted by Jencks and his colleagues. Apparently, the black men who drop out of high school are making rational decisions based on these research observations. Nevertheless, the predictions for success in employment and income seem to be better for black males who go to college. Commenting on this issue, Yankelovich (1979:31) concludes:

> *If you are black and in college and suspect that finishing college is not going to help you economically, you are wrong. Buckle down, hang in there and finish at all costs. If its money and all good job you are after, stay in college, no matter how you do it... Economically it does not matter who you study, how you learn or where you go to college as long as you finish.*

Although data seem to support these assertions, some caution should be exercised in accepting them at face value. Nonetheless, data do show that education, especially at the college level, influences the direction of a number of economic status variables, such as unemployment rates, labor force participation rates, earnings and so forth. Although college education has a positive impact on economic success for black males, it should be noted that only 8.3 percent of them were college graduates in 1979 (see Table 4).

Given this reality, one should expect a high level of economic frustration for the vast majority of black men. The data in Table 5 show that the labor force participation rate for civilian black males has decreased from 83.4 percent in 1959 to 71.9 percent in 1979. For white males, the labor force participation rate was 78.6 percent in 1979. Commenting on the black male participation rate in the labor market, Steward and Scott (1978:84) wrote:

> *One source of frustration of employed black males is the crowding of these workers into low-status occupations of which the associated wages rates are inadequate to provide for a standard of living significantly above the poverty level.*

An examination of the occupational distribution of employed black males indicates that the majority are blue-collar and service workers. In Table5, one can observe that in 1977 over one-half (58 percent) of the employed black males were blue-collar workers, for example, craft, operatives and non-farm laborers-while 17 percent were service workers. It should be noted that 3 percent of black males were employed as farm workers and 23 percent were employed as white-collar workers (U.S. Bureau of the Census, 1979b). In contrast, during the same year, there were nearly twice as many (42 percent) white males employed in white-collar jobs, while less than half (45 percent) were blue-collar workers and 8 and 4 percent, respectively, were service or farm workers.

Not only have the majority of black males occupied lower-status jobs than have white males, but they have also experienced high rates of unemployment over the last several decades. During the period of 1954-1974, the unemployment rate for black males 20 years of age and older was either more than double or slightly less than double that of the white males (U.S. Bureau of the Censes, 1979b). As depicted in Table 5, the unemployment rate for black males 20 years of age and older was 9.1 percent in 1979, but it was only 3.6 percent for white males in this age category. The data in this table also indicate that young black males have had a much higher unemployment rate than has the black male population as a whole. In 1979, the unemployment rate for black males between the ages of 16 and 17 years old was 34.4 percent, but it was only 16.1 percent for white males in the same category. Furthermore, young black male veterans also experienced a high level of unemployment. In all cases, the unemployment rate for black men is substantially higher than that for white men.

When black men are able to find work, their earnings lag behind those of white men. In 1979, black males had a median income that was $4,962 less than that of white males; the median incomes of black and white males, respectively, were $13,068 and $18,030 (U.S. Department of Commerce, 1980a). The gap in median incomes between black and white men was only $3,830 in 1978. The median income of black male-headed families was $13,443, compared to $17,848 for their white counterparts in 1977. Further, in the same year, when wives were also in the paid labor force, the median black family income was $17,078, compared to $20,518 for white families. Studies (Datcher, 1980; Duncan, 199; Miller, 1966; Siegel, 1965) have shown consistently that black men earn lower wages than do white men working in the same occupation. Commenting one wage differences between black and white men, Stolzenberg (1975:300) concluded:

> *It has been found repeatedly that black men are less successful than their white counterparts in "converting" years of schooling into dollars or earnings, even when racial differences in schooling, family background, occupation and other factors are taken into consideration. Numerous analyses have also carried the argument that these racial differences in wage returns to schooling are not merely artifacts of hiring discrimination which keep educationally qualified black men out of the more remunerative occupation; a number of studies have found racial differences in wage returns to schooling within occupational categories.*

Table 3: Educational Profile of Males by Race in the United States

	Black Male	White Male
1. Civilian Labor Force Participation rates for persons 16 years and older, 1979*	71.9	78.6
2. Civilian Labor Force Participation rates for persons 16 years and older, 1969*	76.9	80.2
3. Civilian Labor Force Participation rates for persons 16 years and older, 1959*	83.4	83.8
4. Unemployment rates for civilians 20 years and older, 1979	9.1	3.6
5. Unemployment rates of males Vietnam-era nonveterans 20-24 years of age, 1979*	20.5	9.8
6. Unemployment rates of males Vietnam-era nonveterans 20-24 years of age, 1979*	15.6	6.9
7. Unemployment rates of persons 18 and 19 years old, 1979*	29.6	12.3
8. Unemployment rates of persons 16 and 17 years old, 1979*	34.4	16.1
9. Median family income, male-headed, 1977	13,443	17,848
10. Percentage of employed men who are white-collar workers, 1977	23.0	42.0
11. Percentage of employed men who are blue-collar workers, 1977	58.0	45.0
12. Percentage of employed men who are service workers, 1977	17.0	8.0
13. Percentage of employed men who are farm workers, 1977	3.0	4.0
14. Victimization of rates for persons 12 and older, crimes of violence, 1977	57.4	45.3
15. Victimization rates for persons 12 and older, robbery, 1977	19.8	7.5

SOURCE: U.S. Department of Labor, Employment and Training Report of the President. Washington, DC: Government Printing Office, 1980, pp. 225-226, 230-231, 233-234, 254-255; U.S. Bureau of the Census. The Social and Economic Status of the Black Population in the United States 1790-1978. Washington, DC: Government Printing Office, 1979, p.190, 218; and U.S. Department of Justice. Criminal Victimization in the United States. Washington, DC: Government Printing Office, 1979, p.13.

These data include Black and other racial minorities. Blacks represent about 90 percent of those classified as Black and others.

The economic system generates widespread frustration for many black males. Due to their high level of unemployment, concentration in low-level occupations and low earnings in comparison to white men, other family members- including wives and children are forced to enter the labor market or to seek public assistance in order to augment the earnings of the black male. Even when the wife works, the median income of black families still lags behind that of white families. For example, in 1978 the family income of black male-headed households where the wife worked was about the same as that of white male-headed households where the wife did no work (U.S. Bureau of the Census, 1979b). In fact, regardless of the number of wage earners in the family, blacks earned less than did their white counterparts. Moreover, some data suggest that affirmative action programs in employment have had a negative impact on the economic status of black males. In their analysis of statistics collected by the Equal Employment Opportunity Commission (EEOC), Brimmer and Company (1980:96) observed:

> *White women are winning out over blacks in competing for occupational upgrading... In 1973, white women held 30 percent of the EEOC-reported jobs. By 1978, their participation was up to 31.7 percent... The overall position of black men actually deteriorated in the same period. They filled 6.4 percent of the jobs in 1973 and 2.6 percent of those in 1978.*

It is believed that the black male's frustration with the economic system leads to his disproportionate involvement with America's criminal justice system. It is assumed that there is a relationship between economic conditions and crime against property. Arrest data suggest that blacks are arrested disproportionately for offenses that have a functional relationship to economic frustrations. In 1979, for example, 505,754 blacks were arrested for property crimes. This figure represents 29.4 percent of those arrested for these offenses. In addition, blacks accounted for 56.9 percent of those arrested for robbery, 52.6 percent of those arrested for prostitution and commercialized vice and 67.9 percent of those arrested for gambling in 1979. Similar statistics hold for offenses such as forgery and counterfeiting, fraud, stolen property (burglary, receiving and processing), and weapons and drug abuse violations (U. S. Department of Justice, 1980).

The data in Table 5 summarize the extent to which black males are victimized by the economic system as reflected in the high incidence of crime in black communities. For example, in 1977, the victimization rate for persons aged 12 years and older for crimes of violence was 57.4 percent for black males, but it was 45.3 percent for white males. The victimization rate for robbery was 7.5 percent for white males aged 12 years old and over, and 19.8 percent for black males in that age group in 1977. Moreover, black in general have a much higher rate of incarceration than white have. Further

Table 6. Persons in the U.S. Armed Forces, 1971-1980

Year	Total	White Males	Black Males	White Female	Black Females
1980	2,036,672	1,507,569	358,865	129,374	40,864
1979	1,013,233	1,514,641	348,655	116,994	32,943
1978	2,047,880	1,586,622	327,966	107,775	25,517
1977	2,063,074	1,643,726	301,626	97,555	20,167
1976	2,070,424	1,672,763	288,623	91,165	17,873
1975	2,116,281	1,732,229	287,302	81,681	15,069
1974	2,150,618	1,789,166	286,955	63,562	10,895
1973	2,241,230	1,915,545	270,615	47,995	7,075
1972	2,311,300	2,014,774	525,028	39,279	5,219
1971	2,701,208	2,388,586	270,299	37,656	4,667

SOURCE: U.S. Department of Defense, Equal Opportunity, unpublished data, 1981.

Discussion of the impact of the criminal justice system on black males is contained in Chapter 17. Nonetheless, these data suggest that economic pressures and frustration push a large number of black males into the criminal justice system, which temporarily separates them from the black community and their families.

Many black men who have difficulties dealing with the economic system often join the armed forces. In discussing the involvement of black men in the military, Stewart and Scott (1978:87) commented, "The pressures which push blacks into the penal correction system also push them into the enlisted ranks of the military… Blacks that are nonfunctional in the civilian labor market may still be functional in the military establishment." Table 6 indicates that in 1980 there were 358,865 black males in the military. This figure represents 17.6 percent of the total persons in the military. It is interesting to note that, while the number of white males in the armed forces is on the decline, it has increased for black males. According to Carl Rowan (1980), black volunteers for the armed forces have more formal schooling than do white volunteers.

The military experiences of blacks have both positive and negative components (Moskos, 1973; Moskos & Janowtiz, 1974; Stewart & Scott, 1978). On the positive side, the military provides steady income, good benefits, and opportunity for travel and advancement. On the other hand, black men are overrepresented in the combat and service units. They have a higher expulsion rate than do their white counterparts. As point out in Chapter 18, may black men be incarcerated in the military. According to Stewart and Scott (1978:88), channeling black males into the military, then, complements operations of the public-assistance system in mitigating violent protests against the economic frustrations associated with civilian blacks. Once blacks leave the military, however, they are recaptured by civilian institutional decimation. "The implication is that a large number of black men have negative interactions in the armed forces. Once they return to civilian life, they continue to experience economic frustrations as reflected in the high unemployment rate for veterans, especially those who served during the Vietnam period (see Table 5). Of course, economic frustration will have consequences for the family life of black men as well as for their adaptation strategies.

SOCIAL PARTICIPATION

In developing a social profile of black men, it is important to examine the extent to which they are actively involved in different forms of personal and community associations and activities. Unfortunately, there are not many data on the social participation of black men. The government and other institutions and individuals have collected a great deal of information on family status, income and employment, health status, crime, education, and so forth. More consideration needs to be given to developing a data base on social participation on the part of black men and women, for these data will provide us with the necessary information for developing more functional coping strategies for dealing with the negative institutional outcomes from the majority community.

One type of participation where some data have been collected is in the area of politics. In 1980, 68.3 percent of white men reported that they were registered to vote, compared to only 57.2 percent for black me (see Table 7). In the same year, the majority (60.9 percent) of white men reported that they voted in the 1980 election, but less than half (47.5 percent) of black men reported that they voted. In other words, in 1980, there were 7.3 million black men of voting age, but only 3.5 million indicated that they voted. Furthermore, 3.1 million black men were not registered to vote in 1980. While one can argue that black men have some involvement in political activities the data suggest that the majority of black men of voting age are not very active in the political process in this country. As shown in Table 7, age has an impact on political behavior of both black and white men. Younger men are less active in politics than are older men for both racial groups. It is also assumed that income, education, and family background influence political activities for both white and black men. It is clear, however, that black men are less likely to be involved in political participation than are white men.

One important outcome of the political process is the election of officials. Table 1.8 shows the number of persons elected at the federal government level. In 1979, white men represented 93.1 percent of the persons in the House of Representatives and 99 percent of the persons in the senate. There were no black men in the senate; and they represented only 4.3 percent of the persons in the House of Representatives. The picture is about the same for the 97th Congress (1981); that is. Both houses of Congress are basically composed of white males. Given their population size, black people are distressingly underrepresented in the Congress. A similar pattern exists for high level appointment in all branches of the federal government.

Table 7. Reported Voting and Registration of the Male Population of Voting age by Race,

Age	Percentage Reported Registered		Percentage Reported Voted	
	White Male	Black Male	White Male	Black Male
18-20	45.4	35.6	36.2	25.9
21-24	53.1	42.8	43.5	30.9
25-34	62.4	53.4	55.0	43.8
35-44	70.5	63.4	64.3	54.1
45-54	75.5	62.8	69.3	54.2
55-64	80.4	68.7	74.1	60.1
65-74	81.1	72.2	73.9	63.2
75 and older	77.5	69.6	67.2	54.6
All ages above 18	68.3	57.2	60.9	47.5

Source: U.S. Department of Commerce, Voting and Registration in the Election of November 1980. Current Population Reports (Population Characteristics , Series P. 20, No. 359, advance copy). Washington, DC: Bureau of the Census, January 1981, pp.4-5.

At the state and local levels of government, black people are also underrepresented. In 1979, there were 4, 607 black Americans who held popularly elected offices in the United States; of this number, 80 percent were newly elected (Joint Center for Political Studies, 1979). There has been a significant increase in the number of black elected officials at all levels. For example, in 1969 there were 1,124 black elected officials, but by 1975 there were 3,503. In 1980 there were over 4, 912 black elected officials in 44 states, the District of Columbia, and the Virgin Islands ("Number of Black Elected Officials up by 6.6 Percent," 1980). It should be noted that for federal, state, and local government levels, black elected women held a larger share of black elected offices that white women held. Related to this fact is that the proportion of black men holding elected offices has declined from 88 percent in 1969 to 80 percent in 1980. It is estimated that there are over 490, 265 elected state and local government officials (U.S. Bureau of the Census, 1979a). Given this fact, one can observe that black people are grossly underrepresented at these levels of government. In evaluating the functions of black elected officials, the Joint Center for Political Studies (1979) concluded:

Black elected officials tend to have fewer resources to deal with the problems and needs of their constitutes than do white elected officials. At the top levels of government, where elected officials wield considerable power and are routinely provided a variety of professional support services with which to administer their power, there are relatively few black elected officials.

Table 8.Members of Congress by Race and Sex, 1979

	Male			Female			Total
	Black	White	Total	Black	White	Total	
Congress							
Representatives	14	404*	418	2	14	16	434
Senators	0	99*	99	0	1	1	100
Representatives	14	503	517	2	15	17	534

SOURCE: Joint Center for Political Studies. National Roster of Black Elected Officials, Vol.9. Washington DC: Joint Center for Political Studies, 1979; and U.S. Bureau of the Census. Statistical Abstract of the United States 1979 (100th ed.). Washington, DC: Government Printing Office, 1979, p. 509.

NOTE: Figures exclude vacancies and representatives from the Virgin Islands.

*These figures include other racial groups (1 senators and 36 representatives).

Historically, in the black community, great emphasis has been placed on the importance of participating in voluntary associations (Laying, 1978; Orum, 1966; Ross and Wheeler, 1971; Yearwood, 1980). According to Tomech (1973:99),

Studies.... Shows high participation rates for blacks at all social levels, especially lower class. For whatever reasons, blacks have indeed become joiners. The rise of a wide range of black associations in recent years indicates that voluntary associations are not the preserve of the white

> *middle-class… whatever the case may be, the response of blacks to segregation appears to be quite the opposite of indifference and apathy.*

Often,black people including black men, have used voluntary organizations to solve personal and community problems. In addition, these organizations serve as service centers, information exchanges, forums for job and business-related issues, and support mechanisms in personal development. Hard comparative data on the participation rates of black and white men in voluntary associations are not available. Nevertheless, we are aware of a variety of organizations that a high level of involvement on the part of the black men (see the list of some of these organizations in Table 9).

Black men have not held as many executive positions and offices in traditional professional associations and organizations, such as the American Medical Association, American Bar Association, American Economic Association, American Legion, American Dental Association, Chamber of Commerce of the United States, and the National Rifle Association of America, as have white men. It was estimated that in 1978, there were more than 13, 589 national associations covering a range of areas such as health, social welfare, commerce and business, public affairs, recreation, labor, unions, veterans and education (U.S. Bureau of the Census, 1979a). For the most part, black people do not play important roles in these organizations.

In many cases, blacks have developed their own organizations and associations. The church and fraternal organizations have provided many opportunities for black men to ex-writers

Table 9. List of Selected Organizations with High Levels of Black Male Involvement

---

Business and Commerce
    American Association of Blacks in Energy
    Interracial Council for Business Opportunity
    National Alliance of Postal and Federal Employees
    National Association of Black Accountants
    National Association of Black Manufacturers
    National Association of Broadcasters

National Association of Market Developers
National Association of Minority Contractors
National Association of Real Estate Brokers
National Bankers Association
National Business League
National Funeral Directors an Morticians Association
National Insurance Association
National Newspaper Publishers Association
Opportunities Industrialization Centers of America
United Mortgage Bankers of America

Civic and Civil Rights

Affirmative Action Association of America
Congress of Racial Equality
Congressional Black Caucus
Frontiers International
National Association for the Advancement of Colored Pople
National Black Veterans Organization
National Conference of Black Lawyers
National Conference of Black Mayors
National Urban League
One Hundred Black Men, Inc.
People United to Save Humanity
Southern Christian Leadership Conference
United Black Fund
Veterans Association, Inc.

Fraternal Organizations

Alpha Phi Alpha Fraternity, Inc.
Ancient and Accepted Rite Masons

(Franklin, 1974; Hill, 1972; Staples, 1976) have pointed out the significant role played by black churches in helping black people, including men, to cope with societal pressures and stresses. In Chapter 16, Tinney provides us with specific insight into the role of the church in the life of black men.

Fraternal organizations have been one formal mechanism black men have used to operationalize the value of mutual aid. According mutual benefit societies were the most (important) social institutions in the black community." In his book, The Negro in America, Frazier (1957:378) reached a similar conclusion:

> *The fraternal organizations offered economic relief in*
> *thime of sickness and provided decent burials... The*

> *organizations and growth of mutual aid associations*
> *and secret fraternal societies among Negroes have been in*
> *response to social and economic forces within Negro life as*
> *well as the result of the relations of the races.*

In any social profile of black men, consideration must be given to spots. As with other areas of social participation, there are very little hard data on the participation of the black male in sports except in professional, collegiate, and secondary school areas. But if one drives through any black community and observes, there will be some black males involved in a variety of spots. In the 1975 Health Interview Survey (HIS), there were several questions concerning the participation in sports by adults 20 years old and over (National Center for Health Statistics, 1978). It was discovered that 43.2 percent of white males were involved in at least one type of sport, compared to 29.2 percent for nonwhites. As one would expect, age and income influence the degree to which a person was active I organized sports. Higher-income persons were more likely to be involved in sports than were lower-income parents. As age increases, the level of involvement in sports decreases. Further analysis of data is not possible since the data were not broken down by racial and sex groups. But the data did suggest that black men are more likely to be involved in basketball that they were to be involved in swimming, tennis, or gold. Bowling softball, and baseball are also favorite sports of black men.

Several studies (Anderson, 1976; Liebow, 1967) suggest that black men spend a great deal of their leisure time in unorganized activities, such as playing checkers and chess, shooting pool, and gambling. These recreational activities take place in pool rooms, bars, and barbershops. Moreover, many black men spend time in informal settings with their friends, talking and playing around on "the corner" or on "the block." One has to appreciate the fact that these informal networks provide cognitive and affective services to those men who are in need of help. According to Gary (1978:39),

> *Many black people with personal problems customarily turn*
> *informal organizations.. These informal groups… such as*
> *barbershops, peer groups, gangs, and storefront churches*

> *make up the social network of the black community..*
> *These informal organizations.. have enabled many blacks*
> *to develop the necessary talent for functioning in a hostile*
> *racist environment.*

While these informal networks include recreational activities, many black males are very much involved in professional and semiprofessional sports:

In their book, Jock: Sports and male Identity, Sabo an Runfola (1980) discuss some of the negative consequences of placing so much emphasis on sports in the America society. They examine the interrelationships among sexism, racism, violence, and sports. In most black communities, one can find young black male preparing themselves for the professional world of sports. Many black parents and their male children believe that sports are the most democratic area of our society (Sabo & Runfola, 1980). These parents believe that athletics constitute the main mechanism by which their sons will achieve manhood. The media, especially television, have promoted cultural stereotypes of black males as athletic and sexual supermen. Although professional sports have helped many black males to achieve recognition an to earn good salaries, there is ample evidence that black athletes are victims of racial oppression (Edwards, 1969; Johnson & Marple, 1973; Pacal & Radding, 19720. Commenting on racism in sports, Eitzenn and Yetman (1977:13) conclude:

> *Despite some indication of change, discrimination against*
> *black athletes continues in American team sports; sports*
> *are not a meritocratic realm where trace is ignored.. if*
> *discrimination occurs in a public area, one so generally*
> *acknowledged to be discrimination free and one where a*
> *premium is placed on individual achievement rather that*
> *race, how much more subtly pervasive must discrimination*
> *be in other areas of American life, where personal interaction*
> *is crucial and where the actions of power wielders are not*
> *subject to public scrutiny.*

CONCLUDING COMMENTS

The data in this chapter show that there have been notable changes in the demographic and social characteristics of black men over the past twenty years in comparison to white men. Contrary to myths projected by the media and social science literature, black men are an integral part of black communities. As of 1978, there were 12 million black males, which 7.3 million were adults, that is, 18 years or older. Although there is a growth in the male population, the sex ratio, that is, the number of males per 100 females, had been declining during this century. The imbalance in the sex ratio is particularly problematic for the black community during the marriage and childbearing ages. Moreover, there has been a significant increase in the number of black men who are single compared to white men who are single. Given he employment and income conditions of black men, one can understand why the black family seems to breaking down.

Many black men do not earn adequate incomes to provide for their families, black men have made some gains in higher education and in employment, but data suggest that affirmative action programs directed at white women have eroded some of their advancements. There is much evidence to suggest that the economic frustration of black men has led some of them to engage in criminal activities in order to support themselves and their families. In addition, many black men who have difficulties dealing with the economic system join the armed forces, but once enlisted they continue to experience rapid oppression. They learn some skills in the armed forces, but often those skills are not transferable to the civilian world of work. The data show that the unemployment rate is higher for black than for white veterans. The data also suggest that the basic institutions of our society have developed techniques for systematically making a large percentage of black males useless for fulfilling their obligations.

Although the government has not collected many data on the social participation of black males, we were able to identify some areas where they have had a more positive experience. Black men have developed their own voluntary associations and organizations, especially in the areas of fraternities and benefit societies, civic and professional organizations, and the church. In the political area, black men are grossly underrepresented at all levels of the government.

Also, black men experience considerable discrimination in the area of professional sports. One can conclude that the data indicate that black men, in comparison to white men, have had a difficult time protecting themselves from the pressures of the major institutions in our society, and these institutional outcomes have had negative consequences for family relationships in black communities.

REFERENCES

Anderson, E. A place on the corner. Chicago: University of Chicago Press, 1976.

Brimer and Company. Facts and figures: A statistical profile of Black economic development. Black Enterprise, 1980, 11, 96.

Carter. H., & Glick, P. Marriage and divorce: A social and economic study (Revised edition). Cambridge, MA: Harvard University Press, 1976.

Datcher, L. Effects of community, family and education in earnings of Black and white men. Review of Black Political Economy, 1980, 10, 291-394.

Doddy, II. The progress of the Negro in higher education. Journal of Negro Education. 1963, 32(4), 485.

Duncan, O. Inheritance of poverty or inheritance of race? In D.P. Moynihan (Ed.). Understanding poverty. New York: Basic Books, 1969, 84-110.

Edwards, H. The revolt of the Black athlete. New York: Macmillan, 1969.

Eitzen, D., & Yetman, N. Immune from racism? Blacks still suffer from discrimination in sports. Civil Rights Digest, 1977, 2-13.

Franklin, J. From slavery to freedom: A history of Negro Americans (4th edition). New York: Knopf, 1974.

Frazier, E. The Negro in America (Rev. ed.). New York: Macmillan, 1957.

Gary, L. (Ed.) Mental health: A challenge to the Black community. Philadelphia: Dorrance, 1978

Gary L. & Favors, A. (Eds.). Restructuring the educational process: A Black perspective. Washington, DC: Institute for Urban Affairs and Research, 1975.

Glick, P. Marriage and marriage stability among Blacks, ilbank Memorial Fund Quarterly, 1970, 63, 100-103.

Glick, P. & Norton, A. Marrying, divorcing and living together in the U.S. today, Population Bulletin, 1979, 32,4-38. (Updated reprint)

Gove, W. The relationship between sex roles, marital roles, and mental illness. Social Forces, 1972, 51, 34-44.

Hill.R. The strengths of Black families. New York: Emerson Hall, 1972.

Jackson, J. Where are the men? The Black Scholar, 1971, 3, 30-41.

Johnson, N., & Marple, D. Racial discrimination in professional basketball: an empirical test. Sociological Focus, 1973, 6, 6-18.

Joint Center for Political Studies. National roster of Black elected officials (Vol.9). Washington, DC: Author, 1979.

Jones, D., & Matthews, W. (Eds.). The Black church: A community resource. Washington , DC: Institute for Urban Affairs and Research, 1977.

Layng, A. Voluntary associations and Black ethnic identity. Phylon, 1978, 39, 171-179.

Liebow, E. Tally's Corner. Boston: Little, Brown, 1957.

McPherson, J., Holland, L., Banner, J., Weiss, N., & Bell, M. Blacks in America: Bibliographic essays. Garden City, NY: Doubleday, 1971.

Miller, H. Income distribution in the United States, Washington, DC: Government Printing Office, 1966.

Moskos, C. The American dilemma in uniform: Race in the armed forces. Annals of the American Academy of Political and Social Science, 1973, 406, 94-106.

Moskos, C., & Janowtiz, M. Racial composition in the all volunteer force. Armed Forces and Society, 1974, I, 109-123.

National Center for Education Statistics, Digest of education statistics 1979. Washington, DC: Government Printing Office, 1979.

National Center for Health Statistics. Exercise and participation in sports among person 20 years of age and over. United States. Advance Data, 1978, 19.

Number of Black elected officials up by 6.6 percent. Focus, 1980, 8 (12), 6.

Orum, A.A reappraisal of the social and political participation of Negroes. American Journal of Sociology, 1966, 76, 32-46.

Pascal, A., & Radding. A. The economics of racial discrimination in organized baseball. In A. Pascal (Ed.), Racial discrimination in economic life. Lexington, MA: D.C. Health, 1972.

Ploski, H., & Kaiser, E. The Negro almanac. New York: Bellwhether, 1971.

Raspberry, W. Boys: Endangered species? The Washington Post, March 1979, p. A23.

Rodgers-Rose, L. The Black woman. Beverly Hills. CA: Sage Publications, 1980.

Rosen, B., Goldsmith. H., & Redrick, R. Demographic and social indicators: Uses in mental health planning in small areas. World Health Statistics, 1979, 32 (1), 11-102.

Ross, J., & Wheeler, R. Black belonging: A study of social correlates of work relations among Negroes. Westport, CT: Greenwood, 1971.

Rowan, C. Moshe Dayan insults Black GIs. New York Amsterdam News, December 1980, p.17.

Sabo, D., & Runfola, R. Jack: Sports and male identity. Englewood Cliffs, NJ: Prentice-Hall, 1980.

Siegal, J. Estimates of coverage of the population by sex, race and age in the 1970 census. Paper presented at the annual meeting of the Population Association of America, New Orleans, Louisiana, April 26, 1973.

Siegal, P. On the cost of becoming a Negro, Sociological Inquiry, 1965, 35, 41-57.

Staple, R. Introduction to Black sociology. New York: McGraw-Hill, 1976.

Stewart, J., & Scott. J. The institutional decimation of Black American males. Western Journal of Black Studies, 1978, 2, 82-92.

Stolzenberg, R. Education, occupation and wage differences between white and Black men. American Journal of Sociology, 1975, 81, 299-323.

Tomeh, A. Formal voluntary organizations: Participation, correlates and interrelationships. Sociological Inquiry, 1973, 43(3), 89-110.

U.S. Bureau of the Census. Statistical abstract of the United States: 1979 (100th ed.). Washington, DC: Government Printing Office, 1979. (a).

U.S. Bureau of the Census. The social and economic status of the Black population in the United States 1790-1978 (Special Studies Series P-23), No.80). Washington, DC: Government Printing Office, 1979.b (b)

U.S. Department of Commerce. Social indicators 1976. Washington, DC: Government Printing Office, 1977.

U.S. Department of Commerce. Money, income and poverty status of families and persons in the United States: 1979. Current Population Reports 1980, Series P-60. No. 125, advance report. (a).

U.S. Department of Commerce. Populations profile of the United States: 1979. Current Population Reports, 1980, Series P-20, No. 350, p. 17. (b)

U.S. Department of Commerce. Voting and registration in the election of November 1980. Current Population Reports, Population Characteristics, 1981, Series P-20, No. 359, advance copy.

U.S. Department of Defense. Washington, DC: Department of Defense, Equl Opportunity, 1981. (Unpublished data)

U.S. Department of Justice. Criminal victimization in the United States. Washington, DC: Government Printing Office, 1979.

U.S. Department of Justice. Crime in the United States. Washington, DC: Government Printing Office, 1980.

U.S. Department of Labor. Employment and training report of the president. Washington, DC: Government Printing Office,, 1980.

Yankelovich, D. Who gets ahead in America. Psychology Today, July 1979, pp. 28-34; 40-44.

Yearwood L. (Ed.) Black organizations: Issues and surival techniques. Lanham, MD: University Press of America, 1980.

SOME DEMOGRAPHIC CHARACTERISTICS OF THE BLACK WOMAN: 1940 TO 1975

LA FRANCES RODGERS-ROSE

Many myths exist about the overall status of the black woman in American society. Some scholars would suggest that the black woman has reaped benefits from society while the black male fell farther behind her socially and economically. One way we can begin to piece together the recent history and conditions of the black woman is to analyze her status through the use of government statistics recognizing that statistics are imperfect. One can see the imperfection of government statistics by analyzing the sex ration of the black population. For example, the Census Bureau recognized as early as 1861 that there was an undercount of the black population in the 1860 census. They also admit that the undercount existed in the 1870 and 1880 census, but no corrections were ever made of these statistics. It is them ale population. In viewing the data from Table 2, the reader must keep in mind the general undercount of the black population.

Taking the last official census, 1970, we find that 1.88 million blacks were not counted in that census. This accounted for 7.7 percent of the total black population. For whites, 1.9 percent of the population was missed. It is suggested that one out of every eight black males 20 years and older was missed in both 1970 and 1960. This means that the sex ratio is not as drastic as it might as first appear. Jacob Siegel of the Bureau of the Census, writing in 1973, suggested 627,000 black men between the ages of 20 and 44 were missed by the census in comparison to only 241,000 black (Siegel, 1973). It is in this age group that the greatest discrepancy exists in the male-female ratio. It was data from the 1970 census that led Jacquelyne Jackson to ask the question, "But Where Are the Men?"

Table 1. Undercount of the Black Population, 1970, Ages 20-40 (in thousands)

Age Group	Census Count		Midrange Correction	
	Male	Female	Male	Female
20-24	1,045	1,160	116	54
25-34	1,423	1,673	278	105
35-44	<u>1,106</u>	<u>1,226</u>	<u>233</u>	<u>55</u>
35-44	3,574	4,169	627	214

Therefore, instead of the sex ratio of 857 for this age group, which says that for every 1,000 black women in the age group of 20-44, there are only 857 males in the same age group. The adjusted rate, based on Siegel's data 958. This sex ratio is significantly different from the official 1970 census count.

Table 1. Undercount of the Black Population, 1970, Ages 20-40 (in thousands)

Age Group	Male	Female	Sex Ratio
1820	900,796	870,860	1,034
1840	1,432,988	1,440,660	995
1860	2,216,744	2,225,086	996
1890	3,735,603	3,753,073	995
1890	4,885,881	4,941,882	989
1910	4,885,881	4,941,882	989
1930	5,855,669	6,035,474	970
1940	6,269,038	6,596,480	950
1950	7,269,170	7,757,505	937
1960	9,097,704	9,750,915	933
1970	10,748,316	11,831,973	908
1974	11,452,000	12,592,000	909

*All statistical tables are from the U.S. Department of Commerce, Bureau of the Census, Historical Statistics of the United States: Colonial Times to 1970, House Document No. 93-78; and Current Population Reports, Special Studies Series P-23, No.54, The Social and Economic Status of the Black Population in the United States, 1970, 1973, and 1974.

Analyzing the male-female sex ratio is very important to the survival of black people in general, and the black female specifically. For some people would have us believe that there is a drastic shortage of black males. It is indeed true that there is a difference in the sex ratio, but the difference is not as great as we have been led to believe. Siegel's data also suggest that the sex ratio has not changed significantly since 1940. One should note in Table 2 the significant drop in the sex ratio between 1910 and 1930 and again between 1930 and 1940. Part of the undercount for these censuses must be explained by the changing distribution of the black population. As men and women began the mass migration from the south to the north, many were "lost" in the great exodus north. However, there has been no systematic attempt on the part of the Bureau of the Census to correct these past statistics. Given the data in Table 2, we must be very cautious in accepting census data without careful analysis.

One of the things we can see from the census count of the population is that black females live longer than black males. In part, the differences in life expectancy account for the uneven sex ratio. That is, although more males are born, women live longer than men. The differences in the life expectancy of black men and women can be seen in Table 3. This table also shows the progress blacks have made in the past 70 years in increasing their life expectancy. Specifically, we can see that the black female has gone from a life expectancy of 33.5 years in 1900 to 69.4 years in 1970. On the average, black women are living eight years longer than the white man. The lowest life expectancy rate is for the black man, who is expected to live a little over 61 years. His life expectancy is seven years less than that of the white male.

Most of the increase in the life expectancy of blacks can be accounted for by the tremendous drop in the infant mortality rate that whites reached more than 25 years ago (see Table 4). In 1973, the infant mortality rate was 26.3 for blacks. White had a rate of 15.8 and 1950 the rate 26.8 for white's blacks still fall behind whited in these vital statistics. The poor economic conditions of blacks account for these differences. Without economic resources, blacks cannot afford the doctors needed to maintain health, nor can they buy the kinds of food that would ensure their physical health.

Education is a key factor in determining the economic resources of black people, and white continue to outdistance blacks in education. Rather than the question of whether black women receive more education than black men, the crucial question is to what extend blacks have been able to close the educational gap between blacks and whites. In viewing Table 5, we find that in 1850, more than half of the white population was enrolled in school, compared with less than two percent of the population black population. However, this does not mean that an equal number of blacks and whites finish high school, or that the average number of blacks and whites finish high school, or the average number of years of schools complete is the same. As late as 1940, the black female had completed an average of 6.1 years of school, and the black male had completed 5.4 years. By 1970, the white male and female had graduated from high school, averaging over twelve years of schooling. We can further see that the education attainment of black women did not nor does it differ from black males significantly. That is, what difference does it make, economically or socially, if the black male finished 9.6 years?

Table 3. Expectation of Life at Birth by Race and Sex, 1900-1970.

Year	Male		Female	
	White	Black	White	Black
1970	68.0	61.3	75.6	69.4
1960	67.4	61.6	74.1	66.3
1950	66.5	59.1	72.2	62.9
1940	62.1	51.5	66.6	54.9
1930	59.7	47.3	63.5	49.2
1920	54.4	45.5	55.6	45.2
1910	48.6	38.8	52.0	37.5
1900	46.6	32.5	48.7	33.5

Table 4. Infant Mortality Rates by Race. 1940-1973 (per 1,000)

Year	Black	White
1973	26.2	15.8
1970	30.9	17.8
1965	40.3	21.5
1960	43.2	22.9
1950	44.5	26.8
1940	73.8	43.2

Table 5. School Enrollment Rates Per 100 Population by Sex and Race, 1850-1970

Year	Male		Female	
	White	Black	White	Black
1970	91.9	89.6	89.7	89.1
1960	90.6	86.6	87.3	85.7
1950	79.7	74.7	78.9	74.9
1940	75.9	67.5	75.4	69.2
1930	71.4	59.7	70.9	60.8
1920	65.6	52.5	65.8	54.5
1910	61.4	43.1	61.3	46.6
1900	53.4	29.4	53.9	32.8
1890	58.5	31.8	57.2	33.9
1880	63.5	34.1	60.5	33.5
1870	56.0	9.6	52.7	10.0
1860	62.0	1.9	57.2	1.8
1850	59.0	2.0	53.3	1.8

Table 6. Median Years of School Completed by Sex and Race, 1940-1970.

Year	Male		Female	
	White	Black	White	Black
1970	12.2	9.6	12.2	10.2
1960	10.6	7.9	11.0	8.5
1950	9.3	6.4	10.0	7.2
1940	8.7	5.4	8.8	6.1

Table 7. Percentage of the Black Population Over 25 with At Least Some High School by Sex, 1940-1970

Year	1-3 Years Male	Graduated Female	1-3 Years Male	4+ Years Female	High School Male	High School Female	College Male	College Female
1970	20.6	23.5	22.4	24.6	6.2	6.4	6.8	5.6
1966	20.1	24.0	17.4	21.2	5.3	5.4	5.0	4.4
1959	17.7	19.6	11.5	14.7	3.7	3.5	3.6	2.9
1950	11.6	14.4	7.2	8.9	2.8	3.1	2.0	2.3
1940	7.3	9.8	3.8	5.0	1.6	2.1	1.4	1.2

Table 8. Percentage of the Population Over 25 Who Completed Four or More Years of College by Race and Sex, 1940-1974.

Year	Black		White	
	Male	Female	Male	Female
1974	8.8	7.6	24.9	17.2
1970	6.8	5.6	15.0	8.6
1965	5.0	4.4	13.3	7.7
1960	3.5	3.6	10.3	6.0
1947	2.0	2.6	6.5	4.8
1940	1.4	1.2	5.8	4.0

If one looks at those persons over 25 years of age who graduated from college (Table 7), there is very little difference between males and females. In none of these figures do we see such drastic differences that would call for the kind of theorizing that exists about why black women are more "educated" than black males. Nor do we see the kind of data that suggest that black daughters have been preferred over black sons in terms of education. The fact is that both black men and women have very similar educational levels compared with white men and women have very similar educational levels compared with white men and women. For example, in 1940, 4.0 percent of the white females and 5.8 percent of the white males had graduated from college. This was true for only 1.2 percent of the black females and 1.4 percent of the black males. By1970, the number of black women graduating from college had increased, but so had the number of whites, and the differences by race were still larger than the differences by sec; 5.6 percent black females and 6.8 percent black males had completed four years of college. This was true for 8.6 percent of the white females and 15.9 percent of the white males. What we note in these statistics is the great difference between the white male and female. There had been a tendency for white social scientist to look at near parity in the college education of blacks and see that as a disadvantage for black males, since white females do not graduate from college nearly as often as white males cannot be blamed on the excessive educational advantage of black women.

Table 9. Occupation of Employed Men and Women by Race, 1964, 1974 (in percentages)*

	1964		1970		1974	
	Black	White	Black	White	Black	White
WOMEN						
White-collar workers	23	61	38	64	42	63
Professional & tech.	8	14	11	15	12	15
Teachers, except college	5	6	5	6	5	6
Msgrs. & admin.	2	5	3	5	2	5
Sales workers	2	8	3	8	3	7
Clerical workers	11	34	21	36	25	36
Blue-collar workers	15	17	19	16	20	15
Service workers	56	19	43	19	37	19
Private household	33	5	18	3	11	3
Farm workers	6	3	2	2	1	2
Total	100	100	100	100	100	100
MEN						
White-collar workers	16	41	22	43	24	45
Professional & tech.	6	13	8	15	9	15
Teachers, except college	1	1	1	2	2	2
Msgrs. & admin.	3	15	5	15	5	15
Sales workers	2	6	2	6	2	6
Clerical workers	5	7	7	7	7	6
Blue-collar workers	58	46	60	46	57	46

Service workers	16	6	13	6	15	7
Farm workers	10	7	6	5	4	5
Total	100	100	100	100	100	100

*Percentages may not equal 100 due to rounding.

One must ask what the educational advancement of black women has meant to them. In looking at Table 9, we can see the significant changes that have taken place in the occupational structure of black women. In 1964, more than half of all employed black women were service workers, and 33 percent of service workers had decreased to 37 percent and 11 percent of all black women in private household work. Over the 10-year period there has been little change in the number of white women in service work- 19 percent or the number in private household service from 5 to 3 percent. The number of black women in professional or technical fields rose from 8 percent in 1964 to 12 percent in 1974. For white women, the percentage has remained the same; 15. Very few women, black or white, are found in managerial jobs 2 percent for blacks and 5 percent for whites. There has been an increase of over 100 percent in the number of black women in clerical jobs. The percentage has gone from 11 in 1964 to 25 in 1974; whereas, again, the percentage for white women over the 10-year period has remained about the same, a little over one-third of all employed white women. What we see from Table 9 is that the black woman has seen significant changes in her employment pattern over the past 10 years; she has left the field of service workers in significant numbers and gone into the clerical fields. However, the largest number of black women is still found in service work. From Table 9, we also note that more black women than men are in professional and technical fields. What one must remember is that of the 12 percent of black women who are professional, 42 percent of these were teachers (excluding college). This was true for only 22 percent of the black males.

Table 10. Unemployment Rates by Race and Sex, 1948-1974.

Year	Male		Female	
	White	Black	White	Black
1974	8.4	4.3	10.1	5.9
1970	7.3	4.0	9.3	5.4
1965	7.4	3.6	9.2	5.0
1960	10.7	4.8	9.4	5.3
1955	8.8	3.7	8.4	4.3
1950	9.4	4.7	8.4	5.3
1948	5.8	3.4	6.1	5.9

Although the employment pattern of the black woman has changed, she is still more often unemployed than the black male, white female or white male. Table 10 shows the unemployment rates from 1948 to 1979 by race and sex. First, one can see that the unemployment rate of blacks is much higher than the rate for whites. Further, black women, on the whole, have a higher unemployment rate than black men. Whereas the unemployment rate for whites in about 4.5 percent, it is almost 8.0 percent for blacks. This rate does not reflect the underemployment of black men and women. We know that gains have been made in the occupational and educational fields, but blacks are more often hired in jobs for which they are overqualified.

Table 11. Median Money Wage or Salary Income of Year Round Full Time Workers, by Sex and Race, 1939, 1975.

Year	Male		Female	
	White	Black	White	Black
1975	$10,000	$12,961	$7,486	$7,617
1973	7,953	11,800	5,595	6,598
1970	6,598	9,373	4,674	5,490
1965	4,367	6,814	2,713	3,960
1960	3,789	5,662	2,372	3,410
1955	2,831	4,458	1,637	2,870
1939	639	1,419	327	863

The underemployment of black women and men can be seen in the median income of year-round full-time workers. What one notes in Table 11 is that black women have consistently earned less than white men, black men, and white women. Therefore, it is unfair to suggest that black women have somehow managed to outdistance black men in earnings; this has never been the case. Not only does the black woman earn less than any other group, but, as noted above, she is more often unemployed. For example, in 1975, the white male earned an average of $12,961 per year; the black male earned $10,000. The black female was earning only $7,486 while the while female earned $7,167. Although the earning power of black and white females is near equal, one must keep in mind that black women stay in the economic marketplace longer. Unlike white women, they tend to remain in the job market until their children start. They must work for low wages, even if they do not want to. The economic institution has greater impact on black people in general and the black woman specifically.

Another area of interest to black is political participation (see Table 12). Again, the impression might be that black women are more active in politics than are black men. However, the data collected by the Joint Center for Political Studies show this is far from the truth. In 1975, only 13.1 of all blacks elected officially were female, and the majority of them were in the field of education. Of

Table 12. Black Elected Officials by Sex and Type of Office, May 1975*

Total	Male	Female
4,033	3,503 (84.9%)	530 (13.1%)
U.S Senator and Representatives	18(81.8%)	4(18.2%)
State Legislators and executives	281	35(11.1%)
Mayors	135	9(6.2%)
Others	3,069	482(13.6%)
Country	305	31(9.2%)
Municipal	1,438	203(12.4%)
Law enforcement	387	34(8.1%)
Education	939	214(18.6%)

*SOURCE: Joint Center for Political Studies

The 530 black females elected officials, 241 of them were in education. There is a tendency to pay undue attention to black females who hold high elected positions and to assume they represent what black women are doing nationally. For example, we fail to see that of the 18 U.S. Representatives only four are female. Black women are participating in the political process, but not at the same rate as men. Blacks in general make up less than five percent of all U.S. Senators and Representatives. Therefore, we can begin to see that blacks are severely underrepresented given their population size, and black women are the minority in the elected group that does exist.

Table 13. Percentage Distribution of Black and White Families by Type, 1950-1975

Year	Husband-Wife		Female Headed		Other Male	
	Black	White	Black	White	Black	White
1950	77.7	88.0	17.6	8.5	4.7	3.5
1955	75.3	87.9	20.7	9.0	4.0	3.0
1960	73.6	88.7	22.4	8.7	4.0	2.6
1965	73.2	88.6	23.7	9.0	3.2	2.4
1970	68.1	88.7	28.3	9.1	3.7	2.3
1971	65.6	88.3	30.6	9.4	3.8	2.3
1972	63.8	88.2	31.8	9.4	4.4	2.3
1973	61.4	87.7	34.6	9.6	4.0	2.5
1974	61.8	87.7	34.0	9.9	4.2	2.4
1975	60.9	86.9	35.3	10.5	3.9	2.6

What kind of impact has the above data had on the black family? We find that for the most part, the impact has been negative. Table 13 shows that, since 1950, the number of husband-wife families has dropped from 77.7 percent to 60.9 percent in 1975 a percentage change of nearly 17 points in 25 years. Conversely, the number of black women heading households has increased from 17.6 percent in 1950 to 35.3 percent in 1975. For whites, the change has been only two percentage points from 8.5 percent in 1950 to 10.5 percent in 1975. When one views the increase in the number of females headed households the assumption is, quite often, that the increase is due to the break-up of already existing relationships. Table 14 reveals that the greatest change has come about in the single, never married category, where percentage has gone from 12 in 1960 to 20 in 1973. Over this 13-year period there was a change of 66 percent. The category of separated or divorced accounted for a 25-percent change, going from 40 percent in 1960 to 49 percent in 1973. That is, marital discord does not account for 50 percent of the female headed households. We can see other changes taking place in black families by looking at Table 14, which shows the percentage of ever married women not living with husbands because of marital discord. In 1950, 14 percent of ever-married black women were not living with husbands because of marital discord. By 1960, the percentage has risen to 16 and by 1970 it was 19 percent. It took 20 years to show a percentage point difference of four in this category. However, it took only three years to go from 19 percent in 1970 to 23 percent in 1973.

Table 14. Marital Status of Black Female Heads of Families, 1960, 1967, 1970 and 1973 (in percentages)

Marital Status	1960	1967	1970	1973
Single (never married)	12	12	16	20
Separated or divorced	40	47	48	49
Separated	29	33	34	33
Divorced	11	13	14	16
Husband temporarily absent	6	7	7	4
Armed forces	_	2	2	1
Other reasons	6	5	4	3
Widowed	42	35	30	28
Percentage	100	100	100	100

It is obvious from these data that something is happening in the society which accounts for the drastic ahnges in the number of married black women not living with their husbands because of marital discord. Likewise, we need to study the causes for the large increase in single, never-married black women. We know that a large number of single female-headed households include children: In 1974, 70 percent of all such households included children, and these

Table 15. Percentage of Ever-Married Women not Living with Spouse Because of Marital Discord, 1950-1973

Year	Separated		Divorced	
	Black	White	Black	White
1950	11	2	3	3
1951	9	2	3	3
1952	10	1	3	3
1953	8	2	4	3
1954	14	1	4	3
1955	12	2	3	3
1956	11	2	4	3
1957	10	1	4	4
1958	12	2	3	3
1959	14	2	4	3
1960	11	2	5	3
1961	11	2	5	3
1962	11	2	5	3
1963	11	2	6	3
1964	12	2	5	4
1965	12	2	5	4
1966	11	2	5	4
1967	11	2	5	4
1968	12	2	6	4
1969	12	2	6	5
1970	13	2	6	4
1973	15	2	8	5

Households accounted for 39 percent of all black children under 18 years of age. Further, in 1960, 75 percent of all black children lived with both parents; by 1970, the percentage was down to 64; and for the first time in 1976, less than half of all black children live with both parents. Whites have also seen a change in the number of children living with both parents. In 1960, 92 percent of all white children under 18 lived both parents; in 1970 it was 90 percent, and by 1977 it was down to 79 percent a percentage drop of 11 points in seven years. Some authorities suggest that the changes in the white family are due to the changes in women's status brought on by the women's liberation movement. The same line of reasoning has not been suggested to explain the changes in black families and the lives of black children. Rather, the changes have been viewed as indications of family disorganization without looking for the causes other than the acting individuals. However, we know that the one factor which accounts for the greatest variance in the number of black children living with both parents in income. In Table 16, we can readily see the difference incomes makes in the number of black

Table 16. Own Children Under 18 by Presence of Parents and Family Income, 1974

Income	Black		White	
	Both Parents	One Parent	Both Parents	One Parent
Under $4,000	18	82	39	61
4,000-5999	35	65	56	34
6,000-7,999	53	47	77	23
8,000-9,999	78	22	88	12
10,000-14,999	86	14	94	6
15,000 and over	90	10	97	3

children living with both parents. For families with incomes over $15,000, 90 percent of all black children live with both parents. Since slightly more than half of all black children are in households below the poverty level. For example, the median family income for a black male-headed household was $7,766 in 1974, while a black female-headed household had an income level of $3,576. In 1974, 52.8 percent of all black female-headed households were below the poverty level. This was true for only 24.9 percent for all black male-headed households. What these data show is the black women who are heading households are living in or near poverty and raising children who do not have the basic necessities of life. Rather than malign these women, we need to systematically study their needs and their coping strategies, and help develop ways to give them the income they need to live decent lives.

The data in this chapter show that significant changes have taken place in the lives of black women on a national demographic level. Most of these changes can be tied to the urbanization process. Although poor and living in an oppressive economic system, it would seem that black women and their families were able to maintain certain stabilities within the family. More wives and husbands stayed together and worked to maintain a family. The urban move has meant that black women are still poor, but unlike their forebears they no longer have the land on which to raise their food. The urban environment has imposed a structure which tends to separate wives from their husbands. The welfare state will not "support" struggling families; aid is only given to dependent children. Therefore, from 1940 to 1975, we have witnessed a drastic increase in the number of children living with both parents. In 1976, less than 50 percent of all black children lived with both parents. We know that in the vast majority of case these are poor black children, living with poor black mothers. For example, we see that only 18 per year of all black children living in families with less than $4,000 per year were with both parents, whereas 90 percent of all black children who were families with incomes over $15,000 were living with both parents in 1974. The economic system is destroying the poor black family.

We have also seen that the life experience of black women has changed significantly over the past 40 years. She can expect to live on an average of 70 years. If the black female can survive the first year of life, her life expectancy does not differ significantly from the white female. Also, we noted that there is a difference in the black male-female sex ratio, with more women than men present. However, we say that in every census the black male population is undercounted more often than the female population. When we correct for the undercount, the sec ration is not as drastic as it might first appear.

Finally, it was noted that significant changes can be seen in the educational levels of black women. From 1940 to 1970, the average number of years of school completed increased by four. However, the black had still only completed 10.2 years of school in 1970.

Additionally, changes occurred in the kinds of jobs held by black women. They are no longer exclusively in service occupations. In fact, from 1964 to 1974, the number of women in private jobs declined to 11 percent in 1974. A larger number of black women are now in the clerical field. Only 12 percent of all black female workers are in professional and technical occupations, and nearly 50 percent of them are teachers below the college level. Black women continue to earn less money than black or white men and, although they work more frequently and remain in the labor force longer, they still earn less than white females.

It is very difficult to justify the concept of the positive-negative force of being black and female from these data. One cannot see the positive advantages. The data show that black women still comprise the most destitute group educationally, economically, and politically. These institutions are affecting black women in such a way that the very survival of the black family is being threatened, and the survival of black children is becoming more and more doubtful. Unless our children can survive both physically and mentally, we as a people can no longer survive.

REFERENCES

Farley, R. (1970) Growth of the Black Population: A study of Demographic Trends. Chicago:Markham.

U.S.Dept.of Commerce, Bureau of the Census (1976) Historical Statistics of the United States: Colonial Times to 1970. House Document NO.93-78. Washington, DC: US. Government Printing Office.

______(1979) Current Population Reports, Special Studies Series P-23, No.54, The Social and Economic Status of the Black Population in the United States. Washington, DC: U.S. Government Printing Office.

Siegal, J.S. (1973)" Estimates of coverage of the population by sex, race, and age in the 1970 Census." Presented at the annual meeting of the Population Association of America, New Orleans, Louisiana, April 26.

REVISITING THE DEMOGRAPHICS OF BLACK MEN AND WOMEN

ABA D. ESSUON

Where are the men? This question was posed as recently as April of 2004 in an article in the BBC News Magazine. The article was written in response to the 2021 census which was unable to account for a large portion of young males in their 20s, 30s, and 40s. The gap in the census report suggested that the population estimates were short by one million persons, specifically one million male persons. The birth statistics, however, belied a hypothesis that there were indeed fewer males, for more males than females were and had been born. So, where were the men? The prior question is one that has been posed by many researchers including Dr. La Frances Rodgers-Rose.

The question was first posed and explored by Dr. Rodgers-Rose in her 1989 chapter entitled "Some Demographics Characteristics of the Black Woman: 1940 to 1975." In her investigative chapter, Rodgers-Rose attempted to ascertain the whereabouts of African-American males in the United States. As result of her research, she determined that the 1970's US census report failed to include 1.88 million blacks in its final report. This oversight meant that 7.7% of the total black population had not been presented. In 1973, a census correction reported by Siegel suggested that 627,000 black males between the ages of 20 to 44 and 214,000 black females within the same age range had been excluded from the final 1970 census count. Rodgers-Rose's examination determined that although it is true that black men have not numbered black women since the 1820's, the black male to female ration was not as extreme as the 1970's census data suggested.

The original census report suggested that there were 857 black males per every 1000 females in the 20-44 age range. The corrected census data suggested that this difference was much smaller in that there were 958 black males for every 1000 black females in the 20-44 age range. Her analysis of the 1970's census data highlighted several racial and gender disparities. In her evaluation of the isolate other racial and gender demographic characteristics such as life span expectations, infant mortality rates, education levels, occupation, unemployment rates, income, and marital status which may foster the perception of fewer black males. The year is now 2007 and the United States has undergone three census counts since 1970. The question posed in 2004 BBC News Magazine suggest that the question, "where are the men?" is still variable. From this article it is suspected that the United States has continued to undercount a portion of its population but to what existent? Are you continued population oversights among blacks reflective of the racial and gender differences highlight by Rodgers-Rose? This chapter will attempt to answer this question by offering a comparative analysis of the 1970 data provide in Rodgers-Rose's chapter with the current 2000 US census data by exploring the impact of incarceration and AIDS on the black male/female relationships.

THE CENSUS COUNT

In the United States, nationwide census data is collected once every ten years. The 2000 census report estimates a US population of 281,421,906 persons of which 50.9% where females (n=143,368,343) and 49.1% where males (n=138,053,563) (US Census Bureau, 2000). This estimate reflects a 13.2% increase from the 1990 census data. In 2004, the Centers for Disease Prevention and Control estimated that the population had increased to 293,655,404 persons (CDC, 2004). In that population estimate, 65% were classified as White non-Hispanic, 14% s Hispanic, 13% as Black, non-Hispanic, 4% as Asian or Pacific Islander, and the remaining 1% as American Indian or Alaskan Natives (Chart 1).

Chart 1. US Population 2004
N=293,655,404

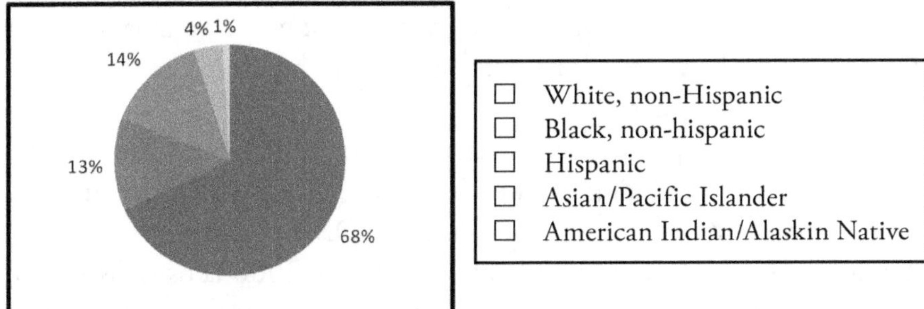

The ratio between the black male and female declined from 1970 to 2005. In 2005, the reported black male to female ratio was 91.2 males per every 100 females, a decree from 95.8 males per every 100 females in 1970 (U.S. Bureau of the Census, 2007). As was the case in 1970, the reported 2005 statistic may be not reflective of the actual black/male dynamic. The 2005, statistics includes only those who self-identified as a single race, thus excluding those who may consider themselves as an "Other" because of bi-racial or multiracial origins but are perceived as black.

One of the most prominent examples of such an individual is the accomplished and multi champion golfer Tiger Woods who was revered as the great black hope of gold at age 21 (Kamiya, 1997; Poe, 1997). Woods had been referred to as an African-American in print, on radio, and on television. It was no until he made an appearance on "Oprah," a national television talk show, to inform the nation that although his appearance may lead one to think that he was black, he was not. It was at this time that Woods made up the term "cablinasian" to describe his black, American Indiana, white, Thai, and Chinese ancestry. Despite making known his preferred racial classification Woods is still perceived as black.

The media has failed to adopt Wood's classification of himself and continues to refer to him as an African-American or as an Asian African-American. Media's reluctance and or inablility to reference Woods differently may have much to do with the fact that he looks black he has the same skin coloring and features as a man self-identified as an African-American. This phenomenon of perception may best be explained by Dr. Delores P. Aldridge in her chapter entitled "Interracial Marriage Empirical and Theoretical Considerations." In this chapter Aldridge explained that the children of black-white marriages were thought to be black by both the black and the white communities despite their mixed heritage.

In 1997, in response to an increasing trend of bi and multi-racial individuals and the dialog sparked by Tiger Woods' racial declaration, the Office of Management and Budget (OMB) change the federal regulation to add a multi-racial category to the 2000 census (Kamiya, 1997; Wikimedia, 2007). The rise in interracial partnerships and transracial adoptions result in noticeable trends. Aldridge's chapter also offered some explanation for the increase in the number of interracial partnerships. In her chapter she discussed the intermingling of young adults on college campus. As a result, with its inherent diversity, college campuses normalize interracial dating and it turn may lay the foundation for some interracial marriages.

In 1990, 14% of 18 to 19 years old were engaging in interracial partnerships. In addition, 15 % of those 20 to 21 and 7% of those 34 to 35 years old were also engaging in interracial relationships (Jayner & Kao, 2005). In response OMB added the category "Other" in recognition of the trend. The use of the term "Other" was by no means an efficient or effective means of classifying the growing multi-racial US population. The United Kingdom, unlike the US, did make an effort to accurately define the multi-racial population. In 2001 census report, the United Kingdom use the terms such as "Mixed White and black Caribbean," Mixed White and Black African" Mixed White and (South) Asia," and "Other Mixed" to classify persons who self-identified to be more than one race (Wikimedia, 2007).

It is estimated that 1.4% of the US population is multi-racial, however, because of the use of the term "Other" to describe this population, Caucasian/African-Americans are grouped with Asian/ American Indians, Arabs, etc. In the 2000 census report, 2.4% of all respondents classified themselves as multi-racial (US Census, 2000). Since the term "Other" manages to capture not only racial but ethnic identities, it is difficult to determine how many of these individuals actually impact the black male to female ration.

SINCE 1970: REVISITING RACIAL AND GENDER DEMOGRAPHICS

Life Expectancy and Infant Mortality

According to the census da the black population has experienced an increase in overall numbers and in life span expectations. Although life expectancy is still greater for whites, the change in life expectation from 1970 to 2000 was higher for black males and females. From 1970 to 2000, white males experienced an increase of 6.9 years where as black males experienced an increase of 7.3 years. In this same time span, white women experienced an increase of 4.5 years and black women experienced an increase of 5.8 years. In addition to experiencing a loner life span, more black babies are surviving. The rate of black infant deaths declined by nearly half between 1973 and 2000 (MMWR, 2001.

Table 1. Expectation of Life at Birth by Race and Sex: 1970 and 2000

Year	Male		Female	
	White	Black	White	Black
1970	68.0	61.3	75.6	69.4
2000	74.9	68.6	80.1	75.2

Source: U.S. National Center for Health Statistics, Vital Statistics of the US. Annual and National Vital Statistics Reports.

Table 2. Infant Mortality Rates by Race, 1973 and 2000 (per 1,000)

Year	Black	White
1973	26.2	15.8
2000	14.0	5.7

Source: Mortality and Morbidity Weekly (MMWR) 2002/21 (27); 589-592

Marital Status

The 2000 US census report estimated that of the 105.5 million households counted, 53% of those households were married families. This number reflected a drop in the number of married couple houses from 69% in 1970 to 53% in 2000. When viewing this data as Rodgers-Rose did in her historic review of black relationship from a female perspective, a trend is found among black female headed households. Her review showed a steady increase in the percentage of black female headed households. Her review showed a steady increase in the percentage of black females who never married. The number of black females never married increased from 12% in 1960 to 1970 the number of separated or divorce black women. From 1960 to 1970 the number of separated black women increased from 29% to 34%. By 1973, the number of separated black females declined (from 34% in 1970 to 33%) and continued to decline reaching 5.90% by 2000. The divorce rate among this population showed a steady increase from 11% to 16% between 1960 and 1973 before declining to 12.8% in 2000.

Table 3. Marital Status: 1970 to 2000

Status	Male				Female			
	1970	1980	1990	2000	1970	1980	1990	2000
Never Married	28.6	29.7	30.1	30.3	22.6	22.9	23.1	24.1
Married	65.7	62.5	60.2	58.6	61.2	57.8	55.6	54.6
Widowed	3.0	2.5	2.5	2.5	12.3	12.3	12.0	10.5
Divorced	2.7	5.3	7.2	8.7	3.9	7.1	9.4	10.8

Table 4. Marital Status of the Black Population Aged 15 and Over by Sex (percentage), 2000

	Total	Now Married		Widowed	Divorced	Separated	Never Married
		Spouse Present	Spouse Absent				
Male	11,691,001	34.2	7.3	3.0	9.5	4.4	41.6
Female	13,626,532	27.5	3.7	10.4	12.8	5.9	39.7

Source: U.S. Census Bureau, Census 2000 special tabulation

Table 6. United Interracial Marriage Statistics- 1970-2000

Year	Interracial Marriages	
	No.	% of all marriages
1970	310,000	0.7
1980	615,000	1.3
1992	1,161,000	2.2
2000	2,669,558	4.9
2005	-	7.0

Source: U.S. Census Report 1993 and 2000.

Similar to the women, the number of black men to never marry also increased from 1970 to 2000 (see Table 3.) The decrease likelihood that black women or black men will never marry as well as the increase prevalence of interracial relationship may prove to be detrimental to the survival of the traditional black male/female dyad. The percentage of interracial marriages in the United States has increased seven folds between 1970 and 2005 (Table 6) (U.S. Bureau of Census, 2000, Wikipedia, 2007). Although interracial marriages are more common among whites, they are somewhat of a rarity among blacks. In 1990 17.6% of all black marriages consisted of a union of a black man or woman with a white man or woman. In these marriages, black men were 2.5 times more likely than black women to marry a white partner. The nearly three to one ration seen in 1990 was still present in 2000. According to the 2000 US census report, 239,477 black males vs. 95,831 black females selected white marriage partners. Black males were also 598% more likely to marry Asian females than black women were to marry Asian men.

The greater propensity for black males to marry outside of their races has resulted in the term "marriage squeeze" (Crowder & Tolnay, 200). The term has been used to describe a social phenomenon that refers to the belief that black women are left with fewer partner options since the most eligible and desirable black men are electing to marry outside of their race. Data from 1980 and 1990 census data, demonstrated a progressive trend towards which may support the "marriage squeeze" phenomenon. In 1980, the percentage of black males without a college degree marrying with their race was higher than those with a college degree (96.5% vs. 94.0%), however education attainment seems to have little bearing on whither black women married within their race. By 1990, the percentage of black males and females with a college degree and greater marrying within their race had declined to 90.4% from black males and 96.4% for black women.

With the number of college educated black females having surpassed the number of college educated black males, black women desiring to marry within their race must often elect to "marrying down" or not marry at all according to the "marriage squeeze" phenomenon which argues that educated women of all races desire to marry a partner within their social and/or economic class (Crowder & Tolnay, 2000). Whether or not one is swayed by the explanation given by the "marriage squeeze" as to why more black women are single, the fact still remains that by the time black women reach their child-bearing years they outnumber the black male by 15%. Disproportionate mortality rates alone account for approximately 85 black males for every 100 child-bearing aged black female. The availability of black males to black women is therefore not only limited by the black male's selection of women from other races but also by social factors.

Table 6. United States Interracial Marriage Statistics-1970-2000

Year	Interracial Marriages	
	No.	% of all marriages
1970	310,000	0.7
1980	651,000	1.3
1992	1,161,000	2.2
2000	2,669,558	4.9
2005	-	7.0

INCARCERATION AND HIV/AIDS

In terms of black male/female relationships, the ration of males to females aged 15 and older is 1:1.2 Despite the relatively small difference in the number of black males to females, black women and researchers alike are still asking, "Where are the men?" In there a shortage of black males? The 1970 as well as the 2000 census data suggest that numerically the black male is present, yet, there are those that would argue differently. The difference in the ration, though seemingly small, is made great by social factor. The nineties War on Drugs and the AIDS epidemic are two social events which contributed to the removal of many young black males from mainstream society.

Incarceration and the War on Drugs

The rate of male incarnation in state and federal prisons as well as in jails is higher for males than it is for females and it is especially high among black males (Harrison & Beck, 2005). From 1990 to 2000, state prisons experienced a growth of 27% among black inmates, 15% among whites, and 70% among Hispanics for drug related offenses (Harrison & Beck 2001). On June 30, 2005, 2.2 million persons were incarcerated in the US (Harrison & Beck, 2005). Of those incarcerated 548,300 were black males between the ages of 20 and 39.

Although the War on Drugs resulted in more black behind bars, evidence suggest that more whites were actually using drugs. The 1998 Substance Abuse and Mental Health Services Administration's National Household Survey on Drug Abuse report reflected that more whites were more likely to use illicit drugs. The survey showed that 9.9 million whites (72%), two million blacks (15%), and 1.4 million Hispanics (10%) constituted all users currently engaging in illicit drugs. Despite a greater prevalence for drugs use among whites, 36.8% of those arrested for drug violations are black, and 58% of those in state prisons for drug felonies are blacks.

Black males have a higher rate of incarceration than any other racial group in the United States. The black male has an incarceration rate of 4,682 per 100,000 which is 2.5 times greater than the Hispanic male with an incarceration rate of 1,856 per 100,000 and 6.6 times greater than the with male with an incarceration rate of 709 per 100,000 (Harrison & Beck, 2005.) Before the mandatory minimum sentences for crack offenses were mandated by War on Drugs policies, the average federal drug offense sentence was already 11% greater for blacks than white in 1986 (Meierhoefer, 1992). Four years following the implementation of the War on Drugs policies, the average federal drug offense sentences were 49% greater for blacks, 4.5 times greater than the pre-War on Drug era.

At the start of the 1990s, there were more black males between the ages of 20 and 29 governed by the US criminal justice system then total in college (Haney & Zimbardo, 1998). The high prevalence of black males in jail and prison as a result of drug related charges is directly related to the fact that when convicted in a state court of a drug felony, white are less likely to go to jail than blacks (Durose & Langan, 2001). In a state court 33% of convicted whites compared to 51% of convicted blacks receive a prison sentence. The differences in sentencing have been justified by prosecutors and lawmakers who have associated crack cocaine use, which is most commonly used by blacks, with dangerous and threatening behaviors which may result in gang shootings, turf wars, and terrorized poor black communities (Hutchinson, 2007). These same prosecutors and lawmakers have attributed non-criminal and non-violent behaviors such as shoplifting, burglary, theft, larceny, money laundering, and transportation of undocumented workers to powder cocaine use.

In some respects, the opposite is true. The majority of those found to deal or use crack cocaine do not poses a propensity toward violence and have no gang affiliation (Hutchinson, 2007). Today's crack user is often poor, increasingly female, young and black. It is actually the powder cocaine user who is more likely to commit an act of violence yet harsher penalties have not been instituted to address these behaviors. Powder cocaine users, who are predominately white, have also been identified as prime dealers of other drugs such as heroin, meth, and crack cocaine and still they treated with compassion, counseling, and drug rehab programs in lieu of prison time. The unequal prosecution of black for similar drug offenses has resulted in the incarceration of 482 black males vs. 36 white males per every 100,000 (Katz, 200).

At the end 2005, 547, 200 blacks were serving time in a state or federal facility. Of those, 374,400 were between 20 and 44 years of age. It is within the 20-to-44-year age range that black women and researchers have noted and greatest felt the absence of the black male. The larger number of black inmates offers some explanation for the perceived discrepancy in the actual number of black males and the assessable of those males to main stream females.

Table 7. Number of sentenced prisoners under State or Federal jurisdiction, by gender, race, and age - 2005

| | Number of sentenced prisons | | | | | |
| | Males | | | Females | | |
Age	Total	White	Black	Total	White	Black
Total	1,362,500	459,700	547,200	98,600	45,800	29,900
18-19	26,300	7,200	11,800	1,200	500	400
20-24	218,700	62,700	94,200	11,900	5,300	3,600
25-29	244,800	67,000	106,600	15,300	6,700	4,700
30-34	224,200	69,800	9,200	17,400	8,100	5,100
35-39	207,200	72,800	81,600	19,400	9,000	6,000
40-44	185,200	70,900	71,000	16,500	7,800	5,100
45-54	189,800	76,300	71,100	13,800	6,500	4,300
>55	63,500	32,900	17,600	3,000	1,800	700

Source: U.S Department of Justice Bureau of Justice Statistics 2006

Table 8. Number of sentenced prisoners under State or Federal jurisdiction, by gender, race, and age - 2005

| | Number of sentenced prisons per 100,000 residents | | | | | |
| | Males | | | Females | | |
Age	Total	White	Black	Total	White	Black
Total	929	471	3,145	65	45	156
18-19	619	274	1,920	29	20	61
20-24	2,016	948	6,345	118	85	248
25-29	2,342	1,098	8,082	153	113	339
30-34	2,234	1,172	7,726	177	138	391
35-39	1,953	1,067	6,630	185	134	435
40-44	1,641	923	5,472	145	102	345
45-54	899	493	3,136	63	41	163
>55	208	697	697	8	6	19

Source: U.S Department of Justice Bureau of Justice Statistics 2006

HIV/AIDS and the US Prison System

By the close of 2002, 75% of those incarcerated were African-American of Hispanic (Rapposelli et al, 2002). Those housed in the US state and federal prisons are five times more likely than the non-incarcerated population to be HIV positive yet there are no comprehensive national testing, prevention, or treatment programs for inmates (Krebs and Simons, 202; Rapposelli et al., 2002; Moran, 2006). Given the high prevalence of HIV among the prison population several studies have been undertake to determine the time of infection. Horshurgh et al. (1990) identified a sample of 1,069 Nevada inmates who tested HIV negative during a mandatory screening at the time of incarceration. Over the course of their study, two of the inmates later tested positive for HIV. Horsburg et al. (1990) concluded an annual seroconversation rate of 0.17%. Brewer et al. (1988) concluded a 0.41% seroconversion rate rated from a sample 393 previously HIV negative Maryland inmates. Castro et al. (1994) studied a sample of 2,400 HIV negative Illinois and concluded a seroconversion rate of 0.3%.

The high rates of HIV in this population have been attributed to a series of high-risk behaviors such as unprotected sex, intravenous drug use, and tattooing while incarcerated (Kerbs and Simmons, 2002). The majority of sex that occurs in the US prison system is unprotected in that only four state jails nationwide permit the distribution and use of condoms. In addition, same sex activities among male inmates often conclude anal sex. Anal sex is significantly more risky than vaginal or oral intercourse because of the greater delicacy of the mucosa lining of the rectum. The lining of the rectum is more likely to tare during sexual activity then are the linings of the mouth or the vagina. Anal sex intercourse among inmates can be consensual or forced. The rate of sexual assault ranges from 3% to 28%.

HIV/AIDS and Black America

Although blacks made-up 13% of the US population they constitute nearly 50% of the US AIDS cases over 50% of all new HIV cases (CDC, 2005; Moran, 2006).

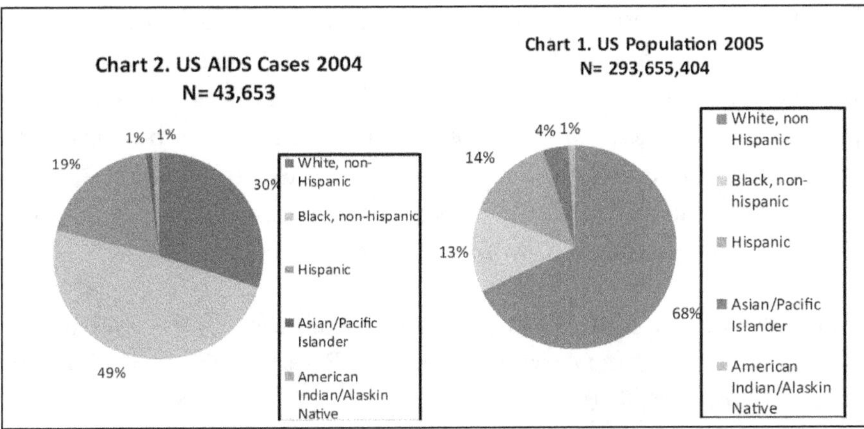

The pie chart on the left illustrates the distribution of AIDS cases reported in 2004 among racial/ethnic groups. The pie chart on the right shows the distribution of the US population (excluding US dependencies, possessions and associated nations) in 2004.

Non-Hipanic whites made up 68% of the US population but accounted for 30% of reported AIDS cases.

More information on the HIV/AIDS epidemic and HIV prevention among blacks and Hispanics is available in a CDC fact sheet at http://www.cdc.gov/hiv/pubs/facts.htm.

There are several key factors which contribute to the effective spread of HIV in black communities the first of these being the disproportionate number of black males in prison. As if it were not enough that a significant number of marriage age black males are incarcerated, many of them have entered the prison system. HIV-negative and exist, unknowingly, HIV-positive. The second factor which has contributed to the spread of HIV among blacks was the lack of federal support for the needle exchange program in the 1990's despite providing effectiveness in other countries in slowing the spread of HIV among intravenous drug users. The likelihood for black males to have multiple simultaneous sexual partners is another reason for the high number of HIV among blacks. The fourth factor is the "down-low" phenomenon. Although the "down-low" life style is not exclusive to black males, it has been used predominately to describe the behaviors of black men, self-identifying as heterosexual despite sexual exploits with other men.

The last factor attributed to the successful spread of HIV among black is the black church which has remained relatively silently. Historically the black church has been a source of political and social activism that has galvanized black communities in numinous causes but has done little to nothing to arrest the rapid spread of HIV among blacks. These factors independently and collectively have resulted in the premature deaths of many black men, women, and children.

Table 9. Estimated Number and Proportion of HIV/AIDS Cases among Adults and Adolescents Attributed to High Risk Heterosexual Contact* by Race/Ethnicity, 2004-35

Areas		
Race/Ethnicity	No.	%
White, not Hispanic	1,862	15
Black, not Hispanic	8,599	68
Hispanic	1,970	16
Asian/Pacific Islander	123	<1
American Indian/Alaska Native	69	<1
Total**	12,683	

CDC data includes persons w/ a diagnosis of HIV infection regardless of AIDS status at diagnosis. Data from 35 areas w/ confidential name-based HIV infection reporting since at least 2000. Data has been adjusted for reporting delays and cases without risk factors information were proportionally redistributed.

Table 10. Estimated # of HIV/AIDS cases By Age Group at Diagnosis 2005—33 Areas

Age (years)	HIV/AIDS Cases in 2005
<13	166
13-14	43
15-19	1,225
20-24	3,904
24-29	4,641
30-34	5,207

35-39	6,247
40-44	6,201
45-49	4,524
50-54	2,879
55-59	1,581
60-64	799
>65	679
Total	38,096

Source: Division of HIV/AIDS Prevention Nation Center for HIV/AIDS, Viral Hepatitis, and TB Prevention. Fata generated as result of point estimates.

Table 11. Estimated # of HIV/AIDS cases By Age Group at Diagnosis 2005—33 Areas

Ethnicity	Estimated # of HIV/AIDS Cases in 2005
White, not Hispanic	11,758

Table 10. Estimated # of HIV/AIDS cases By Age Group at Diagnosis 2005—33 Areas

Age (years)	HIV/AIDS Cases in 2005
<13	166
13-14	43
15-19	1,225
20-24	3,904
24-29	4,641
30-34	5,207
35-39	6,247
40-44	6,201
45-49	4,524
50-54	2,879
55-59	1,581
60-64	799
>65	679
Total	38,096

CONCLUSION

Despite the fact that US census reports continue to under estimate the black population by either failing to count all member or by classifying blacks of mixed heritage as "Other," this population has experienced several positive social changes which would positively impact their population growth. Since 1970, blacks have experienced a decrease in infant mortality and an increase in life expectancy. They have also; however, experienced several social factors that have negatively impacted the male/female dynamic. The census data from 1973 to 2000 showed a decrease in the number of black marital separations and an increase in the number of black interracial marriages (although still relatively small in comparison to interracial marriages among other races), with the greatest increase being among black men electing to marry women of other races.

Other social factors, such as incarnation and disease, which were not evaluated in Rodger-Rose's 1940 to 1975 assessment, arguably has had the most dramatic impact on the male/female dynamic. Both of these social factors have succeeded in limiting the number of eligible black males through isolation, sickness, and premature death. It is these latter factors, coupled with the previous mentioned, which may have steered people to use the question "Where are the black men." Therefore, in conclusion, as Rodger-Rose suggested in her evaluation of the 1970 census data, the 2000 census data also suggest that there is no numeric shortage of black men in the US. The perception that a shortage exist is fueled by census under counting, a disproportionably greater number of black male incarnations, an increase in the number of black males electing to engage in interracial relationships, and elevated level of HIV/AIDS in blacks not seen in any other racial group. In short, the answer to the question as to whiter or not there is a shortage of black men in America is equally yes and no.

REFERENCES

BBC News (2004). Where have all the men gone? Retrieved November 20, 2007 http://news.bbc.co.uk/1/hi/maganize/3601493.stm

Centers for Disease control and Prevention (CDC) (2002), Infant Mortality and Low Birth Weight Among Black and White Infants-United States, 1980-2000. MMWR Weekly, 51(27):589-592.

Durose, M. and Langan, P. (2001) Bureau of Justice Statistics, State Court Sentencing of Convicted Felons, 1998 Statistical tables. Washington, DC: US Department of Justice

Haney, C. Zimbardo, P.(1998). The past and future of US prison policy: twenty-five years after the Stanford prison experiment. American Psychologist 53 (7): 716-718.

Harrison, P. and Beck, A. (2002). Bureau of Justice Statistics, Prisoners in 2001 (Washington, DC: US Department of Justice, July 2002), p.13

Harrison, P. and Beck A. (2006). Bureau of Justice Statistics, Prison and Jail Inmates at Midyear 2005 (Washington, DC: US Department of Justice, May 2006), p.10

Hutchinson, E. (2007). The war on drugs is still a war on blacks. New American Media. Retrieved December 12, 2007 http://www.alternet.org/module/printversion/55403

Jennings, P. (2006). Out of Control: AIDS in Black America. ABC New Internet Ventures. Retrieved December 14, 2007 http://abcnews.go.com/print?id+2346857

Joyner, K. and Kao, G. (2005). Interracial Relationships and the Transition to Adulthood. American Sociological Review 70 (4):563-582.

Kamiya, G. (1997). Tiger Wood's rejection of orthodox racial classifications points the way to a future where race will no longer define us. Salon Retrieved December 12, 2007 http://www.salon.com/april97/tiger9701430.html

Meierhoefer, B. (1992). The general effects of mandatory minimum prison terms: A longitudinal study if federal sentences imposed. Washington, DC: Federal Judicial Center, p.20

Munz, A (2007). U.S. prison population hits all time high. Online NewsHous EXTRA Retrieved April 29, 2007 http://www.pbs.org/newshour/extra/teachers/lessonplans/math/incarceration_story_9-05

Poe,J(1997). Tiger Woods spots lights multiracial identity; golfer star sparks pride in heritage. Chicago Tribune on America Online Retrieved December 12, 2007 http://www.chicago.tribune.com

Rodgers-Rose, L (1989). "Some Demographic Characteristics of the Black Woman: 1940 to 1975." In Black Male-Female Relationships: A resource Book of Selected Materials., Aldridge, D., ed., pp.51-63. Dubuque, Lowa: Kendall and Hunt Publishing Company.

Substance Abuse and Mental Health Services Administration, National Household Survey on Drug Abuse: summary Report 1998, Rockville, MD.

U.S. Census Bureau. Profile of General Demographic Characteristics: 2000. Retrieved April 29, 2007.

U.S. Census Bureau. Census 2000 Demographic Profile Highlights: Selected Population Groups: Black or African American alone. Retrieved April 29, 2007.

U.S. Census Bureau, Census 2000 special tabulation. Marital Status of the Population Aged 15 and Over by Sex, Age, Race, and Hispanic Origin: 2000. Retrieved April 29, 2007.

U.S. Census Bureau, Statistical Abstract of the United States: 2003. Expectations of Life at Birth by Race and Sex: 1900 to 2001. Retrieved April 29, 2007.

Wikipedia Foundation (20070 Demographics of the United States. Retrieved April 29, 2007 http://en.wikipedia.org/wiki/United_States_Census_%2C_2000

Wikipedia Foundtion (2007) Interracial marriage. Retrieved December 15, 2007. http://en.wikipedia.org/wiki/INterractial_marriage

Aba D. Essuon is a postdoctoral fellow at the Morehouse School of Medicine in Atlanta, Georgia. Her specialty is social and behavioral sciences

CHAPTER THREE
Sex and Gender Issues

Algea Harrison sees growing up as a black and as a female to be a dilemma shaped by the political-economic subsystem that lead to the development of feminine and masculine role traits. She discusses how the black female attempts to resolve the dilemma of femininity and dhow achievement goals. A review is made of the black female's aspirations and accomplishments, and an analysis is made of differences between black and white females.

Betty collier-Watson, Louis Williams and Willy Smith investigate sexism and its effects upon gender differences. Gender differences are viewed as both favorable and unfavorable to women. In a systematic sense, women lose because of the inequalities that characterize the operation of social institutions. Conversely, in a vitalistic manner, men lose because their morbidity and morality rates are higher than those of women. It is demonstrated that when men lose, black men lose the most. Thus, sexism is seen as a two-edged sword. Women gain some areas and lose in others. It is concluded that black men and women gain the least and lose the most of the sex-race groups.

Bogart Leashore notes the ways in which racism and ideologies affect the development of racist social policies. This work illustrates how social policies operate to maintain racial inequality, especially with respect to black males. It is shown how domestic policies related to taxes and budget cuts have definitely affected black families and how racism and ideologies have influenced the development of social policies in the United States. Health care, employment and income support, and crime and justice are three areas delineated for alternative social policies.

AN ALTERNATIVE ANALYSIS OF SEXISM: IMPLICATIONS FOR THE BLACK FAMILY

BETTY COLLIER-WATSON
* LOUIS N. WILLIAMS * WILLY SMITH

INTRODUCTION

Over the past two decades since the mid-sixties, it has become quite popular for black writers to engage in debunking of myths concerning the black family. The reasons are obvious. The ideational content of knowledge is always socially determined and human thought has historically served as a critical instrument in the institutionalization of inequality. Thus, it has been incumbent on black social Scientists to inquire, explicate, and reiterate thoughts, ideas, and analyses towards a more accurate understanding of the black family.

Such a task is, however, a difficult one. On societies characterized by inequalities, an epistemological catch-22 exists. On the one hand, various groups within the society may seek to be involved in the advocacy of measures to ameliorate social dysfunction to the degree that such a state is socially produced. Yet, in order to intermediate, a body of knowledge must exist that accurately reflects the magnitude and nature of the dysfunction so that programs and policies can be teleologically related to causes. However, when inequality exists within a society, the inequalities are so far-reaching that the disadvantaged groups are also underrepresented in the production and distribution of knowledge about their own condition. Furthermore, their disadvantaged status is often so psychosocially entrenched that they often fall victim to the same epistemological myopia that tailors the knowledge produced and distributed by the dominant group. The thesis herein is that over the last two decades the stability of the black family and of black male/female relationships has been reduced because black social scientists have failed in promoting accurate discourse about the interactive relationship of race, gender, and class. Indeed, not only white but also black social scientists have promoted the axiomatic view that race and sex have operated and continue to operate as parallel systems of oppression. Such as view has not leapt into black consciousness.

Rather, black scholarship regarding sexism and sex role modeling has tended to play the role of passive beneficiary to the models and paradigms of sexism that have been promoted by white scholarship.

Accordingly, the tasks herein are several. At the first level, the objective of this discussion is that of examining the functioning of sexism between black males and females. To accomplish this task, however, it is necessary to reanalyzes and reconceptualize the functioning of sex role asymmetry in U.S. society.

SEX ROLE ASYMMETRY: A CONTEMPORARY PROFILE

For the most part, black social scientist has adopted what can be called a unilateral model of sexism. A unilateral conception of the operation of sexism postulates that U.S. society is characterized by sex role asymmetry (inequality). Implicit within this conception is the view that this asymmetrical arrangement is one in which females lose and males gain, indeed, inequalities of sex are viewed as constituting a system of male dominance. United States society is also characterized by forms of asymmetry based on race and class. These phenomena are similarly viewed as operating in such a fashion that inequalities emerge with gains accruing to the dominant race and/or class. For the purposes of the analysis herein, inequalities emerging as a consequence of the operation of sex, class, and /or race within a society will be separated into two separate but related categories. Those inequalities that characterize the operation of social institutions can be denoted as systemic inequalities. In contrast, those inequalities that characterize the chances of survival among the members of a given society will be called vitalistic.

Societies exist to enhance the chances of survival of its members. Thus, the ultimate test of the impact of asymmetry on a given group in a society cannot be completely measured by an examination of the asymmetrical functioning of social institutions. Rather, the ultimate impact of asymmetry in that society reveals itself through the impact systematic and vitalistic losses.

Empirical data support this assumption when asymmetries based on social class are examined. In U.S. society individuals of the lower classes experience systemic inequalities. Indeed, they receive unequal benefits from the major pivotal institutions. Such groups receive less income and wealth (Krauss,1976; Miller and Roby, 1977). Additionally, members of the lower classes have less political power and influence (Turner and Starnes, 1976). Such a pattern extends itself into the educational institutions. Children of lower-class families graduate from high school 250% less often, attend college 400% less often, graduate from college 600% less often; and receive postgraduate training 900% less often (Sewell, 1971). Also, the lower classes have more children and more divorces (Krauss, 1976). Such systemic inequalities are directly correlated with a similar vitalistic trend. Lower classes in the United States have lower life expectancies and higher death rates (Tumin, 1967; U.S. Department of Health, education, and Welfare. 1976). Department of Health, Education, and Welfare, 1976). Similarly, individuals within these classes experience a higher incidence of psychosis (Faris and Durham, 1939; Hollingshead and Redlich, 1985). Surveys reveal that lower class individuals report less happiness (Bradburn and Caplovitz, 1965) and more job boredom and dissatisfaction (Chinoy, 1955: Wooten, 1974). Lastly, lower-class individuals experience higher rates of crime as victim and victimizer and higher death rates from all major disease (Collier and Smith, 1981). Indeed, when class asymmetry is examined, the direct relationship between systemic and vitalistic inequalities is most apparent.

Without detailing the data, it can be said that a similar direct relationship between systemic and vitalistic variables exists by race. Not only do minority groups have lower median family incomes, higher levels of unemployment, and disproportionate rates of poverty, but they also have: (1) lower life expectancies, (2) higher rates of crime as victims and victimizers, (3) higher rates of criminal conviction, (4) higher divorce rates, (5) higher death rates from all major diseases, and so on, than do nonminority groups (Collier and Smith, 1981).

When sex role asymmetry is examined from such a perspective, however, and systemic as well as vitalistic variables are considered, a dual system of asymmetry becomes apparent. Systemically, females, for the most part, lose and males gain. Vitalistically, females gain and males lose. When these dual areas are interlocked, there emerges a unique type of asymmetry. More specifically, a bilateral relationship is revealed. Again, a detailed review of data supports these assertions.

The U.S. economy epitomizes an area in which systemic inequalities based on sex prevail. In 1983, for example, median weekly earnings for all families were $470. When the data are stratified by sex, however, significant differences emerge. Married couple families had median family incomes of $27, 286. While single householders of both sexes had median weekly earnings less than those of married couple families, families maintained by women had median family incomes of only $11,789.[1] Similarly, in 1984 34% of female-headed families existed below the poverty level and 44.2% below 125% of poverty, in contrast to 13.1% and 19.8% of all families repectively.[2]

When employment by sex and occupational category is examined, a slightly different form an asymmetry emerges females in contemporary U.S. society are disproportionately white-collar workers and males are disproportionately blue-collar workers. Whereas the overall earnings of males in these various occupational categories exceed those of females, it is not often pointed out that vitalistic losses are incurred by males. In one year, for example, males experienced 92.6 work-related accidents and injuries per 1,000 persons in contrast to 1.8 per 1,000 persons for females.[3] A similar pattern exists when occupational category is further disaggregated by sex. Females constitute only 13.4% of physicians, dentist, and related practitioners, for example.[4] Whereas such occupations are overwhelmingly male, such statuses carry with them one of the highest rates of suicide of all occupational categories as well as average life expectancies below those of males in general.

A brief glance at other pivotal institutions reveals a clear pattern of systemic inequalities from which males gain. Before the 1980 national elections, for example, 417 representatives were male and only 16 were female, and 99 senators were male and only 1 was female. State and local public offices followed a similar pattern. Some 3% of state executive and judiciary officials, 9.2% of state legislators 3.1% of country commissioners, and 7.8% of mayors and city councilpersons were female.[5] this asymmetrical holding of statuses and roles by males extended itself into the religious institution, in which 89% of all religious workers were male.

The educational institution, however, displayed an asymmetrical pattern that was less clear in terms of gains and losses. Some 70% of all non-university and college teachers were female. Again, a disaggregation of the data reveals that 96.8% of prekindergarten and kindergarten, 85.1% of elementary, 49.6% of secondary, and 36.6% of college and university teachers were female.[6] Yet males were disproportionately represented in higher statuses within the educational institution; over 72% of college professors were male.

When this systemic data is conjoined with vitalistic data, the existence of a bilateral pattern of sex role asymmetry becomes most apparent. During the same time period, the life expectancy of females was 78.3 years in contrast to 71.1 years for males.[7] In addition, males died from diseases of the heart 129% more often, from pneumonia 123% more often, from cirrhosis of the liver 200% more often, and from suicide 295% more often than females did (percentages calculated by authors). Indeed, males suffered from all major diseases except cardiovascular diseases, diabetes mellitus, and arteriosclerosis at a greater rate than that for females. [8]

The asymmetry extends itself into other areas. In this same period males were victims of all crimes except rape at a greater rate than that of females. Males were victims of robbery with injury 300% more often, robbery without injury 350% more often, aggravated assault 300% more often, simply assail 172% more often, and personal larceny 128% more often than females.[9] Lastly, males were victims of homicide 300% more often than females. Not only does asymmetry exist in victimization rates, it also exists in rates of arrest and convictions. Males were arrested for crimes 594% more often than females. Finally, since 1979 males have been sentenced to death 8000% more often than females.[10]

Parallel patterns exist in other areas. In 1980, 129% more males than females were in mental hospitals and residential treatment centers. As the disproportionate victims of lung diseases, 240% more males were in tuberculosis hospitals. Similarly, 129% more males were in home and schools for the mentally handicapped, 266% more males were in homes and schools for the physically handicapped, 147% more males were in homes for dependent and neglected children, and 378% more males were in detention homes. Additionally, as would be expected,

5020% more males were in military barracks.[11] The only institutions with disproportionately higher female populations were homes for the aged and dependent and homes for unwed mothers.

Other data could be introduced. However, the data discussed is sufficient to lend validity to the hypothesis that U.S. society is characterized by an asymmetry from which males benefit systemically while losing vitalistically. In contrast, females lose systemically while gaining vitalistically. It is this aspect of sexism that is often underdeveloped in existing literature in the area. Additionally, it is this aspect of sexism that supports as assertion that unlike social asymmetries based on class and race, the phenomenon of sexism operates as a bilateral process. Before an analysis of the relations among sex, race, and class can be presented, it is necessary to address another thematic thread that emerges from the use of the explicit and implicit assumptions of models of sexism that focus on systematic asymmetries. Specifically, the existence of systemic asymmetries. Specifically, the existence of systemic asymmetries is viewed as implying the operation of system of male dominance. Indeed, many social scientists have exonerated white females from responsibility for racial oppression by arguing that white females were merely victims of male dominance.

The notion that the history of women is a history of male dominance is so widely accepted that it too has become an axiom. Examples from literature and religion are used to demonstrate the existence of cultures imbued with sexist ideology (Campbell, 1959; Diner, 1973; Janeway, 1971). Male dominance is also viewed as not only reflecting itself in male control of the major pivotal institutions but also in the generally disproportionate accrual of prestige, power, and privilege to males. Indeed, male dominance is viewed by many as being so thorough and so undisputedly present in all relationships between males and females that sex, like race and class, has come to be viewed as another form of social stratification characterized by the oppression of females by males. This view is well summarized by Sheila Rowbotham (1974:35-46):

> *The social situations of women and the way in which we*
> *learn to be feminine is peculiar to us. Men do not share*
> *it, consequently we cannot be simply included under the*
> *heading of "mankind." The only claim that this word has*

> *to be general comes from the dominance of men in society.*
> *As the rulers they presume to define others by their own*
> *criteria.*

Accordingly, the implications or our bilateral conceptions of sexism for the male dominance thesis must be explored before the relationships between sex, race, and class can be examined. Although the primary focus of the analysis herein is upon the operation of sexism among blacks, the concepts of sex role asymmetry and male dominance have become central themes in black male/female relationships.

SEX ROLE ASYMMETRY: MALE DOMINANCE WITHIN A BILATERAL CONCEPTION OF SEXISM

The existence of systemic sex role asymmetry is widespread in human societies. Similarly, the view that such societies are characterized by male dominance is widespread. The anthropologist W.M. Stephens (1963), in a study of forty-one societies, concluded that males were dominant in 65% of the societies studied, males and females shared power in 26%, and females were dominant in 7%. Such findings have been confirmed in other studies (Gough, 1971; Hunt, 1973; Romeny, 1965). Indeed, the analyses of George Murdock's world ethnographic sample of D'Androde (1966) indicated that 66% of a sample of 565 societies throughout the world were patrilocal, whereas only 14% were matrilocal. Some 80% of the cultures sampled were patrilineal and 99% permitted polygyny but not polyandry. The substantial body of literature on the phenomenon of male dominance from a cross-cultural perspective has been adequately reviewed elsewhere (Parker and Parker, 1979).

An additional glance at the literature reveals that social scientist have also sought to locate the causes of systemic asymmetry and male dominance. A relatively widespread view is that male dominance is a consequence of biological factors (Goldberg, 1973; Tiger and Shepard, 1975). A less well accepted explanation of the alleged existence of male supremacy is the idea that prestate warfare is the causal factor (Divale and Harris, 1974; Hirschfeld, Howe, and Levin, 1978; Lancaster and Lancaster, 1978). The most prevalent explanations, however, view biological factors that emerged into a division of labor by sex as having led to male dominance (Brown 1970; Murdock and Provost, 1973). This view can be examined in greater detail.

For both blacks and whites, sex role asymmetry fulfills several systemic functions. On the one hand, sex roles provide the basis for division of labor and economic specialization. Additionally, critical society functions are fulfilled by the existence of sex roles.

Importantly, sex role differentiation functions as the foundation of marriage and the family. This function is implicit in the definition of a family, which has been described as "a social arrangement based on marriage and the marriage contract, including recognition of the rights and duties of parenthood, common residence for husband, wife, and children and reciprocal economic obligations between husband and wife" (Stephens, 1963:8). The systemic functions of sex role asymmetry via its relationship to the family cannot be over emphasized because such functions relate directly to the themes of sex and class. These points can be examined more closely.

Not only is the family traditionally the basic unit of a society, it and the educational institution are the central mechanisms for preserving the value system of that society (Bell and Vogel, 1968). The division of labor by sex traditionally assigned to females the responsibilities of the socialization of children while assigning to males' primary responsibility for the satisfaction of physical and biological needs of the family (e.g., food, shelter, and protection). These functions of males and females within the family interact in support of the family's role in another critical aspect of the society. Specifically, males and females within a family act out roles that cause the family to act as a major agent for creating and maintaining the existing systems of social stratification. Males are assigned the responsibility for acquiring the artifacts of production and artifacts of power for placement within stratified hierarchy. Similarly, females are assigned the task of socializing the young into those beliefs, values, and practices that correlate to the family's position within the social hierarchy. Thus, both males and females are coparticipants in class and race-based oppression. Such statements do not imply the application of a structural functionalist. (Parsons, 1955) approach to sex role asymmetry and the concept of male dominance. The oversimplification implicit in such a position has been adequately discussed elsewhere (Aronoff and Crano, 1975).

Indeed, a rejection of the view that sex role asymmetry emerged as a functional adaptation of the species as a whole has led to the adoption of other overly simple analyses. Some theorists have suggested that systemic asymmetry and male dominance emerged as a correlate of the development of economic surplus (Gough, 1971). Still others have viewed systemic inequality and male dominance as emerging from a fear of rape (Brwonmiller, 1975). Independent of the causes of the emergency of sex role asymmetry, the accepted position is that sex role asymmetry cross-culturally has led to the emergency of a system of social stratification characterized by male dominance. This system of social stratification is viewed as (1) operating in the interest of males and (2) maintained and supported by males. Additionally, this system of male dominance is viewed, like social stratification based upon race and class, as being supported by sanctions, myths, and other social psychological mechanisms that reinforce existing inequalities. Accordingly, the issue of whether systemic inequalities constitute a system of male dominance is actually subsumed by the issue of whether sex role asymmetry constitutes a system of social stratification. More importantly, it is critical to understand how sex role asymmetry is linked with race and class asymmetries.

Systems of social stratification have been recognized as consisting of inequality in three major components: (1) rights over property, (2) differential power or control, and (3) differential prestige or esteem (Weber, 1958). Such inequalities we have characterized as systemic inequalities in a system of social stratification exists, systemic and vitalistic inequalities together delineate of a set of class interests for the dominant and subordinate groups.

Our analysis of U.S. society, however, demonstrate clearly an inverse relationship between systemic and vitalistic asymmetries for males and females. Although data is not available for measuring and correlating vitalistic asymmetry with systemic asymmetry in traditional societies, existing data support the conclusion that even in traditional societies, females and males do not have separate class interests. Males and females do not separately compete for either property and/or power. Whereas it is true that greater prestige accrues to males, it is critical to our analysis to note that the benefits of property, power, and prestige accrue differentially to family units.

Although intrafamilial relationships may be characterized by various inequalities, these are not so intense as to create a separate set of class interests for males and females.

As other systems of social stratification emerge, such as racism, such systems become sex and gender linked. First, the physical attributes of the sex role model for that society are determined by the physical attributes of the dominant race and/or class. Thus, an interactive relationship exists between sex role asymmetry and other forms of social stratification. Importantly, neither males nor females as a class are the beneficiaries of sex-based system of social stratification. Importantly, neither the family unit becomes the intervening variable through which sex-based roles provide benefits. The family continues to function as the basic unit of social organization based on division of labor and specialization. Each family defends its position in the hierarchy in the struggle for property, power, and privilege. Males and females share class interests. Between males and females, males are allotted legitimate power while females share in their forms of power. An asymmetry does exist. This asymmetry produced benefits and losses for males and females within the family unit and thus must be more appropriately viewed as a system of exchanged based on common goals and common interests. Thus, male/female interaction can be more appropriately characterized as cooperative and accommodative.

In contrast, males and females within families jointly cooperate in a competitive and conflicting interaction with families from other strata (e.g., black versus white families).

Thus, the position herein is that the prevalent view of sex role asymmetry as a system of social stratification characterized by male oppression of females represents tremendous oversimplification. Rather, the positions taken herein can be summarized as follows: (1) Different forms of sex role asymmetry exist for both males and females. (2) Under conditions of stable family units, such asymmetry constitutes a division of labor and specialization that is functional to the survival of the family members. (3) Similarly, when stability of the family exists, male/female asymmetry does not constitute a system of stratification based upon sex, but rather are male/female units act to preserve, in unity, their own race/class interests.

In contemporary U.S. society, however, sex and gender roles are being detached from their function as the foundation of the family unit. Indeed, the numerous factors leading to an increase in single family households was undermined the functioning of sex role asymmetry as a bilateral system of exchange. Within this context, the existence of sex roles achieves an additional importance beyond their impact on self-actualization of males and females.

The increasing shift away from the family as the basic unit of social organization creates a basis for the emergency of class interests by sex. Males and females who choose to exist without attachment to a family unit become responsible for the total need satisfaction of self. Each individual, then, regardless of sex, must be expressive and instrumental in the task performed. Each individual must complete for limited social statuses and scarce economic resources. Because family units benefit from increasing returns to scale, the emergency of one-person social units, as well as single male or female-headed households, a place an additional burden on limited economic resources (e.g., housing, energy, and transportation). Accordingly, it is accurate to conclude that sex-based class interests may be emerging in U.S. society. How such a social phenomenon relates to existing forms of stratification has important implications for social change movements in the United States.

CLASS, RACE AND SEX

If sex role asymmetry is beginning to emerge as a struggle for resources between males and females, the U.S. system of social stratification, already based n class ad race, becomes even more complex. For the most part, unilateral models of sexism view the oppression of females by males as a separate phenomenon that operates across class and across race lines (Beal, 1975). In addition, unilateral models of sexism promote the viewpoint that women experience an oppression that parallels racial and class oppression. Such concepts have led many writers to conclude that

U.S. society, black females, for example, often suffer a triple oppression (Beal, 1975:2-3).

> *Since her arrival on these alien shores, the black woman has been subjected to the worst kinds of exploitation and oppression. As a black, she has had to endure all the horrors of slavery...; as a worker, she has been the object of continual exploitation.*
>
> *In addition, besides suffering the common fate of all oppressed and exploited people, the Afro-American woman continues to experience the age-old oppression of woman by man.*

Although the assertion is often made in the literature that both sexism and racism are products of capitalism (Lewis, 1977; Rowbotham, 1974; Staples, 1979) and some efforts have been made to point out essential differences in the functioning of class, race, ad sexism (Rowbotham, 1974), few systematic efforts have been made to identify the precise relations that exist between asymmetrical relations based on sex and those based on race and class. Thus, the task within this section is that of using our bilateral conceptualization of sexism to examines the interrelations among all three systems of social stratification.

As mentioned earlier, the ideals embody in sex and gender role models are neither class nr race neutral. Sex and gender-based role models prescribe ideal physical and behavioral attitudes for each sex. It has been asserted that losses and gains differentially accrue to individuals on the basis of how closely their physical and behavioral attributes fit the model for their sex. Also, a type of stratification occurs as males and females who closely fit the model choose each other as males (Collier and Williams, 1981). If sex role models are intrinsically race and class based, it follows that the interactive relationship between these three factors function so as to promote and sustain existing patterns of inequality. Studies on similarity attraction not only document that dating and/or marriage occurs disproportionately between those of similar class and race, but also between similar males and females as measured by other criteria. For example, Maslow (1963) pointed out that self-actualizing males tend to marry self-actualizing females. This tendency has since been confirmed by other investigators (King, 1974). Similarly, attraction has also been demonstrated by still other investigations. Males and females of parallel abilities are attracted to each other (Zander and Havelin, 1960). Of course, males and females of comparable socio-economic classes more often marry (Bryne, Cleve, and Worchel, 1966). In addition, physically beautiful females marry economically successful mates (Elder, 1969).

Again, such data assume particular importance since inequalities by class and race are built into the sex role models that operate within U.S. society. Additionally, such data imply that beyond their socialization function, marriage and the family are mechanisms through which class and racial inequalities are perpetuated. Racial and class exploitation, then, serve the interests of both males and females of the dominant race and class. If such a thesis is correct, it would then follow that sexism reinforces patterns of inequality based on class and race. That is, using the assumptions of our bilateral model, we can conclude that sex, race, and class would function in such a way that if the three are interactive, in those areas where males gain, males of the minority race and subordinate class will gain less. Conversely, in those areas in which males lose, the greatest losses would accrue to the victims of social stratification. Similarly, in those areas in which females gain, females of the minority race and subordinate class would gain less and in those areas in which females lose, the converse would occur. Similarly, in those physical and behavioral standards defining sex role models, males and females of the minority race and subordinate class would fall the greatest distance from the norm. Thus, it can be said that sex, race, and class form a comprehensive and interactive system of social stratification within U.S. society. This thesis can also be tested by a brief review of the empirical data. Because the data are unavailable by sex, race, and class, only the interactive effects of sex and race will be examined.

It was mentioned earlier that while men as a class gain systematically from sex role asymmetry, males as a class lose vitalistically. If there exists an interactive relation between stratification by sex and race, this pattern should be evident in vitalistic data by race and sex. And the data are quite clear. When life expectancy data are stratified by sex and race, a telling statistical portrait emerges. White females have a life expectancy 106% greater than that of minority females, 111% higher than that of white males, and 120% higher than that of minority males. Similarly, the age-adjusted mortality rate for minority males are 13.4% greater than that of white males, 169% greater than that of minority females, and 244% greater than that of white females.[12]

When other vitalistic data are included, the interactive effects of race and sex are even more apparent. Minority males dies from diseases of the heart 100% more often than white males, 157% more often than minority females, and 217% more often than white females. Minority males die from malignant neoplasms 128% more often than white males, 168% more often than minority females, and 190% more often than white females.[13]ehen social causes of death such as homicide are included, the pattern continues. Minority males are victims of homicide 682% more often than white males, 480% more often than minority females, and 2072% more often than white females.[14]

When data on crime and crime victimization are examined in greater detail by sex and race, the interactive effects of these two forms of social stratification are equally distinct. Minority males in 1978 were robbed without injury 200% more often than white males, 200% more often than minority females, and 200% more often than white females. Similarly, minority males were robbed with injury 200% more often than white males, 250% more often than minority females, and 600% more often than white females.[15] While males in general are victims of all crimes except rape at greater than the rate for females, the data indicate that minority males in general are more often the victims of serious crime. For example, white males suffer from simple assault 105% more often than minority males, but minority males suffer from aggravated assault 106% as often as the males. In the area of criminal justice administration, this trend is also apparent. Over the period from 1930 to 1979, 3, 862 persons were executed.

Within this group, 54% of those executed were black, 45% were white, and 1% were members of other races. Less than one-tenth of 1% of those executed were females of either ace.[16] Indeed, the data quite clearly support our thesis that in these vitalistic areas in which males lose, the interactive effects of race and sex create additional losses for black males.

As mentioned earlier, sexual asymmetry affects females negatively from a systemic perspective. Again, the data support the assertion that sex and race are interactive social forces. The median income of minority males more nearly approximates that of white males than does the median income of white females. In contrast, the differential between minority females and white males is greatest of all. Similarly, minority male-headed, white female-headed, and minority female-headed families exist in poverty more often than black male-headed families. If the analysis is extended to the political institution, a parallel trend is seen.

Even when systemic asymmetries are examined in combination with vitalistic asymmetries to demonstrate that sex and race are interactive forces, the portrait of the impact of this interaction is incomplete. Sex role models negatively affect the lives of males and females by (1) constraining self-actualization, (2) skewing the distribution of systemic and vitalistic losses and gains, (3) creating a system of rewards and punishments that differentially accrue to individuals on the basis of their physical and behavioral closeness to the ideal. When race and sex are operative forces, individuals are confronted with constraints to self-actualization as a consequence of race and se. As has been demonstrated, systemic and vitalistic losses are compounded. Finally, however, the psychosocial impact of sex role models creates additional trauma for black individuals. Such persons are permanently constrained from being able to achieve the physical and sometimes behavioral attributes of the ideal standard. Thus, additional trauma is created as such persons aspire to the unobtainable while their worth is measured by an implicitly biased model.

CONCLUSIONS AND IMPLICATIONS

Several different yet related reconceptualization in the area of sexism have been highlighted herein. These can be summarized as follows. The first task was that of statistically demonstrating that sex role asymmetry functions in such a manner that females lose systematically while males gain. Simultaneously, data were introduced in support of the thesis that females gain vitalistically from sex role asymmetry while males lose. Second, this bilateral system of gains and losses does not tautologically cause a system of social stratification. Rather, in order for a system of social stratification to emerge, males and/or females as a group must have separate class interests. Third, the point was made that the changing patterns regarding organization of the family have caused a breakdown in the division of labor function of sex roles and have led to a struggle for resources between males and females. Fourth, it was concluded that this struggle for resources does not define sexism as a separate form of social stratification from race and class but rather as an interactive one based on race and class. Fifth, the thesis was introduced that race and class variable condition those attributes incorporated into sex role models. Thus, sexist standards are implicitly racist and class biased. Sixth, it was empirically demonstrated that in those areas in which females lose, black females lose most. Finally, it was pointed out that the existence of sex role models creates special psychosocial problems for those who are black.

In other words, both black males and females are victims of a triple and interactive system of oppression. This interactive system poses psychological, sociological, and economic barriers to black family development and growth.

END NOTES

[1] U.S. Department of Commerce, Bureau of the Census, Statistical Abstract of the United States, 1986. "Median Family Money Income by Number of Earners and Race of Householders, 1983," No.757 (Washington, D.C.: Government Printing Office), 453.

2   U.S. Department of Commerce, Bureau of the Census, Statistical Abstract of the United States, 1986. "Persons below Poverty Level and below 128 percent of Poverty Level by Race of Householders and Family Status: 1959-1984," No. 767 (Washington, D.C.: Government Printing Office).458.

3   U.S. Bureau of the Census, Statistical Abstract of the United States, "Occupations of Work Experienced Civilian Labor Force, by Sex: 1970 and 1980," No.697 (Washington, D.C.: Government Printing Office).600.

4   Center for the American woman and Politics. Women in Public Office: A Biographic Directory and Statistical Analysis, 1980 (New Brunswick, N.J.)

5   Bureau of the Census, 1980 Census of Population.

6   Opt.cit.

7   U.S. Department of Commerce, Bureau of the Census, Statistical Abstract of the United States, 1986. "Expectation of Life at Birth: 1920-1984," No.106 (Washington, D.C.: Government Printing Office), 68.

8   Percentage calculated from data in U.S. Bureau of the Census, Statistical Abstract of the United States, 1986, "Death Rates by Selected Cases and Selected Characteristics: 1960-1982," No.115 (Washington, D.C.: Government Printing Office), 74.

9   Percentage calculated from data in U.S. Bureau of the Census, Statistical Abstract of the United States, "Victimization Rates for Crimes against Persons: 1973-1983," No.284 (Washington, D.C.: Government Printing Office), 169.

10   Percentage calculated from data in U.S. Bureau of the Census, Statistical Abstract of the United States, Capital Punishment, 1982.

11   U.S. Bureau of the Census, Statistical Abstract of the United States, "Population in Institutions and Other Group Quarters, by Sex, Race, and Type of Quarters: 1960-1980," No.73 (Washington, D.C.: Government Printing Office), 48.

12   Percentage calculated from data in U.S. Bureau of the Census, Statistical Abstract of the United States, "Expectation of Life at Birth: 1920-1984," No. (Washington, D.C.: Government Printing Office), 68.

[13] Percentages calculated by the author from U.S. Bureau of the Census, Statistical Abstract of the United States, "Death Rates by Selected Cases and Selected Characteristics," No. 115 (Washington, D.C.: Government Printing Office),74.

[14] Percentages calculated from U.S. Bureau of the Census, "Victimization Rates for Crimes against Persons:1973-1983," Statistical Abstract of the United States, No.284 (Washington, D.C.: Government Printing Office), 169.

[15] Ibid.

[16] Percentage calculated from data taken from the U.S. Department of Justice, Bureau of Justice Statistics, Capital Punishment, 1982.

REFERENCES

Alberle, David, 1966. The Peyote Religion among the Navaho. Chicago: Aldine.

Aronoff, Joel, and William D. Crano, 1975, "A Re-Examination of the Cross-Cultural Principles of Task Segregation and Sex Role Differentiation in the Family." American Sociological Review 40 (February):12-20.

Beal, Frances, M. 1975. "Slave of a Slave No More: Black Women in Struggle." The Black Scholar 6(6, March):2-20.

Bell, Norman W., and Ezra F. Vogel, 1968. "Towards a Framework for Functional Analysis of Family Behavior." In A Modern Introduction to the Family, pp. 1-34. New York: Free Press.

Bradburn, Norman M., and David Caplovitz, 1965. Reports on Happiness: A pilot Study of Behavior Related to Mental Health. Chicago: Aldine.

Brown, J. K. 1970. "A note on the Division of Labor by Sex" American Anthropologist 72:1073-1078.

Brown, Radcliffe, and Alfred Reginald, 1948.the Andamon Islanders. Glencoe, Ill.: Free Press.

Byrne, D.1971.The Attraction Paradigm. New York: Academic Press.

Byrne, D., G. Cleve, and P. Worchel, 1966. "Effects of Economic Similarity- Dissimilartiy on Interpersonal Attraction." Journal of Personality and Social Psychology 19:155-161.

Campbell, J. 1959. The Masks of God: Primitive Mythology. New York. Viking.

Center for the American Woman and Politics, 1980. Women in Public Office: A Biographic Directory and Statistical Analysis. New Brunswick, N.J.: Author.

Chinoy, ely, 1955. Automobile Workers and the American Dream. Garden City, New York: Doubleday.

Collier, Berry J., and Louis N. Williams, 1981. "Towards a Bilateral Model of Sexism." Human Relations 34(2):127-139.

Collier, Betty J., and Willy Smith, 1981. "Racism, Sexism and the Criminal Justice System." National Urban League Review 6 (1, Fall):46-54.

D' Andode, Roy G. 1966. "Sex Differences and Cultural Institutions." In The Development of Sex Differences, Eleanor D. Maccoby, ed., pp. 174-204. Stanford University Press.

Diner, H. 1973. Mothers and Amazon? The First Feminine History of Culture. Garden City New York: Anchor.

Divale, W. and M. Harris, 1974. "Population, Warfare, and the Male Supremist Complex." American Anthropologist 78:521-538.

Duberman, Lucille. 1976. Social Inequality: Class and Caste in America. Philadelphia: Lippincott.

Elder, G.H.1969. "Education in Marriage Mobility." American Sociological Review 34:519-533.

Faris, Robert, and Warren Hurham. 1939. Mental Disorders in Urban Areas. Chicago: University of Chicago Press.

Goldberg, Steven. 1973. The Inevitability of Patriarchy. New York: Morrow.

Gough, Kathleen. 1971. "The Origin of the Family." In the Human Experience (1st ed.), David H. Spain, ed., pp.181-191. Homewood, Ill.: Dorsey Press.

Hirschfeld, Lawrence A., James Howe, and Bruce Levin. 1978. "Warfare, Infanticide, and Statistical Inference: A Comment of Divale and Harris." American Anthropologist 80:110-115.

Hollingshead, Hugh, and Frederick C. Relich. 1958. Social Class and Mental Illness. New York.

Hunt, Robert C. 1973. "Power in the Domestic Sphere." Science Journal 6:68-72.

Janeway, E. 1971. Man's World, Woman's Place. New York: Dell.

King, Mark. 1974. "Sex Differences in Self-Actualization. "Psychological Reports 35:602.

Krauss, Irving. 1976. Stratification, Class and Conflict. New York: Free Press.

Lancaster, Chet, and Jane Beckman Lancaster. 1978. "On the Male Supremacist Comples: A Reply to Divale and Harris." American Anthropologist 80:115-117.

Lenski, Gerhard. 1966. Power and Priviledge: A Theory of Social Stratification. New York: McGraw-Hill.

Levinson, Andrew. 1974. The Working Class Majority. New York: Coward, McCann and Geoghegan.

Lewis, Diane K. 1977. "A Response to Inequality: Black Women, Racism and Sexism." Signs (Winter):3339-361.

Maslow, A.H.1963. "Self-Actualizing People." In The World of Psychology (Vol.2) G. G. Levitz, ed. New York: Braziller.

McKee, J. P. 1959. "Men's and Women's Beliefs, Ideals, and Self Concepts." American Journal of Sociology, p. 64.

Miller, S. M., and Pamela A. Roby, 1977. The Future of Inequality. New York: Basic Books.

Murdock, G.P. 1937. "Comparative Data on the Division of Labor by Sex." Social Forces 15:551-553.

Murdock, George P., and Catherine Provost, 1973. "Factors in the Division of Labor by Sex: A Cross Cultural Analysis." Ethnology 12:203-225.

Parker, Seymour, and Hilda Parker, 1979. "The Myth of Male Superiority: Rise and Demise. "American Anthropologist 81 (2, June): 289-308.

Parsons, Talcott, 1955. "Family Structure and the Socialization of the Child." In Family Socialization and Interaction Processes. Talcott Parsons and Robert F. Bales, eds., pp. 35-131. Glencoe, Ill. Free Press.

Romney, A. 1965. "Variations in Household Structure as Determinants of Sex-Typed Behavior." In Sex and Behavior, F. Beach, ed., pp. 208-220. New York: Wiley.

Rowbotham, Sheila, 1974. Woman's Consciousness, Man's World. Harmsworth: Penguin Books.

Sewell, William H. 1971. "Inequality of Opportunity for Higher Education." American Sociological Review, pp. 793-809.

Sexton, Patrician, and Brendan Sexton, 1971. Blue Collars and Hard Hats: The Working Class and the Future of American Politics. New York: Random House.

Smelser, Neil J. 1963. The Theory of Collective Behavior. New York: Free Press.

Staples, Robert, 1979. "The Myth of Black Macho: A Reponse to Angry Black Reminist." The Black Scholar (March/April):24-36.

Stephens, William, M. 1963. The Family in Cross-Cultural Perspective. New York: Holt, Rinehart & Winston.

Tiger, L., and Shepher, 1975. Women in the Kibbutz. New York: Harcourt Brace Jovanovich.

Tumin, Melvin M. 1967. Social Stratification: The Forms and Functions of Inequality. Englewood cliffs, N.J.: Prentice-Hall.

Turnier, Jonathan H., and Charles Starnes, 1976. Inequality: Privilege and Poverty in America. Pacific Palisades, Calif: Goodyear.

U.S. Bureau of Prisons, 1978. Annual Statistical Report Series. Washington, D.C.

U.S. Bureau of the Census Income Services P-60, No. 125. Money Income and Poverty Status of Families and Persons in the United States (October), p.7.

U.S. Department of Health, Education, and Welfare, 1975. Public Health Service Publication No. 100, Series 10, No. 58. Vital and Health Statistics. Washington, D.C.:Government Printing Office. 1976 Public Health Service. Health-Status of Minorities and Low Income Groups.

U.S. Department of Justice, 1978. National Crime Survey. Washington, D.C.: Law Enforcement Administration. 1979.

SOCIAL POLICIES, BLACK MALES, AND BLACK FAMILIES

BOGART R. LEASHORE

The convergence of some socioeconomic indicators between blacks and whites over the last few decades has prompted some social scientists and others to conclude that the significance of race has declined in the United States.[1] Statistically significant differences between blacks and whites on several socioeconomic measures have declined.[2] However, it is erroneous to conclude therefore that racial inequality no longer exists in the United States. For example, in April 1985 the net seasonally adjusted unemployment rate for black age 16 to 19 years was 37 percent, compared to 14.4 percent for whites in the same age group.[3] Similarly, significant differences exist between blacks and whites on family income, infant mortality, life expectancy, incarceration, the number of children living in poverty, and in other areas.[4] As was recently observed by a white U.S. journalist:

> *It was only yesterday that racial discrimination was legal in vast parts of the country... Racism remains a fact of life in this country- it may be abating, it may be weakening, but it certainly not ready to be mounted for the Smithsonian.[5]*

In short, race remains a critical factor in the quality of life in the United States.

This chapter draws attention to the roles played by social policies in maintaining racial inequality, particularly with respect to black males; why and how this has occurred; and how social policies might be altered to enhance the well-bring of black males. Black families and other Americans as well as black males, are of special interest because of the high-risk status they face compared to white males, and the significant roles they continue to assume in black family males, despite the "feminization of poverty." [6]

TAX INCREASES AND BUDGET CUTS

A comprehensive analysis of U.S. domestic policies observed that between 1980 and 1984 black families, regardless of the presence or absence of a male head, were helped less than or hurt more than were white families.[7] Analysis of the current U.S. tax system indicated that the federal government is taxing the poor at levels "without equal in history."[8] A disproportionate number of blacks-males and females are low wage workers, or working poor and near poor. This group has experienced the sharpest increases in taxes over the past few years, as well as the sharpest cutbacks in social programs. Further, prior to the 1981 tax act, most families in poverty were exempt from federal income tax. In 1978, a family of four at the poverty line paid only $269 in federal taxes, which increased to $460 in 1980 by 1984, a family of four at the poverty line paid $1,076 in taxes.[9]

Since 1980, budget cuts in social programs designed for those with low and moderate incomes have been greater than cuts in programs not designed for this group. Programs designed for low- and moderate-income persons represented less than one-tenth of the federal budget, yet these programs accounted for close to one-third of the total number of cuts in all federal programs. Black Americans comprise 30 percent to 40 percent of the beneficiaries of most of the low-income programs that received the greatest cuts. It has been shown that the 1981 budget cuts cost the average black family three times as much in lost income and benefits as they cost the average white family. This has been attributed to cuts in programs with high participation by blacks. For example, as shown in Table 1, employment and job training programs received the greatest cuts in 1985- and more than 30 percent of the participants in these programs were black.[10]

Table 1. Budget Cuts in Programs with High Black Participation

Program	Degree of Black Participation	Budget Cut
Public Service Employment (CETA)	30%	-100%
Employment and Training	37	-39
Work Incentive Program	34	-35

Child Nutrition	17	-28
Legal Services	24	-28
Compensatory Education (Title I)	32	-28
Pell Grants and other Financial Aid		
for Needy Students	34	-16
Food Stamps	37	-14
Aid to Families with Dependent Children	46	-11
Subsidized Housing	45	-11

Source: Center on Budget and Policy Priorities. Falling Behind: A Report on How Blacks Have Fared under the Region Policies (Washington, D.C.: Author, October 1984), p.12.

RACISM, SOCIAL DARWINISM, AND LAISSEZ-FAIRE IDEOLOGY

The social welfare policies of the United States lag significantly behind those of many countries of the world.[11] For some; the existence of this lag is deliberate and is not coincidental. Claiming that race impacts on the development as well as the implementation of social welfare policies can be a highly controversial position. Nevertheless, it seems clear that blacks disproportionately have to turn to social programs for assistance in providing for their daily needs. Drawing on the premises of social Darwinism and laissez-faire ideology, some social and behavioral scientists, policy makers, and other attribute this disproportionate reliance to the failure of individuals and tend to absolve government from sharing any responsibility.[12]

The paradox of these circumstances becomes more apparent when recognition is given to the role the U.S. government has historically played in promoting and maintaining racial inequality. For example, little more than a decade ago, federal state, and local governments on uniformed black males. The experiment was conducted from 1932 to 1972 and is documented in the work Bad Blood: The Tuskegee Syphilis Experiment.[13] More recently, national efforts have turned to child support enforcement in response to the increasing numbers of families headed by women.[14] Rooted in coercive and punitive social policy, black males are more likely to be the victims of child support enforcement programs because they experience a higher rate of unemployment, receiver lower wages, and area therefore less likely able to pay than white males…

With specific reference to blacks, conservatives and some liberals raise their voices against affirmative action and other federal interventions to promote racial equality. There is an insistence that adequate opportunities are available for those who are motivated toward individual achievement. Pathological views of blacks and the poor suggest that the problems of poverty are rooted in individual deficits, such as indolence. Futile and endless rhetoric continues about the deserving and nondeserving poor. It is assumed that people are poor because they don't try, that governmental assistance is more of a hindrance than help, and that little can be done to improve "the lot of the less fortunate." Little regard is given to the demographics of poverty, which include the following facts: close to one-half of the adult non-aged poor work part time or full time but do not earn enough to escape poverty; others, for health or child care reasons, cannot enter the labor force; and most poor families do not remain in poverty for prolonged periods nor do they perpetuate a "culture of poverty" from one generation to the next. It has been stated that conservative attacks on government-sponsored social programs are "redoubtful assumptions" and that these conservatives "offer no alternative means of bolstering opportunity and advancement for the nation's disadvantaged and working poor."[15]

MOBILIZING FOR ALTERNATIVE SOCIAL POLICIES

Although the United States is hailed as the land of opportunity, and indeed is so for some, too many black Americans continue to face structural barriers that block their entry into the socioeconomic mainstream of the society. Joblessness, low wages, poverty, inadequate medical care, substandard housing, poor education, and incarceration are conditions of life that need to be addressed if the defeminization of poverty is to occur. Too often, these conditions of living have reduced the family availability of many black males…

The probability of being able to function as family provider is related to opportunities for working and receiving adequate financial compensation. Given these highly probable relations, it seems that serious attention should be given to the life circumstances of black males. In the corner of social policies, efforts should be directed toward the elimination of social welfare assaults on black male and others. Special emphasis should be given to the following areas: health care, employment, wages and income support, and crime and justice.

HEALTH CARE POLICY

The overall health status of U.S. continues to lag behind that of whites on several measures. These include higher rates of infant and maternal mortality and shorter life expectancy. Research has shown that black women are more likely than white women to die because of childbirth complications; that low birth weight is more prevalent among black than white infants; that blacks in general and black males in particular live shorter lives than whites; and those whites receive considerably more preventive and routine medical care than blacks.[16]These results ring clear the need for an effective program of national health insurance.

Historically, health care policy has focused on three issues: access to care, quality of care, and cost of care. However, preoccupation with cost has resulted in less interest in access and quality of care. For example, profit-oriented hospitals have been shown to be more expensive than non-profit or public institutions. Those most likely to be without health insurance including Medicaid are women, people of color, and older people. If they cannot pay with, the quality of care is likely to be what has been characterizes as "junk medicine"—for example, unnecessary tests and procedural duplications.[17]

Politicians, labor, religious, service, and charitable organizations and consumer groups should reassert the need for a program of national health insurance with wide coverage and a larger federal financial role. These forces must seize control of the health care industry from the hands of physicians, private hospitals, and private health insurance companies.[18]A universal program of quality health care that is attractive to the nonpoor, as well as the poor, is needed. Broad benefits, public financing, and administration by the federal government should be key features of social policy for national health insurance.[19]Various industrialized nations of the world have implemented a range of programs that guarantee equal access to medical care as a citizen right.[20]That the United States remains without such a health care policy not only defies reason, but also continues to be a source of international embarrassment.

EMPLOYMENT AND INCOME SUPPORT POLICIES

Poverty statistics, economic, and employment differences between blacks and whites have been established. What seems needed are social policies that will reduce and eliminate economic inequality, which is deeply embedded in the structure of U.S. society. Programs increasing the taxes of those with low and moderate incomes while reducing the tax burden of the affluent and big business have done little to improve the U.S. economy. The failure to ensure equal job opportunities for blacks have placed them at the bottom of the U.S. socioeconomic structure. Weakened commitments of government to civil rights and affirmative action have only worsened the situation. Federal policies to create jobs can reduce unemployment and ensure minimal adequate incomes. Moreover, tax credits and wage subsidies designed for low income and low skill workers can be as economically efficient as public employment policies.[21]

Classical economic theory accuses trade unions of pushing wages up, which prices workers out of jobs and thereby keeps unemployment high. On the contrary, other evidence indicates that productivity can be improved by giving workers a formal voice in the workplace. If unions coalesced, broadened their interests, and shifted pressure for wage increases, they could become a greater positive force for full employment. In the lieu of short run wage increase, and organized and cohesive labor movement, egalitarian wage distributions, opportunities for retraining, workplace enrichment and welfare objectives.[22]

Aid to Families with Dependent Children (AFDC) has long been stigmatized as a program for those who do not want to work. As a means-tested program, it separates "them" from "us" and has a history of contributing to father absence and family breakup. Family allowance and cash housing allowances based on family size and family income exist in much of Europe. They are available to all moderate-income families as well as to the poor. The combined allowance has been considered as income support system that guarantees a higher standard of living, especially for those families with special needs (e.g., female-headed families.)[23]

As an expression of important U.S. values, the development of AFDC policy has been consistently directed toward punishing poor parents, especially single mothers, while moving away from promoting the well-being of dependent children. Specifically, values related to capitalism, liberalism, and positivism have been influential in the development of AFDC. The work ethic, individualism, personal freedom, the free market, and the worthiness of individuals have greatly influenced AFDC policy. Racial discrimination against black families in the early days of AFDC further contributed to the humiliating welfare system of today.[24]

A recent historical study of the Society Security system in the United States vividly depicts the process of institutionalizing antipoor biases in the system. Among other things, it is shown why and how the phrase *social security* has come to mean social insurance even though the legislation of 1935 included public assistance. It is concluded that policy development relative to public assistance support.[25] Critical assessments of Society Security Act of 1935 have posited several relations between the state and the economy, or how political power gets translated into economic power. A recent assessment concludes that

> *in a hierarchical state, capitalist groups with varying economic interest exerted their influence at different levels in the hierarchy....Economic power then gets translated into political power through the direct intervention of corporate liberals and through the hierarchical structure of the state, which allows competing factions to petition state managers for direct agendas in social policy.*[26]

Action for Social Security reform should include a comprehensive analysis of the age requirement for receipt of benefits. Particular attention should be given to any disparities between males of color and white males relative to life expectancy and the age at which benefits can be received. Should black and other male of color be eligible for Social Security benefits at an earlier age than white males because the latter have a longer life expectancy?[27] Relative to AFDC all states should be prohibited from using the absence of father in families as an eligibility requirement. In the case of child welfare, federal and state legislation and policies should be modified to include subsidized and legal guardianship as another plan of care for abused and neglected children, in addition to foster care and adoption. Far too many black children, as well as others, linger in foster care.[28] More importantly, efforts need to be directed toward eliminating circumstances that necessitate taking children from their biological families, especially inadequate income and housing. Entitlement programs from the federal government for children, specifically AFDC, continue to lag behind those for other groups (e.g., veterans, the aged, the disabled, and those who are retired). Equal treatment for children through some form of federalized payments is not beyond the capacity of our government.[29]

Cutbacks in federal funds for child day care and nutrition should not only be restored, but increased. Similarly, federal aid for low- and moderate-income college students and food stamps should be restored and/or increased.

CRIME AND JUSTICE

One of the most glaring differences between blacks and whites in the United States is the disturbingly higher involvement of blacks as compared with whites in the criminal justice system.... .

Conditions of prison overcrowding, environmental conditions, idleness, violence, limited staffing, and inadequate medical care characterize many state prisons. Resulting court actions have included order to reduce prison populations, to provide meaningful work, to provide meaningful opportunities for educational and vocational training, to expand prerelease transition programs, to provide medical care and staffing that meet certain standards, and to prevent violence.[30] With specific reference to black homicide, the highest rates have been found among unemployed black youth and young adults. Thus, it can be argued that, the reduction of poverty and other social problems, homicide reduction can be achieved through major political and social problems.[31]

Given the high incarceration rate for black males, new policy initiatives need to be established. These should include sentencing reform, plea bargaining, and employment opportunities for ex-offenders. Regarding the latter, any significant reduction in crime will require better employment opportunities for ex-offenders as well as for delinquents. New policy initiatives for the employment of disadvantaged workers in general.[32] Suggested areas for prevention and intervention concerning homicide include gun control, community organization and education, and more effective responses to prehomicide behavior.[33]

SUMMARY AND CONCLUSIONS

This chapter has focused on social policies and how they have had an impact on black males in particular and black families in general. It is shown how domestic policies related to taxes and budget cuts have differentially affected black families and how racism and ideologies have influenced the development and implementation of social policies in the United States. Attention is called three areas in which there is a need for alternative social policies: (1) health care, (2) employment and income support, and (3) crime and justice. National and local efforts are needed to provide an effective program of national health insurance, full employment, family allowances, and actions to reduce incarceration.

The achievement of the social policy initiatives presented in this chapter will require deliberative efforts on the part of many parties, including blacks and their people of color and supportive whites. In so doing, system-challenging political strategies should be used both within and outside of social institutions. Mass actions and collective efforts by multi-ethnic liberal challenging coalitions can result in social change for female-headed families and others who do not have basic power resources. Strategies that can be used include demonstrations congressional lobbying, and voting. Black leaders and organization can function in a national leadership capacity achieved desired social change.[34] In the meantime, fraternal, business, and religious organizations should implement broad-based supportive and educational programs targeted for black males including those who are institutionalized (e.g., those in prison).

Several conscious strategies should be developed within the black community. These should include an internal black agenda with a recommitment to black community development or institution building. Further, blacks can generate an internal economy with a capacity to absorb the marginally unemployed. Resources can be pooled into economic development institutions that go beyond providing technical assistance to small businesses but can also provide capital for large-scale enterprises that contribute to meaningful employment. An economic development institution could plan the organization and distribution of financial resources in order to promote economic stability and security within black communities. Political activities should include mobilizing the voting power of the black community so that officials are elected who are sensitive to and understand their needs. Black institutions such as churches can establish *priorities* of social needs and can commit resources toward designated ends—as has been the case with a national network of black churches that was organized to provide financial assistance to needy. Black college students. This requires the involvement of organizations cutting across special interests, social classes, and resources so that a sense of community is restored. Special use of mass media can be applied in order to bring leadership together to plan and promote goals and strategies. Local needs should be clearly linked to national issues; similarly, national activities should involve local programming.[35] The mobilization of people of color and others for meaningful social change requires removal of blocks or barriers to power including internal and external political and economic forces that serve to maintain powerlessness among oppressed groups. Though the process of empowerment, blacks and others can exert more influence and overcome obstacles to meeting their needs. Basic to the process of empowerment, blacks and others must understand the consequences of powerlessness. Moreover, there should be an understanding of and an appreciation for the capacity to bring about change.[36] With particular reference to black males, it has been suggested that myths have been perpetuated in response to "an unmitigated fear of black male power."[37] Intertwined with racism and other factors, this fear has resulted in a range of social and economic assaults, which have been operationalized through punitive and coercive social policies and social services.

Black social and behavioral scientists as well as others, should draw attention to research that supports the need for new social policy initiatives. Black scholars and researchers can ill afford the luxury of academic isolation, lest their contributions be minimized. Fresh perspectives and progressive thinking are needed for examining social issues related to the well-being of black people and that of all Americans. This should include a more balanced view of racism that analyzes not only the consequences for the victim, but also the motivations of the perpetrator. Knowledge and understanding are needed regarding why and how racism is nurtured and sustained in the United States, and what mechanisms can be used to eliminate it. In addition, white Americans should be educated about the social benefits which they stand to gain through the enactment of constructive social policies.

END NOTES

[1] William Julius Wilson, *The Declining Significance of Race: Blacks and Changing American Institutions* (Chicago: The University of Chicago Press, 1980); Michael Hout, "Occupational Mobility of Black Men: 1962 to 1973," American Sociology Review, 49 (June 1984), pp. 308-322.

[2] Reynolds Farley, *Catching Up: Recent Changes in the Social and Economic Status of Blacks* (Cambridge: Harvard University Press, 1983); Richard B. Freeman, The Black Elite (New York: McGraw-Hill, 1976).

[3] U.S. Department of Labor, Bureau of Labor Statistics, USDL85-184, Washington, D.C. (May 1985), Table A-3.

[4] Theodore Cross, *The Black Power Imperative: Inequality and the Politics of Nonviolence* (New York: Faulkner Books, 1984); Children's Defense Fund, *Portrait of Inequality: Black and White Children in America* (Washington, D.C.: Children's Defense Funds, 1980): National Urban League, Inc., *The State of Black America*, 1984 (New York: National Urban League, 1984).

[5] Richard Cohen, Racism Recollected," *Washington Post*, August 10, 1985, p. A19.

6   Lawrence E. Gary and Bogart L. Leashore, "High Risk Status of Black Men," *Social Work*, 27 (January 1982), pp. 54-58; Gary and Leashore, "Black Men in White America: Critical Issues," in Color in a White Society, Barbara White (ed.) (Silver Spring, Md.: National Association of Social workers, 1984. pp. 115-125.

7   John L. Palmer and Isabel V. Sawhille, *The Reagan Record: An Assessment of America's Changing Domestic Priorities* (Cambridge, Mass.: Ballinger, 1984).

8   Daniel Patrick Moynihan, "Family and Nation," Cambridge, Mass.: Harvard University, the Godkin Lectures, 1985).

9   Center on Budget and Policy Priorities, *Falling Behind: A Report on How Blacks Have Fared under the Reagan Policies* (Washington, D. C.: author, October 1984).

10 Ibid

11 Robert Kuttner, *The Economic Illusion* (Boston: Houghton Mifflin, 1984).

12 Ibid.; Sar A. Levitan and Clifford M. Johnson, *Beyond the Safety Net: Reviving the Promise of Opportunity in America* (Cambridge, Mass.: Ballinger, 1985, pp. 6-18.

13 James Jones, *Bad Blood: The Tuskegee Syphilis Experiment* (New York: Free Press, 1981).

14 Joyce E. Everett, "An examination of Child Support Enforcement Issues," in Harriette McAdoo and T.M. Jim Parham (eds.), Services to Young Families Program review and Policy Recommendations (Washington D.C.: American Public Welfare Association, 1985), pp. 75-112

15 Levitan and Johnson, *Beyond the Safety Net*, pp. 6-18.

16 *A Cream Deferred: The Economic Status of Black Americans, a working paper* (Washington, D.C.: The Center for the Study of Social Policy, 1983).

17 Michael Clark, "What Hath Reagan Wrought," *Health PAC Bulletin*, 15 (July-August 19874, pp. 3-4.

18 Kuttner, *The Economic Illusion*, pp. 249-250.

19 Theodore R. Marmor, Judith Feder, and John Holahan, *National Health Insurance: Conflicting Goals and Policy Choices* (Washington, D.C.: The Urban Institute, 1980).

20 Kuttner, *The Economic Illusion*.

21 Irwin Garfinkel and John L. Palmer, "Issues, Evidence, and Implications," in *Creating Jobs: Public Employment Programs and Wage Subsidies* (Washington, D.C. The Brookings Institution, 1978).

22 Kuttner, *The Economic illusion*, pp. 136-186.

23 Kuttner, *The Economic Illusion*, pp. 243-247.

24 Jan Mason, John S. Wodarski, and T.M. Jim Parham, "Work and Welfare. A Reevaluation of AFDC," *Social Work 30* (May-June 1985), pp. 197-203.

25 Jerry R. Cates, *Insuring Inequality: Administrative Leadership in Society Security*, 1935-54 (Ann Arbor: The University of Michigan Press, 1983).

26 Jill S. Quadagno, "Welfare Capitalism and the Society Security Act of 1935." *American Sociology Review*, 49 (October 1984), p. 645.

27 Gary and Leashore, *Social Work*, 27 (January 1982), p. 57.

28 Bogart R. Leashore, "Demystifying Legal Guardianship: An Unexplored Option for Dependent Children," *Journal of Family Law*, 23 (1984), pp. 391-400.

29 Moynihan, "Family and Nation," pp. 43-44.

30 Alvin J. Bronstein, "Prisoners and Their Endangered Rights," *The Prison Journal*, LXV (Spring-Summer 1985), pp. 4-5.

31 Darnell F. Hawkins, "Black Homicide: The Adequacy of Existing Research for Devising Prevention Strategies," *Crime and Delinquency*, 31 (January 1985), p. 94-97.

32 James B. Jacobs, Richard McGahey, and Robert Minion, "Ex-Offender Employment, Recidivism, and Manpower Policy: DETA, TJIC, and Future Initiatives," *Crime and Delinquency*, 30 (October 1984), pp. 486-503.

33 Hawkins, "Black Homicide," p. 96.

34 Ronald Walters, "Imperatives of Black Leadership: Policy Mobilization and Community Development," *The Urban League Review*, 9 (Summer 1985), pp. 20-41.

35 Ibid.

36 Barbara Bryant Solomon, *Black Empowerment: Social Work in Oppressed Communities* (New York: Columbia University Press, 1976).

37 Robert Staples. "The Myth of Important Black Male," in *The Black Family: Essays and Studies* (2nd ed.) (Belmont, Calif.: Wadsworth, 1978), p. 99.

THE DILEMMA OF GROWING UP
BLACK AND FEMALE

ALGEA O. HARRISON

The purpose of this paper is to discuss how black females attempt to resolve the dilemma of femininity and high achievement goals. Generally, there has been a reverse relationship between femininity and high need achievement. The objective of this report is to review the nature of relationship between femininity and high need achievement. The objective of this report is to review the nature of the relationship for black females. Since the young black female is presented with different models of life style for womanliness it is expected that her femininity may develop differently from that of her white counterpart. The black female becomes cognizant of the fact early in life that she will not be able to achieve the culturally imposed goals of being soft, clinging and dependent to obtain a man who will support her and provide an array of material possessions. How will she attempt to incorporate femininity as defined by the dominant culture in to her own culture's definition of the female role?

CHARACTERISTICS OF FEMALES

A sex role standard has been defining as a belief shared by the members of the culture regarding the characteristics that are appropriate for males and females (Kagan 1971). Specific behaviors have been ascribed as distinctive of females, i.e., dependency, passivity, conformity, nurturance, submissiveness, etc. A series of studies of overt behavior and/or story telling response indicate more occurrence of affiliative and nurturant behavior and concern with interpersonal relationships among girls than boys (Kagan 1971). An expressive role, skills in

A revised version of a paper presented at the Sixty National Convention of Association of Black Psychologists, August 25, 1973, Detroit, Michigan.

dealing with people, has also been prescribed for women (Reiss 1966). They seem to be better and earlier trained for a commitment to and capacity for romantic love and the subtleties of emotion that lead to strong heterosexual attachments (McCandless and Evans 1973). Therefore, it is not surprising that most studies report greater dependency, conformity, and social passivity for females than males at all ages (Kagan 1971).

Generally, girls are less active physically, displaying less overt physical aggression, and more sensitive to physical pain, have significantly less genital sexuality, display greater verbal, perceptual and cognitive skills, and are better at analyzing and anticipating environmental demands than boys (Bardwick and Douvan 1971). Girls perform less initiative aggression than boys after exposed to aggressive models (Bandura 1965). they usually show more prosocial aggression; however, when anonymity is guaranteed, girls are as capable as boys of delivery aggressive consequences such as electric shock in laboratory experiments (McCandless and Evans 1973).

The role standard has had its most notable effect on the mastery of specific cognitive skills. From kindergarten through grade four, the girl typically outperforms the boy in all areas and the ratio of boys to girls with reading problems ranges from 3 to 1 to 6 to 1 (Bentzen 1963). There seems to be a developmental shift and in the adolescent years, academic and vocational success is viewed as masculine and inappropriate for females. Problems of involving spatial and mechanical reasoning, physics, science logic, and mathematics are viewed as more appropriate for boys than girls. Whenever adolescent or adult subjects are tested on these skills males consistently obtain higher scores than females (Kagan 1971). The adolescent girl, her parents, her girl friends, and her boy friends perceive success as measured by objective, visible achievement as antithetical to femininity (Bardwick and Douvan 1971). It is in the area of need achievement that the black female differs from the general society's expectations of what is appropriate feminine.

Delores P. Aldridge, Ph.D

BLACK FEMALE'S ASPIRATIONS AND ACCOMPLISHMENTS

In spite of the difficulties presented by sex typing the black female has generally emerged with a positive self-concept and high aspirations and expectations. Although a negative self-image appeared to be more characteristic of the black child than of the white child, the black female had more positive self-attitude than the black male (Dreger and Miller 1973). Dreger and Miller (1973:151), in reviewing such studies, found that "Black girls have higher educational hopes than do black boys ... black high school seniors in Kentucky set occupational goals similar to those of whites with the expectation that the black female has higher expectations. The black girls concentrated their occupational expectations among the professions and usually rejected the traditional role of housewife. Out of a total of 52 black female subjects not one wanted to be a housewife. Out of a total of 52 black with 25 percent of the white girls ... an ambitious pattern of aspiration and expectation among black girls was reported with a much greater percentage of black girls than boys actually enrolled in college preparatory programs." In studies designed to measure generalized achievement motivation using the McClelland method it has been found that the black female's achievement motivation is greater than the black male (Smith and Abramson (1962).

In a study conducted by Brazziel (1971), 262 black students completed the Edwards Personal Preference Schedule. The sample was divided geographically into lower-South group, females exhibit significantly higher needs for achievement, endurance and interception, but are lower in deference, autonomy and heterosexuality. On the other hand, there are only two significant differences between the sexes in the upper-South sample, the females score lower on needs for dominance and heterosexuality. What is noticeable is the relative absence of sex differences in this group when compared to the norm group. Sex differences are present in twelve of fifteen variables in the general college norm but are revealed only in two instances in the upper-South and six instances in the lower-South.

Sex differences by social class were not pronounced, in the lower-South, both classes revealed higher female needs for achievement.

Middle income females in the lower-South group revealed higher needs for nurturance and middle-income males in the upper-South groups scored higher dominance.

The high need for achievement and higher educational aims among black females has historically resulted in more black girls enrolled in college than boys. In recent years Jackson (1973:53) notes "Black women and men 25 years of age and older were closer together in 1970 than in 1960 in average number of years of schooling. In the category of college education, however, there were more women. In 1960 the ratio was 100 males to 156 females. In 1970 the ratio rose to 100 males to 161 females." The sex difference in educational achievement varies according to the geographical region. When national statistics are considered, black women have completed a median of 8.7 school years and men 7.7. In the North there was no difference between the sexes in 1950 and by 1965 men were ahead of the women. in the South women still are more highly educated (Billingsley 1968).

Epstein (1973:916) notes that seemingly contradictory figures are reported concerning the total number of graduate and professional degrees earned by black men and women.

> *A study of Negro colleges where the majority of blacks have earned their graduate degrees (Blake, 1971, p. 746) shows that black women earned 60% of the graduate and professional degrees awarded in 1964-65. However, a Ford Foundation study (1970) of all black Ph.D. holders in 1967-68 indicated that of a 50% sample of the total, only 21% were women. Another source covering black colleges in 1964 lists more women than men earning M.A.'s but more men than women earning Ph.D.'s (Epstein, 1973:916).*

I most professional groups, black women constitute larger proportion of the women than the proportion of black men of the men (Epstein 1973). From 1880 to 1960 there has been a larger percentage of black females classified as in professional service than black males, except in 1880 when the percentage of male teachers, 66.4 percent, was greater than female,

33.6 percent (see United State Census, 1880-1960). In the United States as a whole, black women out-number men in the highest job categories, with 10.8 percent of them compared to 8.2 percent of male workers. When we consider the North and West, men slightly outstrip women, but in the South, were school teaching has been traditionally open to black women, the 11.9 percent of women in professional, technical, and managerial jobs considerably outstrips the 6.4 percent of black men. Occupational opportunities are greater for black workers in the North than in the South, and in the South, particularly, they are better or black women than for black men (Billingsley 1968).

it must be remembered that a very small percentage of the black women employed are professional workers, over half are classifies as in domestic and personal services (U.S. Bureau of the Census 1969) It is only when the statistics refer to *nonwhite* employed is there a decrease in numbers of females employed as a private household worker. In 1969, 12 percent of *nonwhite* females employed were in professional, technical, and managerial fields as compared to 11 percent *nonwhite* MALES (U.S. Bureau of the Census 1969).

In 1967 the median income for black females was $3,268 and $4,837 for black males (U.S. Bureau of the Census 1969). At all educational levels the black female's income is approximately $1,000 to $2,000 less than the black male of equivalent education (U.S. Bureau of the Census 19072). This difference in income is most notable when we compare median income of the black female head of the family, $3,341, with that of the black male head of the family, $7,329 (U.S. Bureau of the Census 1972). These findings suggest that although there are slightly more black female than black male professionals, the females are mainly employed in the low-paying and low status professional jobs, i.e., teaching, nursing, etc.

The unemployment rate is also a reflection of difficulties in the labor market for black females. Unemployment was lowest for white adult males, 4.0 percent, and highest for minority teenage girls, 35.5 percent (U.S. bureau of the Census 1972). Minority adult women had an unemployment rate of 8.7 percent compared to 7.2 percent for minority men. Harwood and Hodge (1971) skillfully denounce the myth that black females have had an advantage in the job market when she had to work. Actually, she found a limited range of low paying jobs to choose from, mainly as a servant in a private household. The census data reveal that since 1890 black men have enjoyed greater diversification of jobs that black women.

Black families have been accused of traditionally encouraging their girls to high achievement at the expense of the boys. This practice of stressing achievement for girls has been defended by Grier and Cobb (1968). The black family was concerned about the physical safety and protection they could offer their children. The sons were taught to avoid open conflict with white people and they had to curb their aggression and other behavior considered masculine in American society. For their daughters, the aim was to protect them from the sexual exploitation they might suffer if forced to work as a domestic. The families sought to give them economic freedom through education. Schools were seen as a refuge for the daughter from what was considered a "traditional way of life." Grier and Cobb (1968:124) notes: "If school is seen as a refuge from the white aggressor, and if the black family places its women and children within such safe confines, and if the men turn to face the enemy—pray show me that critic of the 'weak' Negro family." In addition, the black family's major occupation after emancipation was farming and share-cropping the male offspring were necessary to provide a basic economic support for the family. Therefore, the family's educational aspirations were generally centered around the females. The financial resources of the family were limited and in order for a member of the family to attend school, the others had to labor to provide the money. This usually meant that the males of the family pooled their resources and sent the females to school.

The attitude of the current black family has changed very little. Girls are still encouraged to stay in school in the South and urban ghettos as a place of refuge from the problems of modern society. These personal and familial aspirations for achievement of black females have materialized somewhat as expected.

In discussing the role of the black female, the issue of black matriarchy has been listed as a source of conflict with the implication being that the black female's dominance has been destructive to the black community. Robert Staples (1970:8) dismissed this cruel these by noting:

For the black female, her objective reality is a society where she is economically exploited because she is both female and black; she must face the inevitable situation of a shortage of black males because they have been taken out of circulation by American's neo-colonialist wars, railroaded into prisons, or killed off early by the effects of ghetto living conditions. To label her a matriarch is a classical example of what Malcolm X called making the victim the criminal.

BLACK AND WHITE FEMALE DIFFERENCE

The conflict over sex role identity and high need in social achievement distinguishes the black and white females. Generally, females in American society have exhibited lower occupational and educational aspirations. Females have been socialized to succeed in the traditional sex roles and do not maximize the personality traits that are essential for success in the real world, i.e., independence, aggression, competitiveness, leadership, etc. Society does not stress these personality characteristics for females and therefore very few have succeeded in the business and professional world where these skills are essential. There is a difference, however, for black females.

Horner has attempted to explain the phenomenon of low motive to achieve for females in general. Horner (1968) hypothesized the existence of a motive to avoid success (M-) which she defined as the expectancy of anticipation of negative consequences as a result of success in competitive achievement situations. Weston and Mednick (1973) investigated the relationship between Horner's postulated motive and race and social class. Subjects were undergraduate women and the verbal TAT cues such as those used by Horner and a brief questionnaire requesting socioeconomic information were administered. It was found that black college women exhibited fewer M- responses than white college women. There were no social class differences for the black female on the number of M- responses. White lower-class females were not included in the study and no class comparisons were made for whites. Bager (1972:605) found that black college women tended to have higher educational aspirations than white college women. In somewhat related research (Iscoe, Williams, and Harvey 1964) it was found that Negro females (7, 9, 12, and 15 years) were less conforming than white females of the same age when subjected to highly speculative and questionable, i.e., Negro mothers are chief source of authority, Negro females can get away with nonconformity more than can a white female, Negro females are more independent in dealing with whites than are Negro men, etc. Nevertheless, it does suggest that early in life black females probably will be more resistant to efforts to get them to conform to the traditional sex role standard.

In the area of professional success black career women have exceeded their counterparts. Black women constitute a larger proportion of the black professional community. Only 7 percent of white physicians are women, but 9.6 percent of black doctors are women; black women make up 8 percent of black lawyers but white women constitute only 3 percent of all white lawyers; black women accountants, musicians, professional nurses, and social workers exceeded their white female colleagues in earnings (Epstein 1973). black women are more likely to be employed than the white female with equivalent education.

One of the most obvious differences between black and white females is the economic necessity of black females working in order for the family to maintain a middleclass standard of living. Because of the racist economic practice in the general society black men do not have access to higher paying occupations nor do they have any oral control over the economic base. The source of high need achievement for black women may not be solely due to personal aspirations but also economic need. The black female's role in the economic survival of the black community may be compared to that of other women in pre-industrialized and less technologically advanced societies during their pre-industrialized stage development. Women were generally called upon to work in those societies, i.e., pioneer women, Russia, China, etc. Historically black women have had the role of worker with very few accrued benefits.

BLACK FEMALE'S SEX-ROLE IDENTITY

There are two possible explanations of why a larger percentage of black females than white strive toward goals and appear to comfortably function in roles that are viewed by the general society as anti-feminine. One approach is to view her strivings as a result of her feelings of rejection by society. Another view is to see her aims of accomplishment as a result of being exposed to successful, competent, female models in the black community.

The first possibility may result because the black female will encounter problems establishing her sex role that are different from her white counterpart largely because of society's view of what is desirable in womanhood. As Grier and Cobb (1968:32) noted "the first measure of a child's worth is made by her mother, and if, as is the case with so many black people in America, that mother feels that she, herself, is a creature of little worth, this daughter, however valued and desired, represents her scorned self." the black woman is the antitheses of America's idea of a beautiful ideal woman as communicated throughout all strata of society. The ideal all-American is a blond, blue-eyed, white-skinned girl with regular features. This prevailing ideal of womanhood presents problems for black girls as can be easily seen in this typical self-revealing comment:

> *Because I was dark, I was always being plastered with Vaseline so I wouldn't look ashy. Whenever I had my pictures taken, they would pile a whitish powder on my face and make the lights so bright I always came out looking ghostly. My mother stopped speaking to any number of people because they said I would have been pretty if I hadn't been so dark. Like nearly every little black girl, I had my share of dreams of waking up to find myself with long blond curls, blue eyes and skin like milk 9Marshall 1970:26).*

The patterns of marriage in the black community also perpetuate the rejection of the black female. The light-skinned female was viewed as the most desirable marriage partner for black men (Staples 1973a). Interestingly, the reverse skin color was viewed as most sought after by black females. The dark skin black male was preferred more than the light skin who was viewed as self-centered and closely resembling the oppressive white male.

There was no way for the black female to be transformed into a lovely white maiden, hence she did the next best thing. She ascribed to those characteristics that are viewed by society as valuable and she could obtain. Most personality characteristics that are valued by society are possessed by successful persons, usually males, i.e., independence, need for success, self-assertion, ambition, drive, etc. These qualities are earned and acquired and not controlled by the genes like colors of skin, texture of hair, physique, etc. If she could not gain acceptance in the traditional female manner, she would have to be acknowledged for her possession of the other traits on which society places a premium. As a result of society's rejection of her black womanliness she strove for acceptance through avenues that would demand recognition, acquiring some of the traditionally male personality traits.

It has been suggested that a successful woman may be an economic asset and attractive and therefore not as threatening to a black male (Weston and Mednick 1973). Most black families, whether low-income or note, are characterized by an equalitarian pattern in which neither spouse dominates, but share decision-making and the performance of expected tasks (Hill 1972). Her unique qualities facilitated economic gains and made it possible for increasing numbers of black families to move into the middle class. In the professional employment market black females are frequently viewed as less threatening than black males and employers, if they have to hire black, sometimes preferred females (Epstein 1973 and Jackson 1973). Therefore, it was possible for her to obtain measures of success because of her unique position in society.

The attainment of success for the professional black woman seems to have been a double-edged sword. There is a higher rate of divorce and low incidence of marriage for this category of women for various reasons. The major problems seem to be the lack of a large number of equivalently educated black males from which to select a mate, characteristics of females preferred for wives by black male professionals, marital partners with less education, black males marrying white females, etc. (Jackson 1973, Epstein 1973, and Staples 1973a). Bager (1972) conducted a survey of institutional variables predicting marriage for women. He found that for black women in predominantly black institution, being nonwhite and having high degree aspirations were both negatively related to getting married during the undergraduate years (Bager 1972:605). It seems as if the acquisition of "non-feminine" type personalities has presented some difficulties for black females.

Another possible reason for the black female's striving toward success is the type of models she is exposed to in the black community. Modeling is most effected when there is a close similarity between the modeler and the modelee (Bandura 1965). The black models in her community are of women obtaining success is business and professional careers, mothers who are heads of households coping with the many problems of being poor in urban America, and just a daily contact with women who are leading useful productive lives in spite of the pervasive effects of racism in society. Although this is not the appropriate mechanism or time to review her long and rich history it is worth nothing that in West African societies women by custom and tradition play a substantial role in the community. Her role as a mother was considered of primary importance in patrilineal or matrilineal society. Her treatment during slavery and reconstruction has been greatly documented and visibly evident in her present day descendents (Staples 1973a).

The important point is that females in the black community are highly visible and noted for their strengths, accomplishments in the face of obstacles, and personal sacrifices for her family and the black community. The young female, therefore, is exposed to successful females and has models to aspire to emulate. The black female's view of what is appropriately female comes from her own community and not from feelings of rejection from the white world.

Ladner (1971) dismisses the idea that black females depreciate themselves since they have a clear understanding of the root causes of their rejection and place the blame squarely where it belongs. She categorizes the self-hatred thesis as one of "many other myths that are propagated about black people. It falls within the realm of institutional subjugation that is designed to perpetuate an oppressive class" (Ladner 1971:107). Then urban lower-class adolescent girls that were the basis for her study has been exposed to women who played a central role in their households and community. Ladner (1971:132) notes that "it is against this backdrop that the symbol of the resourceful woman becomes an influential model in their lives."

IMPLICATIONS

The dilemma of being a female for the black woman is that she is being urged by society in general o cultivate the traits that lend themselves to feminity, i.e., dependency, passiveness, submissiveness, etc. On the other hand, she is pressured by the political-economic system and survival needs of the black community to develop those traits that are contrary to the ideas of womanhood as prescribed by the sex role standard, i.e., independence, self-assertion, persistence, etc.

Future research should be designed to provide insights into the psychological processes involved in the establishment of the black female's sex role identity. It is obvious from her history of oppression and role in the black community that there is similarity and dissimilarity with the white female. Are the major motivating factor feelings of rejection from the white sex role standard and/or identification with the model of her community?

Regardless of the specifics of the psychological process it is important that appropriate models should be provided by adult citizens. Exposure to and availability of successful black females should be abundant in the young female's life.

The educational system should be aware when they are counseling young black females that her aspirations and needs are different from the typical female's. Her historical role in the community and its impact on her developing personality have to be taken into consideration.

It is also important that the economic –political system acknowledge that in order for the black community to survive black males and females need higher paying jobs. When approximately one-third of the families have females as head of household, supportive systems have to be provided in the community. The status of the black family has altered and public policy must reflect this change. The policy should include a guaranteed income, elimination of sexist discrimination in employment opportunities, community-controlled child care centers, safe and free contraceptives and abortions, and input from the black community in policy making decisions (Staples 1973b).

REFERENCES

Bager, A. 1972. "College Impact on Marriage," *Journal of Marriage and the Family* 34:600-610.

Bandura, A. 1965. "Influence of Model's Reinforcement Contingencies on the Acquisition of Imitative Responses," *Journal of Personality and Social Psychology* 1:589:595.

Bardwick, J. and Douvan, E. 1971. "Ambivalence: The Socialization of Women." In V. Gornich and B. Moran (Eds.) *Women in Sexist Society.* New York: Basic Books

Bentzen, F. 1963. "Sex Ratios in Learning and Behavior Disorders." *American Journal of Orthopsychiatry* 33:92-98.

Billingsley, A. 1968. *Black Families in White America*, Englewood Cliffs: Prentice Hall.

Bazziel, W. 1971. "Correlates of Southern Negro Personality." In R. Wilcox (Ed.) *The Psychological Consequences of Being a Black American.* New York: Wiley: 401-408.

Dreger, M. and Miller, K. 1973. Comparative Psychological Studies of Negroes and Whites in the United States: 1959-1956." In D.R. Heise (Ed.) *Personality, Biosocial Bases.* Chicago: Rand McNally: 125-156.

Epstein, C. 1973. "Positive Effects of the Multiple Negative Explaining the Success of Black Professional Women." *American Journal of Sociology* 78:912-935.

Grier, W. and Cobb, P. 1968. *Black Rage.* New York: Basic Books.

Harwood, E. and Hodge, C. 1971: "Jobs and the Negro Family: A Reappraisal." *The Public Interest* 23:125-131.

Hill, R. 1972. *The Strengths of Black Families.* New York: Emerson Hall.

Horner, M.S. 1968. *Sex Differences in Achievement Motivation and Performance in Competitive and Non-Competitive Situations.* Unpublished Doctoral Dissertation. University of Michigan

Iscoe, I., Williams, M. and Harvey , J. 1964. "Age, Intelligence, and Sex as Variables in the Conformity Behavior of Negro and White Children." *Child Development* 35:451-460.

Jackson, J.J. 1973. "Black Women Created Equal to Black men." *Essence* (November): 56-72.

Kagan, J. 1971. *Personality Development.* New York: Harcourt, Brace & Javanovich.

Ladner, J. 1971. *Tomorrow's Tomorrow: The Black Woman.* Garden City: Anchor Books.

Marshall, P. R. 1970. In T. Cade (Ed.) *The Black Woman.* Signet Books.

McCandless, B. and Evans, E. 1973. *Children and Youth Psychosocial Development.* Hindsdale: Dryden.

Reiss, I.L. 1966. "The Sexual Renaissance: A Summary and Analysis." *Journal of Social Issues* 22:123-137.

Smith, H.P. and Abramson,M. 1962"Racial and Family Experience Correlates of Mobility Aspiration." Journal of Negro Education 31:117-124.

Staples, R. 1970. The Myth of the Black Matriarchy. *The Black Scholar* (January-February). 1973a *The Black Woman in America.* Chicago: Nelson-Hall. 1973b "Public Policy and the Changing Status of Black Families." The Family Coordinator 22L345-351.

U.S. Bureau of Census. 1969. *The Social and Economic States of Negroes in the United States,* 1969. Washington, D.C.: U.S. Government Printing Office:42. 1972. "General Social and Economic Characteristics." Final Report, D.C. C17-C1. *U.S. Summary* Washington D.C.: U.S. Government Printing Office :1-379.

Weston, P. and Mednick, M. 1973. "Race , Social Class and Motive to Avoid Success in Women." I J. Rosenblith, W. Allinsmith, and J. Williams (Eds.) *Readings in Child Development.* Boston: Allyn and Bacon: 308-312.

CHAPTER FOUR
Primary group Issues

Based on research findings, Jacquelyne Jackson presents some interesting ideas to contradict accepted stereotypes about black men in black families and about black husband-wife relationships. There seems to be a clear separation of roles in household activities, with joint decision making on more significant family responsibilities. Some differences exist between older and younger black husband-wife families and the black husband figure demonstrate signs of having a clearly defined role and significant power.

Lena Wright Myers addresses the importance of affect in marital relations and suggests that marital success is based on ability to define marital interaction goals and establish opportunities to carry out these goals in an environment that is flexible without negating the positive aspects of conflict. These conclusions are supported by the perceptions of over 400 presently married or once married black women.

Delores P. Aldridge provides significant information on interracial marriages in the United States covering such topics as incidence, casual factors, characteristics and consequences of interracial marriages concluding with an impressive bibliography to be drawn upon for additional research efforts.

ORDINARY BLACK HUSBANDS: THE TRULY HIDDEN MEN

JACQUELYNE JACKSON

The apparent voluminousness of and persisting myths in most literature about black families have generally been effective in masking its actually sparse, fragmentary, and inconclusive status. For example, any serious search for concrete data and generalizations about ordinary blacks functioning effectively or normally as spouses, parents, and grandparents is almost in vain. The process paucity of much of that literature has been generated primarily by the "culture of investigative property." That is, most of its contributors has been unduly possessed by a homogeneous view of blacks; an overconcentration upon abnormality (and especially upon by-products of sexual intercourse or, indeed, upon the sexual act itself); and apathetic lack of interest in interdisciplinary research; a short attention span; an exaggerated masculinity in defense of their adolescent knowledge; and an inability to defer gratification, as evidenced by their relatively frequent utilization of inappropriate racial comparisons and insufficient data which of course, usually invalid conclusions.

Such traits, analogous in many respects to those commonly ascribed to the "culture of poverty," must be reduced to facilitate acquisition of realistic knowledge about black families in particular and families in general. One step in that direction is very simple: it is merely a description and uncomplicated statistical analysis of ordinary black family members. it recognizes the diversity of black, permits intragroup comparisons of blacks, and can eventually produce a baseline of normality from which deviations can be evaluated to determine if they are only "different strokes for different folks or if they are inherently, structurally, or functionally deficient for their owners and those whose lives they affect.

Presented orally at the 1973 annual meeting of the American Orthopsychiatric Association, New York, this research was partially supported by NIMH Grant #MH16554.

This presentation is a humble step in that direction. It is merely a description and simple analysis of ordinary black husbands who, while numerically larger among black men, represent the truly hidden men from the perpetrators of the "culture of investigative poverty." It is so ordinary, so routine, so humdrum until you may well be bored by the absence of titillation about school drop-outs, street corner winos, drug addicts, muggers, absent fathers, and revolutionaries.

More specifically, this exploratory comparison of instrumental and affective relationships between spouses as reported by two sub-sample sets (i.e., nonmanually and manually employed husbands, and employed and nonemployed or largely retired husbands) from a largely study of roles and resources of older blacks in a southern urban residentially segregated environments was particularly concerned about role allocations for ordinary household maintenance activities and about spouse unilaterality (i.e., decision-making by one spouse).

Following Adam's (1968) definition, *instrumental relationships* consisted of shares activities and mutual assistance patterns between subjects and spouse during the year immediately preceding the interview, the emphasis upon activity type and frequency of occurrence, while *affective relationships* were measured by agreement (i.e., response to "Would you say you and your spouse agree about things you really consider important in life?" of no, very little, to some extent, to a great extent, or completely).

According to Blood and Wolfe (1963). *instrumental relationships* were also measured by ascertaining spouse dominance (i.e., husband only, husband more often than wife, husband and wife about equally, wife more often than husband, and wife only) in specific decision-making situations.

In the largest study, black interviewers, utilizing a modified Kinship Interview Schedule, modeled upon Adams (1968) and Blood and Wolfe (1963), collected data in 1968 and 1969 for approximately 73 percent of all male household heads or all males 21 or more years of age in an urban renewal area, as listed by the local Housing relocation Office, and from 79 percent of adult male subjects randomly selected from designated blocks in areas peripheral to the urban renewal area, and produced a total of 170 male subjects married and living with spouse and included in this report.

Nonmanually (i.e., white-collar or salaried) and manually (i.e, blue-collar or wage-earning) employed subjects were similar in age (about 40 and 46 years respectively) and long-term or indigenous residence in the city. But, whereas well over two-thirds of the non-manuals had completed or gone beyond high school, only about one-third of the manuals had achieved equivalent education. They also differed at the .05 level of confidence in that nonmanual were less likely to be fathers (38 percent of the nonmanual and 19 percent of the manuals were childless) and the manuals were somewhat more likely to be both fathers and grandfathers (true of approximately 35 percent of the manuals and 9 percent of the nonmanual).

The means age of nonemployed or largely retired subjects (about 61 years) was significantly higher than that of the employed subjects (about 45 years). Other significant differences at or beyond the .05 level of confidence also distinguished these two sub-groups: nonemployed subjects with less average education had longer community residence and more children and grandchildren, but they were more likely to be living only with spouse that were the employed subjects. All of these significant differences were, of course, expected, and they are normal.

Interview items, grouped under four major categories of (a) *household maintenance activities* (such as grocery shopping and breakfast preparation), (b) *household decision-making activities* (such as grocery budgeting and disciplining children), (c) *spouse interactive activities* (such as church attendance and family and commercial recreation), (d) *spouse affect* (i.e., agreement tabulated by response frequencies by (1) nonmanually and manually employed, and (2) employed and nonemployed or largely retired husbands, and chi-square analyses were utilized to test for significance differences.

FINDINGS

Nonmanually and Manually Employed Husbands

Among the 23 nonmanually employed husbands, about 70 percent had received more and 22 percent as much education as their wives, whereas approximately 52 percent of the manually employed husbands had received somewhat less education than their wives. Nevertheless, both sets of husbands were not significantly different in their response about *household maintenance activities*. Approximately three-fourths or more of both groups reported the wife as usually preparing her husband's breakfast, washing, ironing, dishwashing, and housecleaning for the family, whereas 90 percent or more of the husbands usually performed the yardwork and household repairs. About 59 percent of the manually employed husbands reported that they most often performed grocery shopping as a couple, whereas about 57 percent of the wives of the nonmanually employed spouses were reported as usually doing the grocery shopping. About 61 percent of the nonmanually and 52 percent of the manually employed couples usually paid bills jointly.

Less role segregations were apparent in *household decision-making activities*. The majority of nonmanually and manually employed husbands reported husband-and-wife joint decisions in deciding about grocery budgets, insurance purchases, physician selections, and residential locations. About 61 percent of the nonmanually and 57 percent of the manually employed husbands also reported joining disciplining of children, but where joint discipline was generally absent, then husbands—and not mother—most often served as disciplinarians for their offspring.

Whereas approximately 70 percent of the nonmanually and 76 percent of the manually employed husbands reported that they determined for themselves whether or not they would accept particular employment initially, a much smaller proportion (47.8 percent and 58.6 percent respectively) determined without spouse assistance if they would continue in that employment. A slightly higher percentage of the nonmanually (65.2 percent) than the manually (55.2 percent) employed husbands indicated that their wives only decided if and when they should work.

Among spouse interactive activities, where the activity had to have been engaged in jointly at least once during the year preceding the interview, nonmanually and manually employed husbands were indistinguishable only by church attendance with spouse. They differed, at or beyond the 0.5 level of confidence, in that nonmanually employed couples were much more likely to have shopped (other than grocery) or vacationed together, engaged in family or commercial recreation, visited relatives jointly, or engaged in other activities.

Manually employed husbands were also significantly more likely to report their wives as usually doing the family letter-writing (72.4 percent) than were nonmanually employed husbands (3.48 percent), and partial factors accounting for that difference may well include differential levels of education and employment statuses among the involved spouses. Although manually employed subjects reported their wives as those most likely to perform family letter-writing, they were not reported as those who usually telephoned relatives. Only about 45 percent of the spouse fell in that category. Among the nonmanually employed spouses, a slightly higher percentage (39.1 percent) were reported as those who usually telephoned relatives than those who usually engaged in family letter-writing.

About 57 percent of the manually and 49 percent of the nonmanually employed husbands reported themselves and their spouse's incomplete agreement about the most important things.

EMPLOYED AND NONEMPLOYED OR RETIRED HUSBANDS

Among the 52 employed subjects (which includes both nonmanually and manually employed subjects compared above), about 46 percent had received more education that wives, as had about 30 percent of the nonemployed or retired husbands. In almost all of the remaining cases, husbands and wives had received equal education. Although educational levels of spouses among the employed group were higher than those among the nonemployed, the two groups were indistinguishable by differences in educational level between husbands and wives in each group.

The typical patterns of *household maintenance activities* reported for nonmanually and manually employed subjects also characterized those employed and not employed. Obviously, similarities would appear for the employed subjects, but what is most interesting is that they also tended to appear for the largely retired group who in the labor force, as compared with employed subjects. Wives were most often reported as usually preparing their husband's breakfast and performing the family's laundry, dishwashing, and household cleaning chores. But two significant differences at or beyond the .01 level of confidence did emerge between the two groups: employed subjects were less likely to report their wives as usually performing household cleaning tasks and more likely to report them as dishwashers. Whereas almost all of the employed husbands reported themselves as the usual person responsible for yardwork and household repairs, a smaller percentage (but still a hefty majority) of the largely retired subjects fell within those categories. About 53 percent of the largely retired subjects reported their wives as the usual grocery shoppers, but the model response (46 percent) to this inquiry from employed subjects was husband and wife, a difference significant at the .01 level of confidence. About 40 percent of the largely retired subjects indicated that they most often paid bills, whereas the corresponding model response from employed subjects (55.8 percent) was husband and wife. Although these two groups were statistically indistinguishable in their reports (irrespective of the source of monies), greater spouse unilaterality was present among the largely retired.

For household *decision-making activities*, employed and nonemployed subjects of resembled each other in spouse responsibility for grocery budgeting, deciding where to live, disciplining children, and physician selection. Joint decisions were most frequent among both groups for living locality and choice of physicians. Those about grocery budgeting were much more characteristics of employed (56 percent) than the nonemployed (35 percnet0, which again reveals some greater spouse unilaterality among the latter.

These two sets of husbands differed critically by employment and insurance decisions. Nonemployed husbands reported greater unilateral power in decisions about their employment for their wives. They also differed in spouse power regarding purchase of life and burial insurance. About 65 percent of the employed and 52 percent of the nonemployed reported joint decisions, while about 35 percent of the former and 30 percent of the latter reported husband only or husband mostly, but almost 18 percent of the nonemployed husbands placed their wives in that category.

Statistically significant differences were most apparent in a comparison of *spouse interactive activities*. Employed subjects were much more likely to report attending church, shopping, vacationing, family and commercial recreation, and other activities with their spouses. Although not statistically significant, they also visited relatives more frequently with their spouses. Their wives were usually more responsible for family letter-writing (53 percent) and somewhat less responsible for telephoning relatives (42 percent), with the reverse pattern typifying nonemployed husbands, where about 47 percent of their wives were usually responsible for family letter-writing, and about 56 percent for telephoning relatives.

DISCUSSION

In general, this description of instrumental activities and perceived spouse agreement revealed the expected conjugal role segregation in household maintenance activities performed within or around the home. Wives engaged in traditional "women's work," and of largely retired husbands were more likely to shop for groceries without their husbands than were their respective counterparts. Spouses were most often jointly involved in paying bills except among the largely retired group.

The reported pattern of household decision-making activities most often indicated joint spouse participation, particularly in activities directly affecting all family members. Data collected about parental responsibility for disciplining children suggested that fathers—and not mothers—in older black husband-wife families most often performed that function. Among younger families, there appeared to be a greater shift toward joint parental responsibility. Such data contradict the usual stereotype of the relative insignificance of the father in black families, and, perhaps more important, the extent of his power within his family. Undue emphasis upon matriarchal black families e.g. has overshadowed patriarchal black families. In a recent comparison of selected research studies about black and white families between 1966 and 1970, it was noted that

> *When the concept of matriarchy is restricted to wife dominance in husband-wife families, existing evidences suggests strongly that matriarchy is most characteristics of white, professional families with unemployed wives. Lower-class intact black families appear to be even more patriarchal (i.e., male dominated) than their white counterparts. That is, black males tend to exercise stronger power within their families than do white males. Clearly, among working-class and middle-class families, black or white, equalitarianism tends to be the dominant pattern, or at least there appears to be a shift towards that pattern (Jackson 1973:437-438).*

Greater spouse unilaterality about the employment statuses for husbands and wives was also more common among older than younger husbands.

With the exception of family letter-writing and telephoning relatives, the data clearly followed expected patterns of greater or more frequent spouse involvement in interactive activities among those in nonmanual than manual employment, as well as among those employed than those not employed. Such differences, of course, are functions of socioeconomic and health variables.

Perhaps more interestingly was the striking amount of agreement reported by these husbands between themselves and their wives on the most important things in life. While these subjects were not asked specifically if they loved their wives, many of them volunteered sentimental comments about their wives to the field interviewers. My impressionistic judgments of many married black couples lead me to believe that love is valued. If so, we must question the validity of such assumptions about love and black couples as that given by Bell (1971:250).

> *There have been a number of studies indicating that husband-wife roles and patterns of interaction in the lower class are quite different from those of the middle class. In the black lower class the notion f love as a prerequisite to marriage and as a condition for its successful maintenance is not a strong value. There is also strong evidence that*

DELORES P. ALDRIDGE, PH.D

> *companionship in marriage is not a strong value or behavior pattern in the lower class. Lack of marital companionship is reflected in the general patterns of sex-segregated activities. For example, lower-class partners tend to maintain old friendship and kinship ties rather than recognize ties after marriage to make the spouse a part of one social network.*

Bell (1971:250) further indicated that "Recent research indicates that the lower-class husband is not only tangential to family functioning but that very often his wife prefers it that way." These exploratory data about ordinary husbands, as well as data collected from many of their wives, but not reported herein, contradict Bell. But they also underscore the problems involved in generalizing about blacks from data unrepresentative of blacks.

Thus, in addition to this description of ordinary black husbands constituting the truly hidden men, obscured, as it were by the "culture of investigative poverty," perhaps the primary purpose of this presentation could well have been that of calling attention anew to the critical need to accumulate meaningful and valid data about the diversities of black families. Except for purposes of demonstrating clearly racial discrimination and its consequences, the current paucity of our knowledge about black families mandates greater concentration upon comparisons of black families with black families, and not with white families.

In any case, these findings, while applicable only to the sample, could well be taken as hypotheses for future investigations of patterns of interaction between black husbands and wives.

REFERENCES

Adams, Bert N. 1968. *Kinship in an Urban Setting*. Chicago: Markham.
Bell, Robert R. "The Related Importance of Mother and Wife Roles among Black Lower-Class Women." *In The Black Family, Essays and Studies*, ed. by Robert Staples. Belmont, California: Wadsworth, 248-255.

Blood, Robert, and Donald M. Wolfe. 1963. Husbands and Wives: The Dynamics of Married Living. New York: Free Press.

Jackson, Jacquelyne J. 1973. "Family Organization and Ideology." In *Comparative Studies of Black and Whites in the United States*, ed. by Kent S. Miller and Ralph Dreger. New York: Seminar Press, 405-445.

ON MARITAL RELATIONS:
PERCEPTIONS OF BLACK WOMEN

LENA WRIGHT MYERS

During the past few years, a number of books have been written about different aspects of human sexuality. "How-to-do" manuals have become best sellers, and books on sex roles and the psychology or social psychology of women (usually whites) have become household items. Recently, a few authors have started discussing the many supposedly profound and difficult dilemmas of intimate relationships and love that are evolving between men and women. And the latter term, love, has been claimed to be so subjective and so elusive that it defies definition. As a matter of fact, there are almost as many ways to love as there are people in the world to be loved or not loved. It is true that expressions of love vary from culture to culture, era to era, and person to person. In some centuries, "real love" had to be romantic and free of the "ugliness" of sex. In other periods of time, sexual expressions were considered the most important ingredient of love.

Attitudes toward intimate expression in the western world have varied between the extreme of an almost total suppression of sexuality—at least on the surface—and a public tolerance of all varies of intimate expression. The mass media have given emotional expressions. But all of us must set our own course for expressing ourselves in an intimate relationship. Maybe some people are "on the fringes" in search of their own personal emotional expression of sexuality (Masters and Johnson, 1974:86).

This study is not an effort to define love among black men and black women, nor it is an attempt to provide a "how-to-do-it" (whatever is that you are doing at a given time) manual. It is simply a descriptive account of social and/or symbolic interaction among black couples as told by 400 black women. Now, what is meant by social and/or symbolic interaction?

AUTHOR'S NOTE: The research reported in this chapter was supposed by a Ford Dissertation Fellowship in Ethnic Studies, 1972-1973, and a National Science Foundation Research Grant, 1974-1976.

Developing and weaving related concepts. Mead (1934 noted that social interaction may be viewed as a conversation of gestures. He suggested that a conversation of gestures includes the mutual adjustment of behavior, where each participant uses the *first* gesture of the other participant's action as a cue for her or his own action. Thus, her or his response becomes a stimulus to the other participant, prompting either a shift in the other's attitude or the completion of the originally intended act. One person may unconsciously respond to the tone of voice or facial expression of the other person may be unaware at a given time. This is called unconscious or nonsignificant conversation of gestures and consists of simple stimulus and response. But most human interaction through the process of socialization becomes symbolic depending upon shared understanding about the meanings of gestures.

People respond creatively to the environment which they are a part through the interpretive process. They do not respond mechanically to the intrinsic qualities of situations. instead, they assign meanings to the given situations and respond in terms of those meanings (Blumer, 1966). The ability to assign meaning to given situation is learned by person while interacting with other persons. Since each person will respond to events in terms of the meanings, he or she assigns to them, each person's action is comprehensible and predictable to others only to the degree that the underlying meanings are *known* (Lauer and Handel, 1977).

Social and/or symbolic interaction is defined in this chapter as a social process which stresses communication through language and gestures (body talk) in the formation and maintenance of personality and social relationships among black men and women. There are many things that are left *unsaid* among black women and men; this may even complement he told cliché that "action speaks louder than words." Some things need to go *unsaid* and *unacted*, too, if there is not shared symbolic meaning among women and men in the form of language and gestures. However, if there are shared symbolic meanings, both verbally and nonverbally, more positive relationships may exist between black women and black men.

Most blacks do not marry in pursuit of a secure financial status, as do whites. However, when they do, they could end up as Ladner (1972) describes:

> *It could be that when black fall in to the "trap" of using the dominant society's reasons for marriage, they become "ipso facto" prone to failure, because in this kind of environment, emotional love cannot counteract joblessness and the multitude of tensions which are frequently present.*

For many blacks the realities of the world cause frustrations that may affect their love lives. Therefore, it may be necessary to find alternatives for coping with the negative influences of society. Let us assume that kind of symbolic or vicarious intimacy ensues which creates an unconscious desire for black married couples to retain their marital relationships rather than resolve them. This form of symbolic intimacy may ensue in spite of negative environmental influences and traditional norms.

In an attempt to explore how black women, perceive their relationships with black men in a marital situation, I used to interview data which collected from two separate, simple random samples each of which included 200 black women from Michigan and Mississippi (N=400) in 1972-1973 and 1974, respectively. These were women who (1) had lived with their husbands for 5 years or more and (2) were divorced or separated. They were 20 to 81 years old. Their educational level ranged from third grade to master's degrees and above. These women had 1 to 15 children, with monthly *family* incomes ranging from $60 to $2,500. The length of residence I the respective areas ranged from 1 to 81 years.

This study describes how these black women saw their social and/or symbolic relationships with their husbands or former husbands.

One of the expressive gratifications sought by married couple sin cathectic affection. In order to examine how satisfied were black women with their cathectic affection, the following question was asked:

> *Cathectic affection has to do with feeling or emotions pertaining to the physical aspect of married life. These may range from the most innocent to the most intimate demonstrations of affection. Now, then, are you generally satisfied—or dissatisfied with this aspect of your marriage or former marriage?*

Table 1 shows the data obtained from the above questions. For both samples, the married women appear more satisfied with the cathectic aspect of their marriages than do the women who are separated or divorced. The difference between the married women and the single women (separated or divorce) of the Mississippi sample is only slight (94 percent and 41 percent, respectively). But for the Michigan sample, the difference between the married and single women is much greater. Ninety –six percent of the married women expressed general satisfaction with their cathectic affection, while 68 percent of the single women expressed the same.

A clearer understanding of the cathectic affection may be found in the examples which follow.[54]

> *Fay is a 47-year-old married woman with four children who lived in Mississippi. With a ray of self-confidence which even the most non-perceptive individual should be able to grasp seemingly she had no problems with talking about her marital relationship with Melvin. She said, "Melvin has a way of looking at me that tells me that he wants to be with me, without having to say one word." She also said that he had another way of looking at her that let her know he did not want to be bothered at times.*

Table 1. Perceived Satisfaction with Cathectic Affection

MICHIGAN	Generally Satisfied		Dissatisfied		Total	
	N	%	N	%	N	%
Married	80	96	3	4	83	100
Separated or Divorced	48	68	23	32	71	100
MISSISSIPPI						
Married	103	94	7	6	110	100
Separated or divorced	68	91	7	9	75	100

> *Somewhat similar is the example of Gerri, a native of Michigan, age 30, a divorcee, and the mother of one child. She talked about how "touchy-feely" both she and Paul*

> *(her former husband) were Gerri made it very clear that*
> *the lack of cathectic affection was not the reason for their*
> *marriage ending in divorce. As a matter of fact, she stated,*
> *"that is one of the things that I miss the most about Paul*
> *and my relationship … we could understand and feel each*
> *other."*

Both cases indicated shared meanings and understandings of emotional expressions between black women and their husbands or former husbands. Even though Faye may not have been very pleased about the way Melvin looked at her he did not want to be bothered at the moment, she must have understood that nonverbal gesture and likely behaved accordingly. An understanding of such gesture could also have aided her in not becoming a "clinging vine" in the marital relationships, as some women do and which some men resent.

For Gerri, nonverbal communication between her and Paul appeared to have been of great importance to their relationship. Being "touchy-feely" toward each other seems to suggest shared meanings and understanding through and about touching.

The fact that black women were satisfied with physical affection shown by their mates is symbolic in that there must have been shared understanding about the meaning of gestures. Satisfaction received from expressions of physical affection has meaning and arouses meaning in the partners to whom these expressions are communicated. This sharing is essential to communication in the symbolic interactionist process. As one writer puts it

> *Each part of the body speaks a silent but intimate and*
> *revealing language. More than mere words—a wink, a*
> *shrug, or a handclasp can be the best clue you'll ever get to*
> *a person's innermost feelings [Callum, 1972].*

The key to nonverbal communication of emotional expression is understanding the *clues*, and one need not to be a sociologist or psychologist to do so. Black people are an expressive people. Data in Table 1 indicate that shared meanings and understandings about such clues did exist between black women and their husbands or former husbands as perceived by the women.

The emergence of body language depends upon an already established form of interaction with the other in a marital situation. The other is the spouse. It is only to language that the individual using the gesture responds in the way the other individual does. In other words, the meaning of what one is saying includes the tendency for the other person to respond to it. As hope to arouse. Each gesture or word serves as a stimulus to them as well as to their spouses. Now, let us examine the women's perception of freedom to communicate with their husbands or former husbands.

Assuming that the "significant other" with a marital situation, at a given time, is the spouse, the women of these samples were asked the following question:

> *Do you feel very free _____ free _____ not so free _____ to confide, talk things over, or discuss anything with your husband or former husband?*

Table 2. Perceived Satisfaction With "Freedom" to Communicate With Spouse

MICHIGAN	Very Free or Free		Not so Free		Total	
	N	%	N	%	N	%
Married	75	89	9	11	84	100
Separated or divorced	40	55	33	45	73	100
MISSISSIPPI						
Married	82	74	28	26	110	100
Separated, divorced						
or widowed	37	49	38	51	75	100

In observing the data in Table 2, we find that the married women of both the Michigan and Mississippi samples felt freer than the separated or divorced women (when these women were married) to communicate with their spouses. Conversely, the separated or divorced women felt less free to communicate with their spouses than did the married women. It is interesting n=to note that the married women of Mississippi felt less free than the married women of Michigan to communicate with their husbands. Could this difference be accounting for by region or social class? This question cannot be answered by this analysis, but is an interesting question to be pursued in the future.

Examples of freedom or lack of freedom to verbally communicate with husbands or former husbands are as follows:

> *Ellen is a 68-year-old mother of four from Mississippi who has been married to George for 47 years. She said, "I never believed in the old saying that woman should be seen and not heard—like some people say about children ... and George knows that."*

> *However, Annette, a 28-year-old mother of two from Michigan, offered an opposing view. She has been separated from Ray for almost three years. "He never wanted me to say much of anything unless he asked me something." Annette said. The lack of verbal communication between Annette and Ray is obvious in that Ray seem to want Annette to do little or no talking to him. One-way verbal communication (as in this case) must have been extremely frustrating—especially for the listener. This alone could account for Annette having felt "not so free" to confide, talk things over, or discuss anything with her former husband.*

What does this imply? It could be that a distinction between verbal and nonverbal communication did not occur among the separated or divorced women and their former spouses. Or, it may be that if distinctions were made, neither form of communications was utilized to its fullest, which may have accounted for their marital relationships having been resolved.

In an effort to assess the husband's readiness to understand what their wives say to them during the process of interacting, data were obtained from the following question:

> *Do you feel that your husband/former husband very readily _____*
> *readily _____ not so readily _____ received or understands*
> *what you are trying to say?*

From Table 3 one can observe that for both samples a greater proportion of the married women than the separated or divorced women said that their husbands very readily received or understood what they were trying to say to them. Conversely, a greater proportion of the separated or divorced women indicated that their former husbands di not readily receive or understand what they were trying to sway to them.

Table 3. Spouses' Readiness to Receive and Understand What Respondents Were Saying

MICHIGAN	Very Readily or Readily		Not so Readily		Total	
	N	%	N	%	N	%
Married	71	85	13	15	84	100
Separated or divorced	32	42	44	58	76	100
MISSISSIPI						
Married	50	49	52	51	102	100
Separated or divorced, or widowed	29	40	44	60	73	100

The difference between the married women and the separated or divorced women is much greater in the Michigan sample than in the Mississippi sample. In other words, the Mississippi women, married as well as separated or divorced, have more in common (49 percent, 40 percent) than do the Michigan women (85 percent, 42 percent) with regard to perceptions of their husband's empathy.

Companionship is a form of expressive gratification which is sought in a marriage. In order to test this, the following question was asked the respondents:

> *Companionship has to do with shared leisure or non-work*
> *time activities, e.g., movies, picnics, parties and dancing.*
> *Are you generally satisfied—or dissatisfied—with this*
> *aspect of your marriage or former marriage?*

Table 4 shows that a greater proportion of married women were satisfied with the companionship in their lives than women who were separated or divorced for both the Michigan and Mississippi samples. Conversely, divorced or separated women were more dissatisfied with their companionship than married women. Here, we observe that the difference between married and single women is greater in the Michigan sample (90 percent and 56 percent, respectively). A 52-year-old divorcee from Michigan said that her former husband was never home long enough to do anything with her and their six children, even when not working. This confirms a common expectation—if separated or divorced women were satisfied with their marriages, they would still be married, especially since companionship is the essence of marriage.

Table 4. Perceived Satisfaction with Companionship

MICHIGAN	Generally Satisfied		Dissatisfied		Total	
	N	%	N	%	N	%
Married	75	90	8	10	84	100
Separated or divorced	40	56	32	44	72	100
MISSISSIPPI						
Married	72	67	35	33	107	100
Separated, divorced, or widowed	37	49	38	51	75	100

Interacting individuals in any situation most constantly the gestures of others and, in so doing, recognize, and adjust their own intentions, wishes, feelings, and attitudes. Similarly, they have to judge the fitness of norms, values, and group prescriptions from the situation indicated by the acts of others. This process of interpretation and redefinition relates to all kinds of interpersonal situations, whether they involve cooperation, love, conflict, hostility, or anger. This notion is examined by using the following questions.

> *How often would you say that you and your husband/ former husband had a big "blow up" and really got angry with each other?*

never

seldom

sometimes

often

very often

Table 5 shows that married women in Michigan sample are more likely than the separated or divorced women to never have marital conflicts. On the other hand, separated or divorced women were more likely to have had conflicts with their former husbands. This conforms to a common-sense expectation. Conflict is negatively related to marital disruption, although some conflict is positively related to marriage.

Table 5. Frequency of Conflict During Marital Relations

MICHIGAN	Never		Seldom or Sometimes		Often or Very Often		Total	
	N	%	N	%	N	%	N	%
Married	12	15	63	77	7	8	82	100
Separated or divorced	2	2	31	40	45	58	78	100
MISSISSIPPI								
Married	0	0	59	74	21	26	80	100
Separated, divorced or widowed	0	0	20	48	22	52	42	100

In the Mississippi sample, we find that neither married nor single women (separated or divorced) had no marital conflicts. The married women (26 percent and 52 percent, respectively).

The notion of conflict in a marital relationship brings to mind an article entitled "Problems Remain the Same" which appeared in a well-known magazine some time ago, noting a request for advice from a marriage counselor.

After ten years of marriage, our problems today are the same as at the beginning. It seems that there can be no compromise. Briefly, our problems are:

1. *He thinks I talk too much detail. He tunes me out, and does not remember things I have told him.*
2. *He says I depend on him too much for little decisions.*
3. *I don't like to argue. I used to cry over misunderstandings, which disgusted him. Now I sulk.*
4. *I have always been more affectionate than he—sometimes too aggressive, which annoys him, I have restrained myself, but this has not made him for affectionate. Signed, Lonely [Home Life, 1972]*

Conflict is often viewed negatively. However, some theorists suggest that conflict has some positive aspects (Simmel, 1955). It can serve as a force which integrates people on opposing sides, bonding them firmly into a group. Granted, this also applies to at least two people interacting. Thus, conflict may be advantageous to some black married couples in that they may refrain from personal abuse and confine a quarrel to issues, thus eliminating points of tension. In addition, it may serve to bring husbands and wives into communication with one another, forcing them to face up to their problems.

In examining reasons for conflict among the women and their husbands or former husbands, the following questions were asked:

What is/was this usually about?

occupational and financial matters or other matters

Thinking back over your married life, what was or is the one thing that you and your husband or former husband have disagreed about most?[55]

Table 6 shows the issues over which women had marital conflicts. For the Michigan married women, "suspicion of husband playing on wife," followed by occupational or financial issues were those over which they had the greatest conflicts. The issues over which they had the least conflicts were discipline of children and infrequent sexual activity on the part of the husband (11 percent each). For the single occupational or financial issues, followed by "suspicion of husband playing on wife." The issues which caused least conflict for single women were "infrequent sexual activity on the part of the husband" followed by discipline of children.

In the Mississippi samples, we find some variations from the Michigan sample. Mississippi married women's greatest marital conflicts appeared to be over child discipline, followed by suspected infidelity by the husband. The issue of child discipline caused less marital conflict in the Michigan sample. The issue over which the least conflict occurred was "infrequent sexual activity on the part of the husband." For the single women, the conflict occurred most frequently over "suspicion of husband playing on wife," followed by occupational or financial issues. The issues over which they had the least conflict were discipline of children and husband's infrequent sexual activity.

Table 6. Major Reasons for Conflict During Marital Relations

MICHIGAN	Occupa tional or Financial		Suspicion of Husband "Playing" on wife		Disciplin ing Children		Infrequent Sexual Activity -Husband		Total	
	N	%	N	%	N	%	N	%	N	%
Married	24	35	30	43	8	11	8	11	70	100
Separated or divorced	47	61	22	29	5	7	2	3	76	100
MISSISSIPPI										
Married	17	28	20	34	23	38	0	0	60	100
divorced	15	35	23	55	2	5	2	5	42	100

SUMMARY AND CONCLUSION

This study is by no means exhaustive—it is merely an effort to describe the social and symbolic interaction among 400 black women who were either married, separated, or divorced. Specifically, we were concerned with the interpersonal behaviors that affect the maintenance of marital relationships. From the empirical findings, one may conclude the alternatives utilized by black married couples in retaining their marital status include perceptions of cathectic affection, perceptions of the opportunity to relate to their husbands (thus having them favorably respond), perceived degree of satisfaction with companionship, and the ability of both partners to use conflict to their advantage in the relationship.

In conclusion, black married and unmarried women may see one function of social and symbolic relationships in marriages as an outlet of emotional support (support system) and concern of someone to confide in. Spouses (mates) seem to fulfill that need which cannot be found in the larger society due to its structure. Let us also realize that being divorced or separated does, in many instances, eliminate social and symbolic interaction between black women and black men in a living arrangement. Although sometimes misunderstood by outsiders, memories of this relationship can remain a part of a former black mate's entire life. This was suggested by the 400 black women from Michigan and Mississippi.

Black women and black men, as reasoning creatures, can relate to each other verbally and through self-disclosure, can learn something about each other and about our own identities as well. In addition, as sexual creatures, we have the ability to express ourselves, our feelings, thoughts, and even our fantasies through physical (nonverbal) communication. It simply becomes an ongoing process of relating sharing, and communicating.

NOTES

[1] Pseudonyms are used to identify the women and their husbands or former husbands for each example since names of the respondents were not secured to assure confidentiality.

[2] It is important to note that open-ended responses to this question were also used in pursuing data on "communication" between the women and their husbands/former husbands, where responses regarding "communicating" occurred.

REFERENCES

Blumer, H. (1996) "Sociological implications of the thoughts of George Herbert Mead." American Journal of Sociology 71 (March.)

Callum M. (1972) Body Talk. New York: Bantam.

Fullerton, G.P. (1977) survival in Marriage: Introduction to family Interaction, Conflict, and Alternatives. Hinsdale, IL: Dryden.

Green, E.J. (1978) Personal relationships: An Approach to Marriage and Family. New York: McGraw-Hill.

Henley, N.M. (1970) "The politics of touch." Presented at the American Psychological Association Meetings, Miami Beach, Florida, September.

—. (1974) "Power, sex, and nonverbal communication." Berkeley Journal of Sociology 18.

Kogan, B.A. (1973) Human Sexual Expression. New York: Hardcourt Brace Jovanovich.

Ladner, J.A. (1972) Tomorrow's Tomorrow: The Black Woman. New York. Doubleday.

Lauer, R.H. and W.H. Handel (1977) Social Psychology: The Theory and Application of Symbolic Interactionism. Boston: Houghton Mifflin.

Maters, W.H. and V.E. Johnson (1974) "The role of religion in sexual dysfunction," in M.S. Calderone (ed.) Sexuality and Human Values. New York: SIECUS/ Association Press.

Mead, G.H. (1934) Mind, Self, and Society (C.W. Morris, ed.). Chicago: University of Chicago Press.

Myers, L.W. (1973) "A study of the self-esteem maintenance process among Black women." Dissertation, Michigan State University. (unpublished)

— (1975) "Black women and self-esteem," in M. Millman and R.M. Kanter (eds.) Another Voice: Feminist Perspective on Social Life and Social Science, Garden City, NY: Anchor/Doubleday.

Simmel, G. (1955) Conflict and the Web Affiliations (K.H. Wolff and R. Bendix, trans.). New York: Free Press.

Walster, E. and G.W. Walster (1978) A New Look at Love, reading MA: Addison-Wesley.

INTERRACIAL MARRIAGES: EMPIRICAL AND THEORETICAL CONSIDERATIONS

DELORES P ALDRIDGE

Interracial marriages have garnered attention periodically since the turn of the century. However, sociopsychological research in the area of intermarriage continues to be scant in spite of increased contact between the races in the 1960s. Social scientists have maintained the study of intermarriage may provide a precise, quantitative measurement of crucial and related questions such as the process of assimilation, the degree of internal cohesion in individual racial, religious, and ethnic groups, and the extent of social distance between groups of these types (Barron, 1946: 249).

Little has been done, however, in the areas which promise so much in understanding social processes. What research that has been done has focused on: the incidence of interracial marriages; casual factors; sociopsychological characteristics; and, the problems encountered by the marriage partners and their children. This paper will summarize the small amount of research which has been done on interracial marriages in the areas mentioned in an attempt to update the body of information. It will also provide directives for future research which should lead a better understanding of black-white marriages and their implications for black people and the larger society.

INCIDENCE OF INTERRACIAL MARRIAGE

The rate of interracial marriage has varied by state since many sates prohibited interracial marriages until the Loving versus Virginia decision in 1967. With this decision all laws against interracial marriages were declared invalid.

Some evidence does exist which suggests that the rate of interracial marriage decreased in the first half of the century and prior to the

JOURNAL OF BLACK STUDIES, Vol. 8 No. 3. March 1978 © 1978 Sage Publications Inc.

1954 Supreme Court decision declaring unconstitutional segregated public schools (Burma, 1962, Drake and Cayton, 1945; lynn, 1953; Panunzio, 1942, Wirth and Goldhamer, 1944). However, data from California indicated that the rate of interracial marriage increased lightly following the court decision of 1954 (Barnett, 1963a). There are other fragmentary statistics which suggest racially mixed marriages may be on the increase in the United States (Powledge, 1963; Heer, 1966: 273; cf. Mayer and Smock, 1960). Data from another study conducted after the 1967 decision found a similar increase as the California study (Aldridge, 1973). Even though data have suggested increases, several surveys of attitudes of blacks prior to the seventies indicated a lack of eagerness for intermarriage. (Pittsburgh Courier, 1958). In the latter 1960s and into the 1970s the emphasis on black pride and racial solidarity has contributed to similar attitudes (Staples, 1973: 123).

CASUAL FACTORS

Numerous social and psychological forces facilitating intermarriage have been set forth by various writers. For example, Barron (1946) took the position that an unbalanced sex ratio and numerically small representation lead some groups into considerable incidence of intermarriage. Another interesting and perhaps more thorough study dealing with casual factors was conducted by golden in 1959. He dealt with propinquity, economic propinquity, and similarity, both occupational and spatial; by close association and common experiences in the amount, type, and locale of education; and by recreational contacts (Baron, 1946).

The intermingling of young adults of different races at the high school and college levels is widely expected to be reflected over the long run in an increased rate of intermarriage. Because of the continual lowering of the average age of dating and entering marriage, high schools will be increasingly faced with mixed racial associations (Barnett, 1963a). And the fact that large numbers of interracial couples meet on college campuses away from home reduces the amount of parental and community control over the   choice of an individual's dating partners. Young people have revolved against traditional institutions and values which have led them to reject the taboos on dating across racial lines (Staples, 1973). While sociologists have theories and hypotheses on the rebellion-projection them explaining the occurrence of inter-marriage, no empirical studies appear to exist.

It seems only logical that an increase in interracial dating would result in an increase in interracial marriages. Using selective data, Heer observed an upward trend in black-white marriage in those areas where residential segregation by race is low and where there are minimal status differences between the white and black population.

While the proportion of black men, dating interracially appears much higher than that of black women, the difference is not so great when it comes to interracial marriages as reflected in 1960 census data. While it appears that black women are deprived of many dates by white women, the vast majority of black males are still available to them for matrimony.

Until recently, many of the black men who married white women were of a higher social status that their wives. Because this social status differential was so common, a theory was formulated about it. Sociologists hypothesized that the black male traded his class advantage for the racial caste advantage of the white bride (Merton, 1941:361-374). But contemporary interracial marriages are more likely to involve spouses from the same social class (Pavela, 1964: 209). Furthermore, when intermarriages involved members of different social classes, there was a pronounced tendency for black women to marry up rather than to marry down (Bernard, 1966: 274-276).

Consequently, one reason that black women marry white men is to improve their social status. Of course, this applies to many homogamous marriages. One notable exception, however, are the marriages of black female entertainers to white men. Because of their close association with white males in the course of their jobs, many of them form interracial unions. Most of the celebrated cases in recent years involved famous black women who married white men who were not equally famous or wealthy (Staples, 1973: 121).

Various motives have been suggested to explain black women/white men marriages. Some students of the subject assert that uneven sex ratios are a basic cause. Wherever a group in nearness to another group has an imbalance in sex ratio, there is a greater likelihood of intermarriage.

If the groups have a relatively well-balanced distribution of the sexes, members will marry their own group (Panunzio, 1942: 690).

In the interracial marriages, there is the tendency to look for ulterior motives. It is a popular notion that people marry interracially because of rebellion against their parents, sexual curiosity toward racially different individuals, and other psychological reasons. It is commonly conceived that there are kinds of unconscious bizarre reasons which propel racially different individuals into marriages. People may marry their "own kind" for the weirdest reasons, yet these reasons do not make each marriages suspect. Perhaps the imputation of ulterior motives to interracial couples says more about the individual making these interpretations and about the society we live in than about the couple who intermarry (Washington, 1970: 303).

CHARACTERISTICS OF INTERRACIAL MARRIAGE

Even though there is some consensus on certain aspects of the interracial marriage phenomenon (Barnett, 1963a), outright contradictions can be found in the literature. This may be attributed to the fact that several studies were conducted at different locales and at different times, and the referent group might be marriages, or married "couples," not randomly selected. Monahan (1970) stresses the point that there is disagreement even on such fundamental point as to whether more black males than black females intermarry with whites more often than black females. But the 1960 census data on married couples show slightly more black females had white spouses than black males had white spouses. Recently, Staples (1974: 6) stated that during the 1960s the black male-white female marriage was common, but the 1970s portend a significant increase in black female-white male marriages. He explains that much of this increase will occur in the south among the college-educated who now have greater opportunity for social interaction than in previous decades.

Pavela (1964) concluded from his Indiana study that, in many respects, the black-white marriages studied contradict the characteristics of such marriages in the public mind or even in much sociology literature.

It would appear that such intermarriage now occurs between persons who are, by and large, economically, educationally, and culturally equal and who have a strong emotional attachment, be it rationalization or real. The following characteristics can generally be discerned from the literature.

1. The religiously less marry persons of different races with a higher frequency than the religiously more devout (Schnepp and Yui, 1955)

2. Persons who have experienced disorganized and stressful parental families are more likely to marry members of other races than those who were raised in cohesive and stable families (Hunt and Collier, 1957; Lynn, 1953; Schnepp and Yui, 1955; Strauss, 1954).

3. Persons living in urban areas cross racial lines to a greater extent that persons living in rural areas.

4. Person crossing racial lines to marry generally chose partners who come from different religious backgrounds (Golden, 1953; Lynn, 1953) and apparently from different socioeconomic levels (Drake and Cayton, 1945; Golden, 1953; Pavela, 1964), however, report that the majority of spouses in interracial marriages come from the same socioeconomic level.

5. Nonwhite males undertaking an interracial marriage appear to have higher-than-average socioeconomic status, and the white male and female and the nonwhite female have a lower-than-average socioeconomic level (Drake and Caton, 1945; Golden, 1954; Wirth and Goldhamer, 1944). However, one study (Lynn 1953) reports that the upper class is greatly underrepresented and the lower class is slightly overrepresented in interracial marriages.

6. In black-white marriages, it is the black make who marries the white female in the majority of cases (Barron, 1946; Burma, 1952; Dake and Cayton, 1945; golden 1953; Lynn, 1953; Risdon, 1954; Wirth and Goldhamer, 1944). For contradictions see Monahan (1970: 62).

7. Among those who undertake an interracial marriage, a greater-than-average number have been married previously (Golden, 1954; Pavela, 1964; Wirth and Goldenhamer, 1944).

8. Foreign-born white males more than native white males and native white females more than foreign-born white females, undertake black-white marriages (Wirth and Goldhamer, 1944).

9. In black-white marriages the family of the black spouse seems to be more willing to accept the couple than does the family of the white spouse (Golden, 1953).

10. American males and females marrying out of their racial group are generally older than the average at the time (Blesanz, 1950; Burma, 1952; Golden, 1953, 1954; Lynn, 1953; Risdon, 1954; Strauss, 1954).

CONSEQUENCES

The fourth and last major kind of research intermarriage has dealt with the consequences of the practice on family life. How do interracial couples and their children fare in personality development and interpersonal relations and success or failure as measured by the criteria of divorce, desertion, and separation? What systematic and empirical data have researchers about the consequences of interracial marriage?

The research is contradictory as to the degree of success attained by mixed marriages as measured by divorce. One study (Cheng and Yamamura, 1957) found that such marriages are less successful than marriages between persons of the same race, while a second study dealing with the rate of divorce in mixed marriages found such marriages to fail less frequently than the average. It seems probable that marriages between whites and blacks would reflect the poorest outcome in view of the particular personal and social problems and the unusual difficulties which confront them, as indicated in many studies (Little, 1942; Drake and Cayton, 1945; Osmundsen, 1965). However, Pavela (1964) makes a point (based on his in-depth study of mixed married couples) that the external pressures faced by interracial couples are often great but certainly do not appear to be overwhelming. Further, except for some nonconforming information on the state of Hawaii, nothing is known statistically to support the thesis of instability (Monahan, 1970).

The literature suggests that in black-white marriages contrary to what might be expected, children do not present a special problem. They are considered to be black by both the white and black communities. The youngsters generally make an adequate adjustment to the black community and thus their problems are the same as those of the children of two black parents (Drake and Cayton, 1945; Risdon, 1954).

The studies of interracial marriage have been fairly unanimous in their assessments of the outstanding problems encountered by couples who enter in such unions. The studies reveal such factors as housing, occupation, and relationships with family and peers as troublesome ones (Drake and Cayton, 1953; Golden, 1954; Risdon, 1954). Staples (1973) explained that among black peers, the sentiment today is clearly against interracial marriages. Many interracial couples are shut out of social life in black circle being forced to seek friends and social intercourse in all white or other interracial environments.

A preliminary survey of the literature on interracially mixed marriages has dealt with both theoretical and empirical considerations from four perspectives: first, the extent to which they occur; second, the casual factors associated with their occurrence; third, problems or consequences of such marriages.

FUTURE CONSIDERATIONS

Though interest has seemingly always existed where interracial marriages are concerned, there continues to be a paucity of meaningful research available. It would be particularly relevant to assess the extent and nature of interracial marriages in the 1970s following the 1967 Loving versus Virginia case. But, perhaps more significant than the 1967 decision as a possible facilitator, is an analysis of interracial marriage with respect to the black movement of the 1960s emphasizing racial solidarity and "black is beautiful." The question, "Why are interracial marriages continuing to occur in the face of a more magnified emphasis on blackness?" therefore, appears to be both apropos and timely.

Since studies are often in contradiction of each other, as earlier pointed out, there appears to be a need for examining in greater depth and research which has already been conducted on black-white marriages. For the most part, research studies from 1930 to 1975 have dealt with fragmented data rather than with a body of data reflecting the entire United States. It would appear, then, that a critical step in research should be to outline precisely the rates of interracial marriages from 1930 to 1975 for determining increases or decreases in racially mixed marriages. Further, research might be undertaken to determine whether the characteristics of interracial marriages approximate those of same-race marriages or appear significantly different. Future researchers might accomplish this by disaggregating data of the American population pertaining to interracial marriage by age, education, income, mobility, origin of birth, fertility and other relevant variables. This data could then be analyzed with respect to current theories and serve as a basis for generating new ones in an area which has not been studied systematically. But, even more importantly, black people will be in a position to determine whether the issue of black-white marriage is a serious threat to the black community and, if a threat, possible methods of amelioration.

REFERENCES

Aldridge, D.P. (1973) "The Changing nature of interracial marriage in Georgia a research note:" J. of Marriage and the Family 35 (November):641-642.

Anderson, C.H. (1971) "Toward a new sociology: a critical view." Homewood,IL: Dorsey Press.

Baber, R.E. (1937) "A study of 325 mixed marriages." Amer. Soc. Rev. 2 (October) 705-716.

Barnett, L.D. (1963a) "Research on international and interracial marriage. Marriage and Family Living 25 (February): 105-107.

—. (1963b) "Interracial marriage in California." Marriage and Family Living 25 (November): 424-427.

—. and J.H. Burma (1965) "Interracial marriage data discrepancy." J. of Marriage and the Family 37 (February): 97.

Barron, M.L. (1946) People Who Internarry. Syracuse: Syracuse Univ. Press.

Beigel, H.G. (1966) "Problems and motives in interracial relationships." J. of Sex Research 2 (November): 185-202.

Bernard, J. (1966a) "Note on educational homogamy in negro-white and white negro marriages. 1960." J. of Marriage and the Family 27 (August): 274-276.

—. (1966b) "Marital stability and patterns of status variables." J. of Marriage and the Family 27 (November): 421-439.

Berry, B (1965) Race and Ethnic Relations. Boston: Houghton Miffliin.

Billingley,A. (1968) Black Families in White America. Eaglewood Cliffs, NJ: Prentice-Hall.

Blau, P and O.D. Duncan (1967) The American Occupational Structure. New York: John Wiley.

Blesanz, J. (1950) "Inter-American marriages on the Isthmus Panama." Social Forces 29 (December): 159-163.

Bogue, D.J. (1969) Principles of Demography. New York: John Wiley.

Brayboy, T.F. (1966) "Interracial sexuality as an expression of neurotic conflict." J. of Sex Research 2 (November) 179-184.

Brooks, M.R. (1946) "American Caste and class: an appraisal." Social Forces 25 (December): 207*211.

Brown, M.C. (1955) The status job and occupations as evaluated by an urban negro sample." Amer. Soc. Rev. 20 (October):564-565.

Burma, J.H. (1963) "Interethnic marriage in Los Angeles. 1948-1959." Social Forces 42 (December):156-165.

—. (1952) "Research note on the measurement of interracial marriage." Amer. J. of Sociology 57 (May):587-589.

—. G.A. Cretser, and T. Secarest (1970) "A comparison of the occupational status of intramarrying and intermarrying couples: a research note." Sociology and Social Research 54 (July):508-519.

Calhoun, A.W. (1917) A Social History of the American Family. Cleveland. Clark Publishing.

Carter, L.F. (1968) "Racial caste hypogamy: a sociological myth?" Phylon 29 (Winter):347-350.

Cash, E. (1955) "A study of negro-white marriages in the Philadelphia area." Ph.D. dissertation, Temple University. (unpublished).

Cavan, R.S. (1971) "Annonated bibliography of studies of intermarriage in the United States. 1960-1970 inclusive." Inter J. of Sociology of the Family 1 (May):157-165.

—. and J.T. Cavan (1971) "Inter. J. Sociology of the Family 1 (May):10-24.

Centers, R. (1949) "Marital selection and occupational strata." Amer J. of Sociology 54 (May): 530-535.

Cheng C.K. and D.S. Yamamura (1957) "Interracial marriage and divorce in Hawaii." Social Forces 36 (October): 77-84.

Chilman, C. (1966) "Marital stability and patterns of status variables: a comment." J. of Marriage and the Family 27 (November): 796-802.

Collins, S.F. (1951) "the social position of white and 'half caste' women in colored groupings in Britain."

Cox, D.C. (1945) "Race and Caste a distinction." Amer. J. of Sociology 50 (March: 360-368.

—. (1942) "The modern caste school of race relations." Social Forces 21 (December): 226-281.

Das, M.S. (1971) "A cross-cultural study of intercaste marriage in India and the United States." Inter. J. of Sociology of the Family I (May): 25-33.

Davis, A.B.B. Gardner and M.R. Gardner (1941) Deep South Chicago: Univ. of Chicago Press.

Davis, K. (1941) "Intermarriage in caste societies." Amer. Anthropologist 43: 376-395.

Day, C.B. (1932) A Study of Some Negro-White Families in the United States. Cambridge: Harvard Univ. Press.

Drachsler, J. (1921) Intermarriage in New York City. New York: Columbia Univ. Press.

Drake, S.C. and H.R. Cayton (1945) Black Metropolis. New York: Hardcourt Brace & World.

Duncan, D.C. (1961) "A socio-economic index for all occupations." in A.J. Reiss et al. Occupations and Social Status. New York: Free Press.

Golden, J. (1959) "Facilitating factors in negro-white intermarriage." Phylon 20 (Fall): 273-284

—. (1958) "Social control of negro-white intermarriage." Social Forces 36 (March): 267-269.

—. (1954) "Patterns of negro-white in intermarriage in Philadelphia." Amer. Soc. Rev. 19 (April: 144-147.

—. (1953) 'Characteristics of the negro-white intermarriage in Philadelphia.' Amer. Soc. Rev. 18 9April): 177-183.

Gordon, A. I. (1964) Intermarriage: Interfaith, Interracial, Interethnic: Boston: Beacon Press.

Heer, D.M. (1974) "The prevalence of black-white marriage in the United States 1960 and 1970." J. of Marriage and the Family 35 (May): 246-258.

—. (1967) "Intermarriage and racial amalgamation in the United States." Eugenics Q. 14 (June): 112-120.

—. (1966) "Negro-white marriage in the United States." J. of Marriage and the Family 27 (August): 262-273.

—. (1965) 'Negro-white marriages in the United States." New Society J. (August:7-9.

Herbert, L. (1939) "A study of ten cases of negro-white marriages in the District of Columbia." Catholic University of America. (unpublished)

Hoffman, F.C. (1896) Race Traits and Tendencies of the American Negro. New York: Macmillan.

Hunt, C.L. and R.W. Collier (1957) "Intermarriage and cultural change: a study of Philippine-American Marriages," Social Forces 35 (March): 223-230.

Kennedy, R.J.R (1952) "Single or triple melting pot? Intermarriage trends in New Haven, 1820-1950." Amer J. of Sociology 58:56-69.

—. (1944) "Single or triple melting pot? Intermarriage trends in New Haven. 1870-1940." Amer. J. Sociology 49:331-339.

Kornacker, M. (1971) "Cultural significance of intermarriage: a comparative approach." Inter. J. of Sociology of the Family I (May): 147-156.

Larason, C. [ed.] (1965) Marriage Across the Color Line. Chicago: Johnson Publishing.

Lazar, R.J. (1971) "Toward a theory of intermarriage." Inter. J. of Sociology of the Family I (May): 1-9.

Lehrman, S.R. (1967) "Psychopathology in mixed marriages." Psychoanalytic Q. 36 (January): 67-82.

Little, C. (1942) "Analytic reflections on mixed marriages." Psychoanalytic Rev. 29 (January): 20-25.

Lynn, A. Q. (1967) "Interracial marriages in Washington, D.C." J. of Negro Education 36 (Fall): 428-433.

—. (1956) "Some aspects of interracial marriage in Washington, D.C." J. of Negro Education (Fall): 380-391.

—. (1953) "Interracial marriage in Washington, D.C., 1940-1947." Ph.D. dissertation, Catholic University of America. (unpublished)

—. (1950) "Interracial marriage: a study of fifteen negro-white marriages in New York City, and the metropolitan area." Catholic University of America. (unpublished)

McDowell, S. (1971) "Black-white intermarriage in the United States." Inter. J. of Sociology of the Family I (May):49-58.

Massaquoi, H. (1956) 'Would you want your daughter to marry one?" Ebony 20 (August): 83-90.

Mayer, A.J. and S.M. Smock (1960) "Negro-white intermarriage for Detroit, 1899-1957." Population Index 26 (July): 210-211.

Merton, R.K. "Marriage across racial lines." J. of Marriage and the Family 35 (November): 632-640.

—. (1971) Interracial marriages in the United States: some data on upstate New York." Inter J. of Sociology and the Family I (March); 94-105.

—. (1970) "Interracial marriages really less table?" Social Forces 48:461-473.

Moore, P. (1975) "Social status: judging people- it's the job that counts." Psychology Today 9 (July) 32, 84.

Osmundsen, J.A. (1965) "Doctor discusses 'mixed' marriage." *New York Times* (November 7): 73L.

Panunzio, C. (1942) "Intermarriage in Los Angeles, 1924-1933." Amer J. of Sociology 47 (March): 690-701.

Pavela, T.H. (1964) "An exploratory study of negro-white intermarriage in Indiana." Marriage and Damily Living 26 (May): 209-211.

Pittsburgh Courier (1958) "Who wants intermarriage? Most courier readers stand against interracial unions." (September 20):6.

Powledge, F. (1963) "Negro-white marriages on rise here." *New York Times* (October 18): I. 18.

Rainwater, L. (1966) "Marital stability and patterns of status variables: a comment." J. of Marriage and the Family 27 (November): 442-445.

Reuter, E.B. (1934) Race and Culture Contacts. New York: McGraw-Hill.

—. (1931) Race Mixture: Studies in Intermarriage and Miscegenation. New York: McGraw-Hill.

—. (1918) The Mulatto in the United States. Boston: Badger Books.

Risdon, R. (1954) "A study of interracial marriages based on data for Los Angeles County." sociology and Social Research 39 (November-December): 92-95.

Roberts, R.E.T. (1956) "A comparative study of stratification and intermarriage in multiracial societies." Ph.D. dissertation, University of Chicago. (unpublished).

—. (1940) "Negro-white intermarriage: a study of social control." University of Chicago. (unpublished).

Rodman, H. (1965) "Technical note on two rates mixed marriage." Amer. Soc.Rev. 30 (October): 776-778.

Sampson, W.A. and PH.H. Rossi (1975) "Race and Family social standing." Amer. Soc. Rev. 40 (April): 201-214.

Sass, H.R. (1956) "Mixed schools and mixed blood." Atlantic Monthly 198 (November): 45-49.

Schermerhorn, R.A. (1966) "Marital stability and patterns of status variables: a comment." J. Marriage and the Family 27 (November): 440-441.

Schnepp, G.J. and A.M. Yui (1955) "Cultural and marital adjustment of Japanese war-brides." Amer J. of Sociology 61 (July): 48-50.

Schuyler, G.S. (1930) Racial Intermarriage in the United States. Girard, K.S.: Haldeman-Julius.

Shaffer, H.B. (1961) "Mixed marriage." Editorial research Reports I (May 24): 381-397.

Smith, C.E. (1960) "Negro-white intermarriage in metropolitan New York: a qualitative case analysis." Ph.D. dissertation, Columbia University. (unpublished)

Staples, R. (1974) "The black family in evolutionary perspective." Black Scholar 5 (June): 2-9.

—. (1973) The Black Woman in America. Chicago: Nelson Hall Publishers.

Stern, C. (1940) Principle of Human Genetics San Francisco: W.H. Freeman.

Stone, A.H. (1908) Studies in the America Race Problem. New York: Doubleday.

Stonequist, E.V. (1973) The Marginal Man. New York: Scribner's.

Strauss, A.L. (1954) "Strain and harmony in American-Japanese war-bride marriages." Marriage and Family Living 16 (May): 99-106.

Svalastoga, K. (1965) Social Differentiation. New York: David McKay.

Toynbee, A.J. (1934) A Study of History. London: Oxford Univ. Press.

Tumlin, M.M. (1967) Social stratification: The Forms and Functions of Inequality. Englewood Cliffs, NJ.: Prentice-Hall.

Udry, J.R. (1967) "Marital instability by race and income based on 1960 census data." Amer. J. of Sociology 72 (May): 673-674.

—. (1966) "Marital instability by race, sex, education, and occupations using 1960 census data." Amer. J. of Sociology 72 (September): 203-209.

United States News and World Report (1967) "Now that mixed marriage is legal." 62 (June 26): 25.

—. (1964) "Intermarriage and the race problem as leading authorities see it." 55 (November 18):84-93.

—. (1958) "What the South really fears about mixed schools." 45 (September 19) 76ff.

Warner, W.L. (1936) "American caste and class." Amer. J. of Sociology 42 (September): 234-237.

Washington, J. (1970) Marriage in Black and White. Boston: Beacon Press.

Wehmann, e.M. (1934) "A study of ten cases of white-negro intermarriage." Smith College. For abstract see 'Abstract of theses." Smith College Studies in Social Work 5 (December): 211. (unpublished).

Wilbert, G.I. and R.J. Hagan (1974) "Alternative sets of occupation score from the 1970 PUS." Public Data USE 2 2 (October): 40-44.

Wilkinson, D.Y. (1975) "Black Male/ White female. New York: Schenkman.

Wirth, I. and H. Goldhamer (1944) "The hybrid and the problem of misconception." in O. Klineberg (ed.) Characteristics of the American Negro. New York: Harper & Row.

CHAPTER FIVE
Economic Issues

Cheryl Leggon explores the double-minority status of black female professionals and finds technical criteria and race as prediction on the job treatment. The author studied medical doctors, attorneys and holders of M.B.A.degrees. Most of the respondents indicated they experienced more discrimination on the basis of race than on the basis of sex. The author also pointed out the ease with which black professional women cope the dual demands of career and home. Leggon concludes that the black professional woman does and gain benefits from the double-negative status.

Betty Collier and Louis Williams examine beliefs concerning differential economic statuses of black males and black females and find such beliefs to be invalid. Their findings indicate social scientists are both victims and offenders in perpetuating misconceptions about the differential status of black men and women. They call for the construction of a black social science based with the reconstruction of social knowledge.

Finally, Delores P. Aldridge explores the relationship between occupational status, educational status and earnings as valid indicators of the position of black females in the labor force. The occupations in which black women participate assessed in terms of the distribution of all women who work. Further, some special problems confronting black working women are presented. Data suggests that while the trend of economic gains for black working women is clear, they have yet to attain equality in the working world.

BLACK FEMALE PROFESSIONAL: DILEMMAS AND CONTRADICTIONS OF STATUS

CHERYL BERNADETTE LEGGON

Everett Hughes, the author of one of the seminal essays on dilemmas and contradictions of status, argued that when

> *new kinds of people in established professional positions are assessed by others, that that assessment of their statuses and the role activity associated with them is likely to be made on the basis of both universally accented technical criteria and in terms of "auxiliary" characteristics carried over from such other social contexts as race and sex [Hughes, 1945:353].*

This, coupled with the fact that in contemporary American society, blacks and women qualify as "new kinds of people in established professional positions,"[56] suggests that the case of elite black professional women should certainly pose an interesting problem for investigation.

The expectations concerning the "auxiliary" characteristics are both created in and reinforced by what Blumer (1958) refers to as the "public arena," which includes public forums, "everyday talk," and the mass media—newspapers, magazines, radio, movies, and especially television.[57] People tend to hold a dual image of professionals: On the one hand, they associate with being a professional, a certain amount of technical skill (for example, specialized training or licensing); on the other hand, they associate certain auxiliary characteristics. For example, when one thinks of a physician, the image of a "Marcus Welby" type comes mind: mature, competent, white, Anglo-Saxon, Protestant, and male. What happens when a potential client encounters a professional who does not fit the image? Hughes' study focused upon the dilemmas occasioned for an individual encountering a status –discrepant professional such as a black physician or a female attorney. My study focuses upon the status-discrepant professional herself rather than on the client.

Hughes argues that when an individual encounters a status-discrepant professional, the outcome of that encounter depends upon the situation: whether or not it is defined as an emergency and/or whether or not another professional (presumably a non-status discrepant professional) is available. If the situation is defined as an emergency or if the individual decides that "there is no other way," then she/he may feel forced to relate to the status-discrepant professional on a purely professional basis. Should the potential client not be forced to relate to the status-discrepant professional on a purely professional basis, what emerges is the fact (pointed out by Hughes) that there are "master status traits"; namely that certain statuses tend to overpower any other characteristic which might run counter to them. For many, race and sex are master status traits; that is, when encountering a status-discrepant professional, the potential client encounters a black or a woman first and a doctor or a lawyer second. What emerges, then, is a status hierarchy with ascribed status (race, sex) on the top and achieved status (for example, professional) below.

According to my findings (and consonant with those of Hughes), not only is there a status hierarchy in which ascribed status placed above achieved status, but within the top stratum of ascribed status the black female professionals whom i interviewed perceive a hierarchy in which race usually ranks above sex. It is my contention that their double-ascribed minority statuses —black and female— place black professional women in what Epstein (1973a) has called "a double bind," in that they share in the economic discrimination patterns based on sex which prevail in American society in addition to those economic discrimination patterns imposed on all blacks; the latter are enforced more strictly than the former. Further, this double bind and its effects are greater than the sum of its parts, the two minority-ascribed statuses of race and sex (Dumont and Wilson, 1957). The black female professional is the product of the confluence of unique sociohistorical, economic, and psychological factors. Although statistics can yield an abundance of useful information, they cannot measure or even delineate the psychological and social psychological problems peculiar to the black female professional. These problems are the focal point of my inquiry.

This study of elite black professional women is more of an ethnographic field study than a verification study of explicit theoretical propositions. The theoretical framework resembles hat Dumont and Wilson (1957) have called a theory sketch.

> *a more or less vague indication of the propositions and initial conditions considered as relevant, but needs 'filling out' to develop into a full-fledged theory. The theory sketch suggests he direction for further required in the filling our process.*

Specifically, my pilot study[58] of elite black professional women sought to determine

1. whether elite black professional women perceived race discrimination as more salient than sex discrimination in their professional experience, and to what extent, if any, there is a cumulative effect from both racial and sexual discrimination in the professions; and
2. the extent to which the status-discrepant individual (i.e., the elite black female professional) recognizes her status-discrepant position and the way(s) in which she attempts to cope with it.

Since there is a great deal of dissension as to which occupations should be included under the category "professions," I chose to examine three of those occupations that are consistently highly ranked on prestige-ranking scales such as that of Hodge and Rossi (see Blau, 1967)[59]: medical doctors, attorneys (who have graduated from law school and passed at least one bar examination), and women with Masters degrees in Business Administration (M.B.A.s).

The pilot study was conducted in the Chicago metropolitan area during the academic year 1974-1975. The Chicago metropolitan area is statistically interested in terms of black professionals: Although Chicago has the largest number of black attorneys of any American city (approximately 330 in 1975), the number of black physicians has decreased 13.5 percent since 1961(Blan and Duncan, 1967). This decrease is partially attributable to the increase in opportunities for black physicians in the United Stated, particularly in the South and West. In 1974, Chicago had 212 black doctors, of which 52.7 percent were over 50 years of age (McClory, 1975: 1). The membership rolls of the Cook County Bar Association, the nation's oldest and largest local black bar association, greatly facilitated the task of estimating and locating the universe of approximately 31 black female attorneys; this task was somewhat more difficult for physicians because most lists contained only last names and first initials—perhaps because many people are wary of female doctors except in "traditionally female" specialties of obstetrics and pediatrics. At the same time my study was being conducted by Comprehensive research and Development, Inc., which independently estimated the number of black female physicians in Chicago to be between 15 and 25; using the snowball technique, I obtained the names of 18. Of these, four were eliminated from y sample because they were foreign-born and raised,[60] and one was eliminated because she suffered a stroke and was unable to be interviewed. It was most difficult to assess the number of black females with M.B.A.s in the Chicago area. Although I am confident that I located all of those who received M.B.A.s from the University of Chicago and who remained in the Chicago area, the Dean's office of the Graduate School of Business of the University of Chicago informed me that the school did not keep records by sex until 1971. The Dean's office of the Graduate School of Business of Northwestern University did not have records of its graduates broken down by race and sex. Therefore, from those names I did receive, I asked each for the name of any other black female M.B.A. they knew. Excepting three who were impossible to locate and one who refused to be interviewed, the sample consisted of six M.B.A.s and one Certified Public Accountant (one of two in the Chicago area, and one of six black female C.P.A.s in the country at that time). Names of doctors, attorneys, and M.B.A.s were obtained from the membership roll of the League of black Women, an organization founded in 1972, whose membership includes women from all area of life and a representative cross-section of professionals. Each woman contacted was asked to name three of four other women (either in her profession and/or others included in the study) whom she recommended the interviewer contact. This snowballing technique proved useful in locating those women not members of organizations and thereby enlarged the population from which the sample was drawn.

The final sample consisted of 12 black female attorneys, six back female doctors, and seven black female M.B.A.s (including one C.P.A.). A matched sample was utilized: Respondents in each occupational category were divided into two groups on the basis of whether they entered their profession before or after 1965 (the year in which Title VII of the Civil Rights Act of 1964 went into effect); this sampling procedure allowed for the detection of age-specific trends across occupations. Due to the complex and sensitive areas probed an in order to reduce interviewer bias, I personally interviewed all of the subjects; this is consonant with basic interviewing techniques based upon the experience of survey research organizations such as the National Opinion Research Center, which finds that the best results are obtained when blacks interview blacks, whites interview whites, and females as opposed to males are the interviewers. My sole instrument of data collection was an interview schedule designed to elicit information that relates the research questions on the professions, women, and blacks implicit in my review of the literature and theoretical sketch of relevant propositions. Over three-fourths of the respondents grew up in the central city of a metropolitan area in the continental United States with a population of more than two million; further, most of the respondents came from families of three or fewer children.

The professionals in my study in both law and medicine tended to be concentrated in specialties traditionally labeled "women's specialties": For law, these specialties are domestic relations (divorce, adoption); for medicine, obstetrics and pediatrics. In business, the traditionally "female preserve" is personnel; the evidence in my study was insufficient to indicate any discernible trend toward concentration because, as a result of being in training for their companies, many of the M.B.A.s were assigned to different departments on a rotating basis. Further, at the time of my study, it was not clear as to which area/subdivision of the company they would ultimately be assigned.

Black female professionals share certain problems with professionals in general—obtaining degrees, meeting licensing requirements, meeting professional standards, and the like. In addition, they share concerns specific to blacks—that is, the problem of racial discrimination in hiring and professional advancement.

Although black female professionals share certain problems/issues specific to blacks, this does not mean that black women can be subsumed under the category "black professionals." To do so would obscure crucial differences between black male and black female professionals:

1. From 1940 through 1960, black male professionals were shown to be more widely distributed than black female professionals among the professions; female professionals were highly concentrated in a few occupations such as teaching, and black female professionals appeared to be the most highly concentrated of all sex-race categories [Glenn, 1963: 443-448].
2. Black females have a greater chance of entering profession designated as open to women than black males have of entering profession designated as open to men ;Glenn, 1963: 443-448].

Some sociologists attribute this phenomenon to the "farmer's daughter effect" (Block, 1969: 17-26). That is, like farm families, black families chose to spend their limited resources to educate daughters rather than sons because, since girl ten to do better than boys in school,[61] they have better chance going on for further training, which improves their chances of getting good jobs and/or marrying well when they migrate to urban areas. In addition, given the limited financial resources of the family, the male children are often pressured to contribute to the family resources, which usually leads to their dropping out of school. Another explanation offered by Jackson (1973) seems more plausible: This theoretical tendency among black families to educate their daughters at the expense of their sons[62] may be interpreted as an effort to keep black women away from domestic work[63] which is and has been, in addition to being a position in which black women could "learn the ropes" of white society, a position of sexual vulnerability (Epstein, 1973B:917).

Although black professional women share certain problems specific to women, such as the problems of maternity leave and its ramifications for professional advancement, this does not mean that black women can be subsumed under the category "female professionals," because by so doing crucial difference between black and white professional women would be obscured. Epstein (1973b) argues that one of these differences is that "because these women are black, they are perhaps not perceived as women; … they may be viewed as sexual objects." Sociohistorical evidence indicates that this argument is invalid; indeed, black women have been viewed legally as well as socially in the United States as *sex objects par excellence* (Hernton, 1965)! Rather than one negatively valued ascribed status (race) cancelling out the effect(s) of the other (sex), my evidence indicates that the two operate to the disadvantage of black professional women. The very fact that most of the respondents were unable to distinguish between race and sex as the basis on which they were being discriminated against indicates that these status-discrepant professionals felt that both are operant. Therefore, it seems to me that the crucial differences between black and white professional women are those of expectations and orientations:

1. A greater percentage of black women than white women work after marriage and childbirth; black women work more years of their lives than do their white counterparts, yet their earnings are lower and their unemployment rate greater (Lerner, 1978).[64]
2. Whereas the majority of white middle-and upper-class women the decision to pursue a career is optional, black women are raised with the expectation that whether or not they marry, whether or not they have children, they will work most of their adult lives; "work to them, unlike to white women, is not a liberating goal, but rather an imposed lifelong necessity (Lerner, 1978).

These expectations are consonant with Epstein's (1973b: 923) generalization that "black women are more concerned with the economic rewards of work than are white women." Further, these orientations help to account for the fact that, as a group, black career women feel less guilt than do their white counterparts about spending less time with their family due to the demands their careers place on their time.

During preliminary conversations with black professional women, the older women tended more frequently than did the younger women to attribute any lack of advancement in their career to racial discrimination. Therefore, I expected that the older women as a group—those entering professions before 1965, (the year in which Title VII of the Civil

Rights Act of 1964 went into effect)—would tend to attribute their perceived lack of professional advancement to racial discrimination; if they mentioned sexual discrimination, I expected that it would be subordinate to racial discrimination. As a whole, I expected the younger women to attribute problems of advancement to sexual discrimination;[65] if mentioned, racial discrimination would be secondary.

My findings indicate that the ability to distinguish discrimination based on race from discrimination based on sex is profession-specific; that is, women in business and law are in a better position than their counterparts in medicine to encounter prospective clients and learn why they do not become actual clients. AS one older physician put it, "I know why those who come to me come, but I don't know why those who don't, don't" A young attorney related an anecdote revealing reasons for one potential client seeking counsel elsewhere:

> *A woman obtained my name from the American Bar association and sent her husband to me. He knew that I was a women, but when he arrived and I introduced myself, and he saw that I am black, he said, "I knew you were a woman, but this is too much," and he turned and left.*

This anecdote supports Hughes' finding that there is a status hierarchy in which ascribed status supercedes achieved status; further, it supports my finding that within the ascribed status hierarchy, the status of race supercedes that of sex. Finally, this anecdote does not lend support to Epstein's (1973b: 914) hypothesis that perhaps "two statuses in combination create a new status (for example, the hyphenated status of black-women-lawyer) which may have no established 'price' because it is unique." Quite the contrary it indicates that the "new" status combination does indeed have a price and a very high one: loss of potential client. Thus, contrary to my initial expectations, most respondents—including more than half of the younger respondents—experienced more discrimination on the basis of race than on the basis of sex, although many respondents added that it is often difficult to distinguish between the two, as young women in business describes:

> *Although it's difficult to distinguish between the two, most*
> *days I think it's sexual because I white women experiencing*
> *the same things, I am … In the matter of salaries, you can't*
> *tell whether it is racist or sexist.*

This quote seems more applicable to business than to medicine and law because (1) discrimination on the basis of sex is probably still more widespread in business than in medicine and law, and (2) women in business see more potential clients than do their counterparts in medicine and, perhaps law. This is due to the tendency for prospective consumers to "shop around" less for medical and legal expertise than for business expertise because, generally, by the time they recognize the need for the former, the problem situation already exists and time presses them for a solution. In other words, those using medical and legal services tend to use them in a remedial way (that is, to remedy an already existing situation), whereas consumers of business services tend to use them in a preventive way. That most of the younger respondents—including all those in business—report that they have personally experienced discrimination more on the basis of race than of sex may be attributed to the fact that civil rights gains made in the 1960s are being checked or even reversed; attempts to retard this process are evident in the attribution of greater importance on the part of the respondents to civil rights for black rather than for women." On the other hand, many respondents may believe that civil rights for blacks include civil rights for black women.

My second hypothesis was that whichever from of discrimination they perceived to have most frequently experienced should dictate which of the two liberation movements, the black or the women's, is most important to them in terms of a coping mechanism for their status-discrepant position. Therefore, if a respondent replied that she has experienced more discrimination on the basis of race than of sex, than the Black Liberation Movement was followed by the Women's Liberation Movement was followed by the Women's Liberation Movement. I hypothesized that younger women would be more likely than older women to feel tension because the Black Liberation Movement and the Women's Liberation Movement, because for older women professional success was viewed as "a credit to the race" and hence consonant with the struggle for racial equality. One unintended consequence of Title VII of the Civil Rights Act of 1964 (which prohibits discrimination in employment based on race, color, religion, sex, and national origin; and which covers discrimination by employee unions and employment agencies) was that many people believed it gave a competitive advantage to black females in that prospective employers could get "two minorities for the price of one." Hernton (1965) points out that while this may be true in the most liberal parts of the North (New York City, Washington, D.C., and Chicago—from which the respondents in in my study are drawn), this does not occur as frequently in the South. For the younger women, then, professional success could be viewed as dissonant with the struggle for racial equality, especially if these women are seen as being (and see themselves as being) in direct competition with black males.

Contrary to expectation, for the younger respondents the Black Liberation Movement is more important the Women's Liberation Movement: That is not to say that black professional women are less concerned about the problems they encounter because of their sex than those they encounter because of their race (even assuming that the two can be distinguished, which they often cannot), but that the Black Liberation Movement does a better job of addressing the latter than does the Women's Liberation Movement the former. As it is presently constituted for the most part, the Women's Liberation Movement addresses more problems of non-black than black women; in response to this, the National Black Feminist Organization (NBFO) was formed in New York City in 1972 and presently has chapters in many major metropolitan areas. Because it was relatively new at the time of my pilot study, man respondents were unaware of but expressed interest in the NBFO. Indeed, comparative research in the two feminist organizations—black and white—would increase knowledge of the points of consensus and dissension between the ways in which black and white professional women deal with the problems engendered by status inconsistency.

My third hypothesis concerns the ease with which black women cope with the conflicting role demands of the professional and the "traditional female" roles. My findings support Epstein's claim that black women experience less guilt than white women over the effects on their children working. This claim is based on two considerations:

1. Since a greater percentage of black women work after marriage and childbirth, having adult female members of the household working has been historically and continues to be more usual experience for blacks than for whites.
2. In contrast to the situation of her white counterpart, work for the black women is not an option, but a necessity if her family is to maintain its precarious middle-class status.

Therefore, rather than viewing her work as taking something way from her family, the black professional women view her career as enabling her to make an even greater contribution to her family's stability and hence to its welfare. This is precisely because for black women in general, work is obligatory rather than optional (as it is for their white counterparts). There is no social role toward which there is no ambivalence. Roles vary in the extent to which it is culturally and psychologically permissible to express ambivalence, to discuss or admit negative feelings toward them. Black women feel less ambivalence about working, precisely because they view their careers as consonant rather than dissonant with the maternal role: Their work contributes rather than detracts from the stability of their family. Consequently, I hypothesized that not only is it easier for black women than for white women to cope with the demands of the role of professional and those of the "traditional female role," but among black women viewpoints of the "female" role along a "traditional-feminist" continuum would be divided along age lines: As a group, the older women would fall more toward the feminist end. While this held so far as agreement with the idea that women always have the "option" of being housewives (whether or not they work), most of the women—regardless of age—expressed at least a moderately feminist viewpoint.[67] This deviation from expectation was caused by older women in business and law expressing strongly feminist viewpoints.[68] This, in turn, is probably due to the fact that black women in business and law would be expected to be more sensitive to discrimination against women and would be more likely to espouse less traditional viewpoints than would their counterparts in medicine. Thus, viewpoint of the female role (traditional or feminist) is a function of the age of the respondent and her profession.

Location of respondents according to viewpoint of the female role along the traditional-feminist continuum is necessary, but not sufficient to ascertain how individuals coped with the strain(s) engendered by their status-inconsistency. It was necessary to inquire (1) whether a respondent anticipated problems before marriage in combining marriage, and perhaps motherhood, with career; and (2) the extent to which their expectations affected the amount of strain perceived and the coping mechanism adopted to deal with the strain. The responses vary with the respondent's age and profession, as discussed in the following sections.

1. *Age.* The older black professional women increased the compatibility or decreased the incompatibility of the role demands of professional and "traditional" female (wife and mother) by deciding a priori that marriage and family would take precedence over their career. Perhaps this type of adjustment was necessitated for this group as a whole by the strength of the societal expectations (prevalent during their youth) that a woman should marry and that home is her primary responsibility whether or not she is working. However the lag between the societal definition of women's role ("woman's place is in the home") and certain economic realities (for example, that realization of the American Dream—a house in the suburbs with a two-car garage—requires both husband and wife to work) affects black women less than white women because societal standards concerning women (including standards of beauty) have been and continue to be based on white women. In addition, unlike whites, most black women are raised with the expectation that whether they marry or not, they will be working most of their adult lives. I found evidence for the older women of the self-fulfilling prophecy. Those who decided marriage would take precedence over career found that that expectation materialized. Further, many of these women attributed to this decision their perceived lack of professional progress (for example, :If I hadn't decided that my family would come first, I would be farther along in my career than I am now.") It is difficult to test the accuracy of this perception although support of it is indicated by the following observations:

a. Most of the older women in medicine were in private practice so that they could set their hours to coincide with family needs; they gave this as one of their most important reasons for going into private practice:

b. Older physicians tended to be in general practice or obstetrics and gynecology rather than in areas characterized by longer training and less flexible hours (for example, surgery);

c. Older attorneys stated the desirability of shorter and more flexible work hours and achieved this end by limiting themselves to cases that require the attorney to spend relatively little time in court (such as in adoption or divorce cases) as opposed to the more lucrative but time-consuming cases (such as criminal or anti-trust).

Because they are able to avail themselves to certain options easier that their older counterparts (for example, living with a mate without benefit of clergy, choosing not to have children), the younger respondents on the whole tend to feel the traditional expectations of marriage and motherhood to be less binding upon them. Nevertheless, that traditional expectations are still felt by today's young women is indicated by a young attorney who is married to an attorney.

> *Many women know that what they are doing is intellectually as important as what their husband do, but they still feel guilty about not doing everything and keeping up the house. In the final analysis, it falls on the women's head if the house is messy.*

2. *Profession.* Regardless of age, many respondents maintain that marriage can be combined easier with business and law than with medicine. Most physicians in my study—married and single—concur, and posit marriage to another physician as the best way for them to combine medicine with marriage. This enables their mate to understand, sympathize, and empathize with the demands medicine makes.

Whether or not they share the same profession, most respondents agree that the greater the personal and professional or occupational security of one's mate, the more able and willing he is to accept and encourage a professional wife, which in turn reduced the tension generated by the demands of profession, marriage, and family.

Taking as the dependent variable the strain(s) engendered by the confluence of the demands of the roles of professional and female, the strength of this strain is a function of the relative degree of commitment to each role: The more the commitment to each role, the greater the resulting strain. Commitment to the role of professional is determined by the amount of sunk costs involved (length of time in training, cost of training, and the like) and is profession-specific; commitment to the role of female—at least, as it has been traditionally defined—is more age-specific, in that current societal consensus on the definition of the female role is weakening and more options (for example, scientific and legal advances making birth control a more viable option) are open to the present generation. The independent variable, social support, can come from many sources: the family of procreation in terms of encouragement to continue (as well as to enter) a profession; spouse (which is a function of his own personal and professional security); relatives; outside help hired for household and/or child care tasks; and others with common experiences who will at least discuss common problems (so that these women know their problems result from larger structural constraints rather than from personal idiosyncrasies) and who will articulate and seek solutions to common problems in long run and try to relieve the tensions generated by these problems in the short run.

The study of elite black professional women affords an unusual opportunity to examine a variety of dilemmas and contradictions of status.

NOTES

1. The first Black female admitted to the bar in the United States was not admitted until 1897 (Lutie Lyttle in Topeka, Kansas); the first Black female to become a physician did so in 1864 (Rebecca Lee, Boston, Massachussets). See Lerner (1973).

2. M.L. Ramsdell's study of 600 hours of eight soap operas in 1971-1972 found that 90 percent of the primary white male characters in one program were either doctors or lawyers (Schrank, 1977).

3. Presently, I am in the process of conducting this study on a nationwide basis to ascertain the generalization of these findings.

4. This is contrary to Epstein's argument (1973b) that two statuses in combination create a new status. For a detailed critique of this argument, see Leggon (1979).

5. The fact that my sample consisted solely of Black women born and raised in the United States, whereas Epstein's (1973b) sample included Black women born and raised in the West Indies, accounts for the differences between her findings and mine. These differences are explored in detail in Leggon (1979).

6. Much of the sociological and social psychology literature on women documents this. For example, see Komarovsky (1945, 1950)

7. Jackson (1973) maintains that there appears to be no evidence supporting the systematic preference of Black parents to educate their daughters at the expense of their sons' education or their sons at the expense of their daughters'.

8. Of all the sex-race categories, Black women are most highly concentrated in the category of domestic service.

9. According to Axel (1977), the percentage of total population 16 years of age and over in the labor force is as follows:

LABOR FORCE PARTICIPATION RATES BY AGE, SEX AND RACE

FEMALE	1950	1960	1965	1970	1975
White	n.a.[a]	36.0	37.7	42.0	45.4
Black, other	n.a.[a]	47.2	48.1	48.9	48.7

10. One reason for this expectation was the fact that since sexual discrimination had recently become at that time a "fashionable" topic of discussion in the public arenas (the mass media; the legislature, both state and national), public attention began to focus on, or at least to recognize, the phenomenon of sex discrimination, whereas heretofore, discrimination in the United States usually referred to racial discrimination.

11. Respondents were asked: "Which do you feel is more important, civil rights for Blacks or women?" Forty-four percent of the older women in law and medicine said that civil rights for Black, 44 percent of the older women in law and medicine said that civil rights for Blacks is as important as civil rights for women; and 11 percent of the older civil rights for women is more important than civil rights for Blacks. In contrast, 88 percent of the younger women in law and medicine and 40 percent of the younger women in business said that civil rights for Blacks is more important, while only 11 percent of the younger women in law and medicine said that civil rights for women was more important.

12. Respondents were asked: "What is your reaction to the following statement: 'Even if she has a career, a woman always has the option of being a housewife'? Response categories strongly agree, agree somewhat, somewhat disagree, disagree strongly, and neutral.

13. Respondents were asked to indicate the extent to which their own views approximate the "feminist" or "traditional" viewpoint. The "feminist viewpoint" stresses greater equality and similarity in the roles of men and women than now exist, with greater participation of women in leadership positions in politics, the professions, and business. The "traditional viewpoint" stresses the difference between the roles of men and women, in which women's lives center on home and family and their job participation is in such finds as teaching, social work, nursing, and secretarial service.

REFERENCES

Axel, H. [ed.] A Guide to Consumer Markets 1977/1978. New York: The Conference Board, Inc.

Blau, P. and O.D. Duncan (1967) The American Occupational Structure. New York: John Wiley.

Blumer, H. (1958) "Race prejudice as a sense of group position." Pacific Sociological review (Spring): 3-7.

Bock, W.E. (1964) "Revolution without ideology: the changing place of women in America." Daedalus 93: 658-670.

Dumont, R.G. and W.J. Wilson (1957) "Aspects of concept formation, explication and theory construction in sociology." American Sociological Review 32: 985-995.

Edwards, G.F. (1959) The Negro Professional. New York: Free Press.

Epstein, C.F. (1973a) "Black and female: the double whammy.: Psychology Today (August) 57-61, 89.

————(1973b) "Positive effects of the multiple negative: explaining the success of Black professional women." American Journal of Sociology (January): 913-935.

Ginzberg, E. (1966) "Some changes in the relative status of American non-white: 1940-1960." Phylon 24: 443-448.

Glenn, N.D. (1963) The Presentation of Self in Everyday Life. Garden City, NY: Doubleday.

Gurin, P and E. Epps (1966) "Some characteristics of students from poverty backgrounds attending predominantly Negro colleges in the Deep South." Journal of Negro Education 35: 336-350.

Hernton, C.C. (1965) Sex and Racism in America. New York: Grove Press.

Hughes, E.C. (1945) "Dilemmas and contradictions of status." American Journal of Sociology 50: 353-357.

Jackson, J.J. (1973) "Black women in racist society." in C. Willie (ed.) Racism and Mental Health. Pittsburg: University of Pittsburg Press.

Komarovsky, M. (1945) "Cultural contradictions and sex roles." American Journal of Sociology 52: 184-189.

————(1950) "The functional analysis of sex roles." American Sociology Review 15: 508-516.

Leggon, C.B. (1979) "Some negative effects of the multiple negative." Chicago Circle: University of Illinois. (unpublished)

Lerner, G. [ed.] (1973) Black women in White America: A Documentary History New York: Random House.

McClory, R.J. (1975) "Fewer Black doctors in Chicago: foreign physicians practice in inner city with some bad side effects." The Chicago Reporter 4: 1.

Rossi, A.S. (n.d.) "The roots of ambivalence in American women." Chicago: National Opinion Research Center Study #483, 34 pp.

Schrank, J. (1977) Snap, Crackle and Popular Taste: The Illinois of Free Choice in America. New York: Delta Publishing.

Staples, R.E. (1973) The Black Woman in America: Sex, Marriage and the Family. Chicago: Nelson-Hall.

THE ECONOMIC STATUS OF THE BLACK MALE: A MYTH EXPLODED

BETTY J. COLLIER * LOUIS WILLIAMS

Reality is not directly available to inquiry. This is indeed no less true in the physical sciences as in the social sciences. Yet, particularly in the social sciences, reality becomes the documented product of our perceptions. As such, reality can be reviewed as the consensually validated intersection of logic, axiology, and epistemology. Thus, even when existing evidence is contradictory, beliefs may continue to influence how we perceive certain phenomena. When such beliefs are further corroborated by erroneous facts, the sustained perpetuation of a distorted perception of reality is all but inescapable. This has been especially true relative to conceptions of the differential economic status of black males and females. In particular is the belief that slavery and oppression so structured the economic basis of black existence that the black man could not find work making it necessary for the black woman to assume economic responsibility for the black family (Moynihan, 1965).

This notion of black male economic inferiority has achieved such legitimacy that it is used axiomatically to explain the economic status of the Black family. (See Rose, 1980; McAdoo, 1981a, 1981b). For instance, Lerner (1973), in *Black Woman in White America: A Documentary History*, noted:

> *The black woman is liberated in her own mind, because she has taken on the responsibility for the black family and she works. Black women had to get the labor force, because black men didn't have jobs [p. 586].*

Robert Staples (1973), in the *Black Woman in America*, integrated this assumption into his analysis:

*Although the black man could not find work, the black
woman returned to her familiar job, working in the white
man's kitchen. She scrubbed, coked, and cared for another
woman's children and home in addition to her own. It
was supposedly her ability to obtain this kind of work that
gave the black woman the advantage over the unemployed
black man [p. 18]*

The assumption of the relative disadvantage of the black male has
penetrated black literature and folklore as well. Martha reeves and
the Vandellas summarized an attitude when in 1967 they sang, "He's
shiftless and he's lazy, he's about to drive me crazy, honeychile."

A careful examination of the assumption under consideration
reveals that it is a conclusion based on several presuppositions. The
first of these is the premise that absolutely more black females work than
black males. Such a premise itself implies either that black men have
extremely high levels of unemployment relative to black women or that
black men have dropped out of the labor force. A second premise is a
belief that even black men work, their earnings are not only absolutely
lower relative to white men but also absolutely lower relative to black
women and white women. A subset of this premise is the notion that
a greater percentage of black women hold professional and technical
positions and that black women have more education than black men,
a belief implicit in an assertion by Whitney Young (1964):

*Historically, in the matriarchal Negro society mothers made
sure that if one of their children had a chance for higher
education, the daughter was the one to pursue it [p. 25].*

A third premise is that white employment opportunities have been
closed to black males, employment as a domestic has always been open
to black females.

Another presupposition often included in this reasoning is the belief
that a majority of black families are headed by a woman, this creating a
structure that places economic responsibility for the support of the family
on the female. This assumption is supported by the belief that black
male/female unions are (1) disrupted by extremely high rates of divorce

and separation and (2) prevented by their being a "shortage" of available black men due to variables such as early death rates, imprisonment, and homosexuality (Jackson, 1978; McAdoo, 1981a, 1981b).

Although each of the suppositions mentioned can be subjected to various degrees of refutation (Collier, Arrington and Williams, 1980), they continue to be accepted and disseminated as truth by both black and white researchers and scholars. Central in this dissemination link are students, for they are passive consumers of the knowledge produced by researchers. Therefore, our aim in this study is to examine the validity of these assumptions about the economic status of black males against existing evidence and to compare this evidence with the degree to which university students accept these assumptions. In doing so, we expect to show that many of these assumptions about black ales persist as fact, even though they can shown to be invalid by documented evidence. Finally, we wish to examine the theoretical implications of this persistent discontinuum between perception and reality. First, however, some attention will be given to the sociological process by which beliefs achieve the status of "facts," thereby deterministically intruding into individual and group behavior.

THE SOCIAL CONSTRUCTION OF "FACT"

SINCE Kant, we have understood that all inquiry is "theory-laden." Thus, reality is not *directly* available to inquiry. This is no less true in the physical sciences as in the social sciences. Indeed, modern physical theory adopts a purely pragmatic stance as to whether reality has an *essential* physical structure independent of measurements. Even ignoring the theory-ladenness of "facts" are never *logical* impositions ascribable to irrefutable internal connections. Thus, ultimately, we are driven to the understanding that just as ideas must be situated within facts, so are facts situated within ideas, and both are constituents of reality as apprehended.

In saying this we bypass the interiority-exteriority, subjectivity-objectivity debate about reality that has plagued black scholarship since the 1970s. More simply, we recognize inquiry as an essentially human enterprise. As such, all inquiry—be it into man or into nature—is socially mediated, and the "realities" so constructed are *socially* constructed.

The process by which facts are produced is a complex one. A confluence of spatial-temporal-quality relationships at apprehension is produced as a situated fact existence. Through conscious acts of the inquirer this fact is inscribed in the public record as a constituent of "primary" sources available to other researchers. Although the "fact" as final product for consumption by researchers may initially have been accompanied by an account and critique of the methodology of its production, it is the fact which achieves the status of "truth." It becomes a factual ingredient which combines with other factual ingredients in the hands of researchers to become new "knowledge" about reality. Some facts even transcend their status as mere facts and become lodged in the public consciousness as elements of folklore. At each stop the fact gains in its power to facilitate the maintenance of the status quo in existing social relations by becoming the lenses through which individuals perceive reality and organize behavior.

Within societies by oppression, the system-serving power elites who control the "factories" which produce the various documents recording facts for the public record also control their dissemination and the uses to which such "facts" might be put. Thus, facts are not only socially produced but are ideologically saturated with the context of that production. *Ultimately, reality itself is appropriated to the terms of the dominant system, and whole universes of critical discourse collapse under the weight of "facts."* We note an advanced stage of this process in contemporary American society where certain questions are no longer asked. (even by black social analysts) in that the facts speak so loudly for themselves. The myths that have developed surrounding the economic status of the black male exemplify this process.

THE ECONOMIC STATUS OF THE BLACK MALE: KNOWLEDGE RECONSTRUCTED

As mentioned earlier, a major conceptual package has been socially produced and "bought" by the American population relative to the economic status of the black male. Although each of the suppositions mentioned are generally accepted as truth, existing evidence does not support them. The fact is that more black men than black women participate I the labor force in an absolute and relative sense. That is, not only does a greater percentage of black men participate in the labor force, but there are absolutely more black men working and/or looking for work than black women (U.S. Department of labor, 1980; 22-23, Table A3). In 1980, 73.9% of black men were either working or looking for work as compared with only 55% of black women (Manpower Report of the President, 1974: 253, 256-257). If one examines the labor force participation rates of black men relative to black women in earlier periods, the difference is even greater. In 1954, for example, 85.2% of the black men participated in the labor force compared to 46.1% of black women. If the 1954 sample is narrowed from all black women in this age bracket, the difference in levels of participation is even greater.

These statistics could be challenged on several counts. The most common charge is that government statistics on unemployment do not accurately reflect true rates of joblessness, since many of the hardcore unemployed drop out of the labor market. Unemployment data are also criticized on the basis that they do not take in to account underemployment, as well as on the basis of other problems of data collection and analysis. The assertion herein is that while such criticisms are valid, such factors do not alter the relative differential in the data between black males and black females. Thus, the statistics presented depict a more or less accurate portrait of relative differences in labor force participation and employment between the black male and female in contemporary American society.

If, then, such statistics are accurate, why are assertions such as the one below found both in academic literature as well as casual conversation?

"In the labor market blacks review low wages, are concentrated in low-skill menial occupations, have high unemployment rates, high turnover rates, and low labor force participation rates for males (through high participation of females)." Statements which use the terms "high" and "low" are innately comparative. The comparisons being made are between the labor force participation of black males relative to white males and black females relative to white females. This distinction is rarely made (even by academicians), and it is precisely the failure to underscore the fact that such conclusions are based on comparisons within the same-sex groupings that has contributed to the distortion.

Even when one compares the labor force participation rate of black males with that of white males, however, the difference is slight. In 1954, the labor force participation rate of black males was 0.4% lower than for white males (Myers, 1978). Today it is only 6.2 percentage points lower (U.S. Department of Labor, 1980). The notion of the "high" labor force participation of black females can be attributed to the fact that in 1954, 46.1% of black females either worked or looked for work as compared with 33.3% of white females (Manpower Report of the President, 1974). Today the differential is 3.7% (U.S. Department of Labor, 1980). Because there are absolutely fewer black women than white women, absolutely more white women than black women worked in 1954 and work today.

An examination of the supporting premises mentioned reveal that these, too, for the most part are either statistically distorted truths or false in their entirety. It is true, for example, that black males have median earnings which are 41% less than white males (U.S. Bureau of the Census, 1979a: 4). The earnings of black males, however, have been historically higher than black females (1979a: 4). Today they earn some 50% more (p. 4). Again, it is true that black women in 1978 had 0.9 more years of education than black males (U.S. Bureau of Census, 1979b: 20). It is not correct that black females hold a larger share of professional jobs than black males. Only 5.4% of all females professionals are black, white 8.7% of all male professionals are black. Furthermore, as late as 1977, more than one-third of black females still worked as service workers (U.S. Bureau of Census, 1979a: 188).

It is true that until World War II, a major source of employment of black women was as domestics. This source of work was nevertheless a limited market. A brief glance at income distribution in American society reveals that inequalities in the distribution of income rendered the proportion of more than black men—82.6% of black women compared to 50% of black men.

Although the survey instrument focused on beliefs about the economic status of the black male, social psychological questions were also asked. Almost 83% of the sample believed that there is a "crisis" between black men and black women. The differential pattern of beliefs between males and females continued. Fully 95.2% of males believed a crisis currently exists compared to 79.1% of females. Although more than half of black families are headed by a couple, 83.8% of respondents believed that most black families are headed by a female. The pattern reversed itself, with a slightly greater percentage of females than males holding this belief. Simultaneously, a slightly larger number of males than females believed that black women do not "respect" black women because of their low earning capacity. The figures were 70% and 64.7%, respectively. An overwhelming 91% of the sample believed that there exists twice as many black females as black males, Again, 95% of the males believed this to be true compared with 88% of the females.

Survey results, then, document two phenomena. First, there exists within the system of black education socially distorted knowledge of the socioeconomic status of black males relative to black females. Second, the results indicate that there exists a slight difference in the acceptance of these myths by black males and females. Black males believed existing myths slightly more than black females.

IMPLICATIONS AND CONCLUSIONS

Sparingly, words are echoed which say it does not matter what is believed so long as proper conduct is followed. Psychology, as a science of behavior, supports the assertion that behavior is a direct consequence of convictions and beliefs as well as experiences. Our findings indicate that social scientists are both victims and offenders in perpetuating misconceptions about the differential status of black men and women. More important, however, the role of scholars in the perpetuation of this documented gap between perception and reality demonstrates that researchers and educators must become even more vigilant in their efforts to resist intellectual imperialism by the larger society. The construction of a black social science based on emancipatory theory and leading to liberatory praxis must begin with the reconstruction of social knowledge. The comments herein are reflective of this emerging trend.

NOTES

Moreover, in 87% of two-earner black families, the husband's earnings far exceed the wives. See Hill (1971).

REFERENCES

Collier-Arington, B.J. and L. Williams (1980) "The myth of economic superiority of the black female." Urban Laegue Rev. 5, 1:66-70.

Hill, R.B. (1971) The Strengths of Black Families. New York: National Urban League.

Jackson J. (1978) "But where are the men?" in R. Staples (ed.) The Black Family: Essays and Studies. Belmont, CA: Wadsworth.

———. (1971) "But where are the men?" The Black Scholar (December): 30-41.

Lerner, G. (1973) Black Women in White America: A Documentary History. New York: Vintage.

Manpower report of the President (1974) Civilian Labor Force Participation by Sex and Color, 1954 and 1973. Washington, DC: Government Printing Office.

McAdoo, H.P. (1981a) Black Families. Beverly Hills, CA: Sage

———. (1981b_ "Upward mobility and parenting in middle-income black families." J. of Black Psychology 8, 1:1-22.

Moynihan, D.P. (1965) The Negro Family: The Case for National Action. Office of Policy Planning and Research, U.S. Department of Labor, Washington, DC: Government Printing Office.

Myers, S.J. (1978) "Economic modeling of the black community." Western J. of Black Studies, 2, 2:95.

Rose, L.R. (ed.) (1980) The Black Woman. Beverly Hills, CA:Sage.

Staples, R. (1973) The Black Woman in America. Chicago: Nelson Hall.

Grabiner, Gene and Virginia E. Grabiner, "Where Are Your Papers" 'Operational Zebra' am d Constitutional Liberties." 333.

Grabiner, Virginia E., see Grabiner G.

Grant, William D., "Racial Attitudes of Hearing-Impaired Adolescents."

BLACK WOMEN IN THE ECONOMIC MARKETPLACE: A BATTLE UNFINISHED

DELORES P. ALDRIDGE

A continuing issue facing the nation is the equal employment opportunities of women and minorities. While there can be no denying that some progress has been made, the plight of black women remains particularly acute. Much of the data presented in this work was taken from massive data categorized as nonwhite. However, since constitute between 92.5 and 95.0 percent of the nonwhites in the United States, it is reasonably safe to assume the data pertaining to nonwhites overwhelmingly obtains for blacks. Note, however, the West Indians, Chinese and Japanese are included in much of the nonwhite data, and they are more likely to be in the higher educational and occupational brackets (Epstein 1973, Moynihan 1971). Thus, gains made by black women may not be as great as they appear. Census data reveal that black women hold the least enviable position on the economic ladder, and industry has a marked absence of black women in the professional, technical and managerial levels. This void has been met by the clamor of black women in recent years over their status in America as many demonstrate their profound dissatisfaction over the nature of their relationships to the American economy.

This response might well be expected in view of the fact that employment status and occupation, more than other factors (more than income, education or family background, for example) contribute to the general social status of an individual (Blau and Duncan 1967). In the labor force, the occupation's position in the hierarchy is an important index to the status of the occupant, generally in society (Ferriss 1973). However, one is forced to question whether this is true where black people are concerned. For example, to be black in

White America in and itself constitutes one status irrespective of the individual's occupation, income or education. To be a professor implies a different kind of status. To be a black professor, suggests yet another status. This latter 'status' might apply to both the larger white society and to values in the more immediate black culture.

It is common to hear utterances of how, indeed, black women have all the advantages going for them in terms of obtaining jobs of significant status and climbing the ladder once they are in an already high-status job. Moreover, it is not unusual for black women to be told in all areas of employment: "You have come a long way, baby." such avowals precipitated this study, for I question seriously whether black women have won the battle.

This paper, therefore, examines the participation of black women in the labor force in relation to occupational status, educational attainment and earnings to assess to what extent they have "made it" in the world of work. Though black women are the focus of the presentation, the occupations in which they participate are analyzed in terms of the distribution of all women who work. Further, some special problems facing black women in society accorded by the occupations in which they work, are evaluated in relation to their position in the total U.S. Population.

LABOR FORCE PARTICIPATION

Black women have gained much more access to higher paying positions than they used to have, but they still have a long way to go before achieving full equality within the economic market in the choice of jobs, opportunities for advancement and other matters related to employment and compensation. Much of this discrepancy can be attributed to direct discrimination. However, it is also the result of more subtle and complex factors growing out of cultural patterns that have been characteristic of most societies through the centuries. In either case, because the possibilities open to black women in general are restricted, they too often are not allowed to contribute a full measure of earnings to their families or to maximize their talents.

In 1971, there were 4.1 million black women in the labor force, or, nearly 50 percent of all black women (43 percent of all white women) who were workers. Numerically, however, the number was much smaller than for white women. Black women accounted for nearly 11 percent of all women 16 years of age and over in the population, but about 13 percent of all women workers. And although the overall rate of labor force participation was higher for black than white women, among teenagers the situation was reversed. The difference in labor force participation between black and white women was greater among those in the age group 25 to 34 years—59 and 44 percent respectively (U.S. Women's Bureau 1972).

THE HISTORICAL PERSPECTIVE

Black women have long been accustomed to working outside the home. They worked as domestics, beauticians, school teachers, librarians, social workers, nurses, secretaries, government employees and much less frequently as doctors and lawyers. To marry was not to become fully employed as a housewife as was the case for many white women. Black women were expected to continue to work because, in a society that measured a black worker's worth as less than that of whites, it was necessary that both partners be employed to make ends meet. This made black woman an anomaly in a country where, until recently, the idealized female role was solely that of homebound wife and mother (Dewitt 1974).

The choice of staying at home or entering the labor force as never a real one for most black women. The casual factor underlying their entrance into the labor force in the past—necessity—continues to exist. However, there have been several developments which have made paid work outside the home an increasingly profitable venture. Other factors are: (1) The increased rate of industrial production, particularly since World War II, which has created a greater demand for labor. The gross private domestic product increased at an annual average rate of 2.2 percent during 1955-60, but stepped up to an annual average rate of 4.8 percent during 1960-65; (1) The Civil Rights Movement and legislation on fair employment practices which was exacerbated by black aggression of the 1960's; (3) The educational attainment of black women has been increasing, thereby improving their employability; (4) Black women have to a large extent always been dependent upon themselves (by choice or necessity) and are becoming even more so, as evidenced by (a) an increase in the portion of single black women, (b) a slight increase since 1960 in the percent of families and households with black female heads (Ferriss 1973, Jackson 1971).

THE WORKING BLACK WOMAN TODAY

Although the decisions of individual women to work outside the home are undoubtedly based on many different factors, the economic factors seem to be overriding importance. The necessity to support oneself or others is one obvious reason but, surprisingly, black adult single women and women who have been separated from husbands or widowed are less likely to be in labor force that are those black women with husbands (U.S. Women's Bureau 1972).

The increase in earnings opportunities, which proved to be such a powerful factor influencing the secular growth of women's participation in the labor force, is a similarly powerful factor influencing the pattern of women's participation at any given time. Thus, education and other training which affect the amount a woman can earn are strongly related to women's work patterns. The importance of education is such that, whether a woman is single, married or separated, the more education she has, the more likely she is to work (U.S. Women's Bureau 1973:95).

Although the probability that a black woman will work seems to vary with education and presence of children in much the same way as it does for all women, there is one very striking difference: the labor force participation of black women is higher. Marked differences are observed when the comparison of labor force participation is confined to married women living with their husbands. In March 1971, about 53 percent of black wives were in the labor force compared to 40 percent of white wives. However, it should be remembered there that numerically there are fewer black wives than white wives. One important reason why this difference in percentages between white and black working wives prevail may be that the earnings of black wives are closer to their husbands than is the case among white married couples. In 1971, black married women worked year-round, full time earned 73 percent as much as black married men who worked year-round, full time. Among whites the percentage was only 51 percent. Behind these relationships is that fact that black men earn considerably less than white men, while black women's earnings are much closer to white women's earnings (U.S. Women's Bureau 1073:96).

OCCUPATIONAL STATUS AND BLACK WOMEN

As mentioned earlier, one of the most important indices of social status is the occupational position one holds, but this has been obscured with respect to blacks who have a singularly constricting status-race. Their status of race tends to dilute whatever other indicators of status are used in measuring their social positions. Clearly, the occupational patterns of black women have witnessed some change over the past three decades. Slowly they are coming into line with white force; but the battle is far from over. The most dramatic and important movement has been away from agriculture. In Table 1, the percentage of black and white women are compared in ten major occupational categories for 1910, 1940, 1950, 1960 and 1970. The data indicate that in 1910, over 85 percent of black women were employed as agricultural laborers or domestics as contrasted with about 25 percent white women in the same occupation.

Between 1910 and 1940, the occupational progress of black women was extremely slight. Although the proportion of black women employed as agricultural laborers declined by nearly three-fourths, apparently many of them moved out of agriculture positions into domestic service as the proportion engaged in the latter showed an increase exceeding 50percent between 1910 and 1940. Such a move was but a horizontal one, for both occupations were equally low in terms of remunerations. White women made significant gains during the same time span. The proportion of white women employed as clerical and sales personnel nearly doubled, reaching one-third of the white female labor force. In addition, the already small proportion engaged in domestics showed a decrease of nearly 4 percent in contrast to the increase among black women.

The decade of the 1940's was more favorable for black women in terms of occupational gains than was the period of 1910-1940. The proportion of black women employed in clerical and sales positions quadrupled, but even so was at only one-twentieth of the total black female labor force. The proportion employed as semi-skilled operatives in manufacturing rose two and one-half times, while the percentage engaged in domestic work declined by 30 percent.

Table 1. Occupational Status of Women 14 Years of Age and Over by Race for 1910, 1940, 1950, 1960 and 1970

Occupational Category	1910 Black	1910 White	1940 Black	1940 White	1950 Black	1950 White	1960 Black	1960 White	1970 Black	1970 White
Professional and Technical	1.5	11.6	4.3	14.7	5.3	13.3	7.7	14.1	10.0	15.5
Managers Officials and Proprietors except Farm	.2	1.5	.7	4.3	1.3	4.7	1.1	4.2	1.4	4.7
Clerical and Sales	.3	17.5	1.3	32.8	5.4	39.3	9.8	43.2	21.4	43.4
Craftsmen and Foremen	2.0	8.2	.2	1.1	.7	1.7	.7	1.4	.8	1.1
Operatives	1.4	21.2	6.2	20.3	15.2	21.5	14.3	17.6	16.8	14.5
Non-Farm Laborers	.9	1.5	.8	.9	1.6	.7	1.2	.5	.9	.4
Private Household Workers	38.5	17.2	59.9	10.9	42.0	4.3	38.1	4.4	19.5	3.7
Service Workers except Private Household	3.2	9.2	11.1	12.7	19.1	11.6	23.0	13.1	28.5	15.1
Farmers and Farm Managers	4.0	3.1	3.0	1.1	1.7	.6	.6	.5	.2	.3
Farm Laborers and Foremen	48.0	9.0	12.9	1.2	7.7	2.3	3.5	1.0	.3	1.3

Source: Data for 1910 from U.S. Bureau of Census, 1940 Census of population, Comparative Occupation Statistics for the United States 1870-1940, Table 15, pp. 166-172. Data for 1940 from U.S. Bureau of the Census 1940 Census Population, Volume III, The Labor Force, Table 52, pp. 87-88. Data for 1950 from U.S. Bureau of the Census of Population, Occupational Characteristics, Table 3, pp. 29-37, Washington D.C., 1953 Data for 1960 from U.S. Bureau of the Census, 1960 Census of Population, Occupational Characteristics, Table 3, pp. 11-21, Washington, D.C., 1963, Data for 1970 from U.S. Bureau of the Census, Social and Economic Characteristics of the Population in Metropolitan and Nonmetropolitan Areas: 1970 and 1960 Current Population Reports U.S.

Government Printing Office: Washington, D.C., 1971 and U.S. Bureau of the Census, The Social and Economic Status of the Black Population in the United States, 1972. Current Population Reports, Series P-23, No. 48. Washington, D.C. Government Printing Office.

From 1950 to 1970, the occupational distribution of black women continued to change marked by appreciable gains. By 1970, there were proportionately nearly four times as many black women employed as clerical and sales workers as in 1950. The percentage of black professional women doubled, while the relative number of domestics declined by more than 50 percent. Nevertheless, the number in this category is still small as compared to white women and white men. Black women are not primarily in white collar occupations as is the case for white women. Too many black women (19.5 percent) are still cleaning white women's houses. Much of whatever gains made can be attributed to the relatively high level of economic activity in

the postwar period, the militant civil rights efforts and subsequent government legislation in the sixties. Additionally, considerable educational gains for black women permitted them to take advantage of available opportunities. However, with the increasing numbers of black females attending colleges and universities, one would expect a more dramatic increase in the percentage of those employed in professional and technical occupations than has been the case.

EDUCATION AND OCCUPATION

It is significant to look at education, even though it has not been accompanied by the increases in top level occupations as it might have been. Like the pattern for whites over 25, black women currently in the labor force have had more median years of schooling than black men, and more of them have been high school graduates. Furthermore, although black men in college now exceed black women, more black women over 25 are college graduates than are men in this age group (Epstein 1973). This fact does not hold for white women, where the case has been that of white men obtaining the college degrees.

While the general measure of high school education is significant in relation to work force, there is little question that higher education is an important determinant of the participation of women in more lucrative employment (Blitz 1974:34). Thus, the educational gains made by black women in part account for their growing access to better positions in the labor market. Epstein (1973) makes this point with respect to black women and professional jobs. However, the gains with respect to white women had graduated from college as black women. By 1970, black women had closed the gap to 353 percent, as reflected in Table 2.

Table 2. Level of Education for Black and White Women in the Labor Force, 1940-70

	Black	White	Black	White	Black	White
1940	7.0	11.7	23.8	4.1	2.0	7.4
1952	8.1	12.1	22.4	2.9	3.6	8.3
1957	9.6	12.2	15.7	2.4	4.3	8.4
1959	9.4	12.2	12.2	2.2	4.6	8.5
1962	10.5	12.3	9.8	2.1	6.7	10.0
1965	11.1	12.3	6.7	1.7	7.8	10.3
1968	11.7	12.4	5.9	1.3	7.8	10.9
1970	12.1	12.5	4.5	1.1	8.1	11.1

Source: Data for 1940 from U.S. Bureau of census, 1940 Census of Population, Volume of Education. Table 17, pp. 75-81, Table 13, pp. 82-85, Washington, D.C., U.S. Government Printing Office. 1943. data for 1952-70 from U.S. Department of Labor, Manpower Report of the President, 1971. Washington, D.C. U.S. Government Printing Office, 1971.

In 1970, an interesting phenomenon surfaced. Black women with relatively high levels of education earned more than white women with comparable levels of education, as seen in Table 3. How is this to be explained? In terms of more fulltime, full-year employment for black than white women? According to the 1960 Census of Population among professional women (mainly occupations requiring some college, and usually college graduation), a higher proportion of whites, 39 percent, worked a full year as compared to about 37 percent for black women. Further, in 1970, 40 percent of all white women worked fulltime, the same proportion as black women (U.S. Bureau of the Census 1971).

Perhaps the explanation is to be found in the fact that 54 percent of all black female professional workers were employed as teachers, as compared to only 39 percent for white female professional workers. And, teaching is a profession in which seniority is directly related to earnings. Data indicate that occupational mobility rates for black women who graduated from college are only 40 percent that of white women (Saben1967). Accordingly, more blacks likely remain with one employer and thus earn higher incomes due to seniority relative to white women.

Indicative of the data in Table 3 is that the ration of black to white earnings has increased for all levels of education from 1950-1970, and that as one moves up the educational ladder, the ratio of black to white income rises. While this suggests that there is less racial discrimination along economic lines against relatively well-educated black women than poorly-educated black women, it may raise another question. Is the decreasing discrimination toward black women reflective of continued or increasing discrimination of black men? Or, is, in fact, discrimination on the way out with respect to all race-sex groups?

Table 3. Income of Black and White Women 25 Years and Over by Years of Education for 1950, 1960, and 1970

Years of Education	1950		Percent Black/ White	1960		Percent Black/ White	1970		Percent Black/ White
	Black	White		Black	White		Black	White	
0-7	$490	$710	69	$732	$1090	87	$1290	$1440	90
8	734	925	80	970	1180	82	1605	1815	86
9-11	807	1110	73	1196	1680	71	2393	2388	100
12	1093	1590	69	1732	2220	78	3491	3380	103
13-15	1247	1680	74	2166	2420	90	4558	3616	126
16 or More	2103	2320	91	3740	3770	99	7744	5995	129

Source: Data from 1950 from U.S. Bureau of Census, 1950 Census of Population, Volume on Education, Table 12, pp. 108-127, Washington, D.C., U.S. Government Printing Office, 1953. Data for 1960 from U.S. Bureau of the Census, 1960 Census of Population, Educational Attainment, Table 7, pp. 112-135, Washington, D.C.: U.S. Government Printing Office, 1963. Data for 1970 from U.S. Department of commerce Current Population Reports, Consumer Income Series, P-60, NO. 80, Income in 1970 of Persons and Families in the United States, Washington, D.C., U.S. Government Printing Office, 1971, Table 49, p. 109.

EARNINGS IN THE LABOR FORCE

One of the most direct indicators of economic status is annual income. The low position of black women in the occupation hierarchy is indicated by their low median income in comparison with men and white women. The discrepancies between the earnings of black women and those of white women and men persist. However, the gap has been narrowing (U.S. Bureau of the Census 1969). In 1939, the median wage and salary income of black women was $246, about one-third that of white women and by 1959 it was still only half as much (U.S. Department of Commerce 1971:129). But in the decade of the 1960's, considerable improvement in the economic status of black women took place. Thus, in 1970, the median wage or salary income of fully employed black women was $3,285 or about 85 percent as much as that of white women and 71 percent as much as that of black men (U.S. Women's Bureau 1972:9). Much of the gains are perhaps directly related to the increasing education of black women. Civil Rights Acts of the 1960's and a relatively healthy labor market up to 1970-71.

The yearly earnings statistics indicate that from 1939-58 the income of black men and women increased at the same rate, but that during the 1960's the income of black women climbed much faster than the income of black men. Accordingly, while black women earned only 39 percent as much as black men in 1959, the earnings of the former increased to 71 percent of the earnings of the latter in 1970.

In 1970, as at every point in American history, black women earned less than white women (with the exception of the highly educated) who, in turn, made less than white or black men. This economic distribution is constant for every category of workers. Of course, that can be attributed to scarcity of any other race-sex group in this work category. These wage differentials, although illustrating the situation of black women, forces an appraisal of black men and their predicament vis-à-vis white men.

RACE-SEX DIFFERENTIALS IN EARNINGS

Looking at the income comparison of white and black men, the statistics are less favorable. From 1945 to 1966, black men earned about 60 percent of the income of white men. Since 1966, black male earnings have increased somewhat faster than the earnings of white males. However, in 1970 black men earned an average of $5,485 from wages and salaries, still one-third less than the $8,254 received by white males (U.S. Department of Commerce 1971:129).

The slow growth in the earnings of black men cannot be accounted for by the lack of growth in their average educational attainment. In fact, from 1952-1970 the median years of education of black men in the labor force increased 3.9 years compared to a gain of 1.6 years for white men (U.S. Department of Labor 1971:244).

A plausible explanation is that employers have preferred to hire black women instead of men because women have always come with a cheaper salary tag. It is also believed in some quarters that a sense of the threat of black men as colleagues and thus intellectual equals has prevented white men from "opening the door" to the potential enemy (Epstein 1973). Moreover, the hiring of black females allows the firm to technically fill two quotas at the same time—sex and Civil Rights Act regarding racial and sexual discrimination in hiring. Therefore, economically this is a smart move.

SOME SPECIAL PROBLEMS OF THE BLACK WORKING WOMAN

Although slowly bettering their loss in terms of better occupational positions, increased earnings and higher schooling, black women have some special problems vis-à-vis all other race-sex groups. They have steadily closed the economic gap in relation to white women, but then, white women compromise but another exploited group so that goals cannot be established with respect to them. It has been suggested that the problem is to close the gap between black women and white men—the possessors of the greatest economic status in the labor force.

But if this is done, then the black women and white men will be the oppressors. The real problem is to change the system so that it ceases to be racist, chauvinistic or capitalistic.

The issue of teaming up with white women in the Women's Revolution Movement is a debatable one. For white women are aiming to get a greater hold on the top-level positions, never having paid any dues in the really low-status jobs. They are ready to come out of the home and take over executive suites while black women have long been in the economic marketplace in large proportions. According to Epstein (1973), black women have no real need to join white women in the struggle for professional jobs—jobs which command the greatest economic status. She states that black women constitute a larger proportion of the black professional community than women in the white professional world. Furthermore, black women are found in professions and occupations known to be hold is attributed to the likelihood that they are more likely to be perceived as serious professionals and not as sexual objects simply women out to get husbands.

While there is agreement that both white and black women need freedom from the white man since he is the "oppressor," there is also black consensus to let white women worry about their own sex hang-ups with white men (Hare and Hare 1970:180).

It is perhaps psychologically easier to deal with the problems concerning white men and women than those relating to the black male. Nevertheless, this is one problem that black women will have to resolve as they continue their battle for economic equality in the labor force.

> *Black men are generally recognized by black women to have been on the rise in recent years, but many women also feel that black men believe they have failed their roles and need to be "helped along" toward full manhood. The black woman anticipates that the rejection of the traditional female role would be psychologically threatening to the black male. She must encourage him and lay as much groundwork for black liberation as he will let her. It is necessary to be patient with black men whenever they engage in symbolic manliness. She must not dominate but merely assist strongly (Hare and Hare 1970:279).*

Some blacks share the view that successful black working women are competitors to black men or at least impediments to the progress of black men (Dewitt 1974:18). Proponents of this view feel that black women should stay in the background, while black men assume significant and primary positions, thus dispelling the image of a matriarchal black society. This suggestion is rooted in western standards and implies that there is only one alternative to the issue. This is fallacy. Still others argue that black women are creative equals to black men, and they have a right, indeed, an obligation, to maximize their skills and abilities (Jackson 1973).

If one is to be guided by the data presented in this paper, it is apparent that black women have only gradually made appreciable gains and no doubt at great costs. Therefore, while they can and do empathize with black men, they are still members of the most exploited group of workers in the American labor force and would strike a negative blow for themselves and black in general were they not to use their skills and work experiences toward continued gains but who goes at all toward the singular goal of liberations for black people. Black men and women must ever be moving forward for the good of all black people.

CONCLUSIONS

Black women have fought against formidable obstacles in the labor force. Undoubtedly, they have not been unscathed by the limits set upon their entry and promotion through the ranks. They have made some gains even though they remain at the bottom of the economic ladder. They continue to be heavily concentrated I service and lower-level occupations, but they are also increasing as a percent of the employees in professional occupations. As a percent of the total in each occupation they are increasing, especially among clerical workers and "other service" occupations, while proportionate increases in the more remunerative professional and technical occupations are at a much slower pace.

Much of the gains made by black women may be attributed to triple force: the Civil rights Movement, educational attainments and a lively and expanding economic market in the last several decades. However, while trends are favorable the position of black women workers is still a precarious one. Black women, as a group, are still very vulnerable to economic changes, despite improvement during recent years in their educational attainment and occupational status. The need continues to exist for increased stress on providing equal employment and training opportunities for black women who cannot afford to get caught up in issues centering around being background figures in deference to black men in the world of work. Black women continue to be plagued by their sex and race with the line often being blurred as to which is more damnable. They must continue to move ahead toward the singular goal of achieving economic parity with those at the top of the economic ladder—white men. The battle of black working women within our overall struggle for liberation is yet an unfinished one.

REFERENCES

Blau, P. and Duncan, O.D. 1967. *The American Population Structure.* New York: John Wiley and Sons, Inc.

Blitz, R.C. 1974. "Women in the Profession, 1870-1970." *Monthly Labor Review* (May):34-39. Washington, D.C.: Department of Labor.

Dewitt, K. 1974. Black Women in Business." *Black Enterprise 5* (August): 14-19.

Epstein, C. 1973. "Positive Effects of the Multiple Negative: Explaining the Success of Black Professional Women." *American Journal of Sociology* 79 (April):912-935.

Ferriss, A.L. 1973. *Indicators of Trends in the Status of American Women.* New York: Russell Sage Foundation.

Hare N. an Hare J. 1970. "Black Women 1970," Pp. 178-181 in Judith M. Bardwick (ed.). *Readings on the Psychology of Women.* New York: Harper and Row Publishers.

Jackson, J.J. 1973. "Are Black Women Creative Equals to Black Men?" *Essence* (November): 56-72. 1971 "But Where Are the Men?" *Black Scholar* (December): 30-41.

Moynihan, D.P. 1971. "Employment, Income, and the Ordeal of the Negro Family." *Essays and Studies.* Belmont, California: Wadsworth Publishing Co., Inc.

Sabern, S. 1967. "Occupational Mobility of Employed Workers." *Monthly Labor Review* 90(June):2—15.

U.S. Bureau of the Census. 1973. *The Social and Economic Status of the Black Population in the United States,* 1972. Current Population Reports, Series P-23, No. 46, Washington, D.C.: Government Printing Office 1-379.

1972. *General Social and Economic Characteristics.* Final Report, D.C.C17-C1. U.S. Summary. Washington, D.C.: Government Printing Office 1-379

1971. *Social and Economic Characteristics of the Population in Metropolitan and Nonmetropolitan Areas:* 1970 and 1960. Current Population Reports, Special Studies. Washington, D.C.: U.S. Government Printing Office.

1969. *The Social and Economic Status of Negroes in the United States, 1969.* Washington, D.C.: U.S. Government Printing Office.

1963a. *Educational Attainment.* Table 7:112-135. Washington, D.C.: Government Printing Office.

1963b. *Occupational Characteristics.* Table 3:11-21. Washington, D.C.: U.S. Government Printing Office.

1953a. *Occupational Characteristics.* Table 3:20-37. Washington, D.C.: U.S. Government Printing Office.

1943a. *Comparative Occupation Statistics for the United States* 1870-1940. Table 15:166-172. Washington, D.C.: U.S. Government Printing Office.

1943b. 1940 Census of the Population. Volume on Education. Table 13 and Table 17:75-85.

U.S. Department of Commerce. 1971. Income in 1970 of Families and Persons in the United States. Current Population Reports, Income Series P-60, No. 80. Table 49:109. Washington, D.C.: U.S. Government Printing Office.

U.S. Department Labor. 1971. Manpower Report of the U.S. President, 1971. Washington, D.C.: U.S. Government Printing Office.

1967. Negro Women in the Population and the Labor Force. Washington, D.C.: U.S. Government Printing Office.

U.S. National Center for Health Statistics. 1967. Suicide in the United States 1950-1964. Public Health Service Publication 1000, Series 20,

No.5. Washington, D.C.: U.S. Department of Health, Education and Welfare.

U.S. Women's Bureau. 1973. The Economic Role of Women. Reprinted from Economic Report of the President, 1973. Washington, D.C.: U.S. Department of Labor.

1972. Facts on Women Workers of Minority Races. Washington, D.C.: U.S. Department of Labor.

1945. Negro Women War Workers. Bulletin 205. Washington, D.C.: U.S. Government Printing Office.

CHAPTER SIX
Religious Issues

James Cone provides a backdrop for understanding the relationship of black theology, black churches, and black women to feminism in different historical periods. He cautions black male ministers and theologians about responsibilities they have in church that affect how women are received and what opportunities are made available to them for the fullest development of their potential for service to God in the church and in society. He ends with suggestions for black men and black women of the church to work more effectively toward the development of each other.

Jacquelyn Grant's work is unique in its data-based focus upon the subsidiary role played by black women in the black church. What is ironical is the non-recognition among scholars of the new black theology to recognize sexism as a viable topic to be confronted. She, like Cone, is particularly adept at shedding new light on the relationship of black men and women in the church and the challenge that black theology faces.

BLACK THEOLOGY, BLACK CHURCHES, AND BLACK WOMEN

JAMES CONE

> *Oh how careful ought we to be, lest through our bylaws of church government and discipline we bring into disrepute even the word of life. For as unseemly as it may appear nowadays for a woman to preach, it should be remembered that nothing is impossible with God. And why should it be thought impossible, heterodox, or improper for a woman to preach, seeing the Savior died for the women as well as the man?*
>
> Reverend Jerena Lee, 1836[1]

> *We'll have our rights. See if we don't. And you can't stop us from them. See if you can.*
>
> Sojourner Truth, 1853[2]

> *To be a woman, black, and active in religious institutions in the American scene is to labor under triple jeopardy.*
>
> Theressa Hoover[3]

> *If theology, like the church, has no word for black women, its conception of liberation is inauthentic.*
>
> Jacquelyn Grant[4]

Although black male theologians and church leaders have progressive and often revolutionary ideas regarding the equality of blacks in American society, they do not have similar ideas regarding the equality of women in black church and community. Why is it that many black men cannot see the analogy between racism and sexism, especially in view of the fact that so many black women in the church and in society have expressed clearly their experience of oppression? What is it that blinds black men to the truth regarding the suffering of their sisters? What is it that makes black churchmen insensitive to the pain of women suffering that we have inflicted on them?

Of course, many black men, like whites in relations to racism, would deny that they are sexist. But an emphatic denial of being prejudiced against black women is no proof that black men are free of sexism: seldom capable of developing criteria to test whether it has been eliminated. The person's best capable of evaluating sexism in the black community and church are black women who are feminists and thus engaged in the struggle to eliminate it from our community. Black churchmen today need not be surprised by militant female voices: black church women have been speaking out for a long time.

NINETEENTH-CENTURY FEMINISM IN THE BLACK CHURCH

Black feminism was developed in the context of the abortionist movement and the rise of white feminism in the second half of the nineteenth century. It is especially important for black men to note that Frederick Douglass, the great abortionist, was also an outspoken advocate of women's right.[5] He was one of the first to see the connection between the freedom of African slaves and the liberation of women. That was why he attended the first women's rights convention, in Seneca Falls, New York, in 1848. Without his unqualified support, the controversial resolution of that convention on women's suffrage would not have been approved.

Nineteenth-century black women did not remain silent on the issue of women's rights. Like white women who became accurately aware of sexism during their involvement in the abolitionist movement, black women also developed a similar consciousness. Sojourner Truth was one of their most outstanding advocates. A former slave, the attended several women's right conventions, giving her support to the cause. She is best known for her famous "Ain't I a Woman?" speech, delivered at the women's convention in 1851 in Akron, Ohio. One clergyman, who spoke at the convention, told women "To beware of selling their birthright of consideration and deference for a mess of equality pottage. What men," he asked, "would help a political or business rival into a carriage, or lift her over a ditch?[6] to which Sojourner replied:

> *That man over there says that women need to be helped into everywhere. Nobody ever helps me into carriages, or over mudpuddles, or gives me any best place! And ain't I am woman? Look at me! Look at my arm! I have ploughed, and planted, and gathered into barns, and no man could head me! And ain't I am woman? I could work as much and eat as much as a man—when I could get it—and bear the lash as well! And ain't I am woman? I have borne thirteen children and seen them most all sold off to slavery, and when I cried on with my mother's grief, none but Jesus heard me! And ain't I am woman?[7]*

Another preacher in the same convention had claimed superior rights and privileges for men on the grounds of the manhood of Christ. "If God had desired the equality of women," he said, "he would have given some token of his will through the birth, life, and death of the Savior."[8] To which Sojourner responded:

> *"That little man in black there, he says women can't have as much rights as men, because Christ wasn't a woman!" Then she paused, with her burning eyes focused on the minister who had made the comment: "Where did your Christ come from?" She repeated her question, "Where did your Christ come from?" Then she answered her own question, her voice ringing like an organ with all the stops pulled: "From God and a woman! Man had nothing to do with him."[9]*

Sojourner concluded her speech with the observation that "if the first woman God ever made was strong enough to turn the world upside down all alone, these women together ought to be able to turn it back, and get it right side up again! And now they are asking to do it, the men better let them."[10]

When there was a debate about black men receiving the right to vote but not women, Sojourner shared the sentiment of other women's right activists who strongly objected seeing it as a bonding of white and black men against women of both colors:

> *There is a great stir about colored men getting their rights, but not a word about colored women; and if colored men get theirs, and not colored women theirs, you see the colored men will be the masters over the women, and it will be just as bad as before. So, I am for keeping the thing going while the things are stirring; because if we wait till it is still, it will take a great while to get it going again."11*

Sojourner Truth was not only nineteenth-century black woman to stand up for women's rights. Harrier Tubman was called the "Moses" of her people because of her leading more than three hundred slaves to freedom. She also attended several women's suffrage conventions and became involved in the National Federation of Afro-American Women. Ida B. Wells-Barnett, a journalist and graduate of Rust College, is best known for her solitary campaign against lynching and her involvement in the work of black club women. Mary Church Terrell, a leading club woman, organized the National Association of Colored Women (1897) and was elected its first president. She was also a charter member of the NAACP (1909), a suffragist and close friend of Susan B. Anthony and Jane Adams, Francis Ellen Watkins Harper, also a club woman and feminist, was a founder and vice president of the National Association of Colored Women.

It is important to note that black women, unlike black men and white women, could not choose between the issues of sexism and racism: they were victims of both. Black feminists today call it double jeopardy. White feminists and abolitionist parted ways at the 1869 meeting of the Equal Rights Association, because of the latter's support of the Fourteenth and Fifteenth Amendments, which excluded franchise for women. White feminists could afford to ignore racism, just as black men could sexism. But black women fought for both rights.[12]

Black women in the church had an additional burden, which led Theresa Hoover to call it triple jeopardy.[82] Although black churches agreed with Sojourner truth, Harriet Tubman, Ida Wells, and other black women regarding the abolition of slavery, lynching, and other forms of white racism, they rejected their views on women's rights.

Black church attitudes toward women ministers were similar to those of white denomination in comparison with some other independent black churches, women were not permitted ordination in the nineteenth century. They were permitted only to exhort and preach without a license. Largely because of their insistence that they were called by God to preach the gospel, the offices of stewardess and deaconess were created in 1868 and 1900, respectively. Although some AME ministers licensed women to preach, the denomination did not make it official until 1884 and limited their preaching to the subordinate office of "evangelist."

Bishop Henry McNeal Turner was publicly reprimanded for ordaining a woman to preach. Later the 1888 General Conference made its position clear:

> *Whereas Bishop H. M. turner has seen fit to ordain a woman to the order of a deacon; and whereas said act is contrary to the usage of our church, and without precedent in any other body of Christians in the known world; and as it cannot be proved by the scriptures that a woman has ever been ordained to the order of the ministry; therefore be in enacted, that the bishops of the African Methodist Episcopal Church be and hereby [are] forbidden to ordain a woman to the order of deacon or elder in our church.*[13]

Despite the limitations placed on black women ministers, several distinguished themselves. Jarena Lee, the first female preacher in the AME Church, was one of the most prominent. Born in 1783, she recorded the story of her conversion and call to preach in *The Life and religion Experience of Jarena Lee.* When she told Richard Allen about her call to preach, his reply was" "As to women preaching…. our discipline knew nothing at all about it—that it did not call for women preachers."[14] But Jarena Lee asked: "If the man may preach, because the Savior died for him, why not the woman, seeing he died for her also? Is he not a whole Savior, instead of a half one, as those who hold it wrong for a woman to preach would seem to make it appear?"[15] Because of her persistence, Allen accepted her as a women preacher even though he did not ordain her. In one year, she traveled over two thousand miles and delivered 178 sermons.

There were other black women of the nineteenth century whose call to the ministry outweighed the rules defined by the black male clergy. When asked "by what authority" she "spoke against slavery" and whether she had been ordained, a woman named Elizabeth replied that although she had not been "commissioned of men's hands, if the Lord had ordained me, I needed nothing better."[16] As black male ministers continue to reject them outright or forced upon them "the extra burden of proving their call," black women found ways to respond to God's call to preach the gospel.

It can be concluded that black churches were similar to white churches in their attitudes toward women during the nineteenth century. The same was true of the black community as a whole at that time.

BLACK FEMINISM IN THE CIVIL RIGHTS AND BLACK POWER ERA

The recent struggle of black women in the churches has drawn not only upon nineteenth-century sources but upon feminist outcry of the 1960s and '70s. The language used to name women's oppression, as suggested in such terms as "patriarchy," "misogyny," and "seism," was developed first by women in the white community. White women initially created the language of contemporary radical left white male groups, such as the Students for a Democratic Society (SDS).[17]

For black women, however, white feminism was not always adequate or appropriate, partly because feminism was sometimes racist and partly because patriarchy had distinctive characteristics in the struggle for racial freedom. Women seldom received the credit they deserved for contributions to the freedom movement of the late 1950s and '60s. They sometimes served as symbols for a brief time, as in the case of Rosas Parks, but seldom did men acknowledged their role in any substantive decision-making process.

Most persons do not know that Ella Baker served as the first executive director of the SCLC and that she was responsible for the founding of the SNCC in the spring of 1960.[18] Many do not know of Anna A. Hedgeman and the role she played in putting race the agenda of the NCC.[19] Seldom mentioned are the contributions of Fanne Lou Hamer in Mississippi,[90] Daisy Bates in the 1957 crisis at Little Rock Central High School,[21] Ruby Doris Robinson and Diana Nash Bevel in the SNCC.[22] Only men—Martin Luther King, Jr., Malcolm X, Andrea Young, Stokely Carmichael, James Forman, and others like them—are given major recognition for their achievements in the black freedom struggle. The invisibility of black women in the freedom movement and the hostility of black men toward women's equality helped drive women to form their own feminist organizations.

A more blatant display of black patriarchy in the struggle for black power was the inordinate emphasis on violence and masculine assertiveness, the stress on black women's passivity and weakness, and the glorification of the pimp and the black male's sexual exploits in such movies as Melvin Van Peeble's *Sweet Sweetback's Baadasssss Song* (1971) and his Broadway play *Ain't Supposed to Die a Natural Death* (1973). In his book, *Soul on Ice* (1968), Eldridge Cleaver thematized rape as a political act, and other black male so-called revolutionaries followed suit. Most of the plays, novels, and movies that were created by black men during the civil rights and black power revolution of the 1960s accented patriarchal values similar to those in white society.

For many black men, freedom meant the assertion of their manhood, which they identified as violence against the black man with guns, rape of the white women, and unlimited physical and mental brutality against the black women. Inasmuch as black women were the most accessible and least capable of defending themselves, black men often made black women victims of displaced anger, doing to their sisters what they really wanted to do white society.

No one was more influential in defining the black consciousness movement than Amiri Baraka, formerly called LeRoi Jones, by his writings and speeches, and in the organizations he headed. But, as is the case of many other radical black men, Baraka's sexism created contradictions in his nationalist philosophy. On one occasion he was asked whether a militant black man could have a white woman companion, and he replied:

> *Jim Brown put it pretty straight and this is really quite true. He says that there are black men and white men, then there are women. So, you can indeed be going through a black militant thing and have yourself a woman. The fact that she happens to be black or white is no longer impressive to anybody, but a man who gets himself a woman is what's impressive. The battle is really between white men and black men. Whether we like to admit it, that is the battlefield at this time.*[23]

Sexism, like racism, encourages violence as a way to subjugate the other. Baraka dramatized his nationalist view in his play *Madheart*. In one scene, the black male protagonist of the play demonstrates his power to use force to subdue the black woman who is urging him to leave the white woman and come to her:

BLACK MAN: I'll get you back. If I need to.

WOMAN (laughs): You need to baby…just look around you. You better get me back, if you know what's good for you…you better

BLACK MAN (looking around at her squarely, he advances): I better?... (a soft laugh) Yes, Now is where we always are... that now.... (He wheels and suddenly slaps her crosswise, back and forth across the face.)

WOMAN: Wha??? What... oh love... please... don't hit me. (He hits her, slaps her again.)

BLACK MAN: I want you woman, as a woman. Go down. (He slaps her again.) Go down, submit, submit... to love... and to man, now, forever.

WOMAN (weeping, turning her head from side to side): Please don't hit me... please... without you, man, I've waited.... (She bends.) The years are so long, without you, man, I've waited... waited for you....

BLACK MAN: And I've waited.

WOMAN: I've seen you humbled, black man, seen you crawl for dogs and devils.

BLACK MAN: And I've seen you raped by savages and beasts, and bear bleach-shit of children of apes.

WOMAN: You permitted it…you could…do nothing.
BLACK MAN: But now I can. (He slaps her…drags her to him, kissing
her deeply on the lips.) That shit is ended, women, you with me,
and the world is mine.[24]

At first women were reluctant to speak the language of feminism, because they did not want to detract from the importance of the struggle of the black community against white racism. Furthermore, they wanted to give black men a chance to "stand up like men" in the presence of white men in order to protect and to provide for the black family. This was also partly due to reaction to the myth of black female matriarchy and partly as a response to black male proclamations of assumed and justified leadership.

In an *Ebony* article, "The Black Woman and Women's Lib," Helen H. King suggested that many black women in the civil rights and black power movements accepted their place behind black men and were proud to see them stand up and demand liberalization for black community.

"We should stand behind our men, not against them," said a black woman opponent of the women's liberation movement.[25] Another is quoted as saying: "This movement won't be any difference from the woman suffrage thing. White women won the right to vote way back then, but black people, including black women, didn't win this right until more than a hundred years later!"[26] Still another black woman opponent characterized the women's movement as "just a bunch of bored white women with nothing to do—they're just trying to attract attention away from black liberation movement."[27]

Prominent black women joined the chorus denouncing the women's movement as a white and middle-class phenomenon, and thus unrelated to the black struggle from freedom. Nikki Giovanni said.

> *I think that it's a moot issue. Just another freedom of white people to find out what black people are doing or to control what we are doing.…They [white women] want "equality" to deal with black women because they're certainly dealt with black men. They're so upset about black women not coming in because they're ultimately trying to control us.*

> *There aren't any other reasons why they could be upset.*
> *Black women consider their firs reality to be black, and*
> *given that reality we know from birth that we are going to*
> *be oppressed—man, woman, or eunuch!*[28]

The well-known poet Gwendolyn Brooks echoed the same theme:

> *Black women, like all women, certainly want, and are*
> *entitled to, equal pay and privileges. But black women have*
> *a second "twoness." Today's black men, at last flamingly*
> *assertive and proud, need their black women beside them,*
> *not organizing against them.*[29]

Although there were a few exceptions,[30] most black women of the early 1970s remained apart from the critical of the women's movement. But when black revolutionaries began "to talk black and sleep white," black women began to question the nature of black men's commitment to the black freedom struggle and to reevaluate their place *behind* the black man. Black women started to realize that to be liberated, from both white racism and male domination, they would have to go the job themselves.

Of course, just as many submitted to racism, many black women accepted the sexist role defined by so-called revolutionary black men. Some black women were willing to walk two steps behind their men and remain silent and passive. Black women wanted to be taken care of by "strong" black men, as white men had supposedly done white for women. Therefore, black women were slow to complain about black male brutality.

Because black men knew that black women were deeply committed to the racial struggle, they did not even take seriously black women's concern for sexual oppression. They merely laughed, treating the hurt and pain of our sisters as a joke. When asked about the role of women in the movement, Strokely Carmichael is reported to have said, "The only position for women SNCC is prone."[31]

Because we were so insensitive, we left black women with no choice but to declare publicly that sexism does exist in the black community and, like racism, it must be eliminated. One of the earlier texts on black feminism is entitled *The Black Woman* (1970), an anthology edited by Toni Cade.[32] But it was not until Ntozake Shange's paly *For Colored Girls ...* (1976)[33] and Michele Wallace's book *Black Macho and the Myth of the Superwomen* (1979)[34] that the idea of a black feminism became widely discussed in the black community...[35]

Although the black church has seldom willing to accept new ideas that were not directly related to the elimination of white racism, the enormous impact of Shange's play and Wallace's book make it impossible for many black women in the church and seminary to avoid the issue of black patriarchy. One does not have to agree with the perspectives of Shange or Wallace in order to know that black women are oppressed by black men, and especially in the church by male ministers.

BLACK THEOLOGY AND BLACK WOMEN

Just as the struggles of the 1960 and '70s reinforced sexism in the black community generally, sexism in the church particularly seemed more blatant in those years. Black clergymen became bold advocates of women's inferiority, emphasizing their supposed lack of intelligence, natural weakness, and passivity. As some white male ministers began to retreat in the face of emerging power of the women's movement in the seminary and church, black clergymen laughed at white men's inability to keep women in their place. At the same time, they mimicked white antifeminist conservatives by preaching about the value of the American family in which wives are subordinate to their husbands. This was the sanctimonious—supposedly biblical—version of the male revolutionary's demand that black women stand behind their men.

Such attitudes limit women's roles in the church. Women are expected to sing in the choir, serve on the usher and stewardess boards, participate in the missionary society, cook in the kitchen, teach children in the Sunday School, and serve in all those positions that men regard as "women's work." But unlike men, women are not encouraged to enter the ministry. Women are tolerated when they insist that God has called them to preach the word. Indeed, a woman's calling is often questioned until her talent and faith remove skeptic's doubts. A man's call is never questioned until a lack of faith or talent or moral integrity create skepticism among the community of believers. A man my live the most immoral life imaginable, be "converted," and still be accepted by the church for service in God's ministry. But an immoral woman who "gets" religion and then receives the call would hardly be given a similar opportunity for service in the church.

In some black churches women are still excluded entirely from the ordained ministry.[36] but even in churches that do ordain women, female ministers do not have the same opportunities as men for the exercise of their ministry. For instance, there is, to my knowledge, only one woman presiding elder, but no bishops, general officers, college presidents, or pastors of major churches in the AME Church.[37] When women push through the male-oriented pattern of expectations and *insist* that God has called them to preach, men often tell them to become evangelists, a ministry with no institutional authority. If women should insist on being pastors, they are usually urged to become assistants to male pastors. If they insist on being the head pastor, the bishop usually appoints them to small churches that men do not want. I n other black denominations, the offices may have different names but the results are the same: men say to women, "This far and no farther."

Turning to theology, it is clear from earlier chapters that black theology arose out of the black church and in response to the black power movement. It is shameful but scarcely surprising that black theology learned the patriarchal bad habits of its progenitors. Only one woman, Dr. Anna Hedgeman, author and staff member of the NCC commission on religion and race, was asked to sign the NCBC "Black Power Statement" of 1966.[38] The NCBC has not been a public advocate of equality for women in the ministry. During my involvement in most of its early history, the issue of women in the ministry was seldom discussed, because the NCBC was controlled by black male theologians and ministers. When the issue was raised most men either laughed or assigned it a low priority in the struggle for black freedom. A woman as served in the position of secretary to the executive director and the board of directors. A few women have even served on the board.

The very name NCBC, with the last letter representing Church—men, indicated clearly the reactionary perspective of black male ministers regarding women's equality in church and society. According to the reports of some black women, the NCBC male leadership, despite repeated appeals, remained adamant in its refusal to replace the word "Churchmen" with "Christians," insisting that the word "men" is generic and not sexist. Only in late 1982 did the NCBC soften its views on the matter and change its name to National Conference of Black Christians.[39]

At first, there were only a few black women theologians who began to criticize black male theology. They included Pauli Murray,[40] an Episcopal priest and lawyer, and Theressa Hoover, an executive of the Board of Global Ministries of the United Methodist Church.[41] But they were the exceptions, and black male theologians and ministers either ignored them or laughed at their arguments. The situation changed, however, I the mid-1970s.

I remember the first time that black men and women at Union Theological Seminary came together to discuss women in the ministry. Because I had been "converted" to women's equality in society, church, and the doing of theology, and because I had just read a paper addressing that theme at Garrett Evangelical Seminary in Evanston (October 1986), Jacquelyn Grant, then a graduate student at Union and now a professor of theology at the Interdenominational Theological Center, asked me to present the same paper to black men and women at Union.

When I now read that October 1976 paper, I am embarrassed by how mildly and carefully I approached the theme of women's equality in the church. It was anything but radical, somewhat analogous to a southern white liberal reflecting on racism. But black male seminarians, almost without exception, were greatly disturbed by my paper. If my paper can be compared to that of a southern white liberal, the reactions of many black seminarians were similar to those of most reactionary southern white racists. They quoted the bible to justify that women should not be obtained, and some even insisted that they should not even be in the pulpit. I was shocked, as were my black colleagues, Professor James Forbes and James Washington. But black women seminarians were not surprised. They were not even aware of the attitudes that kept them subordinate in the church, as well as invisible in black theology.

From like encounters, repeated and multiplied countless times, black women saw the need for black feminist theology. In this project they have had the ambiguous models of black male theology. In this project they have had the ambiguous models of black theology and white feminist theology. Beginning with Mary Daly's The Church and the Second Sex (1968),[42] feminist theology was further developed in the prolific writings of Rosemary Ruether, Letty Russell, Beverly Harrison, Sheila Collins, Judith Plaskow, Carol Christ, and many others.[43] Most black women either ignored these writings or criticized them as irrelevant to black women and the black church. However, as black feminist theology emerges, black women are affirming in varying degrees the value of their white sister's work.

The invisibility of black women in both black and feminist theologies is striking. The most that bought theologies do is to mention in passing the names of Sojourner truth, Harriet Tubman, and perhaps Rosa Parks. But for neither is black women's experience a part of the structure and substance of the theology itself. Black women's experience is merely added to the theologies whose style and content are determined by other experiences. That is why Jarena Lee, Maria Stewart, Frances Ellen Watkins Harper, Ida Wells-Barnett, and Anna Julia Cooper are seldom mentioned in either black male or white feminist theology.

Only black women can do black feminist theology: their experience is truly theirs. Therefore, even if white feminists were not so racist and black males were not so sexist, there would still be a need for black feminist theology. The need arises from the uniqueness of black women's experience. If theology arises out of the attempt to reconcile faith with life, and if black women have an experience of faith in God that is not exhausted by white women so that the universal church can learn from their experience with God. Black women, by giving an account of their faith in worship and living out their faith in the world, create the context for authentic theological reflection.

Among the black women seminarians and professors who have begun to develop a black feminist theology are Jacquelyn Grant, Pauli Murray, Katie Cannnon, Delores Williams, Kelly Brown, and Cherl Gilkes. Although black women's experience is related to some aspects both women and blacks generally, their experience is not exhausted by either group. Black women have begun to feel the need to articulate the uniqueness of their experience *theologically*.

Black feminist theologians in the U.S.A. have been aided by theological reflection arising from the struggles of other minority women in the U.S.A. and women in Africa, Asia, and Latin America.

When black women theologians and ministers encountered third World women in the WCC and other ecumenical settings, they realized that they were not the only women in an oppressed community concerned about women's equality.[44] Meeting Third World women and reading their writings on women's liberation helped black women to recognize the need for the development of a black feminist theology.[45]

Black women may have been reluctant to join in a coalition with white women, but they are less reluctant to express their solidarity with African and other non-European women. the WCC, EATWOT, and other ecumenical organizations have provided many an occasion for dialogues between African-American and Third World women in the church.[46]

A WORD TO BLACK MALE MINISTERS AND THEOLOGIANS

As a male theologian, I am in no position to say what the content and form of a black feminist theology should be. I can only support its development and be instructed by the black women who assume the responsibility to create it. However, I should like to offer some thoughts to black male theologians and ministers whose attitudes range from indifference to mild support of the development of women's fullest potential as human beings in the church and community. There are responsibilities that we have in the church that affect how women are received and what opportunities are made available to them for the fullest development of their potential for service to God in the church and in society.

It is important for black men to realize that women's liberation is a viable issue.[47] We must recognize it and help others in the church to treat it seriously. It is not a joke. To get others to accept it as an issue that deserves serious consideration and discussion is the first step. As ministers in the church, how we treat the issue will affect the attitudes of others in our pastoral care. I realize that many women give the appearance of accepting the place set aside for them by men as is still true many blacks in relation to whites. But just as whites were responsible for creating the societal structures that aided black self-hate, so black men are responsible for creating a similar situation among black women in the church. Saying that women like their place is no different from saying that blacks like theirs.

It is also important that we learn how to listen to women tell their stories of pain and struggle. The art of listening is not easy, especially of oppressors whose very position of power inhibits them from hearing and understanding anything that contradicts their values.

When we try to understand something of the depth of sexism and how it functions in black churches and community, it is helpful to think of racism in American society and white churches. Although racism and sexism are different in many respects, they share many similarities. If black men deny this connection between sexism and racism, it is unlikely that they will recognize the depth of the problem of sexism.

To aid our comprehension of the complexity of the issue, it is necessary to read as much as possible about the history of sexism and women's struggles, especially in the Third World and particularly in the black community and its churches in the in the U.S.A. Just as blacks become impatient with whites who do not take the time and discipline to inform themselves about the history of their brutality against then and their struggle against that brutality, black women will have a similar feeling regarding our failure to study their history.

Black women are beginning to develop their own leadership styles. Black men should support them. But it is already clear that leadership roles and styles of black women will be quite different from those that have been defined for them by black male ministers and theologians. Just as blacks and other oppressed groups develop styles in ministry that are different from those of oppressor whites, so the experience of women provides ways of doing ministry that will be quite different from the patriarchal and authoritarian leadership of men. It is our responsibility as men to be open to new styles of ministry and to help our congregations to be open to them. This will involve the necessity of being critical of our brothers who are opposed to women's taking leadership positions in the church and society. We should be prepared to lose some "friends" as we work for change in the patriarchal structures in black churches and seek to create ones that are humane and just.

Black male ministers should also insist on affirmative action for black women in churches and in the community. The goal should be to have at least as many black women in positions of responsibility in churches and in the community organizations as will reflect their percentage of the overall population. We can never achieve this goal without a plan of action for its accomplishment. Blacks have used this approach vis-à-vis racism; it seems logical to apply it to the situation of black women in our churches and communities. The principle of affirmative actions should be applied to all positions, including those of bishop, pastor, general officer, steward, and deacon.

Finally, it is important for black male ministers to support black women in their attempt to discover role models of the past. In my reading and discussions with black women, they often speak of the lack of role models —both past and present. What is needed therefore is for black women (and also black men) to discover their sisters of the past and to find community with those of the present so they can share experiences with each other and thereby be encouraged to keep fighting for recognition and justice in the church. Through a discovery of their sisters and mothers of the past and the creation of community in the present, self-confidence can be enhanced and the struggle for liberation strengthened.

In addition to the suggestions mentioned above, there are many other things that black men and women can do—both together and separately. My suggestions are intended only to engender serious discussions on the role of black women in the church and in society.

NOTES

1. *The Life and Religious Experiences of Jarena Lee, A Coloured Lady*, in Dorothy Porter (ed.), *Early Negro Writing*: 1760-1837 (Boston: Beacon, 1971), p. 503.

2. From a speech given at the Fourth National Women's rights Convention, New York City, 1853, in Gerda Lerner (ed.), *Black Women in White America: A Documentary History* (New York: Vintage, 1973), p. 568

3. "Black women and the Churches: Triple Jeopardy," in G.S. Wilmore and J.H. Cone (eds.), *Black Theology: A Documentary History* (Marykno;;, N.Y.: Orbis, 1979), p. 377.

4. "Black Theology and the Black Woman," ibid., p. 426.

5. See Benjamin Quarles, "Frederick Douglas and the Women's Right Moment," *Journal of Negro History*, vol. 25, no. 1, Jan. 1940, pp. 35-44. See also the editorial by Douglass published in The North Star," The Rights of Women" 9text in Philip S. Foner [ed.], *The Life and Writings of Frederick Douglass* [New York: International Publishers, 1950], pp. 320-21).

6. Cited in Hertha Pauli, *Her Name Was Sojourner Truth* (New York: Camelot/Avon, 1962), p. 176. For other accounts of the same incident see Jacqueline Bernard, *Journey toward Freedom: The Story of Sojourner Truth* (New York: Dell, 1967), pp. 175 ff.; James Loewenberg and Ruth Bogin (eds.), *Black Women in Nineteenth-Century American Life* (University Park: Pennsylvania State University Press, 1976), pp. 253ff.; *Sojourner truth: Narrative and Book of Life*, Ebony Classic (Chicago: Johnson, 1970), pp. 103ff. All these accounts are based on Elizabeth Cady Stanton, Susan B. Anthony, and Matilda Joseyn Gage (eds.), *History of Women Suffrage*, vol. 1 (Rochester, N.Y.: Susan B. Anthony, 1881).

7. Cited in Loewenberg and Bogin, Black Women, p. 235.

8. Cited in Pauli, *Her Name Was*, p. 176.

9. Loewenberg and Bogin, *Black Women*, p. 236; and Pauli, *Her Name Was*, p. 177.

10. Loewenberg and Bogin, Black Women, p. 236.

11. Ibid., p. 238.

12. On the history of black women's struggles for freedom in the 19th and early 20th century, see Bell Hooks, *Ain't I a Woman* (Boston: South End Press, 1981); Angela Y. Davis, *Women, Race, and Class* (New York: Random House, 1981); Lerner, Black Women in White America; Loewenberg and Bogin, *Black Women*; Dorothy Sterling, *Black Foremothers* (New York: Feminist Press and McGraw-Hill, 1979); Bettina Aptheker , *Woman's Legacy: Essay on Race, Sex, and Class in American History* (Amherst: University of Massachusetts Press, 1982).

13. See her essay "Black Women and Churches: Triple Jeopardy" in Wilmore and Cone, *Black Theology*, pp. 377-88.

14. Cited in Jualynne E. Dodson, "19th –Century AME Preaching Women," in H.F. Thomas and R.S. Keller (eds.), *Women in New Worlds* (Nashville: Abingdon, 1981), p. 287.

15. "The Life and Religious Experience of Jarena Lee: A Coloured Lady (1836)," in *Early Negro Writing* 1760-1837, selected and introduced by Dorothy Porter (Boston: Beacon, 197), p. 503. The full text has been reprinted under the title *Religious Experiences and Journal of Ms. Jarena Lee* (Philadelphia), a 125-page book. No publisher is indicated.

16. "Life and Religious Experience," p. 503.

17. "Elizabeth, A Colored Minister of the Gospel," in Loewenberg and Bogin, *Black Women*, p.133.

18. An excellent treatment of the origin of the modern women's movement out of the civil rights and black power movements is that by Sara Evans, *Personal Politics: The Roots of Women's Liberation in the Civil Rights and the New Left* (New York: Vintage, 1980).

19. Regarding Ella Baker, see Ellen Cantarow, Susan G. O'Mally, and Sharon H. Strom, *Moving the Mountain: Women Working for Social Change* (Old Westbury, N.Y.: Feminist Press, 1980), pp. 52-93; Barbara Omolade, "Black Womanhood—Images of Dignity: Ella Baker and Miriam Makeba, "*The Black Collegian*, April/May 1981, pp. 52-60; James Forman, *The Making of Black Revolutionaries* (New York: Macmillan, 1972), pp. 215-23. Forman is an exception in that he does indicate the important role that women played in the freedom movement. See esp. his tribute to "Strong Black Women" (ibid., pp. 198-202). On Ella Baker, see also her interview with Gerda Lerner in *Black Women in White America*, pp. 345-52; in regard to her role in the founding of the SNCC, see Howard Zinn, *SNCC: The New Abolitionist* (Boston: Beacon, 1964); and Clayborne Carson, *In Struggle: SNCC and the Black Awakening of the 1960s* (Harvard University Press, 1981). For information on Ella Baker, Anna Hedgeman, and Rosa Parks and their roles in the civil rights movement, especially the March on Washington, see Patrice Gaines-Carter, "Women Were Always There," *The National Leader*, vol. 1, no. 17, August 26, 1982, pp. 10f. An important interview of Rosa Parks, "Montgomery Bus Boycott," is found in Joanne Grant

20. (ed.), *Black Protest: History, Documents and Analysis, 1619 to the Present* (Greenwich, Conn.: Fawcett, 1968).

20. On Anna a. Hedgeman, see note 39, below.

21. Most serious accounts of the Civil Rights Movement in the south refer to the dynamic leadership of Fannie Lou Hamer. See her "It's in Your Hands," in Lerner, *Black Women in White America,* pp. 609-14; and her interview with Howell Raines in is *My Soul is Rested* (New York: Putnam, 1977), pp. 249-55. An excellent account of the Fannie Lou Hamer story is found in *Sojourners* (Dec. 1982) with articles by persons who knew and worked with her in Mississippi. See especially the articles by Danny Collum, "The Life of Fannie Lou Hamer," pp. 11-14; and Edwin King, "A Prophet from the Delta," pp. 18-21.

22. See her The Long Shadow of Little Rock (New York: McKay, 1962).

23. Regarding the roles of Ruby Doris Robinson and Diana Nash Bevel, see the studies of Carson and Zinn referred to in note 19, above. See also Diane Nash, "Inside the Sit-Ins and Freedom Rides: Testimony of a Southern Student," in Matthew H. Ahmann (ed.), *The New Negro* (Notre Darne: Fides, 1961).

24. Quoted in Bell Hooks, *Ain't I am Woman,* p. 97.

25. In Leroi Jones and Larry Neal (eds.), *Black Fire: An Anthology of Afro-American Writing* (New York: Morrow, 1968), pp. 583-84. Since Baraka became a Maxist, he has repudiated his earlier nationalist views and his views regarding the subordination of women. See esp. his introduction in his (edited with Amina Baraka) *Confirmation: An Anthology of African American Women* (New York: Quill, 1983), pp. 15-26; and *The Autobiography of Le Roi Jones/ Amiri Baraka* (New York: Freundlich Books, 1984), pp. 300f. In his *Autobiography,* Baraka says, "The women in those 60's and early 70's black nationalist organizations had to put up with a great deal of unadulterated bullshit in the name of revolution" (pp. 300-1). There is a lengthy discussion of his past errors, and it is to his credit that he admits to them in print.

26. Cited in Helen King, "Black Women," *Ebony,* March 1971, p. 68.

27. Ibid., p. 70.

28. Ibid.

29. Ibid., pp. 70-71. Carolyn Roberts is quoted as saying: "The feminist movement is one of the middle-class white women. Of course, these are women whose humanity has been destroyed by their husbands, their fathers, their sons. White women who are housewives have been allowed to remain girls, while the black 'girl' taking care of the house was indeed the woman. White women have been do-nothing dolls and one gathers now that they want to be white *men* or something else. White women with their private schools and summer camps and nursemaids for their children, and mechanical kitchen, want some satisfaction in being a woman. Black women *do* have problems with their men and we are also affected by some of the stereotypes that white women experience, but these are minor irritations when we compare them with our greatest problem—that being one of American apartheid" (ibid., p. 75).

30. Ibid., p. 71.

31. Two prominent exceptions were Congresswoman Shirley Chisholm and the well-known attorney Florence Kennedy, both of whom were strong supporters of women's liberation.

32. Cited in Sara Evans, *Personal Politics* (note 18, above), p. 87. Like Baraka, Carmichael regretted that statement. In fact, several black women testified to the opposite behavior from him. But despite Carmichael's "slip of tongue," his comment does reflect the lack of seriousness that the women's issue received in the black movement. Today Carmichael heads the All-African People's Revolutionary party that explicitly affirms the equality of women. For a typical black male view of women's liberation, see William H. Banks Jr., "Women's Lib: A New Cop-Out on the Black Struggle?" in *Liberator,* vol. 10, no. 9, Sept. 1970, pp. 4-5. My own lack of sensitivity to this issue can be seen in my silence about it in my early writings and the excessively patriarchal language that I used. It as the strong resistance of black women that convinced me of the evil consequences of sexism. Other black men have been convinced as well. See esp. Manning Marable, "in his *How Capitalism Underdeveloped Black America* (Boston: South End Press, 1983).

33. Toni Cade (ed.), *The Black Woman: An Anthology* (New York: New American Library, 1970).

34. There are many outstanding black feminist writers. They include: Alice Walker, *In Search of our Mothers' Gardens* (New York: Hardcourt Brace Jovanovich, 1983); *The Color Purple* (New York: Washington Square, 1982); June Jordan, *Civil Wars* (Boston: Beacon, 1981); Gloria T. Hull, Patricia Bell Scott, and Barbara Smith (eds.), *But Some of Us Are Brave: Black Women's Studies* (Old Westbury, N.Y.: Feminist Press, 1982). I have already referred to B. Hooks, *Ain't I am Woman* and to Angela Y. Davis, *Women, Race and Class,* also important is Claudia Tate (ed.), *Black Women Writers at Work* (New York: Continuum, 1983); see also Maxine Williams, "Why Women's Liberation Is Important to Black Women," and Pamela Newman, "Take a Good Look at Our Problems," published together as a Merit Pamphlet, New York, 1970. *The Black Scholar* has been the chief forum for issues regarding black women in the black community. See esp. the following: Dec. 1971; March/April 1973; March 1975; April 1978; May/June 1979; Nov. /Dec. 1981; Summer 1982. On the relationship between Marxism, feminism, and race, see Gloria Joseph, "The Incompatible Menage a Trois: Marxism, Feminism, and Racism," in Lydia Sargent (ed.), *Women and Revolution* (Boston: South End Press, 1981), pp. 91-107.

35. According to James Tinney, "The first black denomination to ordain women was the AMEZ Church, which ordained it first elder, the Rev. Julia A. Foote, in New York in 1898. But its sister body, the AME church, did not follow suit until 1948, when it ordained the Rev. Martha J. Keys" ("Black Churches Slow to Ordain Women," *National Leader,* Sept. 2, 1982, p. 24). This essay is a good summary of the attitudes of black churches regarding the ordination of women. For black women ministers' accounts of their struggles in the black church, see "The Holy War of the rev. Trudie Trimm," *Ebony,* Sept. 1969, pp. 72-77; Mary R. Johnson, "Black Women in the Ministry," Dollars and Sense, June/ July, 1981, pp. 96-101.

38. See Jeane B. Williams, "Letter to the Editor," *A.M.E. Christian Recorder,* Nov. 1, 1982. This letter was in response to Capt. C.R. Chambliss, "Do you Mean It?" ibid., June 14, 1982. Unlike most AME ministers, Chambliss wrote a strong, supportive letter regarding the equality of women in the ministry. It is unlikely

that Capt. Chambliss, would have written such a strong letter if he had been dependent on an AME bishop, instead of the U.S. Navy, for support of his family. The same applies to my writings. However, unless the AME Church and other black churches create structure of accountability for authority, especially regarding the power bishops and other church leaders, then neither women nor anyone else under their jurisdiction will receive anything close to justice in black churches.

39. See her *The Gift of Chaos* (New York: Oxford University Press, 1977) for her interpretation of her involvement in the NCBC (pp. 152, 159, 162-63). See also her *The Trumpet Sounds* (New York: Holt, Rinehart & Winston, 1964).

40. According to several NCBC members, the name was changed at the 1982 fall convocation in St. Louis. However, the issue of sexism had been raised several women much before that time. Indeed, according to the minutes of the Feb. 20-21, 1975, and the Nov. 17, 1975, board meetings (held respectively in New York and Atlanta), the issue of sexism was discussed. In New York Gilbert Caldwell reported on a consultation on black women in the ministry held at Yale Divinity School: "The women [are] interested in knowing what NCBC is and what it is doing to push issues relating to women's liberation. Sister Mary Kinnard, who attended the consultation, felt that the women raised some significant issues and that they are treated inhumanly in the black church in terms of roles and the way they are perceived. She expects to help them develop a relationship with NCBC." Virgil Wood and Bishop Charles Golden of the United Methodist church "noted that the name of the organization could serve as a deterrent to attracting women and that the organization should again review the need for a name change." At the Atlanta meeting the issue of changing the name was discussed again. "The proposed name change surfaced as an attempt to communicate that the organization is not just for church 'men' but for both sexes. [But] strong opposition was expressed by some to the word 'Christians' as a substitute for 'Churchmen' in our name since the original intent to be 'broadly ecumenical' has never been challenged. When one reads NCBC minutes and listens to black clergymen talk about the problem of sexism in the black

church, there is little difference between such talk and that of white liberals on racism. Black clergymen could enhance greatly their insight on sexism by comparing its close similarity with racism. Of course, black men often strongly resist that comparison, and such resistance only discloses their own sexism.

At a recent convocation on national and international priorities of the black church (see chap. 5, note 37, above), and innovative step was taken by black male ministers regarding sexism in the black church and community. It was, to my knowledge, the first time that black male ministers openly expressed a willingness to listen to black women regarding the problem of sexism in the black church and community, even though it was not a subject area of the convocation. But in planning for the future, the issue of sexism received top priority on the agenda. A resolution was passed that urged the Black theology Project and NCBC to plan a conference in which the only subject would be sexism in the black church and community. To my knowledge, not only did no one resist this solution, but rather all supported enthusiastically. I was greatly surprised but very pleased. Finally, some black male ministers are beginning to recognize the importance of this issue and thus are willing to face it head-on.

41. See her "Black Theological and Feminist Theology: A Comparative View," *Anglican Theological Review,* Jan. 1978, pp. 3-24; also reprinted in Wilmore and Cone, *Black Theology,* pp. 398-417.

42. See her "Black Women and the Churches," in Alice Hageman (ed.), *Sexist Religion and Women in the Church* (New York: Associated Press, 1974), pp. 63-76; also reprinted in Wilmore and Cone, *Black Theology,* pp. 377-88.

43. New York, Harper & Row, 1968.

44. One of the best collections of feminists writing religion is that by Carol P. Christ and Judith Plaskow (eds.), *Womanspirit Rising: A Feminist Reader in Religion* (New York: Harper Forum Books, 1979). See also the important writings of rosemary R. Ruether, *Sexism and God-Talk: Toward a Feminist Theology* (Boston: Beacon, 1983); *New Woman/ New Earth* (New York: Seabury, 1975); *Religion and Sexism* (New York: Simon & Schuster, 1974); Elizabeth Fiorenza, *In Memory of Her: A Feminist Theological Reconstruction Of Christian*

Origins (New York: Crossroads, 1983); Letty M. Russell, *Human Liberation in a Feminist Perspective: A Theology* (Philadelphia: Westminster, 1974); Shelia Collins, *A Different Heaven and Earth: A Feminist Perspective on Religion* (Valley Forge: Judson, 1974); Isabel Carter Heyward, *They Redemption of God: Theology of Mutual Relations* (Washington: D.C.: University Press Of America, 1982); Beverly Harrison, *Our Rights to Choose* (Boston: Beacon, 1983); Mary Day, *Beyond God the Father* (Boston: Beacon, 1973).

45. See esp. *Sexism in the 1970's: Discrimination against Women,* report of a WCC consultation, West Berlin (1974); Constance F. Parvey (ed.), *The Community of Women and Men in the Church: The Sheffield Report* (Geneva: WCC, 1980).

46. EATWOT, an organization of African, Asian, Latin America, Caribbean, and U.S. minority theologians, has been encouraging the development of theologies from perspectives of women in these continents and regions. See esp. Amba Oduyoye, "Reflections from a Third World Woman's Perspective: Women's Experience and Liberation Theologies," in Virginia Fabella and Sergio Torres (eds.), *Irruption of the Third World: Challenge to Theology* (Maryknoll, N.Y. Orbis, 1977); *Women in Dialogue,* An Inter-American Meeting, Puebla, Mexico, Jan. 27-Feb. 13, 1979. In a secular context, Cherrie Moraga and Gloria Anzaldua (eds.), *This Bridge Called Me Back: writings by Radical Women of Color* (Watertown, Mass.: Persephone Press, 1981) is an excellent example of black women joining in coalition with other women of color.

47. It is unfortunate that so many black theologians continue to ignore the issue of the sexist orientation of black theology and the black church. One exception is James H. Evans Jr., "Black Theology and Black Feminism," journal of Religion Thought, vol. 38, no. 1, Spring-Summer 1981, pp. 43-53.

BLACK THEOLOGY AND THE BLACK WOMAN

JACQUELYN GRANT

Liberation theologies have arisen out of the contexts of the liberation struggles of Black Americans, Latin Americans, American women, Black South Africans and Asians. These theologies represent a departure from traditional Christian theology. As a collective critique, liberation theologies raise serious questions about the normative use of Scripture, tradition and experience in Christian theology. Liberation theologians assert that the reigning theologies of the West have been used to legitimate the established order. Those to whom the church has entrusted the task of interpreting the meaning of God's activity in the world have been too content to represent the ruling classes. For this reason, say the liberation theologians, theology has generally not spoken to those who are oppressed by the political establishment.

Ironically, the criticism that liberation theology makes against classical theology has been turned against liberation theology itself. Just as most European and American theologians have acquiesced with the oppression of the West, for which they have been taken to task by liberation theologians, some liberation theologians have acquiesced in one or more oppressive aspects of the liberation struggle itself. Where racism is called into question, racism and sexism have been tolerated. And where sexism is repudiated racism and classicism are often ignored.

Although there is a certain validity to the argument that any one analysis—race, class or sex—is not sufficient universal to embrace the needs of all oppressed peoples, these particular analyses, nonetheless, have all been well presented and are crucial for comprehensive and authentic liberation theology. In order for liberation theology to be faithful to itself it must hear the critique coming to it from the the perspective of the black woman—perhaps the most oppressed of all oppressed.

I am concerned in this essay with how the experience of the black woman calls into question certain assumptions in Liberation Theology in general, and Black Theology in particular. In the Latin American context this has already been done by women such as Beatriz Melano Couch and Consuelo Urquiza. A few Latin American theologians have begun to respond. Beatriz Couch, for example, accepts the starting point of Latin American theologians, but criticizes them for their exclusivism with respect to race and sex. She says:

> *...we Latin America stress the importance of the starting point, the praxis, and the use of social science to analyze our political historical situation. In this I am in full agreement with my male colleagues ... with one qualitative difference. I stress the need to give importance to the different cultural forms that express oppression; to the ideology that divides people not only according to class, but to race and sex. Racism and sexism are oppressive ideologies which deserve a specific treatment in the theology of liberation.117*

More recently, Consuelo Urquiza called for the unification of Hispanic-American women in struggling against their oppression in the church and society. In commenting on the contradiction in the Pauline Epistles which undergird the oppression of the Hispanic-American woman, Urquiza said: "At the present time all Christians will agree with Paul in the first part of [Galatians 3:28] about freedom and slavery that there should not be slaves.... However, the next part of this verse... has been ignored and the equality between man and women is not accepted. They would rather skip that line and go to the epistle to Timothy [2:9-15]."[118] Women theologians of Latin background are beginning to do theology and to sensitize other women to the necessity of participating in decisions which affect their lives and the life of the communities. Latin American theology will gain from these inputs which women are making to the theological process.

Third World and Black women[119] in the United States will soon collaborate in an attack on another aspect of Liberation Theology—Feminist Theology. Black and Third World women have begun to articulate their differences and similarities with the Feminist Movement, which is dominated by white American women who until now have been the chief authors of Feminist Theology. It is my contention that the theological perspectives of black and Third World women should reflect these differences and similarities with Feminist Theology. It is my purpose, however, to look critically at Black Theology as a black woman in an effort to determine how adequate is its conception of liberation for the total black community. Pauli Murray and Theresa Hoover have in their own ways challenged Black Theology. Because their articles appear in this section (Documents 39 and 37), it is unnecessary for me to explain their point of view. They have spoken for themselves.

I want to begin with the question: "Where are black women in Black Theology?" They are in fact, invisible in Black Theology and we need to know why this is the case. Because the black church experienced in general are important sources for doing Black Theology, we need to look at the black woman in relation to both in order to understand the way black Theology has applied it conception in liberation. Finally, in view of the status of the black woman vis-à-vis Black Theology, the Black Church and black experience, a challenge needs to be presented to Black Theology. This is how I propose to discuss this important question.

THE INVISIBILITY OF BLACK WOMEN IN BLACK THEOLOGY

In examining Black Theology, it is necessary to make one or two assumptions: *(1)* either black women have no place in the enterprise, or *(2)* Black men are capable of speaking for us. Both of these assumptions are false and need to be discarded. They arise out of a male-dominated culture which restricts women to certain areas of the society. In such a culture, men are given the warrant to speak for women on all matters of significance. It is no accident that all of the recognized black theologians are men. This is what might be expected given the status and power accorded the discipline of theology. Professional theology is done by those who are highly trained. It requires, moreover, mastery of that power most accepted in the definition of manhood, the power or ability to "reason." This is supposedly what opens the door to participation in logical, philosophical debates and discussions presupposing rigorous intellectual training, for most of history, outside the "women's sphere." Whereas the nature of men has been defined in terms of reason and intellect, that of women has to do with intuition and emotionalism. Women were limited to matters related to the home while men carried out the more important work, involving use of rational faculties.[120] These distinctions were not as clear in the slave community.[121] Slaves and women were thought to share the characteristics of emotionality and irrationality. As we move further away from slave culture, however, a dualism between black men and women increasingly emerges. This means that black males have gradually increased their power and participation in the male-dominated society, while black females have continued to endure the stereotypes and oppressions of an earlier period.

When sexual dualism has finally run its course in the black community I(and I believe that it has), it will not be difficult to see why black woman are invisible in Black Theology. Just as white women formerly had no place in White Theology—except as the receptors of white men's theological interpretations—Black women have had no place in the development of Black Theology. By self-appointment, or by the sinecure of a male-dominated society. Black man has deemed it proper to speak for the entire Black community, male and female.

In a sense, black men's acceptance of the patriarchal; model is logical and to be expected. Black male slaves were unable to reap the benefits of patriarchal. Before emancipation they were not given the opportunity to serve as a protector and provider for black women and children, as white men were able to do their women and children. Much of what was considered "manhood" had to do with how well one could perform these functions. It seems only natural that the post-emancipation black men could view as primary importance the reclaiming of their property— their women and their children. Moreover, it is natural that black men would claim their "natural" right to the "man's world." But it should be emphasized that this is logical and natural only if one has accepted without question the terms and values of patriarchy—the concept of male control and supremacy.

Black men must ask themselves a difficult question. How can a white society characterized by black enslavement, colonialism, and imperialism provide the normative conception of women for black society? How can the sphere of the woman, as defined by white men, be free from the evils and oppressions that are found in the white society? The important point is that in matters relative to the relationship between the sexes, black men have accepted without question the patriarchal structures of white society as normative for the black community. How can a black minister preach in a way which advocates St. Paul's dictum concerning women while ignoring or repudiating his dictum concerning slaves? Many black women are enraged as they listen to "liberated" black men speak about the "place of women" in words and phrases similar to those of the very white oppressors they condemn.

Black women have been invisible in theology because theological scholarship has not been part of the woman's sphere. The first of the above two assumptions results, therefore, from the historical orientation of the dominant culture. The second follows from the first. If women have no place in theology, it becomes the natural prerogative of men to monopolize theological concerns, including those relating specifically to women. Inasmuch as black men have accepted the sexual dualism of the dominant culture they presume to speak for black women.

Before finally dismissing the two assumptions as pertinent question should be raised. Does the absence of black women in the circles producing black Theology necessarily mean that the resultant theology cannot be in the best interest of black women? The answer is obvious. Feminist theologians during the past few years have shown how theology done by men in male-dominated cultures has served to undergird patriarchal structures in society.[122] If black men have accepted those structures, is there any reason to believe that the theology written by black men would be any more liberating of black women than White Theology was for white women? It would seem that in view of oppression that black people have suffered black men would particularly sensitive to the oppression of others.[123]

James Cone has stated that the task of Black Theology "is to analyze the nature of the gospel of Jesus Christ in the light of oppressed black people so they will see the gospel as inseparable from their humiliated condition, bestowing on them the necessary power to break the chains of oppression. This means that it is a theology of and for the black community."[124] What are the forces of liberation in the black community and the Black Church? Are they to be exclusively defined by the struggle against racism? My answer to that question is No. There are oppressive realities in the black community which are related to, but independent of, the fact of racism. Sexism is one such reality. Black men seek to liberate themselves from racial stereotypes and the conditions of oppression without giving due attention to the stereotypes and oppressions against women which parallel those against blacks. blacks fight to be free of the stereotype that all blacks are dirty and ugly, or that black represent evil and darkness.[125] The slogan "Black is Beautiful" was a counterattack on these stereotypes. The parallel for women is the history of women as "unclean" especially during menstruation and after childbirth. Because the model of beauty in the white male-dominated society is the "long-haired blonde," with all that goes along with that mystique, black women have an additional problem with the Western idea of "ugliness," particularly as they encounter black men who have adopted this white model of beauty. Similarly, the Christian teaching that women is responsible for the fall of *mankind* and is, therefore, the source of evil has had a detrimental effect in the experience of black women.

Like all oppressed peoples the self-image of blacks has suffered damage. In addition they have not been in control of their own destiny. It is the goal of the black liberation struggle to change radically the socioeconomic and political conditions of black people by inculcating self-love, self-control, self-reliance, and political participation certainly have broad significance for black women, even though they were taught that, by virtue of their sex, they had to be completely dependent on *man;* yet while their historical situation reflected the need for dependence, the powerlessness of black men made it necessary for them to seek those values for themselves.

Racism and sexism are interrelated just as all forms of oppression are interrelated. Sexism, however, has a reality and significance of its own because it represents that peculiar form of oppression suffered by black women at the hands of black men. It is important to examine this reality of sexism as it is operated in both the black community and the Black Church. We will consider first the Black Church and secondly the black community to determine to what extent black Theology has measured up to its defined task with respect to the liberation of black women.[126]

THE BLACK CHURCH AND THE BLACK WOMAN

I can agree with Karl Barth as he describes the peculiar function of theology as the church's "subjecting herself to a self-test." She [the church] faces herself with the question of truth, i.e., she measures her action her language about God, against her existence as a Church."[127]

On the one hand, Black Theology must continue to criticize classical theology and the White Church. But on the other hand, Black Theology must subject the Black Church to a "self-test." The task of the church according to James Cone is threefold: *()* "It proclaims the reality of divine liberation.... . It is not possible to receive the good news of freedom and also keep it to ourselves; it must be told to the whole world...." *(2)* "It actively shares in the liberation struggle." *(3)* It "is a visible manifestation that the gospel is a reality.... *(3)* It "is a visible manifestation that the gospel is a reality.... If it [the church] lives according to the old order (as it actually has), then no one will believe its message."[128] It is clear that Black Theology must ask whether or not the Black Church is faithful to this task. Moreover, the language of the Black Church about God must be consistent with its action.[129] These requirements of the church's faithfulness in the struggle for liberation have not been met as far as the issue of women is concerned.

If the liberation of women is not proclaimed, the church's proclamation cannot be about divine liberation. If the church does not share in the liberation struggle of black women, its liberation struggle is not authentic. If women are oppressed, the church cannot possibly be "a visible manifestation that the gospel is a reality"—for the gospel cannot be real in that context. One can see the contradictions between the church's language or proclamation of liberation and its action by looking both at the status of black women in the church as laity and black women in the ordained ministry of the church.

It is often said that women are the "backbone" of the church. On the surface this may appear to be a compliment, especially when none considers the function of the backbone in the human anatomy. 9 Hoover prefers to use the term "glue" to describe the function of women in the Black Church. In any case, the telling portion of the word backbone is "back." It has become apparent to me that most of the ministers who use this term have reference to location rather than function. What they really mean is that women are in the "background" and should be kept there. They are merely support workers. This borne out of my observation that in many churches women are consistently given responsibilities in the kitchen, while men are elected or appointed to the important boards and leadership positions. While decisions and policies may be discussed in the kitchen, they are certainly not made there. Recently I conducted a study in one conference of the African Methodist Episcopal Church which indicated that women are accorded greater participation on the decision-making boards of smaller rather than larger churches. This political maneuver helps to keep women "in their place" in the denomination as well as in the local congregations. The conspiracy to keep women relegated to the background is also aided by the continuous psychological and political strategizing that keeps women from realizing their own potential power in the church. Not only are they rewarded for performance in "backbone" or supportive positions, but they are penalized for trying to move from the backbone of the head position—the leadership of the church. It is by considering the distinction between prescribed support positions and the policy-making, leadership positions that the oppression of black women in the Black Church can be seen more clearly.

For most part, men have monopolized the ministry as a profession. The ministry of women as fully ordained clergypersons has always been controversial. The black church fathers were unable to see the injustices of their own practices, even when they paralleled the injustices in the White Church against which they rebelled.

In the early nineteenth century, the Rev. Richard Allen perceived that it was unjust for blacks, free and slaves, to be relegated to the balcony and restricted to a special time to pray and keel at the communion table; for this he should be praised. Yet because of his acceptance of the patriarchal system Allen was unable to see the injustice in relegating women to one area of the church—the pews—by withholding ordination from women as he did in the case of Mrs. Jarena Lee. Lee recorded Allen's response when she informed him of her call to "go preach the Gospel":

He replied by asking in what sphere I wished to move in? I said, among the Methodists. He then replied, that a Mrs. Cook, a Methodist lady, had also some time before requested the same privilege; who it was believed, had done much good in the way of exhortation, and holding prayer meetings; *and who had been permitted to do so by the verbal license of the preacher in charge at the time. But as to women preaching, he said that our Discipline knew nothing at all about it—that it did not call for women preachers.*[132]

Because of this response Jarena Lee's preaching ministry was delayed for eight years. She was not unaware of the sexist injustice in Allen's response.

Oh, how careful ought we be, lest through our by-laws of church government and discipline, we bring into disrepute even the word of life. For as unseemly as it may appear nowadays for a woman to preach, it should be remembered that nothing is impossible with God. And why should it be thought impossible, heterodox, or improper for a woman to preach, seeing the Saviour died for the woman as well as the man?[133]

Another "colored minister of the gospel," Elizabeth, was greatly troubled over her call to preach, or more accurately, over the response of men to her call to preach. She said:

I often felt that was unfit to assemble with the congregation with whom I had gathered. ... I felt that I was despised on account of this gracious calling, and was looked upon as a speckled bird by the ministers to whom I looked for instruction ... some [of the ministers] would cry out, "you are an enthusiast," and others said, "the Discipline did not allow of any such division of work."[134]

Sometimes later when questioned about her authority to preach against slavery and her ordination status, she responded that she preached "not by the commission of men's hands: if the Lord had ordained me, I needed nothing better." [135] With this commitment to God rather than to a male-dominated church structure she led a fruitful ministry.

Mrs. Amanda Berry Smith, like Mrs. Jarena Lee, had to conduct her ministry outside the structure of the A.M.E. Church. Smith described herself as "plain Christian woman" with "no money" and "no prominence."[136] But she was intrigued with the idea of attending the General conference of 1872 in Nashville, Tennessee. Her inquiry into the cost of going to Nashville brought the following comments from some of the A.M.E. brethren:

> *"I tell you, Sister, it will cost money to go down there; and if you ain't got plenty of it, it's no use to go"; ... another said:*

> *"What does she want to go for?"*

> *"Woman preacher; they want to be ordained," was they reply.*

> *"I mean to fight that thing," said the other.*

> *"Yes, indeed, so will I," said another.* [137]

The oppression of women in the ministry took many forms. In addition to not being granted ordination, the authenticity of "the call" of women was frequently put to the test. Lee, Elizabeth, and Smith spoke of the many souls they had brought to Christ through their preaching and singing in local black congregations, as well as their preaching and singing in local black congregations, as well as in white and mixed congregations. It was not until Bishop Richard Allen heard Jarena Lee preach that he was convinced that she was of the Spirit. He, however, still refused to ordain her. The "brethren," including some bishops of the 1872 General conference of the A.M.E. Church were convinced that Amanda Berry Smith was blessed with the Spirit of God after hearing her sing at a session held at Fisk University. Smith tells us that "...the Spirit of the Lord seemed to fall on all the people. The preachers got happy... ." This experience brought invitations for her to preach at several churches, but it did not bring an appointment to local congregation as pastor or the right of ordination. She summed up the experience in this way: "... after that many of my brethren believed in me, especially as the question of ordination of women never was mooted in the Conference." [138]

Several black denominations have since begun to ordain women.[139] But this matter of women preachers having the extra burden of proving their call to an extent not required of men still prevails in the Black Church today. A study in which I participated at Union Theological Seminary in New York city bears this out. Interviews with black ministers of different denominations revealed that their prejudices against women, and especially women in the ministry, resulted in unfair expectations and unjust treatment of women ministers whom they encountered.[140]

It is the unfair expectations placed upon women and blatant discrimination that keeps them "in the pew" and "out of the pulpit." This matter of keeping women in the pew has been carried to ridiculous extremes. At the 1971 Annual Convocation of the National Conference of Black Churchmen,141 held at the Liberty Baptist Church in Chicago, I was slightly amused when, as I approached the pulpit to place my cassette tape recorder near the speaker, Walter Fauntroy, as several brothers had already done, I was stopped by a man who informed me that I could not enter the pulpit area. When I asked why not, he directed me to the pastor who told me that women were not permitted in the pulpit, but that he would have a man place the recorder there for me. Although I could not believe that explanation a serious one, I agreed to have a man place it on the pulpit for me and returned my seat in the sanctuary for the continuation of the convocation. The seriousness of the pastor's statement became clear to me later at that meeting when Mary Jane Patterson, a Presbyterian Church executive, was refused the right to speak from the pulpit.[142] This was clearly a case of sex discrimination in a black church—keeping women "in the pew" and "out of the pulpit."

As far as the issue of women in concerned it is obvious that the Black Church described by C. Eric Lincoln has not fared much better than the Negro Church of E. Franklin Frazier.143 The failure of the Black Church and Black Theology to proclaim explicitly the liberation of black women indicated that they cannot claim to be agents of divine liberation. If the theology, like the church, has no word for black women, its conception of liberation is inauthentic.

THE BLACK EXPERIENCE AND THE BLACK WOMAN

For the most part, black church *men* have not dealt with the oppression of the black women in either the Black Church or the black community. Frederick Douglass was one notable exception in the 19th century. His active advocacy for women's rights was a demonstration against the contradiction between preaching "justice for all" and practicing the continued oppression of women. He, therefore, "dared to not claim a right [for himself' which he would not concede to women."[144] These words describe the convictions of a man who was active both in the church and in the larger black community. This is significant because there is usually a direct relationship between what goes on in the Black Church and the black secular community.

The status of black women in the community parallels that of black women in the church. Black Theology considers the black experience to be the context out of which its questions about God and human existence are formulated. This is assumed to be the context which God's revelation is received and interpreted. Only from the perspective of the poor and the oppressed can theology be adequately done. Arising out of the Black Power Movement of the 1960s, Black Theology purports to take seriously the experience of the larger community's struggle for liberation. But if this is, indeed, the case, Black Theology must function in the secular community in the same way as it should function in the church community. It must serve as a "self-test" to see whether the rhetoric or proclamation of the black community's struggle for liberation is consistent with its practices. How does the "self-test" principle operate among the poor and the oppressed? Certainly, Black

Theology has spoken to some of the forms of oppression which exist within the community of the oppressed. Many of the injustices it has attacked are the same as those which gave rise to the prophets of the Old Testament. But the fact that Black Theology does not include sexism specifically as one of those injustices is all too evident. It suggests that the theologians do not understand sexism to be one of the oppressive realities of the black community. Silence on this specific issue can only mean conformity with the status quo. The most prominent black theologian, James Cone, has recently broken this silence.

> *The black church, like all other churches, is a male-dominated church. The difficulty that black male ministers have in supporting the equality of women in the church and society stems partly from the lack of a clear liberation-criterion rooted in gospel and in the present struggles of oppressed peoples... . It is truly amazing that many black male ministers, young and old, can hear the message of liberation in the gospel when related to racism but remain deaf to a similar message in the context of sexism... .145*

It is difficult to understand how black men manage to exclude the liberation of black women from their interpretation of the liberating gospel. Any correct analysis of the poor and oppressed would reveal some interesting and inescapable facts about the situation of women within oppressed groups. Without succumbing to the long and fruitless debate of "who is more oppressed than whom?" I want to make some pointed suggestions to black male theologians.

It would not be very difficult to argue that since black women are the poorest of the poor, the most oppressed of the oppressed, their experience provided a more fruitful context for doing Black Theology. The research of Jacquelyne Jackson attests to the extreme deprivation of black women. Jackson attests to the extreme deprivation of black women. Jackson supports her claim with statistical data that "in comparison with black male sand white males and females, black women yet constitute the most disadvantaged group in the US, as evidenced especially by their largely unenviable educational, occupational, employment and income levels, and availability of marital partners."[146] In other words, in spite of the "quite insignificant" educational advantage that black women have over black men, they have "had the greatest access to the worst jobs at the lowest earnings."[147] It is important to emphasize this fact in order to elevate to its rightful level of concern the condition of black women, not only in the world at large, but in the black community and the Black Church. It is my contention that if Black Theology speaks of the black community as if the special problems of black women do not exist, it is no different from the White Theology it claims to reject precisely because of its inability to take account of the existence of black people in its theological formulations.

It is instructive to note that the experience of black women working in the Black Power movement further accented the problem of the oppression of women in the black community. Because of their invisibility in the leadership of the movement they, like women of the church, provided the "support" segment of the movement. They filled the streets when numbers were needed for demonstrations. They stuffed the envelopes in the offices and performed other menial tasks. Kathleen Cleaver, in a *Black Scholar* Interview, revealed some of the problems in the movement which caused her to become involved in women's liberation issues. While underscoring the crucial role played by women as Black Power activists. Kathleen Cleaver, nonetheless, acknowledged the presence of sex discrimination.

> *I viewed myself as assisting everything that was done.... . The form of assistance that women give in political movements to men is just as crucial as the leadership that men give to those movements. And this is something that is never recognized and never dealt with.* Because women are always relegated to assistance *and this is where I became interested in the liberation of women. Conflicts, constant came up, conflicts that would rise as a result of the fact that I was married to a member of the Central committee and I was also an officer in the Party. Things that I would have suggested myself would be implemented. But if I suggested them the suggestion might be rejected. If they were suggested by a man the suggestion would be implemented.*

It seemed throughout the history of my working with the Party, I always had to struggle with this. The suggestion itself was never viewed objectively. The fact that the suggestion came from a women gave it some lesser value. *And it seemed that it had something to do with the egos of the men involved. I know that the first demonstration that we had at the courthouse for Huey Newton I was very instrumental in organizing, the first time we went out on the soundtracks, I was on the soundtracks; the first leaflet we put out, I wrote; the first demonstration, I made up the pamphlets. And the members of that demonstration for the most part were women. I've noticed that throughout my dealings in the black movement in the United States, that the* most anxious, the most cager, the most active, the most quick to understand the problem and quick to move are women.[148]

Cleaver exposed the fact that even when leadership was given to women, sexism lurked in the wings. As executive secretary of the Student Nonviolent Coordinating Committee (SNCC), Ruby Doris Robinson was described as the "heart beat of SNCC." Yet there were "the constant conflicts, the constant struggles that she was subjected to because she was a woman."[149]

Notwithstanding all the evidence to the contrary, some might want to argue that the central problem of black women is related to their race and not their sex. Such an argument then presumes that the problem cannot be resolved apart from the black struggle. I contend that as long as the black struggle refuses to recognize and deal with its sexism, the idea that women will receive justice from that struggle alone will never work. It will not work because black women will no longer allow black men to ignore their unique problems and needs in the name of some distorted view of the "liberation of the total community." I would bring to the minds of the proponents of this argument the words of President Sekou Toure as he wrote about the role of African women in the revolution. He said, "if African women cannot possibly conduct their struggle in isolation from the struggle that our people wage for African liberation, African freedom, conversely, is not effective unless it brings about the liberation of African women."[150] Black men who have an investment in the patriarchal structure of white America and who intend to do Christian theology have yet to realize that if Jesus is liberator of the oppressed, all of the oppressed must be liberated. Perhaps the proponents of the argument that the case of black women must be subsumed under a larger cause should look to South African theologians Sabelo Ntwasa and Basil Moore. They affirm that "Black theology, as it struggles to formulate a theology of liberation relevant to South Africa, cannot afford to perpetuate any form of domination, not even male domination. If its liberation is not human enough to include the liberation of women, it will not be liberation."[151]

A CHALLENGE TO BLACK THEOLOGY

My central argument is this: Black Theology cannot continue to treat black women as if they were invisible creatures who are on the outside looking into the black experience, the Black Church, and the black theological enterprise. It will have to deal with the community, Black Theology, therefore, must speak to the bishops who hide behind the statement "Women don't want women pastors." It must speak to the pastors who say, "My church isn't ready for women preachers yet." It must teach the seminarians who feel that "women have no place in the seminary." It must address the women in the church and community who are content and complacent with their oppression. It must challenge the educators who would reeducate the people on every issue except the issue of the dignity and equality of women.

Black women represent more than 50 percent of the black community and more than 70 percent of the Black Church. How then can an authentic theology of liberation arise out of these communities without specifically addressing the liberation of the women in both places? Does the fact that certain questions are raised by black women make them any less black concerns? If, as I contend, the liberation of black men and women is inseparable, then a radical split cannot be made between racism and sexism. Black women are oppressed by racism *and* sexism. It is therefore necessary that black men and women be actively involved in combating both evils.

Only as black women in greater numbers make their way from the background to the forefront will the true strength of the black community be fully realized. There is already a heritage of strong black women and men upon which a stronger nation can be built. There is a tradition which declares that God is at work in the experience of the black woman. This tradition, in the context of the total black experience, can provide data for the development of a wholistic black theology. Such a theology will repudiate the God of classical theology who is presented as an absolute Patriarch, a deserting father who created black men and women and then "walked out" in the face of responsibility. Such a theology will look at the meaning of the total Jesus Christ Event; it will consider not only how God through Jesus Christ is related to the oppressed men, but to women as well. Such a theology will "allow" God through the Holy Spirit to work through persons without regard to race, sex, or class. This theology will exercise its prophetic function, and serve as a "self-test" in a church characterized by the sins of racism, sexism, and other forms of oppression. Until black women theologians are fully participating in the theological enterprise, it is important to keep black male theologians and black leaders cognizant of their dereliction. They must be made aware of the fact that black women are needed not only as Christian educators, but as theologians and church leaders. It is only when black women and men share jointly the leadership in theology and in the church and community that the black nation will become strong and liberated. Only then will there be the possibility that Black Theology can become a theology of divine liberation.

One final word for those who argue that the issues of racism and sexism are too complicated and should not be confused. I agree that the issues should not be "confused." But the elimination of both racism and sexism is so crucial for the liberation of black persons that we cannot shrink from facing them together. Sojourner Truth tells us why this is so. In 1867 she spoke out on the issue of suffrage and what she said at that time is still relevant to us as we deal with the liberation of black women today.

> *I feel that if I have to answer for the deeds done in my body just as much as a man, I have a right to have just as much as a man. There is a great stir about colored men getting*

> *their rights, but not a word about the colored women;*
> *and if colored men get their right, and not colored women*
> *theirs, you see the colored men will be masters over the*
> *women, and it will be just as bad as it was before. So, I*
> *am for keeping the thing going while things are stirring;*
> *because if we wait till it is still, it will take a great while*
> *to get it going again... .[152]*

Black women have to keep the issue of sexism "going" in the black community, in the Black Church, and in Black Theology until it has been eliminated. To do otherwise means that they will be pushed aside until eternity. Therefore, with Sojourner Truth, I'm for "keeping things going while things are stirring... ."

END NOTES

[1] Beatriz Melano Couch, remarks on the feminist panel of Theology in the Americas Conference in Detroit in August 1975, printed in *Theology in the Americas,* ed. Sergio Torres and John Eagleson (Maryknoll, N.Y.: Orbis Books, 1976), p. 375.

[2] Consuelo Urquiza, "A Message from a Hispanic-American Woman," *The Fifth Commission; A Monitor for Third World concerns* IV (June-July 1978) insert. The Fifth Commission is a commission of the National Council of the Churches of Christ in the USA (NCC), 475 Riverside Drive, New York, N.Y.

[3] I agree with the Fifth Commission that "the Third World is not a geographical entity, but rather the world of oppressed peoples in their struggle for liberation." In this sense, Black women are included in the term "Third World." However, in order to accent the peculiar identity, problems, and needs of black women in the First World or the Third World contexts, I choose to make the distinction between black and other Third World women.

[4] For a discussion of sexual dualisms in our society, see Rosemary Ruether, *New Woman/New Earth* (New York: Seabury Press, 1975), chap. 1; and *Liberation Theology* (New York: Paulist Press,, 1972), pp. 16ff. Also, for a discussion of sexual (social) dualisms as related

to the brain hemispheres, see Sheila Collins, *A Different Heaven and Earth* (Valley Forge: Judson Press, 1974), pp. 169-170.

5   Angela Davis, "Reflections on the Black Woman's Role in the Community of Slaves," *The Black Scholar*, vol. 4 no. 3 (December 1971), pp. 3-15. I do take issue with Davis's point, however. The black community may have experienced "equality in inequality," but this was forced on them from the dominant or enslaving community. She does not deal with the inequality within the community itself.

6   See Sheila Collins, op. cit., Rosemary Ruether, op. cit., Letty Russell, *Human Liberation in the Feminist Perspective* (Philadelphia: Wesminster Press, 1974); and Mary Daly, *Beyond God the Father* (Boston: Beacon Press, 1973).

7   Surely the factor of race would be absent, but one would have to do an in-depth analysis to determine the possible side effect on the status of black women.

8   James Cone. *A Black Theology of Liberation* (Philadelphia: J.B. Lippincott, 1970), p. 23.

9   Eulalio Baltazar discusses color symbolism (white is good; black is evil) as a reflection of racism in the White Theology which perpetuates it. *The Dark Center: A Process Theology of Blackness* (New York: Paulist Press, 1973).

10 One may want to argue that Black Theology is not concerned with sexism but with racism, I will argue in this essay that such a theology could speak only half the truth, if truth at all.

11 Karl Barth, *Church Dogmatics,* vol. 1, part 1, p.2.

12   Cone, op. cit., pp. 230-232.

13 James Cone and Albert Clearage do make this observation of the contemporary Black Church and its response to the struggles against racism. See Leage, *The Black Messiah* (New York: Sheed and Ward, 1969), passim; and Cone, op. cit., passim.

14 A study that I conducted in the Philadelphia Conference of the African Methodist Episcopal Church, May 1976. It also included sporadic sampling of churches in other conferences in the First Episcopal District. As for example, a church of 1, 660 members (600 men and 1,160 women) had a trustee board of 8 men and 1 woman and a steward board of 13 men and 6 women. A church of

100 members (35 men and 65 women) had a trustee board of 5 men and 4 women and a steward board of 5 men and 4 women.

15 Jarena Lee, *The Life and Religious Experience of Jenna Lee: A colored Lady Giving an Account of Her Call to Preach the Gospel* (Philadelphia, 1836), printed in Dorothy Porter, ed., *Early Negro Writing 1760-1837* (Boston: Beacon Press, 1971), pp. 474-514.

16 Ibid., p. 503 (italics added). Carol George in *Segregated Sabbaths* (New York: Oxford University Press, 1973), presents a very positive picture of the relationship between Jarena Lee and Bishop Richard Allen. She feels that by the time Lee approached Allen, he had "modified his views on women's rights" (p.129). She contends that since Allen was free from the Methodist Church, he was able to "determine his own policy" with respect to women under the auspices of the A.M.E. Church. It should be noted that Bishop Allen accepted the Rev. Jarena Lee as a woman preacher and not as an ordained preacher with full rights and privileges thereof. Even Carol George admitted that Lee traveled with Bishop Allen only "as an unofficial member of their delegation to conference sessions in New York and Baltimore," "to attend," not to participate in them. I agree that this does represent progress in Bishop Allen's view as compared to Lee's first approach; on the second approach, he was at least encouraging. Then he began "to promote her interests" (p. 129)—But he did not ordain her.

17 Ibid.

18 Elizabeth: A Colored Minister of the Gospel," printed in Bert James Loewnberg and Ruth Bogin, ed., *Black Women in Nineteenth-Century American Lfe* (University Park, Pa.: The Pennslvania State University Press, 1976), p. 132. The denomination of Elizabeth is not known to this writer. Her parents were Methodists, but she was separated from her parents at the age of eleven. However, the master from which she gained her freedom was Presbyterian. Her autobiography was published by the Philadelphia Quakers.

19 Ibid., p.133.

20 Amanda Berry Smith, *An Autobiography: The Story of the Lord's Dealings with Mrs. Amanda Berry Smith,* the Colored Evangelist (Chicago, 1893); printed in Loewenberg and Bogin, op. cit., p. 157.

21 Ibid.

22 Ibid., p. 159.

23 The African Methodist Episcopal Church stated ordaining women in 1948, according to the Rev. William P. Foley of Bridgestreet A.M.E. Church in Brooklyn, New York. The first ordained woman was Martha J. Keys.

The African Methodist Episcopal Zion Church ordained women as early as 1884. At that time, Mrs. Julia A. Foote was ordained Deacon in the New York Annual Conference. In 1894 Mrs. Mary J. Small was ordained Deacon and in 1898, she was ordained Elder. See David Henry Bradley, Sr., *A History of the* A.M.E. *Zion Church,* vol. (part) II, 1872-1968 (Nashville: The Parthenon Press, 1970), pp. 384-393.

The Christian Methodist Episcopal Church enacted legislation to ordain women in the 1970 General Conference. Since then, approximately 75 women have been ordained. See the Rev. N. Charles Thomas, general secretary of the C.M.E. Church and director of the Department of the Ministry, Memphis, Tennessee.

Many Baptist churches still do not ordain women. Some churches in the Pentecostal tradition do not ordain women. However, in some other Pentecostal churches, women are founders, pastors, elders, and bishops.

In the case of the A.M.E.Z. Church, where women were ordained as early as 1884, the important question would be, what happened to the women who were ordained? In addition, all of these churches (except for those which do give leadership to women) should answer the following questions: Have women been assigned to pastor "class A" churches? Have women been appointed as presiding elders? (There is currently one woman presiding elder in the A.M.E. Church.) Have women been elected to serve as bishop of any of these churches? Have women served as presidents of conventions?

24 Yolande Herron, Jacquelyn Grant, Gwendolyn Johnson, and Samuel Roberts, "Black Women and the Field Education Experience at Union Theological Seminary: Problems and Prospects" (New York: Union Theological Seminary, May 1978).

25 This organization continues to call itself the National Conference of Black Churchmen despite the protests of women members.

26 NCBC has since made the decision to examine the policies of its host institutions (churches) to avoid the reoccurrence of such incidents.

27 E. Franklin Frazier, *The Negro Church in America;* C. Eric Lincoln, *The Black Church Since Frazier* (New York: Schocken Books, 1974), passim.

28 Printed in Philip S. Foner, ed., *Frederick Douglass on Women's Rights* (Westport, Conn.: Greenwood Press), p. 51.

29 Cone," Black ecumenism and the Liberation Struggle," delivered at Yale University, February 16-17, 1978, and Quinn Chapel A.M.E. Church, May 22, 1978. In two other recent papers he has voiced concern on women's issues, relating them to the larger question of liberation. These papers are: "New Roles in the Ministry: A Theological Appraisal" and "Black Theology and the Black Church:" Where Do We Go from Here?" Both papers appear in this volume.

30 Jacquelyne Jackson, "But Where Are the Men?" *The Black Scholar,* op. cit., p.30.

31 Ibid., p. 32.

32 Kathleen Cleaver was interviewed by Sister Julia Herve. Ibid., pp. 55-56.

33 Ibid., p. 55.

34 Sekou Toure, "The Role of Women in the Revolution," *The Black Scholar,* vol. 6, no. 6 (March 1975), p. 32.

35 Sabelo Ntwasa and Basil Moore, "The Concept of God in Black Theology," in *The Challenge of Black Theology in South Africa,* ed. Basil Moore (Atlanta, Ga.: John Knox Press, 1974), pp. 25-26.

36 Sojourner Truth, "Keeping the Things Going While Things Are Stirring," printed in Miriam Schneir, ed., *Feminism: The Essential Historical Writings* (New York: Random House, 1972), pp. 129-130.

CHAPTER SEVEN
Psycho-Social Issues

Mwalimu David Burgest and Mary Goosby analyze games of love and power together with their effect upon black male and black female relationships. The authors limit their analysis and evaluation of the games to the specific behavior of the games rather than to a diagnosis of the underlying psychological dynamics. Burgest and Goosby hope the reader may be able to develop and increase self-awareness, self-insight, sensitivity, and human growth from the dynamics provided.

Clyde Franklin identifies two major sources for black male and black female conflict together with suggestions for reducing the conflict. The major sources of conflict are identified as (1) non-complementarily of sex role definitions internalized by black males and black females, and (2) structural barriers in the environments of black males and black females. The suggestions offered for attenuating the conflict include altering three social psychological phenomena: (1) Black male and black female socialization experiences; (2) Black male and black female role-playing strategies; and (3) Black male and black female personal communication mechanisms.

La Frances Rodgers-Rose explores issues that confront black men and women as they interact in a dialectic process of creation and criticism. She, specifically, addresses some myths about black men and women and properties of male-female relationships.

GAMES IN BLACK MALE/ FEMALE RELATIONSHIPS

MWALIMU DAVID R. BURGEST * MARY GOOSBY

As we analyze black male/female relationships, we find that there are numerous negative interpersonal relationship games played that are destructive to sustaining a positive and healthy relationship. Most often, these "games people play" are responsible for the disintegration and disunity existing in black male/female relationships. Eric Berne, in his book *Games People Play* (1964) defines games as a recurring set of transactions, often repetitions, superficially plausible, with a concealed motivation (conscious or unconscious) toward a hidden payoff. In a more colloquial term, he defines games as a series of moves with a snare or "gimmick." It is pertinent to emphasize that the games played may be conscious or unconscious. That is, individuals may not be consciously aware of the games they may be playing, and maybe resistant to having those games brought to consciousness by the nonplayer. Unconscious games are probably the most destructive, in that the player is not aware of the unmet need being aroused, and those unconscious drives are brought into the relationship from early childhood relationships with parents and others.

The hidden payoff noted in the definition above may vary according to the psychological needs of the individual. For example, the hidden payoff may be a desire to attain one-upmanship, inflict pain, control another, seek favoritism, and so on. It is not suggested that all the games being enumerated in this article are unique to the black male/ female experience, for some of these games are generic to any male/ female experience, for some of these games are genetic to any male/ female relationship in that the black experience is part and parcel of the human experience. Nonetheless, the dynamics of all the games outlined in this article will elaborate on the characteristics unique to the black experience.

Games in black male/female interactions must be analyzed and understood from the perspective of prevailing negative myths, stereotypes, and assumptions that affect those relationships. The research and contributions of many scholars help to provide the theoretical and philosophical background necessary to comprehend components of black male/female interaction from a game theory model. Robert Staples (1982) provides a social-scientific appraisal of the myths of black male sexuality dispelling the negative stereotypes and myths that contribute to destructive games. According to Staples, black males and females must recognize that they are both victims of racism and the racist myths; therefore, each must avoid actions that aid and abet these forces and contribute to a dialogue necessary to iron out the differences between black men and women. Contributing to a breakdown in communication and interaction, there are a host of commonly held erroneous assumptions that black women make about black men (Burgest and Bowers, 1981a) and that black men make about black women (Burgest and Bowers, 1981b), in addition to the overall barriers developing genuine and authentic relations between blacks (Burgest, 1980).

The empirical research compiled on the thought, feelings, and aspirations of black men (Gary, 1981) clearly calls for an evaluation of role definition in the black male/female relationship. The exploration of games in the black male/female interaction should help clarify inconsistencies in the definition of role. Moreover, the implication of racism, sexism, and women's liberation (Davis, 1981) cannot be ignored in the dynamics of black male/female communications and interactions. Often, it is the black American's assimilation and identification with the social value and social structure of the American society that contributes to the difficulty in interaction. As we review the makeup of games in the black male/female relationship, it is apparent that racism and stereotypes play an important underlying part in prohibiting genuine communications.

The purpose of this article is to simply highlight, expose, and illuminate some of the games played in the black male/female interaction. It is hoped that the reader may be able to develop and increase self-awareness, self-insight, sensitivity, and human growth from the dynamics provided. We will limit their analysis and evaluation of the games to the specific behavior of the games rather than a diagnosis of the underlying psychological dynamics. It is impossible to do otherwise without understanding the complete background and social histories of the individual(s) involved.

The few games chosen for this manuscript were selected on the basis of their common use and popularity in black male/female interactions; yet some of them are among the more destructive and misunderstood games. These games are misunderstood in that they are not often taken as superficial, and for that reason those game is most destructive. By the same token, the popular and common use of the games provide them with legitimacy; nonetheless, it is those games that continue to foster disintegration and disunity in the black male/female relationship. For organizational purposes only, these games are divided into games of love and games of power.

GAMES OF LOVE

If you love me, you will … A general assumption in male/female relationships is that if you love me, you will … do this, that, or the other. In this instance, love is viewed as a mechanism used in the relationship to bargain, barter, and often manipulate situations and circumstances to one's advantage. The true test of *love* in this game is actualized both by the gratification one received from having someone else do something for them against the other's will, as well as the fulfillment of the unmet need to control and manipulate.

The ultimate social and psychological dangers in this game rest in the manifestation of the "Russian roulette" syndrome, whereby one individual perpetually seeks a heightened reaffirmation of their notion or love: If you love me, you will jump off the building. Implicit in the minds of many is the belief that love is not love unless one's wishes and desires are totally submitted to by the other. Thus, this game makes love one-dimensional and one-directed by subjugating the feelings and desires of the other party. An adequate response to such a game being played is, "If you loved me, you wouldn't ask me that."

Second, the element of testing and bribing is inherent in this game. One party or both may engage in a process to try and measure "how much" love the other party is willing to submit to one's will.

Therefore, if one's partner fails or refuses to acquiesce to the will of the other, an inventory is compiled for later use in the relationship to say "If you loved me, you would have."

One of the primary destructive features of such gamesmanship is that individuals may consciously manipulate another person for their personal gratifications and needs under the rubric of love. The most dangerous element, however, rests with the individual's unawareness that such behavior is a game, he or she truly feels that the authenticity of love in the relationship is legitimized by such interaction.

Authentic and healthy love is not based on testing, manipulations, or bribes as depicted in the "If you love me, you will" game. Love must be based on the assumption of sharing, unity, and compromise, with the capacity for both to give and receive in the relationship. When one gives in the relationship, it should be devoid of persuasion or manipulation. By the same token, when one receives in the relationship, it should not be contaminated with an underlying element or manipulation or bribe. This is not to infer those partners should not please their spouses or mates by doing things to bring them joy or pleasure even though the giver may only be happy by pleasing the mate. Yet, those situations should not be forced by either partner under the rubric or "If you love me, you will."

If it weren't for you, I could ... A common destructive element in relationships is for one partner to blame the other for blocking or prohibiting his or her goals, aspirations, and movement toward self-actualization and self-fulfillment. It is not uncommon to hear one partner boast about what he or she could have accomplished in life "if it weren't for" the other partner, or to boast about what he or she could have accomplished in life "If it weren't for the other party." The perceived obstacles are usually of a nature whereby one partner feels compelled to redirect his or her goals and aspirations to accommodate the other. In some extreme situations, one mate may oppose, reject, and fight the goals, plans, and aspirations of the other mate. Consequently, the mate under attack may decide to abolish his or her present aspirations in order to "keep peace" in the relationship. On the other hand, there is the situation where one mate may feel distressed and burdened by emotional conflicts in the relationship, and is unable to succeed in personal and professional endeavors to these conflicts.

There are probably an endless number of situations where the principles of "if it weren't for you" prevails. Inherent in these dynamics is a love-hate ambivalence whereby the individual who feels cheated and deprived questions the sacrifices he or she made based on the present rewards of the relationship. Nonetheless, the psychological payoff of the "if it weren't for you" game may provide a convenient scapegoat for the internal inadequacies and deficits felt about oneself. The game is to achieve the goal of soliciting sympathy for one's condition or indulging in self-pity. This is not suggesting that goals and plans are not sometimes altered or delayed due to authentic situations and circumstances in relationships. However, the search for fulfillment and actualization in life is a perpetual process requiring that one must psychologically transcend many obstacles and difficulties.

In the case of illness, death, and sickness, "if it weren't for you, I could ..." game must be viewed from a different perspective than the obstacles in interpersonal relationships that one may perceive as destructive to goals. It is the dynamics of the latter that is being addressed her. The underlying problem in this kind of interaction and relationship is one of mutual goals-setting and priorities. One of the intentions of the hidden payoff is to provoke guilt and create a victim in the other party, rather than address insecurities and inadequacies in self.

The bottom line is that no individual can prevent another from attaining goals in life once the other individual has become aware that such games are being played. Therefore, the game "if it weren't for you, I could ..." is inappropriate. Second, there is no need for one individual to feel guilty about his or her achievement sand advancements as long as that individual is aware that he or she did not bribe or manipulate to get there. Again, the manipulation and bribe will not work as long as the other party becomes aware of the game.

Finally, success and happiness in a relationship is dependent on both parties becoming all each can become as individuals, and any subterfuge of this dynamics results in destructive unhappiness.

Why don't you make me happy? One of the greatest myths in an individual's relationships is that one can find another being who can "make me happy." It may be assumed that partners, mates, and spouses can work together for a fulfilled life and hope to move together as interdependent bodies. However, the realities are that individuals seek relationships in order to gain joy, happiness, and fulfillment. It is often misery, rather than love, that pulls individuals together in a relationship. The old adage that "misery loves company" is appropriate here, but few seem to recognize that "*love* loves company" also, and it is difficult for partners in relationship to determine if they come together out of love or misery. There are numerous accounts provided by individuals who say "I met my partner at a time when I was low and he brought me out of it."

As long as people believe the prevailing myth that someone else can make them happy, rather than look at enjoyment and happiness as internal and self-autonomous, the major obstacles to an effective successful relationship will be the need of one individual to be "made happy" by someone else.

On the other side of the coin, "make me happy" syndrome and myth leaves individuals' feelings as though they are responsible for making the other person happy. Yet, the sadness, loneliness, and despair that individuals face may not be related whatsoever to the relationship with the other partner. Many mates are unable to recognize the difference between the "unhappiness" caused by the relationship. Even if individuals recognized the difference, it may be assumed that there are those who would not acknowledge their unhappiness as being internal. Nonetheless, the premise of "Why don't you make me happy?" is not to be confused with loneliness and despair due to internal and individual conflict with self, but conflict in the relationship due to external unfulfilled needs.

In conclusion, the most destructive element in this game of "Why don't make me happy?" rests with fallacy that happiness is something that exists outside of oneself. There is a view that material things, commodities, and circumstances make one happy. For many people, happiness is like a butterfly. The more they chase after it, the more it eludes them; but the moment they sit patiently and get to know themselves, the butterfly comes and lands on their fingertip. Two happy people come together and create more happiness; otherwise, misery will prevail.

You are not like the person I first met. The death of many relationships is cause by the "You are not like the person I first met" assumption. The irony of this attitude is that it is more than usual that the character and disposition of an individual that first attracts another person later destroys the relationship. In other words, the things that most attracted one individual to another become the very same things that may later drive away that individual.

People are usually attracted to someone else because the character of the other person fulfills some deficits the person may see in themselves. Otherwise, there are persons who are attracted to another because the character they perceive is one that is found to be facilitative for their need. A woman may be attracted to a man because he is articulate, analytical, communicative, and intellectual. Those characteristics may be seen as the necessary qualities for conversation and dialogue, as well as the qualities for advancement in the career world. Yet, in the interpersonal relationship, those same qualities and characters may be used by the partner to persuade and coerce. When those qualities influence the interaction in the relationship, the other partner may feel helpless and distraught enough to say, "You are not like the person I first met."

It must be recognized that partners do outgrow each other and may grow in different directions as the relationship unfolds. This does happen. The fact of the matter is no two individuals are the same as they were when they were engaged in a relationship two, three, or four weeks, months, or years ago. The reality of the statement renders the game superficial.

The issues generally being spoken to in such a game is that one partner is feeling that the other is outgrowing him or her mentally, psychologically, socially, and spiritually the underlying assumption being that "my partner is growing 'away' from me." All individuals, like children do not grow at the same speed or rate. "You are not the person I met" should be counteracted with "You might be right … but would you like to take the time to get to know me all over again?"

I am unhappy and I want you to be unhappy. It is an accepted fact that there are unhappy people in the world and their unhappiness is related to internal psychological causes that have little or nothing to do with other people. In other cases, unhappiness may be directly related to dynamics involving other people and circumstances, including problems in the relationship.

When unhappiness prevails in relationship due to any of the above factors, the unhappy person often attempts to make the above person unhappy. It may be that one partner is functioning well in the area of unemployment, promotion, and social relations and the other partner feels jeopardized in those other areas. The unhappy person does all that in within his or her power to dilute the happiness of the other partner. This may be manifested through degrading, minimizing, or placing obstacles in the path of the other partner. The overt behavior and options are plentiful, as is the destructiveness. The unhappy person may exaggerate his or her "unhappiness" as a means of soliciting increased sympathy and avoid participating in the happy moments of the other partner.

One of the inherent dangers in this game is that healthy partners tend to assume the burden and share in the "unhappiness" of their mates in spite of whether or not they are responsible. It is a revelation when the healthy partner liberates himself or herself. The unhealthy cycle is that the partner is not happy unless the other partner is unhappy. This is not to suggest that one person's happiness is dependent on the sadness of the other person, but that some people feels overshadowed by the prevailing joy of their partner. It is only through understanding the dynamics of these interactions that dialogue may develop to resolve the difficulties.

If you don't tell me, you love me, you don't love me. There is a need for many partners to be reminded constantly that they are loved. They need to be told "I love you" by the other partner in the relationship; at the same time, there are individuals who find it difficult to verbalize their love to their partner or mate. A dilemma develops when a couple is composed of one individual who find it difficult to express love verbally and the other has a need to be constantly told "I love you." For the partner who desires to hear repetitiously "I love you," those words are necessary to consummate the affection that binds. There is usually no other action or need that may justify the affection and attitude of love except hearing the words "I love you." Actions and deeds are not sufficient to justify love for the individual who needs always to hear "I love you." There are those who feel that if you cannot say "I love you," then there is no love in the relationship. On the other hand, there are individuals who are unable to verbalize is due to culture, childhood experiences, and family background, which has nothing to do with the feelings and strong emotions that may exist.

As for those individuals who are unable to say "I love you" because of a void feeling for love, the mere verbalization of "I love you" will be nothing more than the "sound of a brass symbol," and thereby are not supported by action. Therefore, the emphasis of this game focuses on the individual who may demonstrate unspoken love in behavior, but never verbalizes "I love you."

Women, more than men, say "I like to hear you say it sometimes." Yet, there are men who either feel uncomfortable saying "I love you" or are just unable to do it. In mature and healthy relationships, the resolution to this game of "Tell me that you love me" can be resolved through the mutual respect for the sensitive emotions of others. This is true not only for one's deep-seated emotions regarding the verbalization of love, but includes other areas in which mutual distance may be needed.

GAMES OF POWER

I pay the cost to be the boss. In today's society many relationships are reduced to a basic economic one in which the transactions are as between partners in business, stockholders, and financial investors. The degree of decision making, collaboration, and feedback in the relationship is determined by the rank in salary. The greatest obstacle to this game is that "paying the cost to be the boss" is not limited to decision making; it is also related to the economic partnership existing in the social and sexual relationship. The under lying danger in the above game is the association of money, income, and salary with power and control. It is the view that if I bring more financially into this relationship than you, "What I say goes."

The hidden dimension of the "paying the cost" game often is the insecurities involving one's self-worth. Males and female's capitalist America tend to associate their self-worth, identity, and self-esteem with their economic and professional status in life. At the same time, power and prestige are associated with one's professional and economic status. Therefore, these artificial variables of self-concepts become intricately interwoven into the fabric of relationships, rather than the relationships being based on the element of human relations.

One must question the use and definition of "power" and "authority" in interpersonal relationships as an equation for such concepts in the economic and political world.

Don't you be here when I get back and don't you be gone. A major dilemma faced by partners in relationships is the double-bind and double-message in communications and actions. In other words, "You are damned if you do and damned if you don't." The underlying payoff is that the other partner is "doomed." Yet, such binds are never communicated so directly and the scapegoat is invariably put in a position to justify and prove his or her worthiness.

A partner may forget the spouse's birthday and try to compensate for it by getting something extra nice for the wedding anniversary. The spouse scolds the partner for forgetting the birthday and chastises him or her for the anniversary by saying "If you didn't get me anything for my birthday, you didn't have to get me anything for the anniversary." On the other hand, the spouse may get home late from work without calling and the partner may accuse him or her of cheating. Yet, when the spouse arrives home early and has the meal ready, the other partner accuses him or her of "operating out of guilt."

The creation of double-bind situations are very serious infringements in interpersonal social dynamics. The perpetrator is usually not aware of his or her behavior and the victim is unable to find contentment and enjoyment in the relationship. Usually, the victims' realization that the game is being played brings about a change. It is the responsibility of the victim to increase somehow the self-awareness of the perpetrator regarding actions in creating double-binds. If the situation of double-binding is severe, the resolution to this problem may require the intervention of a third party to facilitate a change, through counseling or other support groups.

I am dissatisfied, and don't you try to change it. It is a natural tendency for partners in relationships to try and cheer each other up in times of depression and despair irrespective of the causes of the melancholy. By the same token, it is natural that a partner's concern about the welfare of a dissatisfied mate will affect his or her spiritual state. Yet, it is difficult for many partners in interpersonal relationships to accept the realization that their mate may enjoy being dissatisfied and does not want it changed. It is a fact that there are people who are happy when they are complaining, and they seek to be dissatisfied. If you and your mate are out with others to enjoy a movie or theater, your mate will find reasons to be dissatisfied. He or she did not like the seats, the performance, or the length of the show. If you relocate to a different community for a job, your mate will find cause to be dissatisfied with the community. On vacation—and in most other areas of the mate's life—he or she will be dissatisfied and complaining.

The burden of dissatisfaction rests on the shoulders of a spouse or mate who continues to try and provide satisfying experiences and circumstances. When the mate meets the specification of the dissatisfied partner, there will be something else the mate will find dissatisfying.

One partner may be investing all the emotional energy into the relationship; however, the other partner may be interested in ownership of property, a professional career, or travel. As the motivated and inspired partner seeks advancement toward his or her goals, the other partner may proceed to sabotage the accomplishments. Yet, the game is inevitable self-destructive in that the motivated partner will not be satisfied with "staying there" with the other spouse, even if he or she were successful in reaching the goals.

The myth supporting the notion that "I don't want it' you can't have it" rests with the premise that when you help a spouse achieve goals, they will drop you for someone else. There are numerous examples cited about situations when the female worked and helped the male complete law or medical school, after which he terminated the relationship. It is this fear that supports the "stay here with me" or "I don't want it and I don't want you to have it" mentality. The "no-win dilemma" inherent in this game makes it so that the partner playing the game will lose what it was he or she did not want along with the individual he or she was trying to prevent from having it. Needless to say, the issue at hand is for those who play the game of "I don't want it and you can't have it" to resolve the contradiction inherent in the dilemma. If one chooses to withhold support or employ other tactics to cause the other person to remain with him or her, the relationship is bordering on conflict and termination. By the same token, the risks involved in losing a partner through preventing him or her from having what they want must be as great as the risk of supporting a partner and eliminating the "I don't want it, you can't have it (stay here with me)" game.

Getting even. This game occurs when one party, however incorrectly or correctly, perceives that he or she has been wronged by the other party. Therefore, the party who feels the same or similar "wrongful" activity in an attempt to include the same or similar pain in the other person. In a military battle, it is easy to determine the extent of damage needed for "getting even," but in interpersonal relationships the investments and costs cannot be estimated. This is true mainly because of the different ethics, values, and principles that govern individual behavior; consequently, the personal cost that one party would have to pay in order to engage in activities similar to those of the other partner maybe too detrimental. On the other hand, "getting even" may be a mere justification for the need to engage in such activity desired in the first place.

This is not suggested that the first inclination of a partner is to "strike back" at the other, once he or she perceived that they were wronged. The destructiveness of such a game may not be seen in the vicious cycle that is set up. A "pulling of the coat," or opening doors to communications could avoid a prolonged and serious relationship problem.

REFERENCES

Berne, E. (1964) Games People Play. New York: Grove.

Burgest, D.R. (1980) "Black awareness and authentic black-black relations," in M. Asante and A. Vandi (eds.) Contemporary Black Thought: Alternative Analysis in the Social and Behavioral Sciences. Beverly Hills, CA: Sage.

______and J. Bowers (1981a) "Erroneous assumptions black women make about black men." Black Male/Female Relationships 2,5: 13-20.

______(1981b) "Erroneous assumptions black men make about black women." Black Male/Female Relationships 2,6: 13-20.

Davis, A.Y. (1981) Women, Race and Class. New York: Random House.

Gary, L.E. (1981) Black Men. Beverly Hills, CA: Sage.

Staples, R. (1982) Black Masculinity: The Black Male's Role in Society. San Francisco: Black Scholar Press.

BLACK MALE-BLACK FEMALE CONFLICT: INDIVIDUALLY CAUSED AND CULTURALLY NURTURED

CLYDE W. FRANKLIN II

Who is to blame? Currently, there is no dearth of attention directed to black male-black female relationships. Books, magazine articles, academic journal articles, public forums, radio programs, television shows, and everyday conversations have been devoted to black male-black female relationships for several years. Despite the fact that the topic has been discussed over the past several decades by some authors (e.g., Frazier, 1939; Drake and Clayton, 1945; Grier and Cobb, 1968), Wallace's *Black Macho and the Myth of the Superwoman* has been the point of departure for many contemporary discussions of the topic since its publication in 1979.

Actually, Wallace's analysis was not so different in content from other analyses of black male-black female relationships (e.g., Drake and Cayton's analysis was "timely." Coming so soon on the heels of the black movement in the late 1960s and early 1970s, and at a time when many black male-inspired gains for blacks were disappearing rapidly, the book was explosive. Its theme, too, was provocative. Instead of repeating the rhetoric of the late 1960s and 1970s that blamed conflictual relationships between black men and black women on white society, Wallace implied that the blame lay with black males. In other words, the blame lay with those black warriors who only recently had been perceived as the "saviors" of black people in America. Wallace's lamenting theme is captured in a quote from her book: "While she stood by silently as he became a man, she assumed that he would finally glorify and dignify black womanhood just as the white man has done for white women." Wallace goes to say that this has not happened for black women.

Wallace updates her attack on black men in a later article entitled "A Black Feminist's Search for Sisterhood" (1982:9). Her theme, as before, is that black men are just as oppressive of black women as white man. She states:

> *Whenever I raised the question of a black woman's humanity in conversations with a black man, I got a similar reaction. Black men, at least the ones I knew, seemed totally confounded when it came to treating black women like people... . I discovered my voice and when brothers talked to me, I talked back. This had its hazards. Almost got my eye blackened several times. My social life was like guerilla warfare. Here was the logic behind our grandmother's old saying, "A nigga man ain't shit."*

Wallace, however, is not alone in placing the blame on black men for deteriorating relations between black men and black women. Allen (1938:62), in a recent edition of *Essence* magazine, states:

> *Black women have a tendency to be male-defined, subjugating their own needs for the good of that fragile male ego... . The major contradiction is that we black women in our hearts, have a tendency to believe black men need more support and understanding than we do. We bought the Black Revolutionary line that a woman's place was paces behind the man. We didn't stomp Stokeley when he made the statement that the only position for a woman in the movement was prone.*

Such attacks on black men have been met with equally ferocious counterattacks by some black authors (both black men and black women). A few months following the publication of Wallace's book, an entire issue of the *Black Scholar* was devoted to black male-black female relationships. Of the responses to Wallace by such scholars as Jones (1979), Karenga (1979), Staples (1979), and numerous others, Karenga's response is perhaps the most controversial and maybe the most volatile. Karenga launches a personal attack on Wallace suggesting that she is misguided and perhaps responding from personal hurt. Recognizing the complexity of black male-black female relationships, Karenga contends that much of it is due not to black men but to the white power structure. Along similar lines, Moore (1980) has exhorted black women to stop criticizing black men and blame themselves for the disintegrating bonds between black men and black women.

Staples, in his response to Wallace and others who would place the blame on black men for disruptive relationships between black men and black women, points out that while sexism within the black culture may be an emerging problem, most black men do not have the institutionalized power to oppress black women. He believes that the black male's "condition" in society is what bothers black males. Staples devoted much attention to the institutional decimation of black men and suggests that this is the reason for black male-black female conflict. Noting the high morality and suicide rates of black men, the fact that half a million black men are in prison, one-third of urban black men are saddled with drug problems and that 25% to 30% do not have steady employment, Staples implied that black men-black female conflict may be related to *choose*. This means that a shortage of black men may limit the choices that black women have in selecting partners. As Braithwaite (1981) puts it, the insufficient supply of black men places black women at a disadvantage by giving black men the upper hand. In a specific relationship, for example, if a black woman fails to comply with the black man's wishes, the black man has numerous other options, including not only other black women but also women of other races.

In a more recent discussion of black male-black female relationships, Alvin Poussaint (1982:40) suggests that black women "adopt a patient and creative approach in exploring and creating new dimensions of the black male-black female bond." Others, like Ronald Braithwaite, imply in their analyses of relationships with black men and black women that black women's aggressiveness, thought to be a carryover from slavery, may be partly responsible for black male-black female conflict.

Succinctly, by and large, most black male and black female author writing on the subject seem to agree that many black male-black female relationships today are destructive and potentially explosive. What they do not agree on, however, are the causes of the problems existing between black men and black women. As we have seen, some believe that black men are the cause. Others contend that black women contribute disproportionately to black male-black female conflict. Still others blame white racism solely, using basic assumptions that may be logically inadequate (see Franklin, 1980). Many specific reasons for the conflict often postulated include the notions that black men are abusive toward black women, that black men are irresistibly attracted to white women (despite the fact that only approximately 120, 000 black men were married to white women are too aggressive, that black women don't support black men—the list goes on. Few of these reasons, however, really explore the underlying cause of the conflict. Instead, they are descriptions of the conflict-behaviors that are indicators of the tension between black men and black women. But what is the cause of the behavior—the cause of the tension that so often disrupts harmony in black male-black female relationships?

Given the various approaches many black authors have taken in analyzing black male-black female relationships, it is submitted that two major sources of black male-black female conflict can be identified: (1) the noncomplementary of sex-role definitions internalized by black males and black females; and (2) structural barriers in the environments of black males and black females. Each source is explored separately below.

SOURCES OF CONFLICT BETWEEN BLACK MEN AND BLACK WOMEN

Sex-Role Noncomplementary among Black Males and Black Females

Much black male-black female conflict stems directly from incompatible role enactments by black males and black females. Incompatible role enactments by black men and black women occur because they internalize sex-role definitions that are noncomplementary. For example, a black woman in a particular conflictual relationship with a black male may feel that her black man is supposed to assume a dominant role, but she also may be inclined to exhibit behaviors that are opposed to his dominance and her subordinance. In the same relationship, the black man may pay her lip service to assuming a dominant role but may behave "passively" with respect to some aspects of masculinity and in a dominant manner with respect to other aspects.

One reason for role conflict between black man and black women is that many contemporary black man and black women is that many contemporary black women internalize two conflicting definitions of femininity, whereas many contemporary black men internalize only a portion of the traditional definition of masculinity. Put simply, numerous black women hold attitudes that are both highly masculine and highly feminine. On the other hand, their male counterparts develop traits that are highly consistent with certain aspects of society's definition of masculinity, but that are basically unrelated to other aspects of the definition. Thus, in a given relationship, one may find a black woman who feels and behaves in ways that are both assertive and passive, dominant and subordinant, decisive and indecisive, and so on. Within that same relationship, a black man may exhibit highly masculine behaviors, such as physical aggressiveness, sexual dominance, and even violence, but behave indifferently with respect to the masculine work ethic—assuming responsibility for family-related activities external to the home, being aggressive in the work place, and the like.

The reason these incongruent attitudes and behaviors exist among black men and black women is that they have received contradictory messages during early socialization. It is common for black women to have received two messages: One message states "Because you will be a black woman, it is imperative that you learn to take care of yourself because it is hard to find a black man who will take care of you." A second message frequently received by young black females that conflicts with the first message is "your ultimate achievement will occur when you have snared a black man who will take care of you." In discussing early socialization experiences with countless young black women in recent years. I have found that most of them agree that these two messages were given them by socialization agents and agencies such as child caretakers, relatives, peer group members, the black church, and the media.

When internalized, these two messages often produce a black woman who seems to reject aspects of the traditional female sex role in America such as passivity, emotional and economic dependence, and female subordinance while accepting other aspects of the role such as expressiveness, warmth, nurturance. This is precisely why black women seem to be more androgynous than white women. Black women's androgyny, though, may be more a function of necessity than anything else. It may be related to the scarcity of black men who assume traditional masculine roles in male-female relationships.

Whatever the reason for black women's androgynous orientations, because of such orientations black women oftentimes find themselves in conflictual relationships with black men or in no stable relationships at all. The scenario generally can be described as follows. Many black women in early adulthood usually begin a search for black Prince Charming. However, because of the dearth of Black men who can be or are willing to be Prince Charming's for black women, black women frequently soon give up the search for such a black man. They give up the search, settle for less, and "like" what they settle for even less. This statement is important because many black women's eventual choices are destined to become constant reminders that the "female independence" message received during the early socialization process is the correct message. But, because black women also have to deal with the second socialization message, many come to feel that they have failed in their roles as women. In an effort to correct their mistakes, black women often choose to enact the aspect of their androgynous role that is decidedly aggressive and/or independent. They may decide either to "go it alone" or to prod their black men into becoming Prince Charmings. The first alternative for black women often results in self-doubt, lowered self-esteem, and, generally, unhappiness and dissatisfaction. After all, society nurtures the "find a man" message far beyond early socialization. The second message, unfortunately, produces little more than the first message because black women in such situations usually end up in conflictual relationships with black men, who also have undergone a rather complicated socialization process. Let us explore briefly the conflicting messages numerous black men receive during early socialization.

One can find generally that black men, too, have received too conflicting messages during early socialization. One message received by young black males is "to become a man means that you must become dominant, aggressive, decisive, responsible, and, in some instance, violent in social encounters with others." A second message received by young black males that conflicts with the first is, "You are black and you must not be too aggressive, too dominant, and so on, because the *man* will cut you down." Internalization of these two messages by some black men (a substantial number) produced black men who enact a portion of the traditional definition of masculinity but remain inactive with respect to other parts of traditional masculinity that can be enacted within the black culture are the ones exhibited by these black men. Other aspects of the sex role that required enactment external to the black culture (e.g., aggressiveness in the work place) may be related to impassively by black men. Unfortunately, these are aspects of the male sex role that must be enacted if a male is to be "productive" in American society.

Too many black men fail to enact the more "productive" aspects of the male sex role. Instead, "being a man," for many black males who internalize the mixed messages, becomes simply enacting sexual aggression, violence, sexism, and the like—all of which promote black male-black female conflict. In addition, contributing to the low visibility and low salience of "productive" masculine traits among black men is the second socialization message, which provides a rationale for no enactment of the role traits. Moreover, the "man will get you" message serves to attenuate black men's motivations to enact more "positive" aspects of the traditional male sex role. We must keep in mind, however, that not all of the sources of black male-black female conflict are social-psychological. Some of the sources are structural, and in the next section these sources are discussed.

STRUCTURAL BARRIERS CONTRIBUTING TO BLACK MALE-BLACK FEMALE CONFLICT

It is easy to place the blame for black male-black female conflict on "White Society." Several black authors have used this explanatory approach in recent years (e.g., Anderson and Mealy, 1979). They have suggested that black male-black female conflict is a function of America's capitalistic orientation and white society's long-time subjugation of black people. Certainly, historical conditions are important to understand when discussing the status of black people today. Often, however, too much emphasis is placed on the historical subjugation of black people as the source of black male-black female conflict today. Implicit in such an emphasis is the notion that independent variables existing at some point in the distant past cause a multiplicity of negative behaviors between black males and black females that can be capsulized as black male-black female conflict. A careful analysis of the contemporary environments of black men and women today will show, instead, that factors responsible, in part, for black male-black female conflict are inextricably interwoven in those environments. In other words, an approach to the analysis of conflict between black men and black women today must be ahistorical. Past conditions influence black male-black female relationships only in the sense that vestiges of these conditions exist currently and are identifiable.

Our society today undoubtedly remains structured in such a manner that the vast majority of black men encounter insurmountable barriers to the attainment of a "masculine" status as defined by most Americans (black and white Americans). Black men still largely are locked within the black culture (which has relatively limited resources), unable to compete successfully for societal rewards—the attainment of which defines American males as "men." Unquestionably, black men's powerlessness in society's basic institutions such as the government and the economy contributed greatly to the pathological states of many black men. The high mortality and suicide rates of young black men, the high incarceration rates of young black men, the high incidence of drug addiction among black men, and the high unemployment rate of black men are all functions of societal barriers to black male upward mobility. These barriers render millions of black males socially impotent and/pr socially dysfunctional. Moreover, as Staples has pointed out, such barriers also result in a scarcity of functional black men, thereby limiting black women's alternatives for mates.

While some may not be tempted to argue for a psychological explanation of black male social impotence, it is suggested here than any such argument is misguided unless accompanied by a recognition of the role of cultural nurturance factors. Cultural nurturance factors such as the rigid caste like social stratum of blacks in America fosters and maintain black men's social impotence. The result is powerless black men primed for conflictual relationships with black women. If black men in our society were not "American," perhaps cultural nurturance of black people's status in our society could not be translated into cultural nurturance of black male-black female conflict. That black men are Americanized, however, is seen in the outcome of the black movement of the last decade.

The black movement of the late 1960s and early 1970s produced little structural change in America. To be sure, a few black men (and even fewer black women) achieved a measure of upward mobility; however, the vast majority did not reap gains from the black movement. What did happen, though, was that black people did get a glimpse of the rewards that can be achieved in America through violence and/ or aggression. White society did bend when confronted by the black movement, but it did not break. In addition, the few upward mobility doors that were ajar during the height of the movement were quickly slammed shut when the movement began to wane in the middle and late 1970s. black men today find themselves in a position similar to the one black man were in prior to the movement. The only difference this time around is that black men are equipped with the psychological armor of aggression and violence as well as with a distorted perception of a target—black women, the ones who "stood silently by."

Wallace's statement that black women "stood silently by" must not be taken lightly. Black women did this; in addition, the further internalized American definitions of masculinity and femininity. Previously, black women held modified definitions of masculinity and femininity because the society's definition did not fit their everyday experiences. During the black movement they were exhorted by black men to assume a sex role that was more in line with the traditional "feminine" role white women assumed in male-female relationships. Although this may have been a noble (verbal) effort on the part of black men to place black women on pedestals, it was shortsighted and doomed to fail. Failure was imminent because even during the peak of the black movement, societal resistance to structural changes that would benefit black people was strong. The strength of this resistance dictated that change in black people's status in America could come about only through the united efforts of black men and black women.

Unfortunately, the seeds of division between black men and black women were sown during the black movement. Black men bought the Moynihan report (1965) that indirectly blamed black women for black people's underclass status in America. In doing so, black men convinced themselves that they could be "men" only if they adopted the white male's sex role. An examination of this role reveals that it is characterized by numerous contradictions. The traditional white masculine role requires men to assume protective, condescending, and generally patriarchal stances with respect to women. It also requires, ironically, that men display dominant, aggressive, and often violent behaviors toward women. Just as important, though, is that white masculine role enactment can occur only when there is full participation in masculinist American culture. Because black men continue to face barriers to full participation in America society, the later requirement for white male sex-role assumption continues to be met by only a few black men. The result has been that many black men have adopted only a part of the culture's definition of masculinity because they are thwarted in their efforts to participate fully in society. Structural barriers to black male sex-role adoption, then, have produced a black male who is primed for a conflictual relationship with black women. In the next section, an exploration is presented of some possible solutions to black male-black female conflict that arise from the interactive relationship between the noncomplementary of sex-role internalization by black men and black women and structural barriers to black men's advancement in American society.

TOWARD SOLVING BLACK MALE-BLACK FEMALE CONFLICT

Given that societal conditions are extremely resistant to rapid changes, the key to attenuating conflict between black men and black women lies in altering three social psychological phenomenal: (1) Black male and black female socialization experiences; (2) Black male and black female role-playing strategies; and (3) Black male and black female personal communication mechanisms. I first propose some alterations in black male and black female socialization experiences.... .

Black female socialization must undergo change if black men and black women are to enjoy harmonious relationships. Those agents and agencies responsible for socializing young black females must return to emphasizing a monolithic message in young black female socialization. This message can stress warmth, caring, and nurturance, but it must stress simultaneously self-sufficiency, assertiveness, and responsibility. The latter portion of this message requires that young black females must be cautioned against sexual freedom at relatively early ages— not necessarily for moral reasons, but because sexual freedom for black women seems to operate against black women's self-sufficiency, assertiveness, and responsibility. It is important to point out here, however, that this type of socialization message must be imparted without the accompanying castigation of black men. To say "a nigger man ain't shit" informs any young black female that at least one-half of herself "ain't shit." Without a doubt, this strategy teaches self-hate and sets the stage for future black male-black female conflict.

Young black males, on the other hand, must be instructed in self-sufficiency, assertiveness, and responsibility without the accompanying warning opposed to these traits in black males. Such warnings serve only to provide rationales for future failures. To be sure, black men do (and will) encounter barriers to upward mobility because they are black. But, as many black men have shown, such barriers do not have to be insurmountable. Of course, it is recognized that innumerable black men have been victims of American racist policies, but some, too, have been victims because they perceived policies, but some, too, have been victims because they perceived only that external factor hindered their upward mobility and did not focus on some internal barriers that may have thwarted their mobility. The former factors are emphasized much too often in the contradictory socialization messages received by most young black males.

Along with the above messages, young black males must learn that the strong bonds that they establish with their mothers can be extended to their relationships with other black women. If black men perceive their mothers to be symbols of strength and perseverance, they must also be taught that most other black women acquire these same qualities and have done so for generations. It must become just as "cool," in places like urban black barbershops, to speak of black women's strength and dignity as it is now to hear of black women's thighs, breasts, and hips.

On an issue closely related to the above, few persons reading this article can deny that black men's attempts to enact the white male sex role in America are laughable. Black men are relatively powerless in this country, and their attempts at domination, aggression, and the like, while sacrificing humanity, are ludicrous. This becomes apparent when it is understood that usually the only people being dominated and aggressed against by black men and black women (and other black men). Moreover, unlike white males, black males receive no societal rewards for their efforts; instead, the result is black male-black female disharmony. Black men must avoid the tendency to emulate the nauseatingly traditional male sex role because their experiences clearly show that such a role is counterproductive for black people. Because the black man's experiences are different, his role-playing strategies must be different and made to be more complementary with black females' altered role-playing strategies. The black females' role-playing strategies, as we have seen, are androgynous, emphasizing neither the inferiority nor the superiority of male or female sex roles.

On a final note, it is important for black people in our society to alter their personal communication mechanisms. Black men and black women interact with each other in diverse ways and in diverse situations, ranging from intimate to impersonal. Perhaps the most important element of this diverse communication pattern is empathy. For black people in recent years, this precisely the element that has undergone unnecessary transformation. As blacks in America have accepted increasingly white society's definition of male-female relationships, black men and black women have begun to interact with each other less terms of empathy. While black women have retained empathy in their male-female men have become increasingly nonexpressive and nonempathic in their male-female relationships. Nearly 60% of black women (approximately 25, 000) in a recent *Essence* survey cited nonexpressiveness as a problem in male-female relationships; 56% also pointed out that black male nonepathy was a problem (Edwards, 1982). It seems, then, that as black males have attempted to become "men" in America they have shed some of the important qualities of humanity. Some black women, too, who have embraced the feminist perspective also have discarded altruism. Further movement away from empathic understanding in black male-black female relationships by both black men and black women undoubtedly will be disastrous for black people in America.

REFERENCES

Allen, B. 1983. "The Price for Giving It Up." *Essence* (February):60-62, 188.

Anderson, S.E., and R. Mealy. 1979. "Who Organized the Crisis: A Historical Perspective." *Black Scholar* (May/June): 40-44.

Braithwaite, R.L. 1981. "Interpersonal Relations between Black Males and Black Females," In *Black Men,* L. E. Gray, ed. Pp. 83-97. Beverly Hills, Calif.: Sage.

Drake, S. C., and H. R. Cayton. 194. *Black Metropolis.* New York: Harcourt.

Edwards, A. 1982. "Survey Results: How You're Feeling." *Essence* (December): 73-76.

Franklin, C. W. II. 1980. "White Racism As a Cause of Black Male-Female Conflict: A Critique." *Western Journal of Black Studies* 4(1): 42-49.

Frazier, E. F. 1939. *The Negro Family in the United States.* Chicago: University of Chicago Press.

Grier, W. H., and P. M. Cobb. 1968. *Black Rage.* New York: Basic Books.

Jones, T. 1979. "The Need to Go beyond Stereotypes." *Black Scholar* (May/June): 48-49.

Karenga, M. R. 1979. "On Wallace's Myth: Wading through Troubled Waters." *Black Scholar* (May/June): 36-39.

Moore, W. E. 1980. "Black Women, Stop Criticizing Black Men— Blame Yourselves." *Ebony* (December): 128-130.

Moynihan, D. P. 1965. *The Negro Family: The Case of National Action.* Washington, D.C.: U.S. Department of Labor, Office of Planning and Research.

Poussaint, A. F. 1982. "What Every Black Woman Should Know about Black Men." *Ebony* (August): 36-40.

Staples, R. 1979. "The Myth of Black Macho: A Response to Angry Black Feminists." *Black Scholar* (March/April): 24-32.

Wallace, M. 1979. *Black Macho and the Myth of the Superwoman*. New York: Dial.

1982. "A Black Feminist's Search for Sisterhood." In *All the Blacks Are Men, All the Women are White, but Some of Us are Brave*, G. T. Hull, et al., eds., pp. 5-8 Old Westbury, N.Y.: Feminist Press.

DIALECTICS OF BLACK MALE-FEMALE RELATIONSHIPS

LA FRANCES RODGERS-ROSE

One of the most complex and pressing issues in the struggle for black survival is centered in and grows out of the relationship between black men and women. This relationship, in the final analysis, determines how they support each other as men and women and how they will raise their children.

The relationship between black men and women does not take place in a vacuum. They act out their behavior in a society which has clearly defined role behavior. Men are supposed to be aggressive, women passive. With such a definition of role behavior, based on inequality rather than equality, the relationship between men and cannot help but be tenuous. Moreover, any male-female relationship, there are the dialectics of creation and criticism which must take place in an environment of open discussion and sociability (Foote, 1953). This chapter will attempt to look at some of the issues that confront black men and women as they interact in a process of criticism and creation. Specifically, I will discuss some myths about black men and women and properties of male-female relationships.

MYTHS OF THE ROLES AND RELATIONSHIPS BETWEEN BLACK MEN AND WOMEN

If a situation is defined as real, then it is real in its consequences.
W.I. Thomas

Most of what we know about black male-female relationships is a result of the biased research conducted by white social scientists. For example, we hear that in order for black people to succeed, black women must stand behind black men—black women must step back and let the black man lead. The assumption, based on biased

Work of white researchers, is that black women have led their men. But any objective looks at black history will show this has never been the case. Equality between black men and women has been misrepresented as female dominance. What has happened is that some black men and women have internalized the myths of white social scientists, and these definitions of situations have become real in their consequences.

Another myth that some blacks have internalized is that the black male is shiftless, that he does not want to work, that he would rather hang on the corner that look for a job. Objective reading of black history shows the efforts that black men have made to find jobs—jobs that paid very little and were demeaning in nature. Yet another myth in this country is that black women earn more money than black men, that black women can get jobs when black men cannot. U.S> Census Bureau data show that this is not true, nor has it ever been true. In fact, black woman are the lowest paid group in the country: They make less money than white men and women and black men (Ferris, 1971:141). Black women are, in general, the most unemployed and underemployed group. (1971:302-320) A related myth is that black women are generally more educated than black men, and historically this has been the case. However, today this is no longer as true (9171:23).

I am suggesting that a great deal of what is happening to black men and women as the relate to one another is a consequence of definitions based on stereotypes of blacks or biased research, and not from the reality systems of black men and women. Before we can move toward defining black male and female relationships, we must expose false definitions that grow out of thought systems which serve to divide and conquer black people. To the extent that we are unaware of these false reality systems, the black woman is seen as having certain qualities and the black man is seen as lacking these qualities. The black woman is seen as needing little protecting either physically or mentally, while the other black man is seen as needing both physical and mental protection—he lacks the ability to survive in the outside world. The black woman must protect him. Further, the black woman is seen as a dominating matriarch: She emasculates the black man and his character becomes "feminine" in nature. He does not know what to do unless he is told by the women.

Growing out of this myth is the further notion that most black households are headed by women, that the male is absent from the home, and that black children do not have male models. The reality of the situation is that two-thirds of all black households do have both male and female present. In some households, the male is not present to be counted by the census taker. He may be absent for strategic purposes—for example, a needy mother cannot get welfare if there is a man in the home; aid is given only to dependent children, not to struggling intact families. Moreover, white social scientists ignore the fact that black women have boyfriends, fathers, brothers, and uncles who can and do serve as role models.

Finally, the black man and woman are defined as being sexually aggressive. White mythology has asserted that both the black male and female are anxious to have sexual relationships with whites. The female is defined as loose in her morals and out to sell her body to the highest bidder; she wants to establish meaningless relationships with white men at the expense of the black man. Black men seek sexual relationships with white women. Again, when we unmask the myth, we find that less than two percent of all marriages in this country are between black and white people. When blacks are asked to rank the priority of things they want in this country, interracial marriage is ranked last, with economic and political equality ranked first.

As can be seen from the foregoing discussion, it is easy for black people to internalize and use such false definition of themselves. To the extent that an individual has internalized these definitions, his/her mode of interaction with the opposite sex will be affected. Therefore, when a relationship is not going well, the individual will resort to such negative definitions and interpretations as "Black women are too independent," Black men are too possessive," "Black men's feelings are too easily hurt," "Black women are evil," "Black women argue too much," "Black men are weak," "Black men are castrated," and "Black women don't appreciate good treatment." Moreover, these negative definitions have already been supplied and are readily available to the actor. These ready-made definitions keep black men and women from looking inward to what they contribute to the outcome of a particular relationship. One can easily blame the other. Such myths, then, have functioned to divide black men and women, and they have serves as rationalizations for the status quo. Myths keep the individuals focused on criticism rather than on the interplay between the critical and the creative aspects of any male-female relationship.

Properties of Dialectic Relationships Between Black Men and Women

Sociologists have in many cases failed to study the depth of interpersonal relationships between the groups of people they analyze. They have, instead, tended to study the surface areas—those aspects which can be easily defined, codified, and discussed. We know a great deal about deal about financial and sexual aspects of marriage, but we know much less about what attracts one individual to another, what people are looking for in intimate relationships, and what qualities make for viable dialectic relationships. Likewise, we find that men and women are not socialized to look for nor can they articulate their needs in terms of qualities wanted. We are taught to pay more attention to the outward characteristics of a person: education, occupation, and income. Recently, sexual compatibility has been included in these characteristics. Thus, we find people in relationships not realizing what they want form that relationship.

QUALITIES IN MALE-FEMALE RELATIONSHIPS

This chapter is based on interviews of 49 black women and 39 black men. The data were collected in April and May 1975.[153]Each person was asked five question: (1) What qualities do you want in a man/woman with whom you are having an intimate relationship? (2) What behavior/action would show the above qualities? (3) What qualities do you dislike/hate in a man/woman that would make you dissolve that relationship? (4) What behavior/action would show these negative qualities? (5) If you were dating steadily, how often would you like to see that person? The responses to each of these questions were recorded verbatim. Each response was then content analyzed. Background data on age, education, occupation, and marital status were also gathered. Table 1 shows the distribution of males and females by age groups on specific characteristics. As one can see from Table 1, there is a wide range and a similar age span for males and females. The education level is above the national norm. Most are single or separated/divorced. Only 30 percent of the sample presently married, and the professional category is overrepresented in the sample.

Table 1. Distribution of Males and Females by Age Group and Specific Status Characteristics

	Females		Males	
	Under Over		Under Over	
	30 Years 30 Years		30 Years 30 Years	
Characteristics	(N=24)	(N=25)	(N=22)	(N=17)
Mean Age	22.8	42.0	22.0	39.0
Mean Education	13.6	14.4	14.8	15.3
Dates/Week	4.0	2.2	3.4	3.4
Marital Status				
Single	16	1	16	5
Married	3	9	6	8
Divorced	3	4	0	2
Widowed	1	7	0	2
	1	3	0	0
Occupation				
Professional	8	13	8	11
Clerical/Skilled	5	6	5	3
Unskilled	0	5	1	2
Student	7	0	5	1
Housewife	2	0	0	0

The following results were indicated for males and females. In the area of positive qualities, one may not from Table 2 that females under 30 years of age say that the qualities they most want in a man are understanding, honesty, and a person who is warm and gentle. These are the *global* qualities; that is, qualities showing the greatest frequencies. Only qualities mentioned by at least five persons are listed in the tables which follow; however, many other qualities were given. The aim of this study was to show those qualities that have some kind of consensus among age and sex groups. Other qualities mentioned by women under

30 years of age were intelligence, sense of humor, stability, and awareness of self. Table 2 for women over 30 indicates that the most outstanding desirable quality was honesty. This was the only global quality listed, while from women under 30, honesty and understanding had the same frequency. There is a greater consensus among females than males on the positive qualities desired in a person with whom they are having an intimate relationship. For men under 30, the quality having the greatest frequency was independence—a characteristic which men traditionally do not like to see in women. Men over 30 show a global quality of good manners; for example, they mention "acts like a lady," "has good manner of speech," and "the way she carries herself in public." This quality, proper manners, indicates the more traditional way of viewing women. Also, in viewing Table 3, one may note that males over 30 list "character" traits of the individual rather than the "affective" qualities of the person.

When we turn to how these positive qualities are viewed in behavior, the picture changes. Here we find that women under 30 do not ask for a behavioral quality paralleling the qualities of understanding and honesty; rather, they say the person should be respectful and well-groomed. One must raise the following question: Is there an incongruency between stating that the most desired quality is understanding and stating that, behaviorally, one wants respect and a person who is well-groomed? One refers to effect—understanding—and the other talks about character traits—respectful. In general, males and females in this sample found it difficult to give behavioral/actions indicators than general qualities. And in several cases there were people who listed general qualities as behavior/action. It would seem that this is the area in which one needs to be able to identify the action that shows love. As Foote (1953) suggested, love is known by its works. It is an activity, a process. It is one thing to articulate qualities, but an entirely different thing to know that certain behavior/action is love.

To summarize, for women over 30 years we find a consistency in the qualities wanted, "honesty," and the behavior indicated as "open communication." Women over 30 indicate affective behavioral qualities, while women under 30 consider character traits. For men in both age groups there is also a consistency of qualities and behavior. The males under 30 says they want a woman who is "calm"—cool in her behavior, one who is doing something to better herself, such as going to school or being employed. There are behavioral indicators of independence. Males over 30 say they want a woman who has "proper manners"; behaviorally, the global quality is "knowing when to listen," an indicator of proper manners.

In general, there seems to be a distinct difference among the four age groups on the qualities wanted in an intimate relationship. This is true particularly for the global qualities. However, in looking at the various qualities wanted, there is indeed overlap. But the significant point is the priority given the different qualities. It would

---

I. Black Females Under 30 (N=24)

A. Global Qualities	B. Behavioral Global Qualities
1. Ideas	1. Ideas
Aware of Self (6)	Specific goals (7)
Black identity (6)	
Independent (6)	2. Character
2. Affectivity/Character	Respectful (11)
Understanding (14)	Well-groomed (11)
Honesty (14)	
Warm/gentle (10)	3. Affective
3. Character I	Good lover (7)
Intelligent (8)	Responds to my needs (7)
Sense of humor (8)	Encourages me (6)
Positive self-concept (8)	
Stable (8)	
4. Character II	
Nice looking (7)	
Generous (7)	

II. Black Females Over 30 (N=25)

A. Global Qualities	B. Behavioral Global Qualities
1. Affectivity Understanding (9) Aware of my needs (9) Affectionate (8) Aware of others (7)	1. Affectivity Sharing (6) Kind to others (6)
2. Character I Honesty (16)	2. Affectivity Sexually compatible (6)
3. Character II Dependable (6) Down-to-earth (7) Handsome (5)	3. Affectivity Open communication (15)
4. Character III Intelligent (10) Ambitious (11)	4. Affectivity Takes me where he goes (10) Gives self according to my needs (11)

Seem that black males and females differ among themselves and also within groups. In fact, a review of Table 2 and 3 seems to suggest that females over 30 have more in common with males under 30, and that females under 30 have more in common with males over 30. A larger sample is needed before we can be sure of this possible relationship.

Table 3. Positive Qualities Wanted in a Female by Black Males

I. Black Males Under 30 (N=22)	
A. Global Qualities	B. Behavioral Global Qualities
1. Affectivity Loving/tender (13) Understanding (10) Considerate (6) Faithful (6)	Takes care of my needs (5) Sexually compatible (6)
2. Character I Independent (17)	2. Character I Manners (9) Calm (10) Going to school/employed (9)

3. Character II
   Honest (13)
   Clean and neat (11)
   Beautiful (7)

4. Character III
   Strong self-concept (10)
   Aware of self (8)
   Intelligent (11)

5. Character IV
   Open-minded (9)
   Respectful of others (5)

4. Character II
   Independent action (7)

II. Black Males over 30 (N = 17)

A. Global Qualities
   1. Affectivity/Character
      Understanding (8)
      Honest (8)
      Sensitive (7)
      Tender and kind (7)

   2. Character I
      Proper manners (17)

   3. Character II
      Clean and neat (8)
      Independent (8)
      Intelligent (5)

   4. Character III
      Loyal (7)
      Dependable (6)
      Open and truthful (6)

B. Behavioral Global Qualities
   1. Affectivity
      Sexually compatible (4)
      Kissing, holding, responding
      to me (4)

   2. Character I
      Knowing when to listen (9)

   3. Character II
      Active in sports (4)

When we turn to the negative qualities and behaviors disliked in man/ woman, we find that women were able to list more negative qualities disliked in males than vice versa. Whereas females have at least seven negative qualities, males only have four areas of negative qualities. Females under 30 say they dislike a male who dominates or who is selfish and dependent, while females over 30 say they dislike a male who is immature and dishonest. Here again we see a consistency in females over 30 in the things they like in a male ("honesty") and the things they dislike in male ("dishonesty'). This consistency across positive and negative qualities is only true for this age and sex group. For males under 30, the qualities disliked—again, similar to females over 30—were dishonesty and a person who is unaffectionate. Males over 30 showed less of a consensus than any other age or sex group. The highest frequency for any quality dislikes was listed by only five people. Here they list disrespectfulness, rigidity, irresponsibility, and dishonesty. Although listed as global qualities, these are not global in the same sense as other tables showing global qualities. Looking at the behavioral qualities disliked, we find that males over 30 and females under 30 both mentions lying as the behavior most disliked. For women over 30, physical violence is most disliked, and for males under 30 it is a person who is unclean and one who cheats (run around with other men).

It is interesting to note that in listing the qualities liked or the qualities disliked in intimate relationships the traditional variables that sociologists use in studying marriage and the family are not shown. That is, in the global qualities shown no one mentioned occupation, income, education, or sexual compatibility. But rather, qualities dealt more with the inner person—his/her character or the affective aspects of the person.

The preliminary study indicates that if we are to begin to understand the relationship between black men and women, or for that matter women and men in general, we must move beyond the outer status of the person to the inner qualities of the person. When given an open-ended, unstructured question on the qualities liked and the qualities disliked in intimate relationships, this sample of black men and women showed that they are concerned with qualities such as understanding, honesty, warmth, dress, respectability, open communication, sharing, independence, listening capability, dominance, selfishness, lying, unfaithfulness, immaturity, physical violence, lack of affection, and uncleanliness.

Research along this line will add to our knowledge of the relationship between black men and women. Further, I feel that what is true for black men and women will also be true for men and women in general. That is, people are concerned with intangible, hard-to-analyze qualities in a relationship rather than outward status variables. It remains to be seen whether blacks and other racial groups will show the same diversity as this sample, or whether a larger, more random sample will produce the same results between

Table 4. Negative Qualities Disliked in Males by Black Females

I. Black Females Under 30 (N = 24)	
A. Global Qualities	B. Behavioral Global Qualities
1. Character I	1. Affectivity
Dominant (14)	Sexually incompatible (5)
Selfish (14)	
Dependent (12)	2. Character I
	Lying (13)
2. Character II	
Unfaithful (8)	3. Character II
Possessive (8)	Physical violence (9)
Dishonest (6)	Stay-at-home (8)
	Disrespectful (8)
3. Character III	Never show/late (8)
Ignorant (7)	Lazy (7)
Immature (7)	Loudmouth (5)
	Drunken (5)
4. Character IV	
No patience (7)	
No self-respect (5)	

II. Black Females Over 30 (N = 25)	
A. Global Qualities	B. Behavioral Global Qualities
1. Character I	1. Character I
Immature (11)	Physically violent (13)
Dishonest (10)	
	2. Character II
2. Character II	Drunken (9)
No self-respect (6)	
Dependent (5)	3. Character III
	Other women (7)
3. Character III	4. Character IV
Ignorant (5)	Verbal abuse (5)
Selfish (5)	Never show/late (5)
	Gossipy (5)
	Jealous (5)

Black males and females. I am presently pursuing the latter question of a larger, more random sample of black men and women.

I have attempted to show in this brief research study that sociologists who have studied relationships between males and females have failed to study the qualities wanted in persons with whom intimate relations are established. Instead, they have studied the outward special characteristics of income, education, occupation, and sexual compatibility.

Table 5. Negative Qualities Disliked in Females by Black Males

I. Black Males Under 30 (N = 22)	
A. Global Qualities	B. Behavioral Global Qualities
1. Affectivity/Character	1. Character I
Unaffectionate (11)	Unclean (8)
Dishonest (11)	Cheats (8)
2. Character	2. Character II
Selfish (8)	Lying (6)
Irresponsible (8)	Disrespectful (5)
Poor outlook on life (8)	Nags (5)

II. Black Males Over 30 (N = 17)	
A. Global Qualities	B. Behavioral Global Qualities
1. Character	1. Character I
Disrespectful (5)	Lying (9)
Rigid (5)	
Irresponsible (5)	2. Character II
Dishonest (5)	Curses (6)
	Drunken (5)
	Unclean (5)

They have studied the first three properties of intimate relationships—conversation, monetary exchange, and sex—but they have paid little attention to the fourth property of the qualities wanted in a relationship. Further, we know very little about what men and women expect behaviorally from each other. A content analysis of 88 interviews with black males and females show that they are concerned with inner qualities of the individual rather than outward qualities. Even the quality of sexual compatibility does not rank as high as the qualities of honesty, understanding, independence, and proper manners. Additional research along these lines would add to our limited knowledge of black male-female relationships, and perhaps to male-female relationships in general. Further research in this area will begin to lead the way toward the kinds of variables that must be included in any study which seeks to understand the dialectics of male-female relationships. It is imperative that we begin to study the criticism and creativity in male-female relationships.

NOTES

[1.] A search and referral method were used to obtain the sample. The research initially made contact with a small number of black men and women. They in turn were asked to refer the interviewer to another person.

[2.] Interviews ranged from 45 minutes to two hours,

REFERENCES

Alexander, T. and S. Sillen (1972) Racism and Psychiatry. New York: Brunner-Mazel.

Anderson, C.S. and J. Himes (1969) "Dating values and norms on a Negro college campus." Marriage and Family Living 21:227-229.

Bambara, T.C. (1972) "How black women educate each other." Sexual Behavior 2: 12-13.

Beal, F. (1969) "Double jeopardy: to be Black and female." New generations 5: 23-28.

Bernard, J. (1966a) "Marital stability and patterns of status variables." Journal of Marriage and the Family 28: 421-439.

_____(1966a) Marriage and Family Among Negroes. Englewood Cliffs, NJ: Prentice-Hall.

Billingsley, A. (1966) Black Families in White America. Englewood Cliffs: NJ: Prentice-Hall.

_____(1969) "Family Functioning in the low-income Black community." Social Casework 50: 563-572.

Blood, R. and D. Wolfe (1960) Husbands and Wives: The Dynamics of Married Living. New York: Free Press.

Blumer, H. (1940) "The problem of the concept in social psychology." American Journal of Sociology 45: 707-719.

_____(1969) Symbolic Interactionism: Perspective and Method. Englewood Cliffs, NJ: Prentice-Hall.

Bond, J. and P. Berry (1974) "Is the Black male castrated?" in T. Cade (ed.) The Black Woman: An Anthology. New York: Signet.

Bradburn, N. (1969) "Working wives and marriage happiness." American Journal of Sociology 74: 392-407.

Burchinal, L. (1964) "The premarital dyad and love involvement," in H.T. Christensen (ed.) Handbook of Marriage and the Family. Chicago: Rand McNally.

Burgess, E. and P. Wallin (1953) Engagement and Marriage. Chicago: J. B. Lippincott.

Byrne, D. (1961) "Interpersonal auraction and attitude similarity." Journal of Abnormal and Social Psychology 62: 712-715.

Cooley, C. H. (1902) Human Nature and the Social Order. New York: Scribners.

Coser, R. L. [ed.] (1964) The Family: Its Structure and Functions. New York: St. Martin's Press.

Deutscher, I. (1973) What We Say/What We Do: Sentiments and Acts. Glenview, IL: Scott, Foresman.

Donnelly, M. (1963) "Towards a theory of courtship." Marriage and Family Living 25: 290-293.

Drake, S. C. and H. Cayton (1945) Black Metropolis. New York: Harcourt Brace Jovanovich.

DuBois, W.E.B. (1903) The Souls of Black Folks. Chicago: A. C. McClury.

Edwards, G. (1963) "Marriage and family life among Negroes." Journal of Negro Education 32: 451-465.

Farley, R. (1971) "Family stability: a comparison of trends between Blacks and whites." American Sociological Review 36: 1-17.

Foote, N. (1953) "Love." Psychiatry 16: 245-251.

Frazier, E. (1939) "The Negro Family in the United States. Chicago: University of Chicago Press.

Ferris, A. L. (1971) Indicators of Trends in the Status of American Women. New York: Russell Sage.

Geismar, L. (1962) "Measuring family disorganization." Marriage and Family Living 24: 51-56.

Glaser, B. and A. Strauss (1967) The Discovery of Grounded Theory. Chicago: AVC.

Glick, P. and A. Norton (1971) "Frequency, duration and probability of marriage and divorce." Journal of Marriage and the Family 33.

Goode, W. (1956) After Divorce. New York: Free Press.

_____(1959) "The theoretical importance of love." American Sociological Review 24: 38-47.

Gorer, G. (1948) The American People: A Study in National Character. New York: W. W. Norton.

Gouldner, A. (1962) "Anti-minotaur: the myth of value free sociology." Social Problems 9: 199-213.

Habenstein, R. [ed.] (1970) Pathways to Data: Field Methods for Studying Ongoing Social Organizations. Chicago: AVC.

Hannerz, U. (1969) "The roots of Black manhood." Transaction: 6: 12-21.

Hare, N. (1964) "The frustrated masculinity of the Negro male." Negro Digest 14: 5-9.

Harper, R. (1958) "Honesty in courtship." The Humanist 18: 103-107.

Harris, A. O. (1974) "Dilemma of growing up Black and female." Journal of Social and Behavioral Sciences 20: 28-40.

Hernton, D. (1965) Sex and Racism. New York: Grove Press.

_____(1974) Coming Together. New York: Random House.

Herr, D. (1958) "Dominance and the working wife." Social Forces 36: 341-347.

_____(1963) "The measurement and bases of family power." Marriage and Family Living 25:133-139.

Herskovitz, M. (1941) The Myth of the Negro Past. New York: Harper & Row.

Herzog, E. (1966) "Is there a 'breakdown' of the Negro family?" Social Work 11: 3-10.

Hewitt, L. (1958) "Student perceptions of traits desired in themselves as dating and marriage partners." Marriage and Family Living 20: 349-360.

Hill, R. (1945) "Campus norms in mate selection." Journal of Home Economics 37: 554-558.

Hill, R. (1972) The Strengths of Black Families. New York: National Urban League.

Hyman, H. and J. Reid (1969) "Black matriarch reconsidered: evidence from secondary analysis of sample survey." Public Opinion Quarterly 33: 346-345.

Jackson, J. (1971) "But where are the men?" The Black Scholar 2: 30-41.

_____(1973) "Black women created equal to Black men." Essence (November): 56-72.

_____(1974) "Ordinary Black husbands: the truly hidden men." Journal of Social and Behavioral Sciences 20: 19-27.

Johnson, C.S. (1934) Shadow of the Plantation. Chicago: University of Chicago Press.

Ladner, J. (1972) Tomorrow's Tomorrow: The Black Woman. New York: Doubleday.

Kamii, C. and N. Radin (1967) "Class differences in the socialization practices of Negro mothers." Journal of Marriage and the Family 29: 302-310.

King, C. (1954) "The sex factor in marital adjustment." Marriage and Family Living 16: 237-240.

King, K. (1967) "A comparison of the Negro and white family power structure in low-income families." Child and Family 6: 65-74.

Lerner, G. (1972) Black Women in White America. New York: Pantheon.

Lewis, H. (1955) Blackways of Kent. Chapel Hill: University of North Carolina Press.

_____(1965) "Child rearing among low-income families." L. Ferman et al. (eds.) Poverty in America. Ann Arbor: University of Michigan Press.

_____(1967) "Culture, class, and family life among low-income urban Negroes," in A. Ross and H. Hill (eds.) Employment, Race and Poverty. New York: Harcourt Brace Jovanovich.

Liebow, E. (1967) Talley's Corner. Boston: Little, Brown.

Mack, D. (1971) "Where the Black matriarchy theorists went wrong." Psychology Today 4: 86-88.

Mannheim, K. (1936) Ideology and Utopia. New York: Harcourt Brace Jovanovich.

Maxwell, J. W. (1968) "Rural Negro father participation in family activities." Rural Sociology 33: 80-93.

Mead, G. H. (1934) Mind, Self and Society. Chicago: University of Chicago Press.

Miller, S.M. et al. (1965) "A critique of the non-deferred gratification pattern," in L. Ferman et al. (eds.) Poverty in America. Ann Arbor: University of Michigan Press.

Mills, C. W. (1940) "Methodological consequences of the sociology of knowledge." American Journal of Sociology 46: 316-330.

_____(1959) The Sociological Imagination. New York: Oxford University Press.

Morgan, R. [ed] (1970) Sisterhood is Powerful. New York: Vintage Books.

Moynihan, D. (1965) The Negro Family: The Call of National Action. Washington, DC: Department of Labor.

Myers, L. (1975) "Black women: selectivity among roles and reference groups in maintenance of self-esteem." Journal of Social and Behavioral Sciences 21: 34-47.

Nye, F.I. (1957) "Child adjustment in broken and in unhappy homes." Marriage and Family Living 19: 356-361.

Prescott, D. (1952) "The role of love in human development." Journal of Home Economics 44: 73-176.

Parker, S. and R. Kleiner (1966) "Characteristics of Negro mothers in single-headed household." Journal of Marriage and the Family 31: 500-506.

Prescott, D. (1952) "The role of love in human development." Journal of Home Economics 44: 73-176.

Rainwater, L. (1966) "Crucible of identity," in T. Parsons and K. Clark (eds.) The Negro American. Boston: Beacon.

Reid, I. (1972) Together Black Women. New York: Emerson Hall.

Reiss, I. (1960) Premarital Sexual Standards in America. New York: Free Press.

Scanzoni, J. (1971) The Black Family in Modern Society. Boston: Allyn & Bacon.

Schulz, D. (1969) Coming Up Black: Patterns of Ghetto Socialization. Englewood Cliffs, NJ: Prentice-Hall.

Staples, R. (1970a) "The myth of the Black matriarchy." The Black Scholar 1: 2-9.

_____(1970b) "Educating the Black male at various class levels for marital roles." The Family Coordinator 30: 164-167.

_____(1971) The Black Family: Essays and Studies. Belmont, CA: Wadsworth.

_____(1972) "The sexuality of Black women." Sexual Behavior 2: 4-15.

_____(1973) The Black Woman in America. Chicago: Nelson-Hall.

Strokes, G. (1968) "Black woman to Black man." Liberator 8: 17-19.

Sullivan, H.S. (1953) The Interpersonal Theory of Psychiatry. New York: W.W. Norton.

CHAPTER EIGHT
Afrocentric Cultural Issues

One focus of this chapter is Afrocentric cultural consciousness and African-American male-female relationships. The authors, Yvonne R. Bell, Cathy L. Bouie, and Joseph A. Baldwin present findings that support the major prediction that Afrocentric cultural consciousness is positively related to perceptions (values, attitudes) that prioritize an Afrocentric value orientation in heterosexual relationships. Additionally, the findings support the contention that Afrocentric cultural factors may be a sustaining and affirmative force even during difficult times in heterosexual relationships.

Another focus of the chapter is on the hip hop generation with a discussion of African American male-female relationships in a nightclub setting by Janis F. Hutchison. This discussion of the hip hop generation explores popular culture and relationships as manifest in a particular social setting-the nightclub. The conclusions of this study indicate the importance of social status, economic security, and male-female companionship among young adult African American women. It further suggests that African Americans may still be in transition in terms of redefining female-male relationships in the New World Eurocentric environment.

Delores P. Aldridge, Ph.D

AFROCENTRIC CULTURAL CONSCIOUSNESS AND AFRICAN-AMERICAN MALE-FEMALE RELATIONSHIPS

YVONNE R. BELL * CATHY L. BOUIE
* JOSEPH A. BALDWIN

The subject of black male-female relationships is not a new era of focus in psychology. However, the dominant thrust of the existing research has been pathology-centered. It suggests that black heterosexual relationships are characterized by a plethora of conflicts and problems (Farley & Hermalin, 1971), such as instability, disintegration, and pathological weaknesses (Frazier, 1957; Glazier & Moynihan, 1965; Thomas & Sillen, 1972).

In this type of pathology-centered research, it is typically assumed that black heterosexual relationships are based on the same values, beliefs, and life-styles as those governing Euro-American heterosexual relationships. Supportive of this viewpoint is the emphasis on black-white comparisons, and the cross-cultural insensitivity of the item content in the various measures of heterosexuality used in this research (Allen, 1978; Nobles, 1974; Staples, 1971). The various measures have focused on issue pertaining to communication barriers, an egalitarian relationship structure, gender-role differences, and educational-professional status, among other issues (Cazenave, 1983; Fairchild, 1985; McAdoo, 1983). These issues, it has been argued, are a primary focus of relationships in the Euro-American worldview or cultural orientation (Akbar, 1981; Baldwin, 1985; Dixon, 1976; Nobles, 1974). Hence, the dominant conceptual framework suggested by the research on black heterosexual relationships is primarily based on the world-view or cultural orientation of the Euro-American community (Baldwin, 1985; Harper Bolton, 1982, Nobles, 1974).

JOURNAL OF BLACK STUDIES, Vol. 21 No. 2, December 1990 162-189. © 1990
Sage Publications, Inc. Reprinted with permission.

350

THE EURO-AMERICAN WORLDVIEW AND CULTURAL ORIENTATION

The basic principles defining the Euro-American worldview are "survival of the fittest" and "control over nature" (people, objects, material possessions). These principles emphasize the high priority, historically and today, that European people tend to place on individualism and gaining control over the environment or surroundings (people, ideas, objects-property). Mastery is achieved through competition, aggression, materialism, domination and power, oppression, independence, and the transformation and rearranging of objects in nature (Akbar, 1984; Baldwin, 1980, 1985; Carruthers, 1981; Dixon, 1976; White, 1984).

MALE/FEMALE RELATIONS IN EURO-AMERICAN CULTURE

Consistent with the Euro-American worldview, the values of power, competition, material affluence, and physical gratification (or pleasure) have been shown to govern heterosexual relationships in Euro-American society (Akbar, 1981; Asante, 1981; Braithwaite, 1982; Cade, 1970; Karenga, 1978; White, 1984). For example, some researchers (Asante, 1981; Baldwin, 1980, 1985; Nobles, 1978, 1980) have shown that relationships in Euro-American culture are based on the principles of control and domination, or a hierarchy of power. The male is defined as the power-figure in such relationships (Basow, 1980; Beale, 1970; Blood & Wolfe, 1960; Frazier, 1932; Lewis, 1955; Moynihan, 1965; Pettigrew, 1964; Sizemore, 1973). He is expected to be the dominant and controlling family member, the major decision-maker, and/or the primary supplier of the survival-related needs of the family (Basow, 1980; Moynihan, 1965; Podell, 1966, Rainwater, 1966). Thus, his role is defined as superior to the female. The female, on the other hand, is viewed as the subordinate member in Eurocentric heterosexual relationships. Her role is defined as distinct, separate, and subservient (or inferior) to the male (Beale, 1970; Bird, 1968; Cade, 1970; Harper-Bolton, 1982; Nobles, 1974; Sizemore, 1973).

An example of the strong emphasis in Euro-American society on female subordination and male superordination is reflected in the widely held male attitude toward household duties as "woman's work" (Harper-Bolton, 1982; Staples, 1971). Many Euro-American male partners resist assuming or assisting with domestic responsibilities, such as managing the household and rearing the children, even in instances where such support is needed and/or desired (Cade, 1970). Such an attitude on the part of Euro-American men no doubt exists because such responsibilities have been associated with femininity or womanliness, which, as previously noted, suggests weakness and subordination, or a deficit state of being in Euro-American culture (Harper-Bolton, 1982; Ladner, 1971). Another example is reflected in the observation that many women in contemporary America resent and reject their traditional roles as wives and mothers, because these roles have relatively low value in Euro-American culture (Cade, 1970; Karenga, 1978). Many Euro-American women, especially in recent times, tend to think being a parent and/or wife brings them little social respect and sense of dignity or personal gratification (Astin, 1975; Brothers, 1984, Cade, 1970; Hoffman, 1977; Tangri, 1972). These women, therefore, seek "liberation" from their subservient roles in heterosexual relationships, and they advocate "equal rights" with their male counterparts in all sectors of American society (Basow, 1980; Braithwaite, 1982; Hoffman, 1977). Thus, it has been argued that the rigid and hierarchical nature of definitions of heterosexuality and gender roles in Euro-American culture (Nobles, 1978) probably contributes considerably to disharmony in heterosexual relationships governed by this cultural orientation (Cade, 1970; Harper-Bolton, 1982).

The materialistic emphasis of Euro-American culture has been shown to generate high priority for material affluence as a determining factor in the success of male-female relationships (Akbar, 1981; Hampton, 1979; Harper-Bolton, 1982). Studies have found, for example, that socioeconomic status, as indexed by level of income and education, is a major criterion in the mate-selection process and is positively related to material stability in American society (Bernard, 1966; Cater & Glick, 1976; Cruse, 1982; Cutright, 1971; Glick & Norton, 1971; Hampton, 1979; Scanzoni, 1975)/

The emphasis of Euro-American culture on material reality or the accumulation of material wealth has been found to be highly correlated with an overemphasis on physical characteristics, physical appearance, and sexual gratification as primary dimensions of heterosexual relationships (Akbar, 1981; Cruse, 1982; Karenga, 1978). Some researchers, for example, have shown that in American society, physical characteristics and gratification have a higher priority in choosing a mate than many psychological qualities and character traits (Braithwaite, 1982; Cruse, 1982; Fairchild, 1985; Fisher, 1981). Overall, then, the evidence seems to strongly support the contention that heterosexual relationships American society are heavily influenced by the Eurocentric cultural orientation emphasizing individualism, materialism, and physical gratification.

THE IMPACT OF RACIAL/CULTURAL OPRESSION ON BLACK MALE-FEMALE RELATIONSHIPS

In varying degrees, it has been shown that African-Americans manifest some Euro-American cultural values in their relationships with each other (Akbar, 1981; Asante, 1981; Baldwin, 1985; Cade, 1970; Hammond & Enoch, 1976; Karenga, 1975, 1978; Nobles, 1978). This is probably the case because Africa-Americans continue to negotiate their survival in a society where the major institutions are governed by the principals and values of the Euro-American worldview (Amini, 1972; Baldwin, 1979, 1980, 1985; McGee, 1973). Having existed in Eurocentric social reality over several centuries, evidence suggests that African-Americans have become psychologically dependent, in varying degrees, on that reality (Akbar, 1981; Baldwin, 1980, 1985; Nobles, 1976). Consequently, they have accepted an orientation to social relationships which is more consistent in many respects with Eurocentric cultural definitions than with their own Aafrocentric cultural definitions (Baldwin, 1980; Braithwaite, 1982; McGee, 1973). This state of psychological oppression (Baldwin, 1980, 1985) means that many African-American males and females have internalized Eurocentric definitions/values and practice them in their relationships (Braithwaite, 1982; Cade, 1970; Harper-Bolton, 1982).

Support for the contention that black heterosexual relationships are victimized by racial cultural oppression in America comes from research on the values held by black males and females. The research evidence on black heterosexual relationships clearly suggests that many African-Americans (Jewell, 1983; Podell, 1966; Scanzoni, 1975) are influenced in their relationships by values and beliefs that are more congruent with the Euro-American worldview. Eurocentric values of high financial status, physical gratification, gender role differences, and education-professional status tend to play major roles in many black male-female relations (Jewel, 1983; Podell, 1966; Scanzoni, 1975).

Further support that this psychological oppression exists is found in the negative images African-American males and females have of each other (King, 1973). In this regard, American society defines black men and women as being inferior to whites. The electronic media, especially television and film, the mass media, and the American educational system in general have been shown to perpetuate negative black male and female images (Benjamin, 1983; Caution & Baldwin, 1980; Jewell, 1983). Negative black female images such as matriarchal, domineering, emasculating, and aggressive (Benjamin, 1983; Cade, 1970; Staples, 1971; Wallace, 1979) and black male images as "Uncle Tomm," passive, "stud," and criminal, among many others (Burgest & Bowen, 1982; Jewell, 1983), have been popularized by the electronic media. These negative images no doubt affect how many black men and black women view and relate to each other. According to sociological studies, for example, some black males tend to perceive black women as emasculating and aggressive, and conversely, some black females tend to perceive black men as shiftless, passive, and irresponsible (Benjamin, 1984; Houston, 1981; Staples, 1971; Turner & Turner, 1974).

Furthermore, some black males tend to believe that black females are the antithesis of beauty, femininity, and womanhood (Burgest, 1981; Burgest & Bowen, 1982; Nelson, 1975; Turner; 1982). Similarly, some black females tend to believe that white men treat white women much better than black men treat black women (Turner, 1982). This kind of evidence clearly suggests that many black men and women have internalized the negative Eurocentric images of their heterosexual roles, and that these internalized negative images probably contribute to much of the conflict in black male-female relationships (Akbar, 1981; Amini, 1972; Braithwaite, 1982, Cade, 1970; Jewell, 1983; McGee, 1973).

Given the dominance of the Eurocentric worldview in American society (Baldwin,1980,1985), black male-female relationships which prioritize Eurocentric values seemingly would be less stable than black heterosexual relationships with a strong Afrocentric cultural foundation (Akbar, 1984; Asante, 1980, 1981; Baldwin, 1984). There are several reasons why this position seems tenable. One is related to the transient and satiable nature of needs of pleasurable sensations (Akbar, 1981). Physical attractiveness and sexual potency decline with age in both men and women, and sensual pleasure provides only a temporary and intermittent source of self-satisfaction. Hence, while these needs do have a place in relationships, they do not constitute the total experience involved in sustaining healthy, culturally effective, and successful relationships between men and women (Asante, 1980, 1981).

Another reason for the tenability of this analysis concerns the issue of physical attractiveness. This issue is especially critical for African-Americans, given their existence in a society that projects and reinforces Eurocentric standards of beauty (Jewell, 1983; Murstein & Christy, 1976; Turner, 1982). Blacks who assign disproportionate priority to physical attraction/attributes in their relationships are probably more vulnerable to using Eurocentric criteria instead of Afrocentric cultural standards, such as human qualities or personal character. This is, the adoption of Eurocentric standards of physical attractiveness may cause a shift to physical rather than human/character qualities in assessing personal worth (Akbar, 1981; Harper-Bolton, 1982). This contributes to blacks' perception of each other in many instances are deficient and inferior (Burgest, 1981; Jewell, 1983).

A third reason for the tenability of this analysis relates to the materialistic emphasis in relationships. The value of material affluence (prestige) could pose a threat to the establishment of serious and intimate relationships between blacks because of racial oppression. That is, it is probably more difficult for blacks than whites to obtain definitive or absolute security through a self-image based on quantity of material possessions (Karenga, 1978). Furthermore, material affluence does not ensure the presence of those human qualities like strong moral character, mutual respect and sharing, or sacrifice which are so vital to healthy relationships between black men and women (Asante, 1981).

The power emphasis in relationships suggests another basis of support for this analysis. Relationships with a power focus are concerned with hierarchy, manipulation, and control (Braithwaite, 1982). Partners (either one or both) in relationships with this focus tend to objectify competition with and exploitation of each other in order to maintain their self-worth. Thus, power-centered black heterosexual relationships could be considered as maladaptive from the framework of African-American culture, because they lack reciprocity or mutual sharing and support, which define the essence of relationships in African-American culture (Asante, 1980; Nobles, 1974). Blacks in heterosexual relationships with a strong Afrocentric cultural orientation would be more spiritually balanced and thus place greater emphasis on personal-human qualities rather than physical-material qualities. Thus, Afrocentric relationships would be more healthy and culturally successful for blacks. They would also be more resistant to Eurocentric racial cultural oppression, because by virtue of their Afrocentric value base, they should be less vulnerable to manipulation and control by alien cultural institutions (Baldwin, 1984, 1985).

THE AFRICAN-AMERICAN WORLDVIEW AND BLACK HETEROSEXUAL RELATIONSHIPS

An alternative approach in conceptualizing black heterosexual relationships is derived from the African-American worldview. A basic assumption of the Afrocentric conceptual framework, is compared to the Eurocentric/cultural deprivation framework, is that African-Americans have a distinct cultural orientation (Akbar, 1984; Asante, 1980; Baldwin, 1980, 1985; Dixon, 1976). Hence, it is assumed in this model that African-Americans, notwithstanding some Euro-American cultural influences, tend to operate within the framework of the African worldview, which is distinct from the Euro-American worldview (Baldwin, 1985; Harper-Bolton, 1982; Nobles, 1980, 1986). Therefore, African-American scholars contend that a valid understanding of African-American relationships must logically incorporate the values and principles of the African-American worldview (Akbar, 1984; Asante, 1980; Baldwin, 1980, 1981, 1984; Nobles, 1980; White, 1984; Williams, 1981).

The African-American worldview is rooted in the historical, cultural, and philosophical tradition of African people. This worldview interprets black behaviors and psychological functioning from the perspective of a value system which prioritizes the affirmation of black life. The African-American worldview is defined by two guiding principles: "oneness with nature" and "survival of the group" (Baldwin, 1980; Mbiti, 1970; Nobles, 1980. The principle of "oneness with nature" asserts that all elements in the universe (humans, animals, inanimate objects, and natural phenomena) are interconnected (Nobles, 1980). That is, humanity, nature, and the self are conceptualized as the same phenomenon (Baldwin, 1985; Dixon, 1976; Nobles, 1980).

The principle of "survival of the group" prioritizes the survival of the corporate whole (the community), which includes all black people, rather than the individual or some segment of the community apart from the corporate whole (Baldwin, 1985; Dixon, 1976; Nobles, 1980). The essence of both principles is best summarized by the African adage: "I am because we are, and because we are, therefore, I am" (Mbiti, 1970).

Cultural values consistent with the basic principles of the African-American worldview are interdependence, cooperation, unity, mutual responsibility, and reconciliation (Dixon, 1976; Harper-Bolton, 1982; Nobles, 1974, 1980)/ The African worldview, thus, characterizes the natural/normal cultural orientation of black people and no doubt influences their behavior and social relationships.

AN AFROCENTRIC MODEL OF BLACK HETEROSEXUAL RELATIONSHIPS

A model of black heterosexual relationships based on the African-American worldview has been proposed by Asante (1980, 1981). Asante's model defines healthy black heterosexual relationships as those that are governed by an "Afrocentric imperative." By an Afrocentric (or collective cognitive) imperative, he means the spiritual and intellectual commitment of black couples to the cultural affirmation of their people.

Thus, Asante's model emphasized that Afrocentric cultural values should constitute the foundation of black relationships.

Black relationships with an Afrocentric cultural basis, in terms of Asante's model (1981), are based on four major value components: sacrifice, inspiration, vision, and victory. Sacrifice as a value component suggests that partners should prioritize spiritual-communal character qualities in the foundation of their relationships. This component means that couples should use their sense of corporate responsibility and interdependence to benefit their relationship as well as their families and the community at-large. Hence, couples should be committed to giving of themselves, wherever they are located in time and space, for the continued survival and well-being of their families and the black community.

Inspiration as a component of Afrocentric relationships emphasized that partners should relate to each other in a mutually affirmative and/or holistic, as opposed to fragmented, manner (Asante, 1980). In a holistic relationship, each partner provides for the other's physical, intellectual, emotional, and social stimulation. Neither partner exploits the relationship; instead, both encourage, inspire, and support each other in their productive and creative work and responsibilities. Thus, the inspiration component of the Afrocentric relationship identifies mutuality and reciprocity as core ingredients of healthy black heterosexual relationships.

Asante also defines Afrocentric relationships as being visionary. This component emphasizes the couple's role in future planning as related to family-community building. This means that the couple should be committed to goals, accomplishments, and aspirations that are related to the survival that are related to the survival and development of the black family and the black community. This component, therefore, suggests the belief in black community involvement that is designed to revitalize and preserve African-American culture.

Finally, victory as a value component of Afrocentric relationships defines the couple's belief and faith that all goals related to African affirmation are achievable. This component, according to Asante (1980), means that couples celebrate themselves, their achievements, aspirations, and developments as African people, since these are viewed as culturally relevant. This concept of Afrocentric celebration incorporates self-development and/or race-cultural-related accomplishments (e.g., the attainment of joy, peace, and power on behalf of the family and the black community). Hence, family-community participation in the celebration of such accomplishments is more highly valued than (or is certainly considered equal in value to) the material-physical aspects of celebration (e.g., gift-giving). In terms of Asante's model, then, Afrocentric relationships are based on African-American cultural value themes, such as holistic relationships, spiritual/character values, and Afrocentric cultural consciousness.

Based on Asante's (1980, 1981) model, there should be a positive relationship between Afrocentric cultural consciousness and healthy (self-affirming) black heterosexual relationships. Obviously, the value themes in Asante's model are in opposition to those that undergird relationships based on Euro-American values. Hence, African-American heterosexual relationships based on the African-American worldview would be expected to manifest, to a considerable degree, more Afrocentric/self-affirming attitudinal (cognitive) and behavioral orientations. To date, no research to our knowledge has been conducted which attempts to examine this notion or any aspect of Asante's model.

PROPOSED RESEARCH AND HYPOTHESIS

The purpose of this study is to examine the relationship between Afrocentric cultural consciousness and perceptions of male-female relationships among African-Americans. Based on the assumption that Afrocentric cultural consciousness is positively related to healthy black heterosexual relationships, perceptions (values, attitudes and beliefs) of black heterosexual relationships should vary as a function of levels of Afrocentric cultural consciousness. Therefore, it is predicted that Afrocentric cultural consciousness will be significantly related to how blacks perceive heterosexual relationships. More specifically, the hypothesis is that those subjects who exhibit high Afrocentric cultural consciousness will prioritize Afrocentric cultural values in heterosexual relationships, as opposed to Eurocentric cultural values. And conversely, it is hypothesized that those who reflect low Afrocentric cultural consciousness will prioritize more Eureocentric cultural values (e.g., power, prestige, income and/or financial status), or perhaps a diffusion of both Afrocentric and Eurocentric values in heterosexual relationships.

METHODOLOGY

SUBJECTS

The subjects in this study were 88 black males and 89 black females from Gadsden and Leon counties in north Florida. A deliberate effort was made to obtain a cross-sectional sample by selecting subjects at different ages, educational, and occupational levels. Relative to each of these categories, the subjects were selected from four population categories: college students, unskilled workers, professionals, and the elderly. The college students were enrolled in various sections of the introductory psychology course at Florida A&M University. The unskilled workers and professionals were selected from a roster of names and work phone numbers provided by a state employment agency in Florida. Black churches in Gadsden and Leon counties selected the elderly subjects and provided names and phone numbers, with the person's permission. In each category at least 40 subjects were selected, on the basis of whether they were presently or had been involved in a heterosexual relationship and whether they were willing to participate. *African Self-Consciousness (ASC) Scale.* The ASC was developed by Baldwin and Bell (1985) and is designed to assess the black personality construct of African self-consciousness (Baldwin, 1981, 1984). It consists of four competency dimensions that are reflected in the questionnaire's 42 items. The competency dimensions are: awareness and recognition of one's African identity and heritage; recognition of black survival priorities and the necessity for institutions (practices, customs, values) which affirm black life; participation in the survival, liberation, and development of black people and defense of their dignity, worth, and integrity; recognition of how racial oppression hinders the development and survival of black life and resistance to Anti-Black forces. Also included in the ASC Scale are six expressive dimensions: religion, family, education, culture, interpersonal relationships, and political orientation. All statements comprising the ASC Scale reflect some beliefs, opinions, and attitudes of black people which are relevant to important aspects of African-American life and survival requirements. Statements in the ASC Scale are scored as: strongly disagree (1-2), disagree (3-4), agree (5-6), and strongly agree (7-8). The final ASC Scale scores can be computed as either the total score (sum) or the mean total score (sum of score/number of items). The validity estimate for the ASC Scare is $r = .70$, and the reliability estimate is $r = .90$ (Baldwin & Bell, 1985).

Black Heterosexual Relationship (BHR) Survey. This measure was designed to assess the subjects' perceptions (values, attitudes, and beliefs) concerning heterosexual relationships. The structure of the BHR Survey is similar to the Black Male-Female Relations of Survey developed by Fairchild (1985). The BHR Survey consists of four parts:

Ideal Mate (Part 1). This part of the BHR Survey consisted of personal qualities and social traits of an ideal mate that were pre-rated by three expert judges as representing either the Euro-American or the African-American worldview. The qualities and traits pre-rated as representing the African-American worldview derived from Asante's model (1981) of black heterosexual relationships. These were emotional and intellectual stimulation, commitment to the black community, mutual respect and sharing, cultural awareness, unconditional love, and being family-oriented. The qualities and traits pre-rated to represent the Euro-American worldview were: physical attraction, competition and control, independence, sexual compatibility, financial status, educational status, sexual conquests, and professional status. The latter items were taken from Fairchild's survey (1985) of black heterosexual relationships.

Both sets of descriptors were randomly organized in the list to minimize any effects that might be derived from a systematic listing. A final item in Part 1 required the subjects to write in a quality or trait that they viewed as important in heterosexual relationships. The subjects rated each quality or trait on the following scale of importance: not at all (0), a little (1), some (2), very much (3).

Heterosexual Attitudes (Part 2). This part consisted of 20 statements constructed to be consistent in meaning with the four components of Asante's model. Attitudes and perceptions were prepared as projecting either Afrocentric or Eurocentric values in heterosexual relationships. For example, an item reflecting sacrifice was, "In my personal relationship maintaining a workable (useful, positive, growing) relationship with my family and my spouse's family is important." An item reflecting inspiration was, "Each spouse should be approved by both of our parents." An item reflecting vision was, "For black couples, the concept of building a family should definitely include the investment of the couples' productive and financial resources in black institutions, or in efforts to build such institutions." Finally, an example of an item depicting victory was, "In mate selection and/or evaluation, black men and black women should consider black cultural beliefs and values (or cultural consciousness) as a main or primary criterion."

Eurocentric items dealt with such issues as physical attraction, competition, or control. An example of a Eurocentric item was, "A person must have a substantial income before I would consider a serious/ intimate relationship with him or her." These items were modeled after those in the Black Male-Female Relationship Survey developed by Fairchild (1985). Responses were rated on four-point Likert-type scale ranging from strongly disagree (1) to strongly agree (4). On Parts 1 and 2 higher scores indexed a stronger Afrocentric cultural orientation and lower scores indexed a weaker Afrocentric orientation, or a more Eurocentric orientation.

Behavioral Scenario (Part 3). This part consisted of two hypothetical scenarios, one for male subjects and one for female subjects, involving a black relationship dilemma. The scenarios were constructed to symbolize real-life hardships in the African-American community. The scenario for the male subjects depicted a man who is working three jobs to support his family (wife and children). The wife is unable to work due to illness, and because of the nature of her illness, she cannot actively participate in the general management of the home. For leisure activity, she usually spends several hours a day watching television and playing card games with friends. The scenario for the female subjects depicted a woman who is working two jobs to support her family (a husband and three children). The husband is unemployed and remains at home. He has not been able to contribute any financial support to the maintenance of the family but helps his wife with child care and the general duties of managing the home. For leisure activity, he spends a few hours three to four days a week at a local bar talking and drinking with friends.

For each scenario, the subjects were asked to indicate their most likely course of action, from among four choices, if they were the employed partner in the situation described. One of the four courses of action was pre-rated Afrocentric and the other three were pre-rated as Eurocentric in value projections. The Afrocentric alternative involved being totally supportive of the mate in hardship, while the Eurocentric alternatives ranged from partial to total withholding/withdrawing of support.

Personal Background Information (Part 4). This las section of the BHR Survey was used to obtain background data on the subjects relative to their age, sex, social class status, educational level, and occupational-professional status, where appropriate.

PROCEDURE

The ASC Scale and the BHR Survey were hand-delivered simultaneously to the subjects by the researcher. The subjects were instructed to complete the ASC Scale and the BHR Survey. They were told that the questionnaires would be collected in five days at the same place where they were delivered. The college students received and returned both instruments in their psychology classes. All of the elderly subjects and some of the professional and unskilled workers received and returned the instruments in their homes. Some other professionals and unskilled workers received and returned the instruments at their places of employment. Some of the unskilled workers and elderly subjects indicated that they would have difficulty reading and comprehending the ASC Scale and the BHR Survey. These subjects were assisted by the researcher in their homes. On two separate occasions, the researcher assisted these subjects with the completion of the ASC Scale and the BHR Survey, respectively.

RESULTS

The primary data in this study consisted of the total scores obtained on the ASC Scale, and Parts 1 and 2 (Ideal Mate and Heterosexual Attitudes) of the BHR Survey. The frequency of

TABLE 1
Means and Standard Deviations for
The ASC, Ideal Mate, and Heterosexual Attitudes Scores

Measure	N	*Mean*	*Standard Deviation*
ASC	177	240	48
Ideal Mate	177	46	9
Heterosexual Attitudes	177	59	13

NOTE: ASC refers to the African Self-Consciousness Scale developed by Baldwin and Bell (1985).

Afrocentric versus Eurocentric responses to Part 3 (the Behavioral Scenario) of the BHR Survey and responses to the background data section were included as primary data in these results.

Correlation and chi-square analyses were used to evaluate the data. The Pearson product moment correlation coefficient was computed to assess the magnitude of the relationship between ASC scores and scores on the Ideal Mate and the Heterosexual Attitudes scores and scores on the Ideal Mate and the Heterosexual Attitudes measures. A significant positive correlation was obtained between ASC scores and Ideal Mate scores, $r = .44$, $p < .001$. High ASC scores tended to be associated with high Afrocentric Ideal Mate scores. The analysis of ASC scores and Heterosexual Attitudes scores also yielded a significant positive correlation, $r = .53$, $p < .001$; high ASC scores correlated with high Afrocentric Heterosexual Attitudes scores.

The chi-square test was computed to compare the frequencies of high and low ASC Scale scores with the frequencies of high and low scores on the Ideal Mate and the Heterosexual Attitudes measures. Scores that were one standard deviation above the mean on each of these measures were designated high scores, while scores that were one standard deviation below the mean were designated low scores. Table 1 summarizes the means and standard deviations for these measures.

TABLE 2

Frequency and Percentages of High and Low ASC Scores by High and Low Ideal Mate and Heterosexual Attitudes Scores

	High	ASC	Low
Ideal Mate[a]			
High Afrocentric	11 92%	1	8%
Low Afrocentric	1 10%	9	90%
Heterosexual Attitudes[b]			
High Afrocentric	14 100%	0	
Low Afrocentric	0	10	100%

NOTE: ASC refers to the African Self-Consciousness Scale developed by Baldwin and Bell (1985).

    a. X^2 (1, N = 22) 14.67, $p < .001$

    b. X^2 (1, N = 24) 24.00, $p < .001$.

The chi-square analysis for the ASC and Ideal Mate scores yielded a significant value, $X2$ (1, N = 22) = 14.67 $p < .001$. Ninety-two percent of the students with high ASC scores obtained high Ideal Mate scores. Also, 90% of the subjects with low ASC scores obtained low Ideal Mate scores. The chi-square value for ASC scores by Heterosexual Attitudes scores was also significant, $X2$ (1, N = 24) = 24.00, $p < 001$. This analysis indicated that all of the subjects with high ASC scores also obtained high Heterosexual Attitudes scores. These results are summarized in Table 2. Overall, both the correlation and chi-square analyses indicate that a significant relationship exists between Afrocentric cultural consciousness and an Afrocentric values orientation in perceptions of black heterosexual relationships.

To further substantiate the role of cultural values in heterosexual relationships, additional chi-square analyses were computed to assess the relationship between scores on the Behavioral Scenario were designated high-scoring subjects and those who selected one of the Eurocentric alternatives were designated low-scoring subjects.

TABLE 3
Frequency and Percentages of
Afrocentric vs. Eurocentric Behavioral Scores by High
And Low ASC, Ideal Mate, and Heterosexual Attitudes Scores

| | Behavioral Scenario Measure | | | |
	Afrocentric		Eurocentric	
ASC[a]				
High	27	100%	0	0%
Low	2	8%	22	92%
Ideal Mate[b]				
High Afrocentric	26	96%	1	4%
Low Afrocentric	6	16%	31	84%
Heterosexual Attitudes[c]				
High Afrocentric	22	92%	2	8%
Low Afrocentric	2	8%	22	92%

NOTE: ASC refers to the African Self-Consciousness Scale developed by Baldwin and Bell (1985).

    a. X^2 (1, N = 51) = 43.52, p < .001

    b. X^2 (1, N = 64) = 40.04, p < .001.

    c. X^2 (1, N = 48) = 33.33, p < .001.

The results of the chi-square analysis between ASC Scale, Ideal Mate and Heterosexual Attitudes scores, and the Behavioral Scenario measure are summarized in Table 3. The ASC x Behavioral Scenario analysis indicates that all of the high-ASC subjects chose the Afrocentric response to the Behavioral Scenario measure: $X2$ (1, N, = 51) = 43.52, p < .001. Contrastingly, 92% of the low-scoring subjects on the ASC Scale did not choose the Afrocentric response. The analysis of the relationship between the Behavioral Scenario measure and the Ideal Mate measure was also significant: $X2$ (1, N = 64) = 40.04, p < .001. This analysis indicated that 96% of the subjects who obtained high Ideal Mate scores chose the Afrocentric alternative on the Behavioral Scenario measure. The chi-square value for the Behavioral Scenario measure and the Heterosexual Attitudes scores was significant was well: $X2$, (1, N = 48) = 33.33, p < .001. This analysis indicates that the subjects with Afrocentric Heterosexual. Attitudes scores also chose the Afrocentric alternative on the Behavioral Scenario measure.

TABLE 4
Frequency and Percentage of Demographic Data Related to the Behavioral Scenario Measure

| | Behavioral Scenario Measure | | | |
	Afrocentric		Eurocentric	
Age[a]				
Nonelderly	17	41%	24	59%
Elderly	34	79%	9	21%
Occupational status[b]				
Students	19	43%	25	57%
Unskilled	58	70%	25	30%
Professional	19	37%	32	63%
Educational level[c]				
Primary/secondary	56	71%	12	29%
College/college graduate	38	40%	58	60%
Socioeconomic status[d]				
Lower	73	66%	38	34%
Middle/upper	23	36%	41	64%

a. X^1 (1, N = 84) = 12.44, p < .001
b. X^2 (1, N = 178) = 16.25, p < .001
c. X^2 (1, N = 175) = 17.08, p < .001
d. X^2 (1, N = 175) = 14.58, p < .001

The chi-square analysis was also computed for the demographic data in relation to performance on the Behavioral Scenario measure. These results are presented in Table 4. The age x Behavioral Scenario measure analysis generated a significant chi-square: $X2$ (1, $N - 84$) = 12.44, p < .001. This indicates that 79% of the elderly subjects as compared to 41% of the nonelderly subjects chose the Afrocentric response to the Behavioral Scenario measure. The chi-square value for occupational status (student, unskilled, and professional) and performance on the Behavioral Scenario measure was also significant: $X2$ (2, $N - 178$) = 16.25, p < .001. this analysis reveals that 70% of the unskilled subjects chose the Afrocentric response, as compared to 43% of the students and 37% of the professionals. Additionally, educational level and the Behavioral Scenario measure generated a significant chi-square value: $X2$ (1, $N - 175$) = 17.08, p < .001. Seventy-one percent of the subjects with a primary/secondary education, as compared with 40 % of the subjects with a college education, choose the Afrocentric response. Finally, the chi-square value for socioeconomic status and performance on the Behavioral Scenario measure was also significant: $X2$ (1, $N-175$) = 14.58, $p < .001$. This analysis indicates that 66% of the subjects with a lower socioeconomic status, as compared to 36% of the subjects with a middle-upper socioeconomic status, chose the Afrocentric response to the Behavioral Scenario measure. The chi-square analysis did not indicate a significant relationship between sex and performance on the Behavioral Scenario measure.

DISCUSSION

It was hypothesized in this study that Afrocentric cultural consciousness is significantly related to perceptions of heterosexual relationships among African-Americans. The present findings support this prediction. The correlation analysis indicated a positive and stable relationship between Afrocentric cultural consciousness and an Afrocentric value orientation in perceptions of heterosexual relationships. The chi-square analysis also supported this finding in terms of frequency (or percentage) of subjects.

Specifically, these findings suggest that subjects with high Afrocentric cultural consciousness tended to prioritize their ideal mate in terms of emotional and intellectual stimulation, commitment to the black community, mutual respect and sharing, black consciousness (awareness), unconditional love, and family orientation. In contrast, subjects who manifested low Afrocentric cultural consciousness prioritized such ideal-mate qualities as physical attraction, competition and control, independence, sexual compatibility, financial status, emotional status, sexual conquests, and professional status.

Additionally, subjects with high Afrocentric cultural consciousness tended to place more value on heterosexual attitudes (or perceptions) that were consistent in meaning with Asante's four components of healthy black relationships. That is, the subjects were more inclined to endorse the idea that partners should relate to each other in a reciprocal manner, as well as family-community building and recognition and respect for each partner's achievements, aspirations, and development.

On the other hand, those with low cultural consciousness were more in favor of attitudes and perceptions reflective of Eurocentric cultural values in heterosexual relationships (e.g., competition, physical-material gratification). Overall, then, these findings strongly suggest that Afrocentric cultural consciousness is positively related to an Afrocentric value orientation in black heterosexual relationships.

The present findings also support the position that Afrocentric values play an affirmative role in black heterosexual relationships. This contention is strongly supported by the performance of the subjects on the Behavioral Scenario measure. All of the subjects with high ASC scores indicated that they would remain with and be totally ASC scores indicated that they would remain with and be totally supportive of their mate when the latter was ill or without employment. The same alternative was chosen by subjects who manifested an Afrocentric orientation on the Ideal Mate and the Heterosexual Attitudes measures. The exact reversal of this response pattern occurred for the subjects who manifested a less Afrocentric or more Eurocentric cultural orientation. Less Afrocentric subjects indicated that they would withhold either partial or total support of the mate suffering hardship. Thus, the highly Afrocentric subjects reflected a stronger commitment to the relationship during a hardship or crisis involving the other partner.

This consistency in performance on the Behavioral Scenario measure by the high and low groups on ASC, Ideal Mate and Heterosexual Attitudes measures strongly suggests that Afrocentric values may constitute a much more reliable predictor of stable and affirmative black heterosexual relationships than the prominent literature has indicated. Regarding this point, it should be emphasized that only one of the four response alternatives on the Behavioral Scenario measure indexed an Afrocentric cultural orientation. The subjects were provided with more opportunities (three) to choose a Eurocentric alternative. Therefore, the strong preference for the Afrocentric alternative among the Afrocentric subjects tends to further support the affirmative nature of Afrocentric values in black heterosexual relationships. In this regard, the present findings are consistent with Asante's (1980) model. His model argues that the successful attainment and/or maintenance of goals related to the survival and well-being of these relationships (e.g., economical stability, personal-social adjustment) are contingent upon the mates having and maintaining an Afrocentric cultural/value base. The performance of these subjects on the Behavioral Scenario measure, in particular, seemingly provides good support for Asante's contention.

With the exception of sex, all of the other background factors (age, socioeconomic status, educational, and occupational ranks) differentially affected performance on the Behavioral Scenario measure. The elderly subjects and the low-ranking educational, occupational, and socioeconomic subject groups indicated a stronger preference for the Afrocentric alternative than did their younger or higher-level counterparts. This result may be linked to the fact that the elderly and low-ranking groups share a more peripheral or marginal status in (i.e., social and psychological distance from) Euro-American-controlled institutions than the latter groups. For example, the elderly subjects experienced their formative socialization and received their education, at least the early part of it, during the segregation era of American social policy. The elderly subjects' education and sociocultural experiences in general are probably products of a more Afrocentric experience than the younger subjects (Billingsley, 1968; Nobles, 1974, 1978). Thus, the difference observed in this finding may have been influenced to some extent by the sociohistorical factors of American life. The present findings might also be interpreted as supporting the notion that Euro-American institutions (education, employment) tent to have a culturally alienating effect on black heterosexual relationships.

IMPLICATIONS OF THE STUDY

As discussed earlier, previous research on black heterosexual relationships, for the most part, has been governed by the cultural deficit perspective (Asante, 1981; Baldwin, 1985). Such research tended to be guided by the erroneous assumption of the dominant culture that black heterosexual relationships are governed by the same Eurocentric values, beliefs, and life-styles that govern Euro-American relations (Allen, 1978; Baldwin, 1980; Nobles, 1974; Staples, 1971). Therefore, most of the previous assessments of African-American heterosexual relationships emphasized the deviations from Euro-American norms and standards for healthy relationships (Cazenave, 1983; Fairchild, 1985; McAdoo, 1983). Since a cultural deficit perspective has dominated this area of research, the observations generated have mostly reflected the influence of racial and cultural oppression on black heterosexual relationships, rather than the role of African-American culture as a legitimate system of values and standards governing such relationships. In contrast to the deficit-oriented literature, it is important to reiterate that the present findings suggest an entirely different research focus by documenting the importance of Afrocentric cultural consciousness and Afrocentric values in black heterosexual relationships. Thus, the findings of this study help to broaden the knowledge base related to a fuller understanding of black heterosexual relationships.

The findings relating background variables to Afrocentric vs. Eurocentric value orientations on the Behavioral Scenario measure suggest that these orientations may vary consistently with age and occupational, educational, and socioeconomic ranks. Afrocenetric value orientations in heterosexual relationships may be moderated to some extent by these kinds of background factors. In light of this suggestion, it seems that future research should focus on comparing the relative contributions of background factors, such as those in this study, to variance in cultural values regarding heterosexual relationships. Such research could strengthen the knowledge base undergirding intervention strategies (therapeutic and educational programs) that are directed toward fostering healthy black relationships.

The present findings also direct attention to the socialization process, especially as the latter relates so sex-role definitions in the black community. In this regard, one implication appears to be that it might be healthier, at least from the vantage point of heterosexual relationships, for black males and females to internalize sex-role definitions that are consistent with African-American culture rather than Euro-American culture (Harper-Bolton, 1982; Nobles, 1974). It seems that future research in this area might also be designed to investigate the nature of heterosexual relationship patterns in black youth as a function of socialization factors (e.g. child-rear patterns, parental heterosexual relationship values, family structure) in African-American families. Seemingly, additional research such as this is needed to strengthen our knowledge base relative to the impact of socialization on the development of heterosexual cultural values. It should also help to generate models for fostering healthy relationships among African-American men and women.

CONCLUSIONS

The findings of this study support the major prediction that Afrocentric cultural consciousness is positively related to perceptions (values, attitudes) that prioritize an Afrocentric value orientation in black heterosexual relationships. Additionally, the findings support the contention that Afrocentric cultural factors may be a sustaining and affirmative force even during difficult times in black heterosexual relationships. In this regard, the findings are supportive of Asante's model of culturally based black heterosexual relationships.

The analysis involving background factors may magnify the potential importance of culturally affirmative experiences in culture values preferences related to black heterosexual relationships. That is, as an explanation for the stronger Afrocentric cultural orientation manifested by the elderly subjects and low-ranking educational, occupational, and socioeconomic groups, it was speculated that these group may be more psychosocially distant from the European-American sociocultural reality than the younger and higher-ranking subject groups. The latter groups manifested a more diffuse or more Eurocentric cultural orientation. In contrast to the deficit-oriented thrust of previous research related to black heterosexual relationships, the present findings reflect support for an alternative paradigm for conceptualizing such relationships. One which emphasized the importance of Afrocentric cultural consciousness and Afrocentric cultural values to healthy black heterosexual relationships.

Given the reality of the experience of racial and cultural oppression among African-Americans, it is suggested that a continued research effort is needed in this area to further refine our understanding of the role of cultural variables and related factors in black heterosexual relationships. Such research should result in more culturally valid intervention planning geared toward fostering healthy African-American relationships in general, and healthy male-female relationships in particular.

REFERENCES

Akbar, N. (1981). Reconciliation of the African American woman and man. *Black Male/Female Relationships, 5,* 60-64.

Akbar, N. (1984). Africentric social sciences for human liberation. *Journal of Black Studies, 14* (4). 395-414.

Allen, W. (1978). The search for applicable theories of Black family life. *Journal of Marriage and the Family, 35,* 117-128.

Amini, J. (1972). *An African frame of reference.* Chicago: Institute of Positive Education.

Asante, M.K. (1980). *Afrocentricity: A Theory of social change.* Buffalo, NY: Amulefi.

Asante, M. (1981). Black male-female relationships: An Afrocentric context. In L. Gary (ed.), *Black men.* Beverly Hills, CA: Sage.

Astin, H. (1975). *Women and work.* Paper presented at the Conference for New Directions for Research on the Psychology of Women, Madison, WI.

Baldwin, J. (1979). Education and oppression in the American context. *Journal of Inner City Studies, 1*(1), 62-83.

Baldwin, J. (1980). The psychology of oppression. In M.K. Asante and A. Vandi (Eds.), *Contemporary Black thought. Alternative analyses in social and behavioral science.* Beverly Hills, CA: Sage.

Baldwin, J. (1981). Notes on an Africentric theory of Black personality. *Western Journal of Black Studies, 5*(3), 1972-1979.

Baldwin, J. (1985). Psychological aspects of European cosmology in American society. *Western Journal of Black Studies, 9*(4), 216-223.

Baldwin, J., & Bell, Y. (1985). The African self-consciousness scale: An Africentric personality questionnaire. *Western Journal of Black Studies, 9*(2), 61-68.

Basow, S. (1980). *Sex role stereotypes.* Belmont, CA: Wadsworth.

Beale, F. (1970). Double jeopardy: To be Black and female. In T. Cade (Ed.), *The Black woman: An anthology.* New York: New American Library.

Benjamin, L. (1983). The dog theory: Black male/female conflict. *Western Journal of Black Studies, 7*(1), 49-55.

Bernard, J. (1966). Marital stability and patterns of status variables. *Journal of Marriage and the Family, 28,* 358-367.

Billingsley, A. (1968). *Black families in White America.* Englewood Cliffs, NJ: Prentice-Hall.

Bird, C. (1968). *Born female.* New York: Durd McKay.

Blood, R., & Wolfe, D. (1960). *Husbands and wives: The dynamics of married living.* Illinois: The Press of Flencoe.

Braithwaite, R. (1982). Interpersonal relations between Black males and females. *Black Men,* 83-95.

Brothers, J. (1984). *What every woman ought to know about love and marriage.* New York: Ballentine.

Burgest, D., & Bowen, J. (1982). Erroneous assumptions Black men make about Black women. *Black Male/Female Relationships, 6*(Winter), 13-19.

Burgest, M. (1981). Theory on White supremacy and Black oppression. *Black Books Bulletin, 7*(2), 26-30.

Cade, T. (1970). *The Black woman: An anthology.* New York: New American Library.

Carruthers, J. (1981). Reflections on the history of the Afrocentric worldview. *Black Books Bulletin, 7*(1), 4-25.

Carter, H., & Glick, P. (1976). *Marriage and divorce: A social and economic study* (rev. ed.). Cambridge: Howard University.

Caution, G. L., & Baldwin, J. A. (1980). *Television as projection of the European worldview.* Unpublished manuscript.

Cazenave, N. (1983). Black male-black female relationships: The perception of 155 middleclass Black men. *Family Relations, 32,* 341-350.

Cruse, H. (1982). The crisis in Black sexual politics. *Black Male/Female Relationships, 1*(Autumn), 27-40.

Cutright, P. (1971). Income and family events: Marital stability. *Journal of Marriage and the Family, 33,* 291-306.

Dixon, V. (1976). Worldview and research methodology. In L. M. King (Ed.), *African philosophy: Assumptions and paradigms for research on Black persons.* Los Angeles: Fanon Research and Development Center.

Fairchild, H. (1985). Black singles: Gender differences in mate preferences and heterosexual attitudes. *Western Journal of Black Studies, 9,* 69-73.

Farley, W., & Hermalin, A. (1971). Family stability: A comparison of trends between Blacks and Whites. *American Sociological Review, 36,* 1-17.

Fisher, H. (1981, April). Female sex appeals an asset even in prehistoric times. *Jet,* p. 43.

Frazier, E. (1932). *The Negro family in the United States.* Chicago: The University Press.

Frazier, E. (1957). *Black bourgeoisie: The rise of a new middle class in the United States.* Glencoe, IL: Free Press.

Glazier, N., & Moynihan, D. (1965). *Beyond the melting pot.* Cambridge, MA: MIT Press.

Glick, P., & Norton, A. (1971). Frequency, duration and probability of marriage and divorce. *Journal of Marriage and the Family, 44,* 307-317.

Hammond, J., & Enoch, J. (1976). Conjugal power relations among Black working class families. *Journal of Black Studies, 8*(1), 107-128.

Hampton, R. (1979. Husband's characteristics and marital disruption in Black families. *Sociological Quarterly, 20,* 255-266.

Harper-Bolton, D. (1982). A reconceptualization of the African-American woman. *Black Male/Female Relationships, 6*(Winter), 33-42.

Hoffman, L. (1977). Changes in family roles, socialization and sex differences. *American Psychologist, 32,* 644-657.

Houston, L. (1981). Romanticism and eroticism among Black and White college students. *Adolescence, 16,* 2 63-272.

Jewell, K. (1983). Black male/female conflict: Internalization of negative definitions transmitted through imagery. *Western Journal of Black Studies, 7*(1), 43-48.

Karenga, M. (1975). In love and struggle: Toward a greater togetherness. *Black Scholar, 3,* 16-28.

Karenga, M. (1978). *Beyond connections.* Los Angeles: Kwaida.

King, M. (1973). The politics of sexual stereotypes. *Journal of Black Studies and Research, 4*(4-7), 12-23.

Ladner, J. (1971). *Tomorrow's tomorrow: The Black woman.* Garden City, NY: Doubleday.

Lewis, H. (1955). *Black ways of Kent.* Chapel Hill, NC: University of North Carolina Press.

Mbiti, J. (1970). *African religions and philosophy.* New York: Doubleday.

McAdoo, H. (1983). *Extended family support to single black mothers.* Final report submitted to National Institutes of Mental Health. Rockville, MD: U.S. Department of Health and Human Services.

McGee, D. (1973). White conditioning of Black dependency. *Journal of Social Issues, 29*(1), 53-55.

Moynihan, D. (1965). *The Negro family: The call for national action.* Washington, DC: U.S. Department of Labor.

Murstein, B., & Christy, P. (1976). Physical attractiveness and marriage adjustment in middle-aged couples. *Journal of Personality and Social Psychology, 34,* 537-542.

Nelson, C. (1975). Myths about Black women workers in modern America. *Black Scholar, 3,* 11-15.

Nobles, W. (1974). Africanity: Its role in Black families. *Black Scholar, 5,* 10-17.

Nobles, W. (1976). Black people in White insanity: An issue for Black community mental health. *Journal of Afro-American Issues, 4*(1), 21-27.

Nobles, W. (1978). The Black family and its children: The survival of humaneness. *Black Books Bulletin, 6*(22), 7-14.

Nobles, W. (1980). African philosophy foundation for Black psychology. In R. Jones (Ed.), *Black psychology.* New York: Harper & Row.

Nobles, W. (1986). *African psychology: Towards its reclamation, reascension and revitalization.* Oakland, CA: The Institute for the Advanced Study of Black Family Life and Culture.

Nobles, W., & Goddard, L. L. (1984). *Understanding the Black family: A guide for scholarship and research.* Oakland, CA: Institute of Black Family Life and Culture.

Pettigrew, T. (1964). *A profile of the Negro American.* Princeton, NJ: Van Nostrand.

Podell, L. (1966). Sex and role conflict. *Journal of Marriage and the Family, 28*(2), 163-165.

Rainwater, L. (1966). Crucible of identity: The Negro lower-class family. In Lengine & Brombley (Eds.), *White Racism and Black Americans*. Chicago: Schnekman.

Scanzoni, J. (1975). Sex roles, economic factors, and marriage solidarity in Black and White marriages. *Journal of Marriage and the Family, 37,* 130-144.

Sizemore, B. (1973). Sexism and the Black male. *Black Scholar, 4*(6-7), 2-11.

Staples, R. (1971) *The Black family: Essays and studies,* Belmont, CA: Wadsworth.

Tangri, S. (1972). Determinants of occupational role innovation among collage women. *Journal of Social Issues, 28,* 177-199.

Thomas, A., & Sillen, S. (1972). *Racism and psychiatry.* New York: Brunner/Mazel.

Turner, B., & Turner, C. (1974). Evaluation of women and men among Black and White college students. *Sociological Quarterly, 15,* 442-456.

Turner, R. (1982). The ordeal of the ugly Black woman. *Black Male/ Female Relationships, 6*(Winter), 21-29.

Wallace, M. (1979). *Black macho and the myth of the superman.* New York: Dial.

White, J. (1984). *The psychology of Blacks.* Englewood Cliffs: NJ: Prentice-Hall.

Williams, R. (1981). *The collective Black mind: An Afrocentric theory of Black personality.* St. Louis, MO: Williams & Associates.

THE HIP HOP GENERATION: AFRICAN AMERICAN MALE-FEMALE RELATIONSHIPS IN A NIGHTCLUB SETTING

JANIS FAYE HUTCHINSON

In examining black male-female relationships, Bell, Bouie, and Baldwin (1990) noted that most of the research is pathology-centered. This research focuses on a worldview or cultural orientation whose center is Euro-American. It is assumed that black heterosexual relationships are based on the same values, lifestyles, and beliefs as those of Euro-American heterosexual relationships. To support this belief, the research emphasizes black-white comparisons that are not cross-culturally sensitive to variation (Allen, 1978). Any deviation from the Euro-American pattern is considered abnormal.

Asante (1980) proposed that African American cultural orientation is distinct from that of Euro-Americans. African American cultural orientation and worldview are situated in the cultural, historical, and philosophical tradition of African people. This worldview is defined by two principles: "oneness with nature" and "survival of the group." In this holistic perspective, each partner provides for the other's intellectual, emotional, physical, and social stimulation. Neither partner exploits the relationship (Bell et al., 1990).

Other social scientists, such as Page (1997), Hutchinson (1997), and Michaels (1995), discussed the heterogeneity and variation within African American communities. For example, Michaels used a historical examination of writers such as Paul Lawrence Dunbar, Zora Neal Hurston, and W.E.B. DuBois to discuss variation among African Americans. Page also suggested that promoters of the traveling photographic exhibit *Songs of My People* showed only the positive attributes of African American life from a Eurocentric perspective. She believed the exhibit did not present the heterogeneous nature of African American communities. Hutchinson provided an

JOURNAL OF BLACK STUDIES, Vol. 30 No. 1, September 1999 62-84 © 1999 Sage Publications, Inc. Reprinted with permission.

Examination of negative portrayals of African Americans and their varied responses to these portrayals. In doing so, she described African Americans as socially and economically varied and continually changing within and among their communities.

This study should be interpreted within the context of a socially heterogeneous population of young adult African American women in a low-income urban environment. The aim of the ethnography was to identify perceptions of female-male relationships from the viewpoint of African American women and to provide a context for understanding these perceptions by examination of theory.

METHODS

The ethnography took place at a local gangsta rap nightclub (Club X, fictitious name) in Houston, Texas, from May 1993 to the summer of 1995. This nightclub is not unique among blacks or the general population of Houston. It is similar to other black clubs in terms of age and gender composition and percentage of non-whites (small numbers of whites and Hispanics).

Only a few clubs in Houston play gangsta rap music. It is the controversial type mentioned in the local news. These rappers espouse themes of killing, use of guns, extremely derogatory statements about women, and explicit sexual statements. The music also portrays realistic views of life in the African American society. This music appeals to diverse groups of younger African Americans. Club X was chosen because it has the previously discussed characteristics and because many young African Americans frequent this club. A former student who frequented the club introduced me to the club. She was infected with HIV by one of the "regulars" at the club. Through discussions with her, I learned about sexual transactions in her network and that this club was a focal point for their interactions.

PARTICIPANT OBSERVATIONS

Ethnographers describe cultures or certain aspects of a culture and attempt to understand the culture from the perspective of the people attempt to understand the culture from the perspective of the people living within it. The ethnography involved participant observation on Thursday, Friday, and Monday nights. Observations focused on female-male interactions and the general atmosphere of the club. Public interaction at the nightclub was concerned with issues such as: What do they do at the club? How do men approach women and how do women respond? I observed interactions, listened to people's conversations, and talked to women about men (this usually took place in the restroom).

INTENSIVE INTERVIEWS

Five African American women between the ages of 25 and 32 years old were intensively interviewed. Interviews lasted between 1 and 4 hours and were conducted at their homes, my biocultural laboratory at the University of Houston, at a park, and at a McDonald's restaurant. Intensive interviews dealt with determining who to date, categorization of men, sexism, dancing, personal appearance, economics, female-male relationships, use of the word "bitch," rap music, and condom use and nonuse. The interviewed women were students with no children (Latasha, 22 years old, and Yvonne, 25 years old), La Quita (28 years old) was unemployed and on welfare with three children, Shontele was a 25-year0\-old woman with one child who lives with her parents, and the eldest was Anna, a 32-year-old professional working woman with no children (all names are fictitious).

RESULTS

CATEGORIZATION OF MEN AND WOMEN

Categorization of men by women was based on a number of criteria. For instance, a student informant stated that different areas of the club are allocated to certain drug dealers, and men form a hierarchy. Drug dealers are at the top and are ranked by the amount of money they spend at the club. Rappers who have recorded an album and next in the ranking, and men who work for the drug dealers are beneath the rappers in rank, followed finally by the regulars—men who do not fall into the other categories (they have a regular job)—who are at the bottom of the hierarchy. Certain women are associated with different groupings of men and also form a hierarchy based on the men's rank. There is desire among some women to date men in the upper echelon of the club. This means dating the top drug dealers and their friends or rappers.

Shontele said:

> You're in it but you're looking out. Yeah, I know I'm hanging out with these people. That's not me. I'm in the front of all of them. I'm not in the back of them or in the middle. So I have a better chance of getting out. Some women still get respect because of boyfriends they used to have.

Unfortunately, "to get in front of them," you have to date the high-level drug dealers. This is an attempt at social elevation and an economic categorization that symbolizes the attempt at upward mobility.

Another way women categorize men is through their personal appearance. This includes physical attractiveness and clothing. Clothes add to a man's physical attractiveness and also provide a clue about economic status (although women reported that this sometimes can be misleading). Finally, women group men based on their potential as a husband or sexual partner. A potential short-term sexual partner is one who is a good dancer, spends money, and may have money (as shown by a Lexus or Tommy Hilfiger clothes). Potential husbands are men with an education, those who spend money and appear to have money, and who do not appear to have a lot of women. As a mate, women want someone they can talk to (compatible with) and someone they feel will "treat me right."

Manning (1973) stated that these symbols represent sensory and ideological poles of meaning. The sensory pole contains clusters of meaning related to the physiological, for instance, physical attractiveness and dancing. At the other end of the spectrum is the ideological (education, employment status, and perceived sex experience). Whereas education and employment status attest to a man's positive motivation and show maturity and responsibility, perceived sex experience is not viewed as a negative attribute for me. Men can have a number of sexual liaisons as long as they are not perceived as a "player," someone with a number of sexual partners at the same time.

Concerning reputations, Yvonne said "I don't like one-night stands. But plenty of it goes on." Women who frequent the club weekly may get a bad reputation.

Some men they'll say like I slept with her. My homeboy slept with her. They do get reputations being in there all the time. Some women don't care about their reputation. They're having a good time and trying to see what they can get out of someone. Or saying, "Hey I met this guy in a Suburban and I met a guy in a Lexus and he took me to breakfast and we went to the hotel" and things like that. Some people like that. It's a status thing. It raises their status. Then you have some people with real low self-esteem. So, when they go out and have guys approaching them, and say "Well, I'll do this and that for you and I have this and that," it makes them feel I am something. I am somebody. At one time I had low self-esteem. Now I'm at the point where I can dress the way that I want to dress and it doesn't bother me if anyone talks to me or if not. Women feel that if no one talks to them then maybe I'm not cute enough maybe this or that is not right with me. They feel like something is wrong with them. So next time I come I'll wear something different and I'll do this or that. (Latasha)

My roommate sleeps with a lot of men. I said to my roommate "Don't you worry about your reputation?" She said, "Girl I don't care. I do what I want to. This is my body." Things like That. (Latasha)

Some women have bad reputations, because, as Anderson (1990) noted, not only must young men have sexual conquests, but also, they must prove it. Therefore, they must talk about sex and girls with other young men (Anderson, 1990). Others have reputations because of their sexual orientation. Anna said,

It's a girl, I don't know her name but she's a lesbian, right. I see her all the time and I never knew she was one, I see her talking to males and females. This guy told me like, see her, she's a lesbian. She come in here all the time and she talked to this person and that person.

The standards for marriage and nonmarital relationships are different. Marriage at Club X is with the "good girl." For nonmarital relationships, the ideal woman may be identified at the club by frequency of attendance, skimpy clothing, and sexual dancing. Women believe that men perceive these women as "hard up" and desperate for a man.

SEXUAL DANCING

The dancing is very sexual at Club X and, to some degree, mimics the physical act of sex. "Sexual dancing" takes place on the dance floor and while standing around watching people dance. Off the dance floor, some women dance in front of their boyfriends. For example, one night a woman was dancing with her back to her boyfriend. She put her "butt" in his crotch and proceeded to move in a circular motion against his genital area. He was not dancing, just standing. She took his beer out of his hand and took a few swallows and then handed it back to him. Then she continued dancing, which was really a grinding of his crotch area. Later, she turned around and danced face-to-face with him.

LaQuita said,

> It's just something they just like to do. I just dance regular. I hear guys say she can roll her body good. I bet she's good in bed. I might see a guy dancing and say "Ooh, he's something else" and I might say a little something. Dancing is an indication of something else. Guys says, "Oh, she can get down. I'm going to try to get with her." I've seen it where a guy is laying on the floor and a girl is on top of him. Just dancing and stuff. I wouldn't do that, it's degrading.

> Guys look at the way you dance. The guys check it out. Guys watch the way you dance. Guys watch the way you move when you dance. They figure if you can move like that on the dance floor you can do that in bed. It is important in terms of finding someone. If you can dance and move like that, they are going to try to talk to you, even if you're ugly.

Dancing is part of the public performance in attracting a partner. The dance floor is a place to display and to pique the interests of potential suitors. Manning (1973) STUDIED RECREATIONAL CLUBS IN Bermuda and described similar sexual dancing at clubs where men and women dance in sexually suggestive manners.

DATE SELECTION

In terms of selecting a date, attractiveness must be considered. Factors involved in attractiveness include not only biological appearance, but economic status and personality. Anna said,

> I look at the way they're dressed, casual, decent, not too much jewelry. Then if he tries to talk to me, I check out his attitude. See if he has that "ladies" man attitude." Does he think he's got it going on? Have I seen him with this girl and that girl every time I come. I watch the guys, what they do, how they talk, and how they act. I ask if they're talking to somebody else. If he says he doesn't have a girlfriend we can talk. I would have to get to know him before I got to bed with him. I'll tell him we need to be friends right now.

In describing the clothes men wear, Latasha said that,

> Guys wear the Tommy Hilfiger, it's a little emblem on the shirt. You buy them at places like Palais Royal. The shirt runs from $65 on up. They are nice shirts, similar to the polo shirt, but it's Tommy Hill. They like to wear the Guess jeans and the Tommy Hill jeans. Then you have a few who like to put on some slacks and nice shirt. Then you have ones that like to throw on jeans and a T-shirt. Sometimes people try to tell how much money they have from what they wear. But you know what I've come to realize, like I might look at a guy and I'll be like he's dressed really sharp. He probably has a

little money and what have you. But then once you get to know them, they really don't have anything.

As for the women,

> I've noticed some of the women like me like to put on a nice casual type outfit. Some of them like to wear the short, daisy dukes you'd call them, I guess, with a little halter top to show off their breast, figure, what have you. You have some of them that don't wear anything… . When I dress casual with bell bottoms, guys will be attracted to me. They'll be like, "Hi, how are you doing?" But I noticed when I put on my daisy dukes, the men are "Ooh baby you look so cute" and I have men coming from everywhere. All out the woodwork with the daisy dukes on. I get a lot of stares for my physical appearance. But I don't want them to like me for that. I want them to like me for what I am on the inside. (Anna)

Dress varies at the club. To some degree, this determines the likelihood that a man will approach a woman and also if the women will be responsive. Manning (1973) noted that women in clubs used clothing as a symbol of sexuality:

> Women's fashions, in addition to projecting the mod and Afro images, are designed to enhance sex appeal. Flesh-clinging dresses with plunging neckline, miniskirts that suggestively expose the thighs, two-piece ensembles that daring bare the midriff, hot pants outfits that accentuate the pubes, hips, and buttocks, and tight-fitting pants suits that gloriously contour the cantilevered dimensions of their weavers, are popular attire. (p. 157)

This raises the issue of how men think about women who wear little in the way of clothing. Latasha said some men look at them as "Ooh, they're cheap."

> Some men look at them like that and some don't. Most of the men, I come to realize now, they're into sex. You know what I'm saying. That's all they think about is sex. So when they see a woman dressed like that they're like "Wow, she'll probably give it up easy." So they go after her and try to pursue her and see what she's all about and if they feel they can take her home they will. That's when I noticed a lot of them will pull out their money. "Well here, I'll buy you and your friends a drink." That's supposed to make you go "Wow. He has money so I might talk to him and go home with him." Men love it. Most guys go "She's a whore. She can give it up." They look at another person, "She's decent. She's nice." (Latasha)

So, depending on how you are dressed, men and women classify women as "decent" and "whore." A decent person is someone with whom you have a relationship and a whore is someone you can go to bet with anytime.

> Women know they're getting a reputation but they figure they can get anybody they want. Some women wear the shorts real short. We call them "whore shorts." Women like the attention. All eyes are on them. They catch all the men. They like the attention. When guys say that looks fine on you. They love the attention. (Anna)

For women, attention seems to be fair focus. They dress in skimpy clothes although they may create a negative image. Then again, who determines that it is negative image? To them, it is positive. They get the attention they desire.

Brooks (1995) discussed the "centerfold syndrome" and its impact on sexual relationships. The basic thesis of the syndrome is the belief among men (and women) that physically attractive women's bodies are magnificent and men are destined to desire them. The centerfold syndrome has five components: voyeurism, objectification, the need for validation, trophism, and the fear of true intimacy. In terms of voyeurism, the unique features of a woman's or man's physical appearance—the outline of a man's biceps or contour of a woman's breast in a dress—can be strong sexual stimuli. The harm is this is that glorification of the body leads to unreal images of women, creates an obsession with visual stimulation, and minimizes other aspects of a healthy psychosexual relationship (Brooks, 1995).

Objectification is related to voyeurism. In the centerfold syndrome, men observe women and therefore women are the object and men are the objectifiers. In American society, men have the right to look at women and women are expected to accept the role of visual stimulators for men. When men see women as objects, imperfect women (those with varicose veins, cellulite legs, etc.) are less appealing. Also, one fantasy woman is not enough, because images that were exciting can soon cease to be so (Brooks, 1995). Outward physical features, clothes, jewelry, hairstyle and hair texture, and biological features are used to objectify both genders at Club X.

Men crave validation of their masculinity and view women's bodies as an avenue for that validation. A woman has tokens to manhood (sex) that she can dispense whenever she likes. Although women may have little power in other spheres, women do have power in the sexual arena; this sets the background for misunderstandings and antagonisms between women and men (Brooke, 1995).

> When women are viewed as objects, they also become trophies, testaments of a man's power and skillful performance. The trophy hunting man must realize that his prize eventually will lose her irresistible allure. Also, he can never be sure that the trophy will remain his (Brooks, 1995).

According to Brooks (1995), the centerfold syndrome "prevents real intimacy, mature discourse, and honest interpersonal connection, it creates barriers to understanding and becomes a significant obstacle to healthy relationships." (p.12).

ECONOMIC INTERACTIONS

Part of the social interaction involves economic power plays. In *Sexual games in Black Male/Female Relations,* Burgest (1990) discusses a variety of games played between black men and women. Burgest calls one game "if you dance to the music, you got to pay the piper." The aim of the performance is to create indebtedness in black women to black men. This is accomplished through economic and financial dependency. In return for economic favors provided by black men, the woman is to provide sexual favors (Burgest, 1990). This may be observed in the simple offer to buy a woman a drink (and maybe her friends a drink). "Some men think if you buy them a drink, they have to be with them all right." Yvonne said she tells them that "If you buy me a drink it doesn't mean that I'm going to be with you all night.' A guy told me that if I buy you this drink, well I think you need to be with me. I told him, 'Well, that's okay. I'll get my own drink.'"

Latasha had the following experience:

> At [Club X]. I had an experience with this guy that I had been knowing. He was kind of drunk. He bought me a drink and I was walking around, you know, looking for my friends and he saw me. He grabbed the drink out of my hand and poured it out. He just poured it out. He

said, "Well, I wanted you to be with me," and I didn't want to be with him. [She laughed]

He thought, that she should be attentive to him because he bought her a drink.

> Others don't mind, they just want to buy you a drink. Some women at [Club X] might go to bed with someone because they bought them some drinks. It's a dollar bill. One of my roommates probably feels obligated to go to bed with him if he buys her drinks and clothes. (Latasha)

> This popular among black men who value property and economic resources. They use these resources as a means to manipulate and control women (Burgest, 1990).

Another game, played mainly by women, is "I won't … if you don't or you can't … if you don't." black women negotiate with their bodies for favors in the relationship. Black men and women view sex as a commodity (Burgest, 1990). Women at Club X discussed money and clothes in exchange for sex. They look at the clothes men wear and the cars they drive to determine their economic potential.

> Other guys may feel that you owe them if they buy you clothes or give you money. Others are girls who come out strictly to meet someone to go home with. I see them and they are always talking to the guys in the flashy cars. Every time you see them. It's certain ones. I see them. One week she may be talking to somebody in a Lexus. Next time I see her she's talking to somebody in a BMW. My roommate will say something like, "Girl, we're going to go out tonight and I'm going to meet me a man in a Lexus." She doesn't necessarily go to bed with them, but that is what she is looking for. Some women do that. We call them "car hoppers."

> They're not necessarily considered whores, but maybe.
> If someone acts, you know what I'm saying, if she likes
> flaunting herself, dressed like a slut. They are whores.
> (Anna)

> I see girls that are like a real wild. I don't know what
> they do. But just from fearing the conversation as I pass
> by, a guy might say, "Well, I want to take you home
> tonight," and he looks like a big spender. So, the female
> might to home with him. Then you have some people
> like me who just like to go out and have fun. I'm a
> people person and I just like to go out, dance, socialize.
> (Yvonne)

There is a continual bartering system in black female-male relationships.

MALE-FEMALE RELATIONSHIPS

I Asked questions about the importance of a relationship and whether it is a status symbol.

> It's security. I just got out of a relationship. I like to be
> in a relationship because of sexwise I don't like to have
> a lot of partners. I like to have one main partner and
> he's with me and no one else. Then again, he could be
> with someone else. I always use protection. Security.
> Sometimes I wouldn't have money for rent and he'd
> say okay I'll pay your rent for you this month. I don't
> fool with a lot of females. So, when I come home from
> work I'll talk to my boyfriend. This happened today.
> He knows that I'm talkative so if I come home and I'm
> quiet he's like, "What's wrong?" it's fun to do things, go
> to the movies, double date. (Anna)

So, there are a variety of reasons for being in a relationship: security, companionship, and sex. It is also a status symbol. When asked this question, they all said, "Yes, pretty much so."

> A prestigious guy might marry a woman because she has a degree and if we get together and get married, we'll have X amount of dollars. It's prestige thing. Then I see it leads to an unhappy marriage if they get married for the financial thing. (Yvonne)

> Women don't want to be along. They want someone to hold them and tell them it's going to be all right. You have to have a man. Everyone looks down on you if you're not in a relationship. They ask why you're not married yet. "Are you going to get married?" What do they say in the Bible, fornication is a sin? I would love to get married. Most people just go form one person to the next. It's a cycle. It's all about money. The younger generation are about he's going to do this for me. Give me this, buy me this. If he's not going to buy it, then the next person will. (Anna).

Also, if you're not in a relationship, women feel that men think you're a whore.

> When guys see that some women don't want to be in a relationship or want to be single, guys think that they're whore hopping. They want to be with that man and that man. If you're not in a relationship, you may be whore hopping. In terms of power in the relationship, men have the power. (Yvonne)

LaQuita said it is hard to say no to a man when you love him.

Hard to say "No, you can't come over here." I do want to see him. It's hard to say no when you're in love. It's hard to say no you can't kiss me. That's how it is when you're in love. That's how weak you get when you're in love. If he's in my face it's hard for me to say no. if we're on the phone, no. Face to face is hard.

Most men have the upper hand. I figured if you know how to do it you can work it. If a man can satisfy you, they have the upper hand because they know you want it. If a man is good in bed, then he has control. Men have control because they have more money. For women if you don't have that car and job, they don't want you. Men are the same way. Whoever has those things can be in control. If the man is good in bed, it's hard to say who has control. They may be controlling each other.

I noticed that it is difficult for women to say no during my interviews, as I noted in the journal I kept during the study:

One woman agreed to do the interview and then didn't show up. I paged her and she never returned my call. I'm not going to page her again. If she didn't want to take part she could have said so, but she didn't. I wonder how they can negotiate condom use and sex when they can't tell someone they don't even know that they don't want to be interviewed.

One woman felt that it is extremely important for a woman to be with a man.

> There is no woman who wants to be alone without a man. Someone to hug, someone to care for them. Someone to be there for them. (Yvonne)

> The man feels that he has power but I look at it as the woman has power. I've had several men say, "I don't want to use a condom." Well, if you don't want to use a condom, then you don't want to have sex. But you do have some individuals who feel, "Well, I don't want to lose this guy so I'll just go along with what he says so I won't use a condom this time. (Yvonne)

> This attitude goes along with the game, "if you love me, you will." It is played by black men and is usually introduced by young lovers who attempt to coerce a partner into a sexual encounter. The outcome of this game is for black men to gain satisfaction against the explicit wishes of the woman (Burgest, 1990).

Women feel that men are going to have more than one woman and there is nothing they can do about it. "Some men are never satisfied with one woman."

My roommate has been with this guy for 3 years. The second year into the relationship he told her he had been dating someone else. He made that particular person his girlfriend, but he's still messing with her. I feel like this, if you let it happen it will happen. I don't like to play second fiddle. I like to be number one. But my momma told me, you may be number one but you're not the only one. I believe it because a man is going to do what he wants to do. Some of them you can talk to them, mold them in a sense, but some of them: "I'm going to do this." I've come to realize it's a big ego thing too. "I had this girl this week and (Latasha)

"This guy told me that sometimes I have to have more than one woman. It takes more than one woman to satisfy me." LaQuita said she believes it.

Sometimes you lose the attraction. You don't lose the feelings for the person you're with, but there's something different. I caught my boyfriend with another girl. He told me that the feeling wasn't there anymore. He said he loves me, but the feeling wasn't there anymore. He said I still love and care for you, but the feelings aren't there. It's something different. He said he wanted to be single. We were going to break up and I agreed to it. He told me he loved me and didn't want me to be with anyone else. When I caught him with the girl he said the girl doesn't mean anything to him. They're just friends. Now he said he wants to be with her. I said, "Last week you said something different. Why did you lie?" He said I didn't lie. He can cut me off. He still calls me and comes by. He said it's just something different. He came over yesterday.... . I would take him back because I'm in love with him. For four and a half years it was me and him. I can't be with him while he's with another woman. I can't accept that. He said he was happy with this girl. I said, "Didn't I make you happy?" He said, "You did, but the feeling isn't there anymore." I would

> still take him back because I miss him. I miss the time we spent together. Him taking me places. It's hard for me to start over. I think it was because he didn't have a decent job and wasn't dressed. Now he has a new car and he's dressing nice. He's getting a lot of attention now. (LaQuita)

> All men are going to have someone else. My dad is like that. He's married. He's been married for 17 years, but he's out there. He has another woman. Stepmom might know and it's security. She came up with hardly anything. My dad's a chemical engineer. He brings home a lot of money. He has her living in a nice two-story house. She's driving a Jag. He has a BMW. It's security. As long as she's bringing home the money he can do whatever. Then again, she might be naïve and don't know. My dad's always going out of town. "Well, I'm flying to Dallas." He doesn't take her. Sometimes he does but a lot of times he doesn't take her. When I was little, I don't know if he knew I wouldn't tell or what, but I remember meeting a number of his girlfriends. One of them claimed that she was pregnant and he had a blood test and it wasn't his. (Shontele)

Although they are young, one participates sees herself as "spoiled" and that she must get a mate before no one wants her. Shontele said,

Men are more interested in what's untouched, in what's pure. They are not interested in a woman with a baby. Some men are more interested in women who are untouched, more pure and clean. Most men like women with the perfect measurements, no children, no sex or they only had a little sex, but you don't know a lot about sex. You don't have to have a mind or brain, you can be dumb, but you have the looks, the body. If I knew then what I know now my children would come a whole lot later and I wouldn't have had as much sex as I did. I'm old him now. I'm going to be really old as far as a spouse or partner is concerned in a few years. I'm worried about that. I worry about it all the time.

Women strive to show that they had little in the way of sexual experience. In the recreational clubs studied by Manning (1973), there was no stigma from extramarital affairs. This is not true for women at Club X. Although some women admitted having past relationships with married men, such affairs are not considered acceptable behavior. The married man can provide short-term and long-term economic support, but they cannot provide the status symbol of "Mrs."

Women at Club X may see the individual only for the night or have a longer-term relationship. However, a longer-term relationship with one individual does not necessarily exclude sexual contact with others.

BABY'S MOTHER

"Baby's mother" is a special category. Two of the interviewees in this study were baby's mother. Anna explained it the following way:

> They are not called girlfriends. Your girlfriend is someone else, a completely different person. Everybody's got one. Everybody has a baby's mother. They have no plans to marry these people buy they will do everything they can to be nice to them so they won't file child support.

> Many poor black women have a profile philosophy, and abortion is often not an option. Children are wanted regardless of the circumstances, and the child is genuinely valued. A baby brings a woman praise, a welfare check, and some independence (Anderson, 1990). Adult status is placed on women who become mothers (Collins, 1990).

Baby's mother is a good position to be in for financial reasons and also because the woman has an ongoing relationship with the father. Baby's mother is a socially prestigious position, and she may or may not date other men. Shontele said,

You're sort of like property then. The father can always go back and sleep with the baby's mother. It's like a given. He'll say I'll give you money. She'll say if you give me money. I won't file child support. It's sort of like an intricate bartering system.

> Anderson (1990) argued that because such men are unemployed or underemployed, they could not form economically self-reliant families, the usual marker of the transition to manhood. As a consequence, young men's peer groups stress sexual activity to prove manhood, and a baby is proof of sexual activity. Young girls are lured to have sex by the hopes of love and marriage and may become pregnant and abandoned. Some view this as an opportunity to be eligible for welfare that allows them to establish their own households and to attract other men who need money. Anderson views it as cultural manifestation of persistent urban poverty. Although the sexual codes of the youth in this ethnography probably do not differ from those of other young people, the consequences vary by social class. Exploitative sexual relationships are prevalent in all social classes, but middle-class youths have stronger interest in their future and realize that a pregnancy can derail that future (Anderson, 1990).

> The girls have a dream, the boys a desire. The girls dream of being carried off by a Prince Charming who will love them, provide for them, and give them a family. The boys often desire sex without commitment or babies without responsibility for them. It becomes extremely difficult for the boys to see themselves taking on the responsivities of conventional fathers and husbands in view of their employment prospects. Yet the boy knows what the girl wants and plays that role to get sex. In accepting his advances, she may think she is maneuvering him toward a commitment or that her getting pregnant is the nudge he needs to marry her and give her the life she wants. What she does not see is that the boy, despite his claims, is often incapable of giving

her that life. For in reality, he has little money, few prospects for earning much, and no wish to be tied to a woman who will have a say in what he does. (Anderson, 1990, pp. 113-114)

This scenario outlines the dilemma faced by both genders in trying to form a sexual relationship. The bartering system has short-term gains but long-term disadvantages. Consequences of the bartering system for women are unplanned pregnancies, increased prevalence of sexually transmitted diseases (STDs), continued poverty, and lowered quality of life, especially unhappiness.

DISCUSSION

Families in the United States have undergone significant demographic changes. These important changes include an overall decline in marriage rates, older ages at first marriage, a higher prevalence of births to unmarried women, increases in female-headed households, more children in female-headed households, and a larger percentage of children living in poverty. Although these trends affect both blacks and whites, black families are disproportionately affected. In 1993, more than half of black men (58%) and women (61%) in the United States were not married, compared with 41% of white women and 38% of white men. A large proportion of this decline in marriage occurred because of an increase in the percentage of those who were never married (Taylor, Tucker, Chatters, & Jayakody, 1997). Relative to other groups, blacks will spend a greater percentage of their lives as singles (Tucker & Taylor, 1997). The declines in marriage have been offset by increases in cohabitation (Taylor et al., 1997). McLanahan and Casper (1995) suggested that because marriage differentials between white and black women is equally high for mothers as for nonmothers, the cause of the decline in marriage is similar for all women, not just mothers.

A number of theories have been put forth to explain the relatively high prevalence of "unmarriedness" among African Americans. These same theories may help elucidate observed patterns of male-female interpersonal relationships.

SEX RATIO IMBALANCE

There is a gender imbalance among whites and blacks, but not Hispanics. For example, the gender ratio in 1991 was 100 to 100 among Hispanics, 95 to 100 among whites, and 88 to 100 for African Americans. This scarcity of men is more marked among young, sexually active age groups. The gender ratio imbalance for those below the poverty line is more striking than the overall figures. For instance, the gender ratio for those below the poverty level is 73 to 100, whereas the ratio drops to 69 to 100 among African Americans living in poverty (Aral, 1996).

Guttentag and Secord (1983) advanced the argument that societies with gender ratio imbalance have different patterns of marital values and social organization; shortage of men is related to more divorce, singlehood, adultery, out-of-wedlock births, transient relationships, less commitment among men to relationship, lower societal value on family and marriage, and a rise in feminism. They also argued that a shortage of men among African Americans is associated with an increase in extramarital childbearing and marital decline. Second and Ghee (1986) also argued that this gender ratio imbalance destabilizes existing relationships because viable alternative mates are always available to the gender in short supply.

The gender ratio hypothesis considers how gender ratio imbalances interact with gender inequality to influence marriage patterns. Members of the scarcer gender have a bargaining advantage because they have more potential mates (Guttentag & Secord, 1983). But how members of the scarcer gender use their advantage depends on their structural power and control of economic and political resources. It is assumed that women depend on marriage for financial support and therefore use their bargaining power when potential mates are abundant to marry, and they marry men with higher status than they otherwise could attract. Men are more likely to marry when the gender ratio is near 100. When women are scarce (i.e., when the ratio is less than 100), men are less likely to marry, and when men are in short supply (less than 100), they are also less likely to marry because they do not need commitment to gain sexual relationships (Guttentag & Secord, 1983).

Low gender ratios are also believed to weaken husband's commitment to marriage because men do not place great value on marriage. Therefore, husbands provide fewer benefits to wives, which results in lower marital satisfaction for women than for men. A consequence of this scenario for married couple sis higher risk of separation and divorce (Guttentag & Secord, 1983).

The African American gender ratio has declined since the 1920s. this disparity between the number of women and men is partly due to higher male mortality and increased female longevity (Taylor et al., 1997). However, researchers such as Epenshade (1985) noted that although black gender ratios declined since the 1920s, marital decline did not begin until the 1960s.

ECONOMIC FACTORS

The declining economic condition of black men also has been cited as a causative factor in the decline in marriage and bonding. The decline in the industrial sector, which provided employment for black men without higher education, resulted in black men being less attractive as potential husbands and also made them less confident that they could financially support a family (Dairy & Myers, 1987; Wilson, 1987). Another economic explanation of marital decline is the growing disparity between black female and male income levels and increased economic independence of women. Research indicates that the most economically independent black women, those most highly educated, are more likely to marry than less educated women (Taylor et al., 1997). The effects of the gender ratio and employment on marital status are more evident under conditions of poverty (Taylor et al., 1997).

FEMINIST THEORY

Those who espouse the view that black men experience more severe oppression than black women and that therefore black women must support black male sexism do not consider the overarching gender ideology that constrains both blacks and whites (Collins, 1990).

Objectification of subordinate groups is part of domination and is central to female oppression.

The foundations of complex social hierarchy become grounded in the interwoven concepts of either/or dichotomous thinking... .[D] omination based on difference ... impl[ies] relationships of superiority and inferiority, hierarchical bonds that mesh with political economies of race, gender, and class oppression. African American women occupy a position whereby the inferior half of a series of these dichotomies converge, and this placement has been central to our subordination. (Collins, 190, p. 70)

Eurocentric gender ideology objectifies both genders. Some African American men believe that they can only be men by dominating black women (Collins, 1990). Sexism and internalized sexism play major roles in the dynamics of black male-female relationships.

CONCLUSIONS

Attributes of women's beliefs and behaviors described in this article can be found in any club and among any ethnic group. These young people are not afraid to say how they feel. They want to have fun. They are "the hip hop generation," a generation that is concerned about pleasure and enjoyment, and they are not afraid to say so. During the hippie movement, people talked about free love. However, they discussed it in political and liberation tones. Today, young people are living a free love devoid of the political rhetoric, sometimes pretentious, of the 1960s.

Karenga (1978) discussed black female-male relationships. He said the dynamics of black love fall within one of the following categories: dependency connection, flesh connection, and the cash connection. According to Karenga, the root of social problems in black male-female relationships rests on these stereotypical connections. However, these connections are probably more widespread and real than simply stereotypical. These connections form the base for many female-male relationships. In a society where women, especially black women, have little social and economic status and power, these connections are survival strategies in a Eurocentric-structured world.

The study indicates the importance of social status, economic security, and male-female companionship among young adult African American women. The bartering of materials resources, companionship, and social status in exchange for sex within a sexist context are driving forces in black sexual interpersonal interactions. Although all men are viewed as unfaithful, women have unprotected sex because the relationship is more important than the perceived risk of STDs, including HIV. Having a baby is another way, like sex, to gain attention, social status, companionship, and economic security. It may be that African Americans are still in transition in terms of redefining female-male relationships in the New World Eurocentric environment. Poor black women often use male-female bonding to attain companionship, social status, and economic security.

REFERENCES

Allen, W. (1978). The search for applicable theories of Black family life. *Journal of Marriage and the Family, 35,* 117-128.

Anderson, E. (1990). *Streetwise: Race, class and change in an urban community.* Chicago: University of Chicago Press.

Aral, S. O. (1996). The Social context of syphilis persistence in the southeastern United States. *Sexually Transmitted Diseases, 23(1),* 9-15.

Asante, M. K. (1980). *Afrocentricity: A theory of social change.* Buffalo, NY: Amulefi.

Bell, Y.R., Bouie, C. L., & Baldwin, J. A. (1990). Afrocentric cultural consciousness and African-American male-female relationships. *Journal of Black Studies, 21* 162-189.

Brooks, G. R. (1995). *The centerfold syndrome: How men can overcome objectification and achieve intimacy with women.* San Francisco: Jossey-Bass.

Burgest, D. R. (1990). Sexual games in Black male/female relations. *Journal of Black Studies, 21,* 103-116.

Collins, P. H. (1990). *Black feminist thought.* New York: Routledge.

Darity, W., & Myers, S. (1987). Public policy trends and the fate of the Black family. *Humboldt Journal of Social relations, 14,* 134-164.

Epenshade, T. J. (1985). Marriage trends in America: Estimates, implications, underlying cause. *Population and Development Review, 11,* 193-245.

Guttentag, M., & Secord, P.F. (1983). *Too many women: The sex ratio question.* Beverly Hills, CA: Sage.

Hutchinson, J.F. (1997). *Beyond connection: Liberation in love and struggle.* New Orleans, LA: Ahidiana.

Manning, P.E. (1973). *Black clubs in Bermuda.* Ithaca, NY: Cornell University Press.

McLanahan, S. S., & Casper, L. (1995). Growing diversity and inequality in American family. In R. Farley (Ed.), *State of union: America in the 1990s* (Vol. 2, pp. 1-45). New York: Russell Sage.

Michaels, W. B. (1995). *Our America: Nativism, modernism, and pluralism.* Durham, NC: Duke University Press.

Page, H. (1997). Visual images of the postcolonial blues on the corner of Toulouse and Royal: Discord and identity in songs of my people. In J.F. Hutchinson (Ed.), *Cultural portrayals of African Americans: Creating an ethnic/racial identity* (pp. 75-111). Westport, CT: Bergin & Garvey.

Secord, P., & Ghee, K. (1986). Implications of the Black marriage market for marital conflict. *Journal of Family Issues, 7,* 21-30.

Taylor, R. J., Tucker, M. C., Chatters, L. M., & Jayakody, R. (1997). Recent demographic trends in African American family structure. In R. J. Taylor, J. S. Jackson, & L. M. Chatters (Eds.), *Family life in Black America* (pp. 14-62). Thousand Oaks, CA: Sage.

Tucker, M. B., & Taylor, R. J. (1997). Gender, age, and marital status as related to romantic involvement among African American singles. In R. J. Taylor, J. S. Jackson, & L. M. Chatters (Eds.), *Family life in Black America* (pp. 79-94). Thousand Oaks, CA: Sage.

Wilson, W. J. (1987). *The truly disadvantaged: The inner city, the underclass, and public policy.* Chicago: University of Chicago Press.

CHAPTER NINE
Conclusion

The conclusion provides a summary of some of the major facets of the individual chapters while setting forth implications for research. This is done in an effort to underscore what is seen as the last hope for black male-female relationships—greater understanding. An understanding of how these relationships have developed and can be changed for healthier lives of black people is, indeed, set forth as the last hope for black survival in America. For only through understanding the nature of a problem can relevant solutions be provided and embraced. Numerous topics are explored which include: black sex ratios, black families, black marriages, economic well-being of black people, religion in the black community, conflict in relationship, and Afrocentric cultural issues.

CONCLUSION

Black Male and Female Relationships:
Implications for Research and Action

This assembled text of various works represents an attempt to provide a context for understanding black male – female relationships. In doing so it maintains that our last chance for healthy male-female relationships is anchored in understanding the many interpersonal and institutional factors that contribute to shaping them. Too often, the tendency for white scholars has been to conduct research on black males that ignores the structural inequalities that permeate the lives of black men. This is not to say, however, that research on black females has not been conducted. On the contrary, recent interest in studying the lives of black women has generated significant research on this topic. However, research that explored the personal relationships of black males and females in the context in which they develop has not been extensive. In this selection of articles, research that black scholars conducted about black males and females has been included to highlight important issues. Chapter Two focused on demographic issues such as the availability (or lack thereof) of black men, levels and types of educational attainment, employment and income, social participation, marital and family status, and how the life experiences of black women have changed. Chapter Three focused on the issues of sex and gender issues that face the black family, black men, and black women such as sexism, femininity, and the intersection of social policies and racism.

Chapter Four highlighted the primary group issues that black men and women face, including the role that black men play in black families and black husband-wife relationships, marital success of black couples, and various aspects of interracial marriages. Chapter Five presented the economic issues that black men and women face. Issues addressed included the position of black men and women in the labor face, factors that possibly explained the differential economic statuses of black males and females, and the double-minority status of black female professionals. Chapter Six examined the religious issues facing black men and women, such as the treatment of black women in the black church and black theology. Chapter Seven explored the psycho-social issues that black men and women face, such as games of love and power, major sources of conflict between black males and females, and the myths about black men and women. And, Chapter Eight examined Afrocentric cultural issues with focus on Afrocentric cultural consciousness and African-American male-female relationships. In addition, it provided research on the Hip Hop Generation and the nature and dynamics of male-female relationships in a nightclub setting.

Specifically, the issues addressed in this edition included the black sex ratio, the black family, black marriages, the economic well-being of blacks, religion in the black community, conflict in black relationships and Afrocentric cultural issues. The following issues will be addressed in the preceding paragraphs.

Black Sex Ratio

The availability of black men for black women has been and still continues to be an issue. Jacquelyne Johnson (1971) tackled the issue in Chapter Two, using statistics from the 1970 United States Census to show that there were approximately 91 black males forever 100 black females. Based on statistics, she showed that the black sex ratio declined steadily from the year 1850 to 1970. As sociologist William Julies Wilson (1987) later argued in *The Truly Disadvantaged,* the male marriageable pool index (MMPI) in the black community showed a scarcity of black men that black women could marry. As Lawrence E. Gary (1981) showed, the black sex ratio is the largest, and therefore, the most problematic during the childbearing and marriage ages of the early twenties to the mid-40s. Furthermore, the sex ratio differs depending on the city, state, and region. However, as La Francis Rodgers-Rose (1980) argued, the undercounting of 1.88 million blacks in the 1970 U.S. census may have accounted for some of the perceived gap in the black male-female ratio. Although the extent to which the black sex ratio exists may be contested, it is evident that its existence has implications for black and female relationships. Particularly important is the update on male-female ratios provided by Aba D. Essuon. The factors of the high rates of incarceration of black males and HIV AIDS are new variables impacting the relationships which were not central to discussions more than a decade ago. How these complicating factors are dealt with will weigh heavily on future relationships.

The Black Family

Black males and females both experience a triple system of oppression in which race, class, and gender interact to shape their life experiences and abilities. As a form of social stratification, this triad of oppression is problematic because of the important roles that both black men and women hold in the black family. As long as this system exists, the black family will face psychological, sociological, and economic barriers to its development and growth. For example, 1981 budget cuts disproportionately impacted the black family negatively. Compared to the average white family, the budget cuts cost the average black family three times more. As Chapter Three showed, this unequal effect results from the type of programs that were cut. Data from the Center on Budget and Policy Priorities showed that programs with high black participation were cut, such as employment and job training programs. Thirty-seven percent of the participants in the program were black, and the program received a 39 percent budget cut. This problem highlights the disconnection that sometimes occurs between policy design and outcome. According to Leashore (1986), there are far-reaching effects of cuts to programs in which blacks participate. Cutting costs in job training and employment programs undermines the ability of black men and women to provide for their families through work.

Black Marriages

Outside pressures from the greater society may influence black women and men to seek a support system that allows them to deal with the triple oppression they face on a daily basis. In Chapter Four, Myers' (1980) research highlighted the possible interpersonal sources of support that facilitate the maintenance of black marital relationships. These sources include physical, verbal, and nonverbal communication of emotional expression. Aside from contributing to the positive emotional aspect of black marriages, black husbands and wives must collaborate in the household. Jackson's study of manually/non-manually and unemployed/ employed husbands investigated the extent to which household maintenance activities, household decision making activities, spouse interactive activities, and spouse affect were shared between spouses. The study found that both husbands and wives usually participate in household decision-making activities. It also found that men and women perform the expected household maintenance activities and many agree on important life issues. When interracial marriages between a black and non-black couple are considered, issues that potentially impact their lives include those surrounding housing, occupation, and interpersonal relationships with family members and friends.

Economic Well-Being of Blacks

Although both black males and females may face substantial barriers to economic progress, they occupy different status roles in terms of economic progress. Contrary to the widely held and disseminated belief that black men are disadvantaged compared to black women, the authors concluded that women are more disadvantaged. Black men, Collier and Williams (1982) argue, earned 50% more than black women during the time of their research. Furthermore, black men occupied more of the professional occupations: 8.7% of all male professionals were black. It is important to note that it is often difficult for black women to determine whether or not their race or sex is the most important factor in determining their experiences in the work force. Aldridge (1975) concluded that black women still occupy a low economic status when compared to white men, black men, and white women. Nonetheless, even though black women have experienced gains in education and have fared better in the economic market, economic parity has not yet been reached. (1999)

Religion in the Black Community

The experience of black women in the church has historically been one of support, not leadership. As Cone shows, the progressive AME Church refused to ordain women preachers in the nineteenth century. Although women were granted the opportunity to obtain licenses to preach in 1884, their preaching was limited to one of subordination, or "evangelist". Grant argues that those black women who attended seminary school often were questioned about the authenticity of "the call" they received to join the ministry. Unlike women, male preachers have not had their authenticity called in question. Regardless of the limitations imposed on them by the black church, some black women have been ordained as ministers. Instead of occupying major leadership roles, black women have generally been the "backbone" of the church. They have occupied such roles as choir member, Sunday school teacher, cook, and all other traditional women's roles. As Grant suggests, the treatment of black women in the church is mirrored in the status of black women in the community. The lower status of black women in the church was also reflected in the black theology movement. This movement drew on the patriarchal nature of the black power movement from the 1960s and rendered the black woman invisible. This invisibility was achieved through the way the black theology was structured outside of the black woman's experience. Black theology and feminist theology both ignored the important role of black women. It is important that black feminist theology be further constructed so that the unique experiences of black women are articulated.

Conflict in Black Relationships

According to Clyde Franklin (1984), conflict between black men and women in relationships stems in part from two sources. Both the structural barriers imposed on black men occupy create conflict in black relationships. The structure of American society is such that black men are powerless in institutions such as the government and the economy. Their caste like social status in America contributes to this conflict because black men are unable to experience upward mobility. Instead, black men face high mortality rates, high suicide rates, high unemployment rates, and high rates of drug addiction. Franklin argues that conflict is also due to the black woman's internalization of two competing definitions of what it means to be a female. During early socialization through caretakers, relatives, peers, the black church, and the media, black women were taught that they needed a black man to take care of them. This socialization towards a feminine role directly contradicts with the message they also receive that says they must be independent. Both Franklin and Algea O. Harrison (1974) suggest that black women seem to occupy roles that are generally viewed as anti-feminine. In order to counteract these contradictory messages, black males and females must be socialized differently, change the way they role-play, and change the way they communicate with each other.

Afrocentric Cultural Issues

Afrocentric cultural consciousness and African-American male-female relationships is an important approach to understanding how identity influences the development and sustainability of relations among black males and females. According to Bell, Bouie and Baldwin, given the reality of the experience of racial and cultural oppression among African-Americans, there is a continued need for research to further refine our understanding of the role of cultural variables and related factors in heterosexual relationships. Likewise, the contemporary hip-hop generation provides an ever-increasing black males and females and the impact of these values on the development of healthy relationships. Janis F. Hutchinson with qualitative measures explains how this generation and its approach to relationships is one of the most pressing areas for further research.

The book ends as it began, our last hope for healthy black male-female relationships depends upon our understanding the factors which influence and shape our lives—both interpersonal and institutional as pointed out in the Aldridge Lens Model.

Understanding is key. What we do with that understanding is *our choice* and *our hope.*

CHAPTER QUESTIONS

CHAPTER ONE
Toward an Understanding of Black Male-Female Relationships

"Approaching the Study of Black Male-Female Relationships"

Delores P. Aldridge

1. Did this work point directions for conceptualizing and naming a model to explain male-female relationships among black people in the USA?
2. What is the importance of male-female relationships?
3. What are the components of the structural framework for examining the male-female relationship?

"The Structural Components of Violence in Black Male-Female Relationships"

Delores P. Aldridge and Willa Hemmons

1. How are the terms "violence" and "male-female relationships" defined?
2. What are the major components of the Lens Model? Does the figure illustrating the model capture the components in a meaningful way? If so, how?

3. Does the operationalizing of the Lens Model provide greater clarity for understanding the ideas presented in "Approaching the Study of Black Male-Female Relationships?" Does the work demonstrate the importance of placing a specific behavior in the context of ta theoretical model or framework? How so?

CHAPTER TWO
Demographic Issues

"But Where Are the Black Men?"

Jacquelyne Jackson

1. Does the trend of increased white women-headed households that Jackson noted in 1970 still hold today?
2. What sociological explanations other than population composition illuminate the author's statement that white females have greater access to black men that black women doe to white men?
3. Although the author provides many solutions to solving the problems of "where are the black men" she does not give new policy suggestions for achieving this goal. How can new policy increase the life expectancy of black men? How can it reduce the number of black men available to white men? Is this a feasible suggestion, given the implications of this policy?
4. Use question number three to assess the assumptions that are implicit within Jackson's argument.
5. Do the observed trends of increased black female-headed households still hold currently?

"A Social Profile"

Lawrence E. Gary

1. In 1997, only 8.3 percent of black men were college students. What were the implications of the affirmative action policies in higher

education for higher educational attainment along black males? Will this pattern of increased access still hold once these policies are revoked (i.e. California and the public education system).

2. What tie exists between incarceration of black males and voting? In other words, if prisoners who have been convicted of a felony are ineligible to vote based on law in many states, how does this inability to vote impact Gary's statistics that in 1980, 7.3 million black men were voting age but only 3.5 million actually voted? How would taking this into account have strengthened or weakened his argument?

"Some Demographic Characteristics of the Black Woman: 1940 to 1945"

La Frances Rodgers-Rose

1. Why do black women tend to disproportionately work in the service industry, in education (as teachers) and as clerical workers? Linda Grant's (1994) work on the social roles of young black girls in classrooms found that black girls worked as helpers, enforcers, and interpreters in the classroom. Explain the degree that socialization at a young age can impact occupation at an older age.

2. Since Rodgers-Rose does not support the belief that black women substantially out number black men, how would she explain the increased number of black women headed households? She argues: the urban environment has imposed structure which tends to separate wives from their husbands" (62). To what degree would she attribute this change in black female-headed households to urbanization?

3. Can you classify Rodgers-Rose as a black feminist? Why? Why not?

"Revisiting the Demographics of Black Men and Women"

Aba D. Essuon

1. To what extent are the demographics the same as/different from those presented by Jacquelyne J. Jackson, Lawrence Gary and La Frances Rodgers-Rose?
2. What new factors influence the male-female ratios? What does the future portend?

CHAPTER THREE
Sex and Gender Issues

"An Alternative Analysis of Sexism: Implications for the Black Family"

Betty Collier-Watson,
Louis N. Williams, Willy Smith

1. What theoretical framework (s) does this work draw upon?

"Social Policies, Black males, and Black Families"

Bogart R. Leashore

1. Does the author reject the culture of poverty thesis in his argument? Does the author believe that structure or individual characteristics explain the state of black men in America?
2. Do black immigrants experience the same social problems that black Americans face? How does immigrant status impact the ability to overcome these structural issues? Are structural issues something that black Americans and/or black immigrants overcome?

"The Dilemma of Growing Up Black and Female"

Algea O. Harrison

1. How does the theoretical framework of symbolic interaction explain findings in this article?
2. Does the DuBois' concept of double consciousness apply to the experience of black women?

CHAPTER FOUR
Primary Group Issues

"Ordinary Black Husbands: The Truly Hidden Men"

Jackquelyne J. Jackson

1. What could account for the shift between older black families and younger black families from fathers disciplining children to joint parental responsibility?

"On Marital Relations: Perceptions of Black Women"

Lena Wright Myers

1. How accurate is the statement that "black people are an expressive people"? If one accepts this, how do black people become expressive? Through socialization?

"Interracial Marriages: Empirical and Theoretical Considerations"

Delores P. Aldridge

1. Many black male entertainers, actors, athletes, politicians, and intellectuals marry white women currently. How would the observations of intermarriage as it relates to social status change if current trends were included?

2. How does the one-drop rule confirm/deny the finding that children of interracial marriages "are considered to be black by both the white and black communities?"

3. Provided an explanation for why rates of interracial marriage vary by region and why the Est has the highest rates of interracial marriage."

CHAPTER FIVE
Economic Issues

"Black Female Professionals: Dilemmas and Contradictions of Status"

Cheryl Bernadette Leggon

1. Leggon argues that clients of status-discrepant professionals react in different ways to their presences depending on the situation. If it is an emergency and there is no alternative, then clients may feel forced to interact with the status discrepant professional as a professional. The other outcome is that black female professionals are viewed as black or female first, then their respective profession. Are the situational outcomes that black women professionals experience types of overt, covert, or subtle discrimination?

"The Economic Status of the Black Male: A Myth Exploded"

Betty J. Collier and Louis Williams

1. What data do Collier and Williams draw upon to show that 83% of the sample believed "that there is a 'crisis' between black men and black women"? Is it problematic that the link between theory, method, and data is not fully explained? How does this strengthen or weaken their argument?

"Black Women in the Economic Marketplace: A Battle Unfinished"

Delores P. Aldridge

1. Aldridge argues that the usual factor that impacts a black woman's entrance into the labor force is necessity. Is necessity still important today?
2. Black feminist Deborah K. King argued that black women viewed the ability to stay at home and be a housewife as a luxury while white women viewed the ability of black women to enter the workforce as a measure of independence and a luxury. With this idea in mind, discuss the idea of entrance into the workforce as a necessity for black women.

CHAPTER SIX
Religious Issues

"Black Theology, Black Church and Black Women"

James Cone

1. Cone argues that black women who are feminists are the people most capable of evaluating sexist in the black community and church. Similar to feminist Deborah K. King, he also argues that only black women "can do black feminist theology". Why do you think he only selects black women feminists as capable of this position? What is a black feminist" Who can be a black feminist? Only black women?

"Black Theology and the Black Woman"

Jacquelyn Grant

1. How can the black woman be the "most oppressed of all the oppressed?" Use examples from other articles in the book to answer this question.
2. What contributes to the continuing invisibility of black women in society, black feminism and black theology?

CHAPTER SEVEN
Psycho-Social Issues

"Games in Black Male/Female Relationships"

Mwalimu David R. Burgest and Mary Goosby

1. Compare and contrast this article with the section on black male and female relationships in Chapter One by Aldridge.

    "Black Male-Black Female Conflict: Individually Caused and Culturally Nurtured"

    Clyde W. Franklin II

1. To what degree can rational choice explain the rejection and acceptance of certain feminine characteristics that black women embrace?

    "Dialectics of Black Male-Female Relationships"

    La Frances Rodgers-Rose

1. What role does structure, racism, and sexism play in black male and female relationships?
2. What could account for the differences in preferred qualities among different age groups of black men and women?

CHAPTER EIGHT
Afrocentric Cultural Issues

"Afrocentric Cultural Consciousness and African-American Male-Female Relationships"

Yvonne R. Bell, Cathy L. Bouie, Joseph A. Baldwin

1. What are the defining features of the Euro-American Worldview and Cultural Orientation?
2. How does the African-American Worldview and Black Heterosexual Relationships differ from that of the Euro-American Worldview and Cultural Orientation?
3. What are the major conclusions reached in this study of Black Heterosexual Relationships?

"The Hip Hop Generation: African American Male-Female Relationships in a Nightclub Setting"

Janis Faye Hutchinson

1. What was the major focus of this work? How does it support/reject findings of the previous study by Bell, Bouie and Baldwin?
2. This work tends to embrace much of the psychological and cultural literature. However, in the discussion there is considerable emphasis on sex ration imbalance and economic factors which are structural components of the society. How might attention to these variables at the outset of the work been valuable for understanding the nature of relationships?

NOTE: Tiffany Davis, my graduate research assistant contributed significantly in the development of the questions for each chapter.

INDEX

A

Abuse iii, 55, 62, 98, 106, 137, 178
Affective relationships 158
African centered 22
Afrocentric vii, ix, 1, 5, 17, 22, 23, 26, 35, 221, 324, 325, 330, 331, 333, 334, 335, 337, 338, 339, 340, 341, 342, 343, 344, 345, 346, 347, 348, 349, 351, 375, 376, 377, 381, 393
Afrocentric cultural consciousness 324, 334, 335, 341, 343, 344, 346, 347, 348, 349, 351, 375, 376, 377, 381, 393
Afrocentric cultural consciousness 324, 334, 335, 341, 343, 344, 346, 347, 348, 375, 377, 381
Aldridge, Delores P. iii, iv, v, vi, 1, 2, 17, 20, 35, 93, 156, 182, 195, 223, 383, 388, 389
Association 64, 66, 67, 69, 71, 73, 183

B

Baldwin, Joseph A. vii, 324, 325, 393
Bell, Yvonne R. vii, 324, 325, 393
Black church 73, 102, 103, 238, 239, 240, 243, 249, 250, 252, 259, 260, 263, 268, 272, 273, 299, 377, 380, 381
Black female professionals 201
Black male-black female conflict 297, 298, 301, 302, 303, 304, 305

Black theology vi, 238, 239, 249, 250, 252, 256, 260, 261, 262, 263, 264, 266, 267, 272, 273, 274, 277, 278, 279, 280, 377, 380, 381, 391
Bouie, Cathy L vii, 324, 325, 393
Burgest, Mwalimu David R. vi, 282, 392

C

Capitalism 1, 6, 17, 20, 21, 24, 141, 258
Centerfold syndrome 360, 361, 375
Centers for Disease Control and Prevention 106
Collier-Watson, Betty v, 108, 109, 387
Cone, James vi, 238, 239, 266, 267, 273, 278, 279, 391
Connections 13, 14, 32, 215, 350, 374
Crime 62, 64, 75, 108, 112, 123, 129, 134, 137, 138, 141
Cultural Orientation 325, 326, 327, 328, 331, 332, 338, 344, 345, 347, 348, 352, 393

D

Demographic v, xii, 4, 37, 50, 71, 74, 76, 87, 90, 91, 106, 221, 342, 370, 375, 377, 384, 385
Dialectics vii, 309, 320, 392
Differential socialization 1, 8, 9

E

Economic disparity 27
Economic issues vi, xii, 195, 377, 389